THE OFFICIAL®

2004

BLACKBOOK PRICE GUIDE TO UNITED STATES COINS

FORTY-SECOND EDITION

S0-CFR-606

BY MARC HUDGEONS, N.L.G.
& TOM HUDGEONS, JR.
& TOM HUDGEONS, SR.

HOUSE OF COLLECTIBLES

RANDOM HOUSE REFERENCE • NEW YORK

Published by House of Collectibles, 1745 Broadway, New York, New York 10019. Distributed by the Random House Reference, a division of Random House Inc., New York, and simultaneously in Canada by Random House of Canada Limited, Toronto.

House of Collectibles is a registered trademark and the colophon is a trademark of Random House, Inc.

Buy It • Use It • Become an Expert is a trademark of Random House, Inc.

www.houseofcollectibles.com

Printed in the United States of America

ISSN: 0193-9610

ISBN: 0-4000-4805-2

10 9 8 7 6 5 4 3 2 1

Forty-second Edition: June 2003

CONTENTS

OFFICIAL BOARD OF CONTRIBUTORS

The authors would like to express a special thank-you to:

Q. David Bowers at The Bowers and Merena Galleries, Inc., Wolfboro, NH 03894, for his article on "Coin Auction Sales" and modern commemorative photographs,

Dale H. Cade, Rancho Palos Verdes, CA, for his article on "Civil War Tokens,"

Tom Culhane of The Elusive Spondulix, Union, NJ 07083, for his article and pricing information,

Mike Ellis at C.O.N.E.C.A. (Combined Organizations of Numismatic Error Collectors of America), Donalsonville, GA 31745, for his article "Errors and Varieties,"

Stephen Bobbit at The American Numismatic Association, Colorado Springs, CO 80903, for the Official ANA Grading Section,

and to **Michael White at The Department of the Treasury,** United States Mint, Washington, DC 20001, for photographs and mintage figures.

SHARE YOUR KNOWLEDGE

We would be interested in your questions and comments regarding <u>buying and selling</u> one piece or an entire collection.

OR

You may have information that would be of interest to your fellow collectors. In either case please write to:

Marc and Tom Hudgeons, PO Box 690312, Orlando, FL 32869-0312

<u>Please send a SASE for a reply.</u>

Are you interested in becoming a

CONTRIBUTOR?

If you would like to join our Board of Contributors and have <u>your name printed in the next edition,</u> please let us hear from you.

Please send a SASE for more information to: Marc and Tom Hudgeons, PO Box 690312, Orlando, FL 32869-0312

INTRODUCTION

By Tom Culhane

1933 TWENTY DOLLAR GOLD PIECE

Welcome to the new 2004 Blackbook Price Guide to United States Coins and the pleasures you should derive from collecting with this guide book in hand! The individual coin which generated the most press and buzz in the hobby during 2002 was no doubt the 1933 Saint Gaudens. The firm of Stacks combined with Sotheby's to sell the coin as a single lot auction in July. As expected all price records were shattered as this uniquely monetized twenty realized the lofty sum of $7.59 million (surpassing the old record of $4.2 million for an 1804 dollar.)

Coin collectors may view this specimen which is now on public display just a few blocks from Ground Zero in lower Manhattan at the ANS Museum. While this piece will apparently hold the price record for the foreseeable future, other newsworthy rarities may now seem relatively cheap by comparison. At the start of 2003 the sale of a 1913 Liberty nickel took place at private treaty above the former price record for the date. With just four coins known to exist and two of those impounded in museum collections, the coin likely sold at or above the $2 million mark. Truly great numismatic rarities continue to bring higher prices.

MODERN COINS

Modern commemoratives (1982 and onwards) continue to be shipped off in quantities to the grading services in search of those lofty grades, such as Proof 68 Cameo and above. Collectors are willing to pay premiums for high and certified pieces; well above prices generated by those left ungraded in original government packaging. It is readily apparent that many of these original government holders have done a less than adequate job of preserving the coins, and after a number of years the coins just seem to pale in comparison to those stored in NGC holders.

The modern bullion eagle series in silver, gold, and platinum are also shipped off by the thousands to the grading services. These seem to be graded to meet the needs of TV promoters who are selling incredible volumes of coins. It is important to understand that despite the grading services' (primarily NGC and PCGS) efforts to educate the collectors through their population reports that the numbers reported only reflect those coins which have been certified. Neither service has published reports as to how many hundreds of thousands of coins have been rejected due to spotting, scratches, dull surfaces, etc. The massive numbers of rejected coins which fail to meet minimum grades is left unreported. Therefore, those not actively involved in modern coins may be under the misconception that the percentage of top grade specimens is so high since so few are graded less that 67. The high percentage of rejects on certain dates is not yet published, but some day they may be compiled as a useful resource.

STATE QUARTERS

The state quarter program has fueled the modern market and brought tremendous numbers of new hobbyists, many of them internet savvy. Tennessee led 2002 with a design featuring its musical tradition thus being the first state to highlight the arts. Its three stars represent the three regions and three musical traditions. Ohio quarters were produced in the midst of a closing of the Philadelphia Mint for weeks due to health concerns, thus leaving the Ohio P quarter with a significantly lower mintage (217,200,000 P vs. 414,832,000 D).

Louisiana's quarter featured the tremendous land expansion of our country with the Louisiana Purchase approximately doubling the size of the U.S., and eventually splitting into thirteen states. The race car superimposed over the state map of Indiana was the first quarter to feature sports as a topic. There was no doubt plenty of Hoosiers who would have preferred it if a certain basketball player wearing number 33 had made it onto the design instead. Certainly that coin would have been a big seller at the Boston Coin Show too! Mississippi featured a rather uninspiring entry with its magnolia blossoms and leaves which visually seems especially hard to distinguish.

2003 saw the series get off on the right foot with a coin artistically superior to any from 2002. A young Abe Lincoln framed by the Illinois state map seems to be the right size to have the initial arms length impact of a central design. A closer look at the background from a farm view to Chicago's skyline makes for a very impressive and appealing design. I felt the poorest design of 2003 was undoubtedly the Missouri coin. Despite some mint improvements to the design its discombobulated mixing of the Saint Louis arc seemily there during the Lewis and Clark expedition makes it look more like some backwoods vagrant slopping through some mudhole behind a hamburger joint. I believe this coin to be the low point of the series artistically though I would rate it above only the Connecticut quarter because of the poor choice of the Charter Oak's symbolism.

While many people are awaiting the two huge states' entries, Texas and California, to spur the series, Iowa may release a coin with the artistic merit and historical significance equal to the highlight of the series so far, the New Jersey quarter. Iowa is considering a design featuring the five Sullivan brothers who sacrificed their lived during WWII on the ship U.S.S. Juneau. The moving rendition is currently under consideration along with four other designs. Readers of the Blackbook wishing to get involved with the state quarter program should contact the governor of Iowa in support of the Sullivan brothers design. The price one family paid losing five brothers represents the cost American servicemen paid for our freedom and would make a great coin!

COPPER

In early coppers, 1793-1839, half cents and large cents, little is available on the market and auctions seem to be commanding most of the coins. Here bidders frequently pay exceptional premiums, particularly whenever nice problem free planchets are evident.

The collectible coin market has rebounded after the effects of 9/11. Perhaps people want to return to something they can enjoy after watching stocks decline. The strengthening price levels of key dates are very notable throughout the Lincoln section. Color is primarily the main collector focus as opposed to years back when strike was more in vogue. And the color collectors have been demanding is full original red which does bring healthy premiums, even among dates from the forties and fifties. A 1963 Lincoln cent started off the 2003 auction season with an incredible jump when it fetched $39,000! By a factor of less than 200, this 1963 cent may make the 1933 $20 look cheap at 7 and a half mil!

NICKELS

The Buffalo nickel charts are far and away the most active of the nickel section. Increases are show in virtually every early date from good to gem! Of particular note, the rare 18D over 17 is now valued at $550 in good with wholesale buyers eager to pick up specimens at $450. While last year's edition of the Blackbook had fines under $1,000, the overdate has now jumped to $1,500. More than half of the dates from the teens and twenties in XF have plussed. The 1927-D in MS 65 made a major move all the way up to $5,750, thus nearly doubling in value during the last 12 months.

Liberty nickels were also up strong with common date gems up 15% to 25%. Finding selected dates for sets in gem proved difficult with the 1907 increasing from just about common last year to the $850 level. Five new dates broke the $1,000 barrier including three from the 1890s. Liberty nickel sets are being sought once again!

Proof Jefferson nickels are bringing higher prices and the 1997-D Specimen 5c has evidently had strong demand and is now approaching $200. As more collectors join in the hunt for full step nickels, it is readily apparent that quite a few dates including some mid-date S mints are seldom available.

DIMES

Mercury dimes in proof are no longer the stagnant laggards of the past few years and interest is currently strong. Several of the top mint state complete collections in existence had been broken up a few years ago and those appear to have been absorbed into the market.

Barber dimes were one of the few areas of weakness in this year's Blackbook. Fewer set collectors weakened prices for a number of dates. Virtually all demand comes from type coin collectors, and perhaps the series will continue to go the way of Liberty Seated dimes as the sight of Barber coinage in circulation now fades from the collective memory of today's hobbyists.

QUARTERS

Washington quarters continued as one of the hottest series in all of coins. Newsworthy prices were reported throughout the year for finest graded examples. Demand seemed unabated for both key and semi-key dates in choice to gem condition.

Be sure to check through the Standing Liberty quarter pages for a goodly number of price increases in the midgrades. Lesser price adjustments took place among the Liberty Seated and Barber coinage as the circulated market was relatively stable.

HALVES

No one can deny the popularity of Bust halves and their appearance at a bourse table. There really aren't enough of them for the big-time promoters to market them, so Bust halves remain somewhat available to collectors in decent VF and XF condition at affordable levels. Who can not like a large silver coin approaching 200 years old in very presentable condition for less than the price of a good ticket to a basketball game!

Seated halves saw the XF columns increase across the board as a type coin. Many dates were left unchanged as not enough coins were available for trading. Common date

Walking Liberty halves in gem continued to break out of the doldrums and now show some price increases. The tougher pre-1934 dates when available in MS 65 are taken off the market in a hurry. Finally, the proof Walkers as have the proof Mercs from the same era started their rebound and this year's edition shows new strength in this area.

MS 65 Franklins from the sixties have continued to drop as more certified coins have been made and exceeded current demand. The lofty levels these coins first experienced a few years back was likely due to the fewer number of people bothering to search through their bags and rolls for gems.

Kennedy halves as is the case with many of the modern issues are currently very strong. The U.S. Mint, naturally the world's largest coin dealer, decided to cash in on this market and, instead of releasing 2002 halves for circulation, sold them at a premium above face value to collectors.

DOLLARS

Bust $1.00's were among the most active of all early type series this past year. Demand continued strong for them into 2003, and certainly more coins could have been sold had they been located.

One observation I had noticed while at a number of major coins shows was the almost complete lack of Binion silver dollars on the bourse floors. A few years ago a hoard of this size would have been very noticeable and quite a few would have been evident at many dealers' tables. The Binion hoard, however, seemed to make its way through intelligent marketing right into the strong hands of serious collectors and virtually bypass the dealer to dealer trading on the bourse. The more than 100,000 coins were labeled by NGC with the Binion pedigree and most if not all were quickly sold. The silver dollar market has certainly become more efficient due to a number of factors including third party grading, the Internet, and professional marketing.

Ike dollars recently joined the upsurge in modern series, and you will notice significant price increases in that section. The government also decided in 2002 not to release Sac dollars for general circulation. The Mint sold, probably, in excess of 10 million Sac dollars in rolls and bags. Compared to the more than one billion coins issued in 2000, the first year of the series, perhaps the 2002 will become the key to this series. There exists very minimal commercial demand for the Sac dollar, and it is generally considered a failure as a circulating coin. Most Americans have yet to receive one in change.

COMMEMORATIVES

While the modern issues of the commemoratives heat up, there has not been much activity in the older silver (1892-1954) pieces. It remains to be seen how much longer these historically interesting lower mintage coins will be ignored.

GOLD

2002 saw the year end with a strong upwards movement in the spot price, as gold returned to over the $350 level for the first time in years. With a Venezuelan oil strike and war once again looming with Iraq people have returned to that old standby store of value.

2003 has seen the beginnings of a number of issues increasing in trading volume which bodes well for the gold market. Primarily considered generic coins, the MS 60/63 market appears to have a surer foundation with the rise in bullion.

As I mentioned last year, rare proof gold had not recovered, and with the falling stock market, the thin market for these high priced rarities seems a bit stretched. This is not an area of panic selling by any means, since the coins reside with financially sound players in the first place. Activity is, however, down and more pieces are being put onto the current market.

U.S. PHILIPPINES

Truly a collector dominated area of the market with few dealers able to carry a significant inventory of Philippines, especially in choice condition. Collectors continue to seek out rarer pieces for set completions. A good number of noticeable gains can be seen throughout the series with key dates rapidly advancing. The NGC and PCGS certified specimens are competitively sought after as a number of top collectors vie for the finest sets.

Tom Culhane, a coin dealer since 1979, operates his coin store, The Elusive Spondulix, at 954 Stuyvesant Avenue, Union, NJ 07083. He is an authorized ANACS dealer as well as a PCGS dealer for more than ten years. The television program *Jeopardy* has consulted with him as a coin expert to verify its numismatic questions. Culhane is a member in good standing with most major numismatic organizations, including NLG, ANA, and FUN.

Culhane offers regular, fixed price lists and auction representation as well as maintains tables at national and regional coin shows. He is a buyer of all types of U.S. coins, in addition to being an expert on Irish coins. Culhane has competed in both professional arm wrestling and fighting tournaments.

Tom Culhane was actively involved in getting two U.S. commemorative postage stamps issued in 1999. His proposal for the James Cagney stamp was approved with the assistance of several senators, congressmen, and governors, as well as a letter of support from the White House. He also worked in conjunction with most major Irish-American organizations to get the Irish Immigration stamp issued. Culhane presently has a proposal for 2002, calling for a St. Patrick's Day stamp depicting General Washington kneeling in prayer with his troops to mark the day. Since the majority of Revolutionary War troops were Irish, Washington ordered the Continental Army to celebrate St. Patrick's Day as a holiday.

U.S. TERRITORIAL COINAGE

PHILIPPINE COINAGE

The United States held sovereignty over the Philippines after paying $20 million to Spain at the end of the Spanish-American War and issued their coinage from 1903 to 1945. Proof coins were struck in Philadelphia from 1903 to 1908, while business strikes were minted in San Francisco. By 1920 the United States had opened a branch mint in Manila, and Philippine coinage was struck there. During WWII, production shifted back to the U.S. mainland.

For more information on Philippine coinage, please refer to *The Official Price Guide to World Coins.*

	ABP	F-12 FINE	EF-40 EX. FINE	MS-60 UNC.	MS-63 UNC.
PHIL ½ CENT					
☐ 1903	1.50	2.00	4.25	15.00	30.00
☐ 1903 Proof	35.00			45.00	78.00
☐ 1904	2.00	3.00	5.00	15.00	30.00
☐ 1904 Proof	40.00			50.00	75.00
☐ 1905 PF	115.00			150.00	250.00
☐ 1906 PF	75.00			100.00	210.00
☐ 1908 PF	75.00			100.00	210.00
PHIL ONE CENT					
☐ 1903	.75	1.00	2.25	16.00	25.00
☐ 1903 PF	45.00			55.00	85.00
☐ 1904	1.00	1.50	3.50	20.00	32.00
☐ 1904 PF	50.00			60.00	85.00
☐ 1905	1.00	2.00	4.25	20.00	37.00

	ABP	F-12 FINE	EF-40 EX. FINE	MS-60 UNC.	MS-63 UNC.
☐ 1905 PF	100.00			135.00	225.00
☐ 1906 PF	80.00			95.00	210.00
☐ 1908 PF	75.00			90.00	190.00
☐ 1908 S	2.00	3.00	9.00	30.00	50.00
☐ 1908 S/S Horned S					
	22.00	28.00	50.00	115.00	225.00
☐ 1908 S/S/S	20.00	30.00	55.00	130.00	250.00
☐ 1909 S	10.00	15.00	25.00	75.00	125.00
☐ 1910 S	2.00	3.00	8.00	30.00	55.00
☐ 1911 S	2.00	3.00	8.00	28.00	45.00
☐ 1911 S over S	20.00	30.00	60.00	95.00	235.00
☐ 1912 S	7.00	10.00	15.00	40.00	90.00
☐ 1912 S over S	15.00	20.00	40.00	70.00	100.00
☐ 1913 S	2.00	3.00	9.00	25.00	45.00
☐ 1914 S	2.00	3.00	9.00	25.00	60.00
☐ 1914 S over S	15.00	20.00	40.00	75.00	125.00
☐ 1915 S	25.00	35.00	55.00	275.00	485.00
☐ 1916 S	8.00	12.00	21.00	85.00	160.00
☐ 1916 S over S	18.00	25.00	40.00	135.00	200.00
☐ 1917 S	3.00	5.00	10.00	45.00	70.00
☐ 1917/6S	45.00	60.00	85.00	375.00	850.00
☐ 1918 S	4.00	6.00	10.00	40.00	60.00
☐ 1918 Med S	8.00	10.00	12.00	55.00	110.00
☐ 1918 Large S	325.00	375.00	475.00	1100.00	3300.00
☐ 1919 S	4.00	6.00	10.00	40.00	60.00
☐ 1920	6.00	8.00	14.00	60.00	90.00
☐ 1920 S	12.00	15.00	32.00	120.00	275.00
☐ 1921	1.00	2.00	6.00	35.00	55.00
☐ 1922	1.00	2.00	6.00	35.00	65.00
☐ 1925	.75	.90	4.00	20.00	40.00
☐ 1926	.75	.90	3.50	19.00	35.00
☐ 1927 M	.70	.90	3.50	28.00	42.00
☐ 1928 M	.70	.90	3.25	25.00	36.00
☐ 1929 M	.70	.90	3.25	25.00	36.00
☐ 1930 M	.70	.90	3.25	25.00	38.00
☐ 1930 M/M	7.50	10.00	25.00	100.00	175.00
☐ 1931 M	.70	.90	3.00	25.00	36.00
☐ 1932 M	.70	.90	3.00	25.00	36.00
☐ 1933 M	.70	.90	3.00	25.00	36.00
☐ 1934 M	.70	.90	3.00	25.00	36.00
☐ 1936 M	.70	.90	3.00	20.00	36.00
☐ 1937 M	.70	.90	3.00	18.00	28.00

	ABP	F-12 FINE	EF-40 EX. FINE	MS-60 UNC.	MS-63 UNC.
☐ 1938 M	.70	1.00	3.00	21.00	28.00
☐ 1939 M	.70	1.00	3.00	21.00	28.00
☐ 1940 M	.70	1.00	3.00	16.00	22.00
☐ 1941 M	1.25	2.00	4.00	25.00	52.00
☐ 1944 S	.25	.50	.90	3.00	4.50
☐ 1944 S Doubled					
	2.00	3.00	6.00	25.00	45.00
5 CENT					
☐ 1903	1.00	2.00	4.00	18.00	30.00
☐ 1903 PF	35.00			55.00	100.00
☐ 1904	2.00	3.00	7.00	28.00	40.00
☐ 1904 PF	50.00			65.00	140.00
☐ 1905 PF	100.00			125.00	210.00
☐ 1906 PF	75.00			100.00	190.00
☐ 1908 PF	75.00			110.00	200.00
☐ 1916 S	30.00	40.00	85.00	400.00	650.00
☐ 1917 S	4.00	6.00	14.00	80.00	180.00
☐ 1918 S	4.00	6.00	14.00	100.00	235.00
☐ 1918 S Mule	400.00	500.00	950.00	4200.00	7500.00
☐ 1919 S	4.00	7.00	14.00	85.00	160.00
☐ 1920	4.00	7.00	14.00	95.00	160.00
☐ 1921	4.00	7.00	14.00	90.00	160.00
☐ 1925	7.00	10.00	25.00	125.00	175.00
☐ 1926	5.00	8.00	16.00	110.00	150.00
☐ 1927	5.00	8.00	15.00	110.00	130.00
☐ 1928	3.00	5.00	12.00	95.00	125.00
☐ 1930	1.00	2.00	4.00	55.00	92.00
☐ 1931	1.00	2.00	4.00	55.00	92.00
☐ 1932	1.00	2.00	4.00	60.00	100.00
☐ 1934	1.00	2.00	4.00	75.00	110.00
☐ 1934 Doubled MM					
	7.00	10.00	15.00	100.00	210.00
☐ 1935	1.00	2.00	5.00	90.00	125.00
☐ 1937	.70	1.50	3.00	35.00	60.00
☐ 1938	.70	1.50	3.00	28.00	45.00
☐ 1941	1.00	2.00	5.00	30.00	50.00
☐ 1944 P	.70	1.00	2.00	3.00	6.50
☐ 1944 S	.25	.50	1.00	2.00	5.00
☐ 1945 S	.25	.50	1.00	2.00	5.00
10 CENT					
☐ 1903-S	10.00	15.00	32.00	150.00	275.00
☐ 1903	2.00	3.00	5.00	32.00	65.00

	ABP	F-12 FINE	EF-40 EX. FINE	MS-60 UNC.	MS-63 UNC.
☐ 1903 PF	60.00			75.00	145.00
☐ 1904	20.00	25.00	40.00	60.00	120.00
☐ 1904 S	3.00	4.00	8.00	45.00	75.00
☐ 1904 PF	60.00			80.00	120.00
☐ 1905 PF	100.00			125.00	285.00
☐ 1906 PF	80.00			110.00	240.00
☐ 1907	1.00	2.00	5.00	50.00	95.00
☐ 1907 S	1.00	2.00	4.00	45.00	95.00
☐ 1908 PF	100.00			125.00	200.00
☐ 1908 S	1.00	2.00	5.00	50.00	80.00
☐ 1909 S	10.00	15.00	32.00	240.00	375.00
☐ 1911 S	3.00	6.00	10.00	80.00	150.00
☐ 1912 S	3.00	6.00	10.00	90.00	165.00
☐ 1912 S/S	20.00	25.00	40.00	200.00	485.00
☐ 1913 S	3.00	5.00	11.00	90.00	825.00
☐ 1914 S Long Class					
	10.00	15.00	26.00	235.00	575.00
☐ 1914 S	7.00	10.00	20.00	185.00	400.00
☐ 1915 S	10.00	15.00	25.00	225.00	550.00
☐ 1917 S	1.00	2.00	4.50	25.00	55.00
☐ 1918 S	1.00	2.00	4.50	25.00	50.00
☐ 1919 S	1.00	2.00	4.50	25.00	45.00
☐ 1920 M	2.00	3.00	8.50	90.00	150.00
☐ 1921	.70	.90	2.10	20.00	35.00
☐ 1929	.70	.90	2.10	15.00	32.00
☐ 1935	.70	.90	2.10	15.00	32.00
☐ 1937	.70	.90	1.50	12.00	25.00
☐ 1938	.70	.90	1.50	12.00	25.00
☐ 1941	1.00	2.00	3.00	15.00	25.00
☐ 1944 D	.35	.50	.80	3.00	6.00
☐ 1945 D	.35	.50	.80	3.00	6.00
☐ 1945 D/D	7.00	10.00	18.00	55.00	80.00
TWENTY CENT					
☐ 1903	2.00	3.00	7.00	40.00	80.00
☐ 1903 S	10.00	15.00	32.00	210.00	365.00
☐ 1903 PF	60.00			75.00	180.00
☐ 1904	20.00	28.00	42.00	100.00	175.00
☐ 1904 S	3.50	5.00	8.00	50.00	95.00
☐ 1904 PF	60.00			75.00	195.00
☐ 1905 S	15.00	20.00	35.00	300.00	650.00
☐ 1905 PF	150.00			200.00	265.00
☐ 1906 PF	135.00			165.00	325.00

	ABP	F-12 FINE	EF-40 EX. FINE	MS-60 UNC.	MS-63 UNC.
☐ 1907	2.50	4.00	8.00	35.00	100.00
☐ 1907 S	2.50	4.00	6.50	32.00	100.00
☐ 1908 S	2.50	4.00	8.00	32.00	90.00
☐ 1908 PF	125.00			160.00	325.00
☐ 1909 S	12.00	18.00	35.00	250.00	500.00
☐ 1910 S	15.00	20.00	40.00	250.00	565.00
☐ 1911 S	12.00	18.00	35.00	230.00	450.00
☐ 1912 S	8.00	12.00	22.00	125.00	375.00
☐ 1913 S	7.00	12.00	22.00	100.00	225.00
☐ 1914 S	10.00	13.00	25.00	185.00	465.00
☐ 1915 S	12.00	15.00	35.00	200.00	550.00
☐ 1916 S	7.00	12.00	20.00	150.00	350.00
☐ 1917 S	2.00	4.00	7.00	62.00	110.00
☐ 1918 S	2.00	4.00	7.00	62.00	125.00
☐ 1919 S	2.00	4.00	7.00	75.00	140.00
☐ 1920 M	5.00	8.00	10.00	90.00	180.00
☐ 1921	1.00	2.00	7.00	42.00	70.00
☐ 1928/7 Mule	10.00	14.00	52.00	525.00	1150.00
☐ 1929 Repunch Date					
	10.00	14.00	45.00	60.00	90.00
☐ 1929	1.00	2.00	4.00	20.00	35.00
☐ 1937	.70	1.50	4.00	18.00	29.00
☐ 1938	.70	1.50	4.00	18.00	29.00
☐ 1941	.70	1.50	4.00	28.00	55.00
☐ 1944 D	.45	.75	.90	2.00	6.00
☐ 1944 D/S	15.00	20.00	45.00	110.00	200.00
☐ 1945 D	.45	.75	.90	2.00	4.00
FIFTY CENT					
☐ 1903	4.00	6.00	15.00	75.00	150.00
☐ 1903 PF	75.00			100.00	200.00
☐ 1904	25.00	35.00	64.00	135.00	225.00
☐ 1904-S	8.00	12.00	22.00	110.00	210.00
☐ 1904 PF	100.00			135.00	225.00
☐ 1905 S	180.00	26.00	40.00	260.00	450.00
☐ 1905 PF	225.00			300.00	475.00
☐ 1906 PF	165.00			200.00	375.00
☐ 1907	2.50	4.00	12.00	100.00	195.00
☐ 1907-S	2.50	4.00	12.00	100.00	195.00
☐ 1908-S	2.50	4.00	12.00	100.00	225.00
☐ 1908 PF	175.00			260.00	400.00
☐ 1909 S	7.00	10.00	28.00	260.00	475.00
☐ 1917 S	5.00	8.00	21.00	165.00	400.00

	ABP	F-12 FINE	EF-40 EX. FINE	MS-60 UNC.	MS-63 UNC.
☐ 1917 S Broken 7					
	9.00	15.00	30.00	285.00	550.00
☐ 1918 S	3.50	5.00	9.50	45.00	125.00
☐ 1918 Inverted S					
	25.00	35.00	65.00	190.00	350.00
☐ 1919 S	3.50	5.00	9.00	50.00	145.00
☐ 1920	3.50	5.00	8.00	50.00	95.00
☐ 1921	2.00	3.00	6.00	25.00	45.00
☐ 1944 S	1.85	2.25	3.00	5.00	7.50
☐ 1944 S/S	25.00	35.00	55.00	110.00	165.00
☐ 1945 S	1.85	2.25	3.00	5.00	8.00
☐ 1945 S/S	35.00	45.00	65.00	120.00	185.00
PESO					
☐ 1903	15.00	18.00	28.00	175.00	365.00
☐ 1903 S	8.00	12.00	21.00	110.00	275.00
☐ 1903 PF	140.00			190.00	420.00
☐ 1904	60.00	80.00	125.00	225.00	400.00
☐ 1904-S	10.00	14.00	23.00	100.00	215.00
☐ 1904 PF	160.00			200.00	475.00
☐ 1905-S	12.00	18.00	28.00	225.00	450.00
☐ 1905-S Straight Serif					
	45.00	60.00	75.00	750.00	190.00
☐ 1905 PF	450.00			600.00	1100.00
☐ 1906 S	1000.00	1200.00	2150.00	7000.00	13500.00
☐ 1906 PF	350.00			425.00	800.00
☐ 1907 S	6.00	8.00	15.00	85.00	185.00
☐ 1908 S	5.50	8.00	13.00	80.00	175.00
☐ 1908 S/S	50.00	70.00	95.00	200.00	385.00
☐ 1908 S Double Diz & Inverted MM					
	75.00	100.00	130.00	350.00	700.00
☐ 1908 PF	325.00			400.00	700.00
☐ 1909 S	8.00	12.00	18.00	75.00	165.00
☐ 1909 S/S	25.00	35.00	55.00	150.00	265.00
☐ 1909 S/S/S	55.00	80.00	100.00	200.00	450.00
☐ 1910 S	15.00	20.00	30.00	125.00	260.00
☐ 1911 S	25.00	35.00	70.00	1300.00	4500.00
☐ 1912 S	25.00	35.00	85.00	1500.00	4500.00
COMMEMORATIVE					
☐ 1936 50 C	27.00	32.00	50.00	75.00	120.00
☐ 1936 Murphy Queyer					
	45.00	55.00	80.00	135.00	215.00
☐ 1936 Roosevelt Queyer					
	45.00	55.00	85.00	150.00	225.00

COIN AND PAPER MONEY COMPUTER SOFTWARE

by Tom Bilotta,
Carlisle Development Corporation

The use of computer software to assist in organizing a coin or paper money collection is an excellent way to enhance your enjoyment of collecting. In addition to helping you to catalog your collection, coin collection software can aide you in identifying collection objectives that are aligned with your interests and financial resources. Software for coin and paper money collectors can be grouped into two broad categories; inventory software and educational software.

Most commonly when collectors think of using computer software to assist with their collecting, they first think of an inventory program. Their goal is to catalog their collection and then use this information to generate a variety of printed reports. These reports include a variety of sorted and filtered listings to assist in managing your collection, want lists which identify items you are seeking, sales lists of items to be sold or traded, detailed inventories for insurance purposes, as well as many other purposes.

Once familiar with inventory programs, collectors often seek educational programs to enhance their collecting skills. These include general historical information about their collecting interest, software to assist in grading collectibles, and special topics to extend their effectiveness in acquiring collectibles.

7

RECENT TECHNOLOGY TRENDS IMPACTING COIN AND CURRENCY COLLECTORS

Over the past several years, usage of the Internet has continued to grow. The number of coin and currency sites has grown exponentially. Web sites may be found covering almost any imaginable specialty of coin or currency collecting. These sites are often maintained by very knowledgeable sources. The American Numismatic Association (ANA) maintains a major website dedicated to coin and currency collecting (www.money.org). This site offers a variety of useful information, and links to many other coin & currency related websites. Most major mints have a strong web presence. The United States Mint, for example, has a highly successful website (www.usmint.gov) which has become the preferred way for its customers to purchase current offerings.

High quality images of coins for sale have become commonplace and are rapidly becoming expected by many online buyers. Users have more powerful computers with very large storage, allowing them to retain hundreds or thousands of high quality coin images. Printers, inks, and specialty papers are now commonly available which allow collectors to print very high quality images of their collection for the purpose of sharing or cataloging. Scanners have continued to improve in quality such that the average collector can now obtain a high quality digital image of a coin in their collection.

The impact of computer technology on coin and paper money collecting is only limited by your imagination. It can be used to obtain specialized information from numismatists throughout the world, to communicate with collectors you would otherwise never meet, or to buy and sell items from a variety of dealers and collectors.

ORGANIZING YOUR COLLECTION WITH COIN & PAPER MONEY INVENTORY SOFTWARE

Collectors of coins and currency fall into several categories. There is the serious coin collector who enjoys the hobby and pursues personally defined collecting objectives. Accumulators retain many of the coins that they receive in normal commerce and build up large quantities of unsorted coins. Investors use coin collecting to build portfolios intended to produce profits. Inheritors receive a coin collection or accumulation from their families and must decide how they will handle a potentially valuable asset.

All of these collectors have a common need to catalog their items and understand their value. Most collectors also have accumulated many items with a very wide range of values.

A modern inventory program can adapt to meet the needs of all types of users from novice collectors to experienced experts. It will incorporate a comprehensive database of coin and or paper money to assist the user in identifying and defining their collections as well as a flexible set of functionality to enable them to organize their collection in a manner consistent with their collection methodology.

Most collectors will want to organize their collections into several groupings. The collector will want to create collections that mirror their physical collection. For example, someone with coin albums of common series such as mercury dimes, statehood quarters, or buffalo nickels will want to have software albums organized in similar fashion. Other coins might be grouped into coins for sale, duplicates, partial collections for other family members, or any other categorization which suits the collector.

USING YOUR TIME WISELY

When using computer software to catalog a coin or paper money collection it is important to use it in a manner consistent with your purposes and which will enhance your enjoyment. You should spend your time, therefore, working with the portions of your collection in which you have the most interest or where the primary financial value exists.

For example, if you are collecting a complete set of Mercury dimes, you may wish to scan an image of each individual piece so that you can print picture catalogs of your collection. For these coins, you might choose to enter in complete information including purchase price, source, certification information, origin, etc. For this type of grouping you will also likely want to include coins you don't have that are required to complete your collection, enabling you to generate want lists. This will also assist you in identifying the cost to complete your collection and planning your approach.

For large quantities of relatively inexpensive items or coins worth only bullion content and where you have no particular collecting interest, you might choose to only enter a single line item and not bother to take the time to list each coin individually. For example, if you have several hundred silver Washington quarters in circulated condition from the 1950's and 1960's you might enter a single line item 225 Washington Quarters with a date range and average value. In this way, large accumulations can be tracked with minimum effort and your attention can be focused on your real collecting interests. Your coin inventory program should adapt to all of these possible approaches to organizing your collection.

EVALUATING COIN AND PAPER MONEY INVENTORY SOFTWARE

The quality of the software that you purchase will greatly impact the success of your efforts.

One of the most important parts of a coin inventory program is the database. The database contains standard information about coins and paper money and saves the user from having to type this information manually. The greater the amount of information in the standard database, the easier the task of data entry. A modern coin collecting program, at a minimum should include coin type, date, mint mark, denomination and variety. Comprehensive programs, such as those made by Carlisle Development Corporation also include such information as designer/engraver, coinage metal, size, weight, edge, and mintage. The organization of the database should reflect commonly used groupings and thereby provide user with guidance in organizing their collection.

Some inventory programs include current market values. It is important that these are updated frequently and produced by reliable sources. Coin values should evolve to include areas of high market interest. For example, over the past year, the market interest in high grade recent coin issues has become very high. It is also important to allow the user the ability to extend the database to include items that are not listed. These may be specialized varieties, private mint products, or other coin related collectibles.

Ability to share data with other programs and people is

also very important. Most computerized collectors are connected to the Internet and will want to share some information with other collectors and dealers. The ability to export listings in common text readable formats for transmission over the Internet or for input into a word processor or spreadsheet is of great value in buying and selling coins and paper money.

Carlisle Development's inventory software, Collector's Assistant provides a comprehensive database of all coins ever minted by the United States Mint. This includes all type coins by date and mint mark, bullion coins, sets, old and new commemoratives. Recent additions to the database are the 50 states circulating quarters and the new Sacagawea Dollar. Coin values are licensed from Coin World, Inc., an industry leader in providing coin valuations. Quarterly updates are available by subscription allowing collectors to maintain trends of their values. Carlisle Development's Currency Collector's Assistant has a complete database based on Friedberg's Paper Money of the United States, 16th Edition. This database includes all U.S. Paper Money, including Confederate notes and Encased postage stamps. A relationship with CDN, publisher of the Greensheet, makes value information available to the paper money collector in electronic format.

For collectors of ancient coins, Carlisle offers an add-on database containing color images of several hundred ancient coins and a specialized interface containing data entry fields appropriate for ancient coins. For example, the date field can handle and sort mixed AD/BC dates and has long fields for obverse and reverse inscriptions. The most recent additions to Carlisle Development's databases include the Euro Coin Database and World Currency Database.

REPORT GENERATION

Once you have entered your coin collection into an inventory program, the most important function will become its ability to generate a wide array of reports and/or exports for informational purposes.

You will probably want to have a detailed listing, identifying items, their value, and where they are stored for insurance purposes. You will want to generate partial lists of your collections for sales and trading. You may want to generate labels to aid in identifying your coins. You may want to look at your collection in many different ways such as sorted by value or metal content or collection completeness.

One common need of coin collectors is the printing of inserts for 2" flips. Once catalogued, computer softare can allow you to produce customized flip inserts in a standard format of your own design.

Report generation is the subset of an inventory program which produces the listings that you view on the screen, print on paper, or export to other computer applications. Its flexibility will greatly impact its utility. For example, you may want to generate two listings of coins that you have for sale, one which includes your cost and target price (your copy) and one which does not include this information for general distribution to prospective buyers.

At various times, you will probably want to be able to list any subset of the information fields, filter based on a wide array of parameters and sort using different criteria.

OTHER FUNCTIONALITY YOU SHOULD EXPECT FROM YOUR INVENTORY SOFTWARE

Inventory software should be able to store all of the information in which a collector is interested. Specific fields will vary based on collector interest and purpose. Some will require detailed certification and descriptive information, others comprehensive purchase & sales history. Some collectors will want to have comprehensive recording of storage location and insurance information. Modern programs provide sufficient information fields to meet all of these needs.

Backup and restore functionality should allow the user to easily protect the data they have meticulously entered. History charting enables the user to track the changes of value of a part of their collection over time.

Good software must be easy to use and supported by context sensitive help which provides the user with detailed instructions in a "how-to" format on all of the basic functions that they will wish to perform.

AVAILABILITY OF TIMELY UPDATES

Once you have taken the time to catalog your collection in a computer program, you will want to preserve your investment by having access to database updates incorporating information on new coin releases as well as changes in value. Your supplier of inventory software should have a timely program for availability of annual database and value updates.

INVENTORY SOFTWARE FOR INHERITORS OF COIN COLLECTIONS

The inheritor is usually faced with a daunting task, often having to sort a large number of coins and then decide on their disposition. Often this task is undertaken with little knowledge of coin collecting.

One of the first challenges faced by someone who inherits a collection is the identification of the coins that they have received. Modern inventory programs typically incorporate a comprehensive picture catalog enabling visual identification. Once identified, tables of values assist the heir in deciding which coins may have substantial value and should be analyzed closely and which coins are relatively commonplace and not sufficiently valuable to warrant a significant allocation of time.

Once the coins are divided, time can be focused on the coins with greatest potential value and the remainder quickly sold at a fair price.

Educational computer software can be of particular value to the inheritor, who must build his knowledge of coin collecting in a very short period of time.

EDUCATIONAL SOFTWARE FOR COLLECTORS

Adding significantly to your enjoyment of collections are electronic information sources that exploit the power of the computer to present you with high quality information in an easily accessible format. These programs can provide comprehensive knowledge of all aspects of coin collecting, detailed information on grading coins, and specialized information such as collecting coin varieties.

COIN GRADING

Most coin collectors will want to be able to grade their coins, at least to an approximate grade. This enables them to have an understanding of value as well as identify coins that might be appropriate for certification. Coin grading skill is built up through time and experience.

The Grading Assistant, offered by Carlisle Development is based on the official Grading Guide of the American Numismatic Association. It enables the user to view side-by-side images of their own coins along with various grades from the ANA grading set. These images are supported by detailed descriptions of the wear points for each grade. Using software such as the Grading Assistant, a user can develop their skill in grading coins and establish approximate grades for their collection.

VARIETY COLLECTING

The collecting of coin varieties is an exciting area of the hobby currently experiencing some growth. Varieties are the result of differences in the minting process or dies which produce design differences and or errors. These include such effects as doubling of some of features or letters, extra pieces of metal on the coin surface and die breaks. Variety collecting requires the collector to identify subtle differences in coin designs.

The Morgan dollar series is one of the most commonly collected and is categorized by many varieties. Carlisle Development offers a Top 100 Morgan Dollar CD, based on the book written by Michael Fey and Jeff Oxman. This work provides pictures, identification information, and values for the most sought after and valuable Morgan dollar varieties. It provides a spectacular set of high quality pictures to assist you in identifying these coins and also the full text and information provided in this work.

GENERAL EDUCATIONAL WORKS ON COLLECTING

There is much to learn about coin collecting, whether it is technical knowledge such as grading and authentication or practical knowledge such as buying and selling coins, attending trade shows, or participating in auctions. Educational computer software offers advantages over printed works in that the contents may be searched and indexed allowing the user to rapidly retrieve valuable information.

Carlisle Development offers the *Coin Collector's Survival Manual,* an interactive edition of the work by Scott Travers. This work provides a set of information that every collector of coins should have. The entire contents of this book are provided in a searchable, interactive format. This allows the user to easily locate information based on word searching, topics, illustrations, bookmarks, a table of contents, or index. In addition to the contents of the book, a set of high quality NGC PhotoProof images have been included for such topics as identifying MS-63, MS-65, MS-67 coins and toning. An interactive grading calculator brings to life the grading methods described in the book.

WELL DESIGNED COMPUTER SOFTWARE WILL ADD TO YOUR ENJOYMENT OF COLLECTING

Carlisle Development Corporation publishes the most comprehensive line of collector software available, especially regarding coins and paper money.

Central to Carlisle's product line is the Collector's Assistant, the most advanced and comprehensive collection software available. It is sold in a variety of configurations to serve collectors of over thirty collectible types from autographs to toys. Most extensive is support for coins and paper money. The Collector's Assistant family includes:

- **United States Coin Database**—complete listings of all U.S. coinage from 1793 to the present. 50 State quarter program and Sacagawea dollar are recent additions. This also includes Colonial and Hawaiian coinage.
- **World Coin Database**—A listing of over 5000 coin types from over forty-five countries, which may be extended by the user.
- **Ancient Coin Database**—includes several thousand listings of Byzantine, Judaic, Roman and Greek coinage along with several hundred images. Data entry screens

are optimized for ancient coin collectors including long fields for inscriptions and preloaded choice lists of rulers, ancient denominations, towns, mints and others.

• **United States Currency Database**—A complete listing of all United States currency based on Friedberg's 16th Edition, Paper Money of the United States. This also includes 120 high quality color images of early US currency.

To learn more about Carlisle Development's product line, visit our website at www.carlisledevelopment.com. You will find current product information and may also place orders. You can reach us by e-mail at support@carlisledevelopment.com or by phone at 800-219-0257.

COIN AUCTION SALES

By Q. David Bowers

Auctions are perhaps the truest test of coin values. One can talk about "bid" and "ask" prices in various numismatic publications, but do actual transactions occur at these figures? The bottom line is that a coin is worth what someone will pay for it. An auction price, assuming that the sale is conducted in a professional manner, that "reserves" are disclosed, that the catalog is widely distributed, and that the sale is publicized, represents what a given coin, token, medal, or piece of paper money is worth in a given moment of time. For example, if I were to state to you that a certain coin in Very Fine grade fetched $1,200 at a recent sale, you would be hard pressed to argue that it was only worth $500 or, conversely, it was worth $3,000. Rather, $1,200 represents the current market value at the moment.

However, sometimes in the case of "name" sales, coins will bring more than their normal prices at auctions. Let me explain:

Auction "Fever"

There are a lot of interesting stories that can be told with regard to auction sales. A number of years ago, the New Netherlands Coin Company conducted an auction in which some Uncirculated examples of early Lincoln cents were offered on an individual basis. A 1915 Philadelphia Mint cent surprised spectators by selling for four or five times what everyone thought it would fetch. Later, it developed that both bidders were competing for what they thought was a differ-

17

ent lot! The auction record price was publicized (without explanation of the bidding mistake), and, overnight, the price of the 1915 Lincoln cent in Uncirculated grade multiplied in catalogs and reference books!

In another instance, I recall offering a 1909-S V.D.B. cent in one of my own auction catalogs. I attended the sale and was amazed as the price went over current retail levels, then double retail, and then even further. Both buyers were people I knew, so after the sale I asked them for the rationale of their bidding. Both stated that they wanted a coin pedigreed from the sale and illustrated in the catalog, and this was more important than buying it for a reasonable price!

Similarly, in our sale of the Garrett collection for The Johns Hopkins University, 1979–1981, a common Washington-Carver commemorative half dollar, worth perhaps $15 at the time, sold for several hundred dollars because of its pedigree! *The New York Times* illustrated and featured this otherwise common coin, sold at a spectacular price, in one of the articles concerning the event. The Eliasberg Collection, sold by us in 1996 and 1997 and containing the fabulous 1913 Liberty Head nickel, saw many unbelievable prices for other coins as well.

HOW TO BE A SMART BIDDER

How should one participate in an auction? In my opinion, it is best to plan in advance. I recommend contacting different auction firms requesting sample copies of their catalogs, but please bear in mind that often a charge must be paid as catalogs can be very expensive to publish. Review the catalogs, paying particular attention to the Terms of Sale as they fluctuate from firm to firm. Issues to be concerned with are buyer's fees, return privileges, bidding options, etc. You are legally bound to those terms, and they are put into the catalog for a specific purpose—not just for entertaining reading. Do not take them lightly or fail to read them!

Then determine the type of coin offered and subscribe to the catalogs you find to be best. If you have a specialty—such as tokens, medals, obsolete paper money, or the like—you may find that one or two firms issue specialized catalogs. If your interests are simply the general U.S. series, then you have a very wide selection. In any event, I recommend that you subscribe to multiple auction catalogs so that you can get a "feel for the market." After a sale takes place, you will receive a copy of the prices realized list, which will guide you in future bidding.

A typical auction firm will issue a catalog describing each lot in detail. If you have a question about a piece, that question can often be answered on the telephone. Many firms will gladly accommodate your request for a phone description. Furthermore, if you are an established collector with a history of successful coin buying, and are known to the auctioneer, an arrangement may be made whereby the coin can be sent

to you for inspection, providing that the coin is returned the same day and that you pay postage and insurance both ways. This courtesy is commonly referred to as "mail inspection."

Participation in an auction sale can be by mail or in person. Before each auction, there is a lot viewing period during which each lot can be personally inspected. Most auctioneers firmly state that anyone who has had a chance to view lots beforehand, or anyone who is a floor bidder, cannot return a coin for any reason whatsoever, with the exception of authenticity. So do your homework earlier, not later!

Bidding by Mail

If you plan to bid by mail, send in your bid sheet as early as you can. Most auction firms accept bids via mail, fax, and telephone. If you are unknown to the auction house, you may be required to send a deposit and/or references to secure your bids. This is a normal procedure which protects the auction house and consignors by eliminating competition that is not real.

When compiling your bids, first determine the lots you are interested in and the amount which you are willing to pay for each. Be aware of current price levels. If a certain variety of Morgan silver dollar generally brings $500 on the retail market, the chances aren't very good that a bid of $300 will make you the owner. Conversely, there is no particular point in bidding $800 for it if you can buy one somewhere else for $500, unless you like the pedigree, toning, or some other aspect which differentiates the piece. Many auction houses offer a reduction in the top bid if competition permits, but not all companies follow this practice. In any event, it is best not to count on this for if you bid $1,000, you may very well be charged $1,000.

Once your bids are compiled, you can determine whether to utilize some of the special bidding options offered by the auction house. These special options help the mail bidder place as many potentially winning bids as possible.

Floor Bidding

As sales to floor bidders are usually final, it is important to study each piece carefully during the lot viewing time permit-

ted before the sale. I suggest viewing some coins that are not in the mainstream of your collection specialty but, at an appropriate price, might still prove to be a good buy. For example, there is nothing more frustrating than to be a silver dollar specialist who has looked only at Morgan and Peace dollars, and to be sitting in the auction room when a gorgeous Liberty Seated silver dollar comes up, only to realize that you did not take the time to look at the lot before the sale.

Bidding strategy at the sale itself has furnished the topic for endless discussions. Should I sit in the front? Or, will I better know what is going on if I sit in the back? Or, perhaps on the side would be best. There are no rules. Pick your favorite.

Most auction houses furnish bidders with paddles or cards with printed numbers. Some bidders flick their paddles almost unnoticeably while others hold them up in the air like a banner. Personal preference is the key, but be sure the auctioneer knows what you are doing. If the auctioneer misses your bid, call out right at the time the lot is being sold. Generally the auctioneer at his discretion may reopen a lot if he feels that a legitimate mistake has been made on the auction floor, but he will not do this on a consistent basis for the same bidder who isn't paying attention.

After the sale, check with the accounting department of the firm and make payment. You may wish to take the coins with you, or you may wish to have the auctioneer ship the coins to your home or office. Unless you have a resale permit, you will be liable for city or state sales tax in the area in which the auction was held.

YOUR ROLE AS A SELLER— FINDING THE RIGHT AUCTIONEER

If you have a group of scarce and rare coins to sell, and the coins are valued at several thousand dollars or more in total, auction may be the route for you. By exposing your coins in an auction catalog, thousands of potential bidders can become acquainted with them. On the other hand, if you have miscellaneous coins of low value, or bullion-type coins, a dealer with an over-the-counter business may offer a better price to buy such items for store stock.

How to choose an auctioneer? Here are some questions you should ask:

What is the commission rate? What is the buyer's fee? Some auction houses will offer a reduced commission rate but an increased buyer's fee.

What do I get for this rate? Are there any extra charges? Are catalog illustrations extra? What about photography? What about advertising? It is a practice for some auction houses to give a "minimum price" or cut-rate fee, and then charge extra to bring the service up to "normal." Find this out in advance.

Once the auction takes place, when will the settlement date be? How will I receive payment? Can I receive a portion of the expected realization in advance? If so, what interest rates are charged? What is the financial reputation of the company? Does the company have adequate insurance? How can I be sure that my valued coins and other numismatic items are in truly safe hands?

Does the auction house allow reserves? Can I bid on my own coins? What is the anticipated market for my consignment? What happens if someone bidding on my coins fails to pay his auction bill?

What type of coins has the firm handled in the past? Does the company specialize only in certain areas or does it offer many different services? How large is the staff and what are the qualifications of the individual staff members?

What is the reputation of the firm? What do past consignors think of the performance of the auction house? Is the company familiar with die varieties, great rarities, and obscure coins in addition to ones normally seen?

What do the firm's catalogs look like? Are the descriptions appealing? Are the descriptions authoritative? What is the quality of the mailing list? Does it contain proven bidders? What type of advertising will be done for the catalog featuring my coins?

In what town or city will the event be held? What are the facilities like?

I suggest that each of the preceding questions be answered with care and you may well think of other questions in addition.

IT'S THE BOTTOM LINE THAT COUNTS

Several years ago, I and another member of the Auctions by Bowers and Merena staff traveled to visit with the heirs to a very large collection of U.S. and world coins. Our firm offered a 10% commission rate to sell the pieces, stating that they would be presented in a Grand Format™ color-illustrated catalog with no expense spared when it came to advertising, publicity, and the like.

While the owners of the coins seemed to be very impressed with our track record, the appearance of our past catalogs, our reputation, and other factors there was one problem: a competitor had offered to do it for no commission rate at all! It was stated that the competitor's profit would be determined only by the buyer's fee.

To make a long story short, the coins were awarded to a company whose main expertise was not in coins but rather in art and furniture. The sale came and went, and instead of realizing the approximately $1.5 million that the heirs hoped for (and which I felt could be achieved with proper presentation), only about half that amount was obtained! Dealers at the sale had a field day, for few collectors had received a copy of the catalog. I later reviewed a copy of the prices realized and noted that many issues sold for fractions of what I felt they could be sold for by my firm or, for that matter, by other leading *rare coin* auctioneers. Virtually no advertising was placed by the other auction firm. And, apparently many of the catalogs went to people who were not proven buyers of the type of coins being offered.

To expand upon this further, if an auctioneer sells a coin for $1,000 hammer price and charges you 10%, thus netting you $900, it might be a much better deal than if another auctioneer sells your coin for $600 and charges you no fee at all—netting you $600. If you were considering having surgery done, or having an architect design your house, or having your portrait painted, I cannot envision you saying "I am looking for the cheapest rate." Rather such considerations as past performance would be more important. So it should be with coins as well. As I believe John Ruskin said, "the bitterness of poor quality lasts much longer than the sweetness of low price."

A LASTING TRIBUTE

There are some aesthetic considerations to selling at auction. A finely prepared catalog can be a memorial to you and your collecting activities. Although the coins once owned by you are in new hands, the catalog will remain a lasting tribute to your collection for you to enjoy. In addition, most people who have spent many years collecting coins enjoy the pride and satisfaction that comes with the recognition a beautiful catalog provides when their collections are sold.

If you form a collection over a long period of years, and if you enjoy numismatics to its fullest extent, selling your collection by auction can be the high point of your accomplishments.

Meanwhile, as you build your collection, auctions provide an interesting and exciting way to acquire pieces that you need.

Have fun!

AUCTIONS BY BOWERS AND MERENA

Auctions by Bowers and Merena, Inc., has had the good fortune of being in the forefront of numismatics for many years. We have received more "Catalog of the Year" honors awarded by the Numismatic Literary Guild than all of our competitors combined. Of the top three most valuable

U.S. coin collections ever to be sold at auction, we have catalogued and sold all three—the $44,900,000 Eliasberg Collection, the $25,000,000 Garrett Collection, and the $20,000,000 Norweb Collection.

If you would like an "Auction Kit" which will include a current auction catalog and a full-color brochure on consigning your coins to auction, please send $10 to Auction Kit, Auctions by Bowers and Merena, Inc., PO Box 1224, Wolfeboro, NH 03894.

If you'd like immediate information on the most profitable way to sell your coins call Q. David Bowers, Chairman of the Board, at 1-603-569-5095. Contacting us today may be the most financially rewarding decision you have ever made.

EXPERT TIPS ON BUYING AND SELLING COINS

Intelligent coin buying is the key to building a good collection at reasonable cost. Today, with the added confusion of split grading, slider grading, and the devious practices of some coin sellers, it is more necessary than ever to be a skilled buyer.

In the interest of supplementing the coin pricing and identification in this book with practical advice on astute buying, the editor presents the following article. It reviews major pitfalls to which an uninformed buyer might succumb and gives specific suggestions on getting the most for your money when buying coins.

The editor wishes to state clearly that the exposure of questionable practices by some coin sellers, as detailed below, is not intended as a general indictment of the coin trade. The vast majority of professional coin dealers are ethical and try to please. Moreover, it can be safely stated that if the hobbyist restricts his buying exclusively to well-established coin dealers, he runs very little risk.

UNSATISFACTORY SOURCES OF COINS

Unsatisfactory sources of coins—those entailing a higher than necessary degree of risk—include flea markets, antiques shops, garage sales, private parties who are unknown to you, auction sales in which coins are offered along with non-numismatic merchandise, and advertisements in magazines and newspapers published for a general readership rather than for coin collectors. This advice is given to benefit the nonexpert buyer and especially the beginner. Advanced collectors with full confidence in their coin buying skills will sometimes shop these sources to find possible bargains.

Mail-Order Ads in National Magazines

The sharp rise in coin values during 1979 and 1980 encouraged many promoters to deal in coins. (Promoters are persons who aren't coin dealers in the accepted sense of the term, but who utilize coins for large-scale mail-order promotions.) The objective, nearly always, is to sell coins to buyers of limited knowledge and thereby succeed in promising more, and charging more, than would a legitimate professional coin dealer. Undoubtedly such promotions are extremely successful, to judge from the number of such ads that appear regularly.

Here are some examples of the headlines they use:

"Genuine Silver Dollars Struck by the U.S. Mint . . ."

"Real John F. Kennedy Silver Half Dollars . . ."

"Cased Set of U.S. Mint Morgan Dollars . . ."

"Unbelievable But True: U.S. Silver Dollars at Only $21.95 . . ."

The ads look impressive and sound impressive. They show enlargements of the merchandise. They quote facts and figures, often with historical data. They present a variety of guarantees about the coins, and there is no misrepresentation in those guarantees. You do receive genuine coins struck by the U.S. Mint. They really are 90% silver if you order Morgan or Peace dollars. But the price you pay is from twice to three times as much as if you bought from a *real* coin dealer. In the legitimate coin trade, the coins sold via these ads are looked upon as "junk coins." They command a very small premium over their silver bullion value. They are not only the most common dates but are usually in miserable condition.

To lend credibility, the promotors will normally use a company name which gives the appearance of being that of a full-time coin dealer. There is nothing illegal in doing this, but it does contribute to the misleading nature of such ads.

Let's examine some of the specific methods used in today's ever-increasing deceptive coin ads. You will soon see why coins, especially U.S. silver coins, have become a favorite of mail-order promoters: they can be "hyped" in a most convincing manner, without making statements that are patently false. Thus, the advertisers skirt around—though narrowly—allegations of mail fraud. (Fraud cannot be alleged on the basis of price, as a merchant is free to charge what he pleases for whatever he sells.)

1. *Creating the impression that the coins offered originate from a hidden or sequestered cache not previously available to the public.* This is accomplished by the use of such phrases as, "Just found, 2,367 specimens," or "Now released to the public . . ." The assertion that they were "just found" is not wholly inaccurate, however. The advertiser has, more than likely, located a dealer who could supply wholesale quantities of junk coins. The coins themselves were never lost or hidden. "Now released to the public" has nothing to do with official government release nor release by a court. It simply means the advertiser is selling them.

In a very few isolated cases, in which mail fraud charges were brought, ads have gone beyond this kind of assertion-by-innuendo. They actually stated that the coins were from secret government stockpiles. One of them wove an elaborate tale of silver dollars being taken to special storage locations by the army during World War I. Such an event never occurred, and that is the basic difference between prosecutable and nonprosecutable ads. If an advertiser merely hints at something, but does not state it as fact, he is usually within the law.

2. *Leading the potential customer to believe the coins are scarcer or more valuable than they really are.* This is done via numerous techniques. Among the favorites is to compare the advertiser's selling price against prices for other coins of the same series. An ad offering Morgan dollars for $27.50 may call attention to the fact that "some Morgan dollars have sold for $20,000, $50,000, and more." Yes, they have. They are the rare, desirable dates in UNC, not the common, circulated coins you receive from the advertiser.

When half dollars are offered, it will be said that "you just can't find them in circulation any longer." It's entirely true that Walking Liberty halves, Franklins, and the lone 90% silver Kennedy half (1964) cannot be found in day-to-day circulation. But coin dealers have them by the roll and sell them for less than you will pay through such an ad. The fact that these coins are not found in circulation is not an indication of rarity. Many coins carrying very little premium value over their face value cannot be found in day-to-day circulation.

3. *Emphatic guarantee that the coins are genuine.* On this point the advertiser can speak with no fear of legal repercussion. His coins are genuine and nobody can say otherwise. But, even where absolute truth is involved, it can be—and is—presented in such a manner as to give a false impression. By strongly stressing the coins' authenticity, the message is conveyed that many nonauthentic specimens exist and that you run a risk in buying from someone else. Such is far from the case. Any large coin dealer can sell you quantities of perfectly genuine Morgan dollars, Peace dollars, or any other coins you want.

4. *Implication that the coins offered are in some respect "special," as opposed to specimens of the same coins available at coin shops.* This presents an obvious difficulty for the advertiser, as his coins are just the opposite of special: usually heavily circulated, often with actual damage such as nicks, gouges, etc. It is not, however, insurmountable. The advertiser can keep silent about the condition of his coins and present them as some sort of special government issue. Usually this is done by selling them in quantities of four or five and referring to them as "U.S. Mint Sets," "Government Mint Sets," or something similar. The uninformed reader believes he is ordering a set assembled and packaged by the Mint. The Mint *does* assemble and package sets, as everyone knows. But it had no part in these! Assembling and packaging was done by the advertiser. Regardless of how attractive the box or case may be, it is not of official nature and lends absolutely nothing to the value. The Mint has never issued cased or boxed sets in which all the coins were of the same denomination. In these hard-sell sets you will find such combinations as two Morgan dollars and two Peace dollars, four Morgan dollars, or three half dollars. Dates are a purely random selection. And, we repeat, the coins are in well-worn, circulated condition.

5. *Failure to state actual silver content.* This falls under the heading of deception by silence. The potential customer is left to draw his own conclusions and the advertiser knows full well that those conclusions will be wrong. Provided, of course, the ad is worded in such a way that it lends itself to incorrect conclusions. Typically this sort of advertiser is selling Kennedy halves dated from 1965 to 1970. During these years the Kennedy half contained some silver but not very much—just 40% (after 1970 it contained no silver at all). Its silver content was less than one half that of 50-cent pieces struck prior to 1965. In fact, it was even less than the silver content of pre-1965 quarters. Very few individuals, aside from coin hobbyists, are aware of this reduction of silver content in half dollars from 1965 to 1970. When *silver* coins are advertised they automatically think in terms of 90% silver. Yet the advertiser is legally within his rights in referring to 40% silver coins as silver. As the 40% silver coins look just like their 90% silver predecessors, few purchasers will suspect they've overpaid. Until they have them appraised.

6. *Creation of gimmicked names for coins.* By calling a coin something different than its traditional numismatic name, it is made to seem more unusual or special. Everyone is familiar with Kennedy half dollars but what about "Kennedy Silver Eagles"? This is a promoter's name for the Kennedy half, used in an effort to glamorize it. It is highly inappropriate.

7. *False references.* Advertisements of this type are sometimes accompanied by doubtful or fairly obvious fake references on the advertiser's behalf. Taking his cue from legitimate coin dealers, whose ads nearly always refer to their membership in coin organizations and often carry other easily verifiable references as well, he feels he must present similar assurances of his background and reliability. Since he has nothing too convincing to offer in the way of genuine references, he manufactures them. He invents the name of a mythical coin organization, of which he is either a member in good standing, an officer, or perhaps even president. If he chooses not to go quite that far, as he might be caught in the deception, he can take a less volatile course and claim membership in "leading coin collector and dealer organizations" without, of course, naming them. This is just like the ads for questionable diet aids which say, "Tests at a leading eastern university have shown . . ." No one is likely to check all 500 or more eastern universities, or enter into a debate about which ones are leading, or what they may be leading *in*.

Of the various other unsatisfactory sources of coins, the dangers they present should be fairly obvious.

RECOMMENDED SOURCES OF COINS

As a general rule, coin purchasing should be confined to the following sources:

1. Professional coin dealers who sell coins at a shop and/or by mail order.

2. Auction sales conducted by professional coin dealers or auction houses making a specialty of coins.

3. Shows and conventions for coin collectors.

Another acceptable source, though unavailable to many coin hobbyists, is the fellow collector with duplicate or surplus specimens to sell or trade. This source is acceptable only if the individual is known to you, as transactions with strangers can result in problems.

If a coin shop is located in your area, this is the best place to begin buying. By examining the many coins offered in a shop you will become familiar with grading standards. Later you may wish to try buying at auction. When buying from dealers, be sure to do business only with reputable parties. Be wary of rare coins offered at bargain prices, as they could be counterfeits or improperly graded. Some bargain coins are specimens that have been amateurishly cleaned and are not considered desirable by collectors. The best "bargains" are popular coins in good condition, offered at fair prices.

The dangers of buying from sources other than these are overgraded and consequently overpriced coins; nongraded and likewise overpriced coins; coins that have been doctored, "whizzed," chemically treated, artificially toned, or otherwise altered. Buying from the legitimate, recommended sources greatly reduces but does not absolutely eliminate these risks. The buyer himself is the ultimate safeguard, if he has a reasonably thorough working knowledge of coins and the coin market. In this respect experience is the best teacher, but it can sometimes be costly to learn from bad coin buying experiences.

COIN BUYING GUIDELINES

Smart coin buyers follow certain basic strategies or rules. They will not buy a rare coin that they know little or nothing about. They will do some checking first. Has the coin been frequently counterfeited? Are counterfeits recorded of that particular date and mint mark? What are the specific grading standards? What key portions of the design should be examined under magnification to detect evidence of circulation wear?

The smart coin buyer may be either a hobbyist collecting mainly for the sport of it, or an investor. In either case he learns not just about coins but the workings of the coin trade: its dealers and auctioneers and their methods of doing business. It's essential to keep up to date always, as the coin market is a continual hotbed of activity.

When buying from the recommended sources there is relatively little danger of fakes, doctored coins, or other obviously unwanted material. If such a coin does slip through and escape the vigilance of an ethical professional dealer, you are protected by his guarantee of authenticity. It is highly unlikely that you will ever be "stuck" with a counterfeit, doctored, or otherwise misrepresented coin bought from a well-established professional.

Merely avoiding fakes is, however, not the sole object of intelligent coin buying. It is, in fact, a rather minor element in the overall picture. Getting the absolute most for your money in terms of properly graded coins at fair prices is the prime consideration. Here the responsibility shifts from seller to buyer. It is the dealer's responsibility not to sell fakes or misidentified coins. But it is the *buyer's* responsibility to make certain of getting the best deal by comparing prices and condition grades of coins offered by different dealers. Quite often you *can* save by comparison shopping, even after your incidental expenses are tabulated. The very unique nature of the coin market makes this possible.

Prices do vary from one dealer to another on many coins. That is precisely the reason—or at least one of the primary reasons—for the *Blackbook*. If you could determine a coin's value merely by checking one dealer's price, or even a few dealers' prices, there would be minimal need for a published price guide. The editors review prices charged by hundreds of dealers to arrive at the median or average market prices that are listed in the *Blackbook*. Prices are matched condition grade by condition grade, from UNC down the line. The results are often little short of astounding. One dealer may be asking $50 for a coin priced at $30 by another. And there are sure to be numerous other offerings of the coin at $35, $40, $45, and various midpoint sums.

It is important to understand why prices vary and how you can utilize this situation to your advantage.

Some readers will remark, at this juncture, that prices vary because of inaccurate grading.

It is unquestionably true that personal applications of the grading standards do contribute to price differences. What one dealer sees as an AU-55 is AU-50 or AU-52 to another, with a corresponding difference in price. It is one reason for nonuniform prices. *It is not the only one.*

Obviously the lower-priced specimens are not always those to buy. Smart numismatic buying calls for knowing when to take bargains and when to bypass them. Low price could result from something directly concerning the coins. Or it may be tied to matters having nothing to do with the coin or coins. A dealer could be oversupplied, or he may be offering coins in which he does not normally deal and wants to move them quickly. He may have a cash flow imbalance and need to raise funds, in which case he has probably reduced most of his prices. He may be pricing a coin low because he made a fortunate purchase in which the coin cost him very little. In all of these cases—and examples of all can be found regularly in the coin trade—the lower than normal price is not a reflection upon the coin's quality or desirability. These coins, if properly graded, are well worth buying. They do save you some money and cause no problems.

Personal circumstances of the dealer are, to one degree or another, reflected in the prices of most of his coins. A dealer cannot very well charge $1,000 for a 1948 Lincoln cent just because he needs the money. The traffic would not bear it. But within reasonable bounds a dealer's pricing structure for his stock reflects his circumstances. If the dealer has substantial operating costs to meet, such as shop rent and employee salaries, his overall pricing structure will reflect this. Yet his prices are not likely to be too much higher than the average, as this class of dealer is intent on quick turnover. Also, there is a certain degree of competitiveness between dealers, particularly those whose advertisements run in the same periodicals. Unfortunately, this competitiveness is sometimes carried to extremes by some dealers, resulting in "bargains" that are sometimes overgraded.

Condition has always played a major role in coin prices. Even in the hobby's early, far less sophisticated days, collectors would pay more for a bright, shiny uncirculated coin than for the same coin in worn condition. The undeniable difference in value and desirability of coins in different condition grades led gradually to adoption of grading standards. In a sense, grading standards are comparable to the "scale of one to ten." Some circulated coins show more wear than others, so it is not sufficient to merely call a coin circulated. Even among uncirculated coins or UNCs, there can be differences in condition and desirability. While UNCs show no circulation wear, the majority do have tiny hairlike or lintlike scratches on both surfaces. You will not see these on casual examination, only if you look closely or, in some cases, only if a magnifying lens is used. These are the "average" UNCs. Uncirculated coins having very few surface abrasions are scarcer, and many buyers are willing to pay extra for them. This increases their market value. Occasionally an uncirculated coin has no surface abrasions. It is then regarded as Mint State Perfect, for which the designation on the grading scale is MS-70. A correctly graded specimen in MS-70 will sell higher than any other grade of condition, sometimes much higher.

COIN GRADING

The grading guidelines used for U.S. coins (no grading guidelines exist for foreign coins) are those adopted by the American Numismatic Association and are included in summarized format in this book. Any U.S. coin can be graded by these guidelines, from the very oldest obsolete types to those in current production. The principle behind the grading guidelines is simple.

A coin's design always has certain vulnerable areas. Some parts of the design are more highly raised than others. These show wear the quickest. Likewise, some of the engraved lines are shallower than others and more quickly obliterated with day-to-day handling. By carefully examining a coin and checking these vulnerable areas, one can determine if the coin grades Circulated or Uncirculated. If it grades Circulated, its vulnerable areas will also establish its specific grade, by the amount of wear they've absorbed. Anyone can learn to grade coins, but the process does call for patience, good lighting, a magnifying lens, and objectivity. Objectivity is essential. There is always a natural tendency to believe one's coins are a shade better than they really are. This is true even of a collector who has no intention of selling and takes no particular interest in resale potential. It applies to a greater degree when the person doing the grading has intentions of selling.

Values, as you will see in this book, often jump sharply from one grade to the next higher grade. The difference in price between an AU-55 and MS-60 specimen is not 10% or 20%. It is more often 100%, 200%, or more, depending on the coin, its scarcity, age, and other considerations. Hundreds, or even thousands, of dollars can be riding on the clarity of one tiny portion of its design. Even when a coin is not really rare or expensive, it will be worth quite a bit more in the higher grades of condition than in the lower.

While grading as practiced today is very precise and scientific compared to numismatics' early years, it is not foolproof. The human element still comes into play to some degree. So do situations not specifically accounted for in the grading guidelines. The human element is the great intangible. Two or three persons of equal competency may grade a coin identically. A dozen are not likely to. Someone will believe, honestly and without motive, that the coin is a grade higher or lower than the others consider it. The person who grades it differently is not necessarily careless. He may, in fact, be the most careful observer in the group. His close attention has revealed something overlooked by the rest.

Some coins invite variations in grading, for any of various reasons. These include Circulated and Uncirculated specimens as well as coins that appear to fall directly on the borderline between these categories. What makes certain coins more difficult to grade than others? First we have the coins, usually very old ones, that have not followed the normal patterns of wear. For reasons not always satisfactorily explained, the more vulnerable portions of their designs show less wear than other areas. By strict adherence to the established ANA standards they would grade in the higher ranks of circulated condition. A truly objective grader would hesitate to place them here. He would drop them down a bit, though just how far to drop is, in cases of this nature, mostly a matter of opinion.

Then there are coins which can be matched up easily with their proper condition grade so far as wear is concerned, but which have problems not related to wear. The ANA guidelines apply to circulation wear or its absence *only*. There are no provisions under these guidelines for grading coins with rim nicks, bruises, discoloration, oxidization, porosity, or any other defect not related to circulation wear. Such coins, which are encountered frequently, are treated in different ways by different dealers. Many will grade the coin for wear, then insert a note calling attention to its defect. Some will just grade the coin a little lower and let it go at that.

SLIDER GRADING

According to the ANA grading guidelines, a coin that does not fully meet the requirements for a grading level must be dropped down to the next lower category. If a coin cannot squeeze by as an AU-55 it has to be called AU-50, with the corresponding inevitable difference in retail value. As the guidelines are hardly enforceable by law, however, they are bent at will by anyone who wishes to do so. One of the by-products is so-called *slider grading*, which has become widespread. The use of slider grading is so commonplace today that some of its critics of a few years ago are adopting it. Coin dealers have an entirely logical reason for doing so. Even if a certain dealer is personally opposed to slider grading, he is in effect placing himself at a disadvantage by declining to utilize it. If his fellow dealers are slider grading their coins, his will seem inferior by comparison. His MS-60 price will be the same as another dealer charges for MS-62. Many customers, looking simply at price and the claim made for condition, will order the MS-62. So slider grading is done defensively just as much as offensively.

A slider grade is any grade outside of the accepted guidelines. It is an unofficial grade that exists in the seller's eye and which he hopes will exist in the purchaser's when he examines the coin. It is unofficial because there are no published guidelines for it. Presumably an AU-52 coin is a shade nicer than AU-50, but grading of this sort is very subjective. A great deal of personal opinion comes into play and that is directly contrary to the purpose of grading standards. They were established to remove personal opinion as much as possible from coin grading. It is certainly understandable that anyone, whether dealer or collector, would be reluctant to grade a coin AU-50 when it seems finer than most specimens of that grade. Under the present guidelines, however, there is no alternative provision for such coins. However one may feel about slider grade coins, one thing is certain: if you pay a premium for them, you take a risk. A dealer who buys your coin collection at some future time will not pay extra for your sliders. He will pay no more than for specimens in the next lower condition ranking.

SPLIT GRADING

Also prevalent today, to make intelligent coin buying even more challenging, is *split grading*. Split grading is seen in advertisements and coin dealers' catalogs as AU-50/55, MS-65/60, and so on. The coin is given two grades instead of one. The first stated grade, which would be AU-50 in our example of AU-50/55, refers to the front or obverse of the coin while the second refers to the back or reverse. Under normal circumstances, both sides of a coin show the same degree of surface wear or smoothing down of their designs. Nearly all coins in Circulated condition have received their wear from being handled day after day, carried in pockets and change purses, taken in and out of cash drawers, and rubbing against other coins. Whatever happens to one side of a coin generally happens to the other as well, so the wear on both sides will be equal in 99 out of 100 coins. Yet there is that problematical 100th coin, which is slightly—never more than slightly—better preserved on one side than on the other.

If the coin is very old and quite rare, the sort that would have appealed to collectors of generations ago, its unevenness of wear will be attributed to a phenomenon called *cabinet friction*. Today most hobbyists store their coins in albums or individual holders made of paper to inert plastic. In the 1800s and early 1900s it was quite the fashion to keep coins in wooden cabinets with pull-out trays or drawers. This is still done in Europe by wealthy collectors. The coins rested in little slots on beds of velvet, sometimes merely on the bare wood (a very bad practice!). Collectors almost always kept all their coins face up, so for decades and decades a coin might be absorbing friction on one side, as the tray was pulled in and out. The side facing up did not rub against anything and absorbed no friction. Consequently many such coins showed greater deterioration on their reverse side than on their face. Perhaps the difference was not noticed by hobbyists of that uncritical era. Today, when every coin is meticulously inspected, the effects of cabinet friction become apparent. This is not to say that cabinet friction is the only possible explanation for unevenness in wear. There could be other causes that would be difficult to speculate upon without knowing the actual history of the coin, how it was handled and stored, and so forth. Obviously, in the case of split grade *uncirculated* coins, cabinet friction does not come into play. These coins do not show evidence of wear on either side. They are true UNCs, but their grading is split, such as MS-63/60, because one side has fewer "bag marks" or fine hairline scratches than the other. One may even, occasionally, encounter a coin graded Mint State Perfect on one side but not on the other. This can appear in any of various ways: MS-70/68, MS-67/70, MS-70/69, etc.

There is no denying the fact that split grading, confusing though it is, is a legitimate grading practice when the coin calls for it. The alternative to split grading is to grade the coin into the lower category; in other words, use the side showing more deterioration as the grading criteria. In doing this, an AU-55/50 coin would become merely AU-50. This is objected to by most sellers, including not only dealers but private parties selling coins from their collection, on grounds that the coin is better than a plain or straight AU-50 and deserves to sell for a premium or at least attract more attention. Some individuals solve this dilemma by use of the slider grading discussed previously. They would call an AU-50/55 coin AU-52 or AU-53 without entering into further explanation. This, however, is the least acceptable of the potential methods of describing such coins. Most collectors seem to agree that coins with real condition variations from one side to the other, ought to be graded into split grades. The key word here is "real." The middle 1980s witnessed an undeniable misuse of split grading, not only on the part of some professional coin dealers but collectors, investors, auctioneers, even writers of numismatic books and magazine articles. It has become trendy to split grade a coin, as if the use of split grading indicated extra careful attention on the grader's part. Literally tens of thousands of older coins that passed through the market with a standard grade in the late 1970s reappeared later as split graders. More are sure to follow.

The time may well be coming when the majority of all 18th- and 19th-century U.S. coins carry a split grade. Nor would it be terribly surprising, considering the proliferation of split and slider gradings, to see an onslaught of finely split grades such as AU-50/51, MS-62/63, and the like.

As with coin grading in general, split grading can be helpful to both seller and buyer in judging the desirability and cash value of a coin. It can also be utilized to confuse, mislead, and overcharge a potential buyer, so once again it becomes a matter of the care and integrity of the person doing the grading. Several precise conclusions can be drawn with regard to split grading. The true split grade coin—that is, the coin which truly merits such a grading and would be so graded by most astute persons—is not nearly so plentiful as today's market would lead one to believe. Of true split graders, those in Circulated condition will generally be in better grade on the front or face.

As to quantities, here is a rough summary:

18th-Century Uncirculated Coins. Here the proportion of genuine "splitters" runs rather high, as it includes coins which are Uncirculated on one side but show some slight wear on the other. These coins were kept in cabinets for many years, enduring the previously mentioned cabinet friction. The percentage of true split graders among UNCs of the 18th century would run at least 20%. Some of them are coins that were simply better struck on one side than the other, which technically should not enter into grading considerations—but it does. Many of these coins have uneven toning from one side to the other, which is another result of cabinet storage for long periods of time. One side was in continual contact with a possibly acid or moisture-emitting substance—such as wood—while the other was not.

18th-Century Circulated Coins. The proportion of true split graders found in this category is lower than for 18th-century UNCs but higher than for circulated coins of the 19th or 20th centuries by quite a wide margin. The total would probably be from 15–20% of all specimens if we group together copper, silver, and gold. It will always be slightly higher on gold coins, as their surface softness invited uneven wear. They suffered the most and the quickest from cabinet friction, with silver coins coming next and copper suffering least of all. Hence, in all the time periods there will be somewhat fewer split grade copper coins, or coins composed of other so-called base metals. It is not just the greater durability of these metals which resisted uneven wear. Though that was a factor, a more important one was circumstances in the coin hobby. In the earlier days of coin collecting in this country, say up to about 1870, relatively few of the advanced collectors were taking an interest in copper or other base metal coins, regardless of age or rarity. They preferred the more prestigious gold and silver. Copper coins such as the Large cent were regarded as good material for a starter collection or juvenile collection. Thus, few copper coins went into cabinets to absorb friction wear.

19th-Century Uncirculated Coins. Among these you will find a moderate number of true split graders in the rarer and more popular types, such as Bust dollars and the $10 gold pieces from the earlier part of the century. They also occur on the Double Eagles but not as frequently. The percentage of split graders with one side UNC and the other side Circulated is rather substantial for the groups just mentioned, though negligible in such groups as the silver 3 cent, Large cent, 10 cent, and most others. Even when these smaller coins were stored in cabinets, which was not as frequently, their lighter weight worked in their favor to reduce friction.

19th-Century Circulated Coins. A considerably lower percentage of true split graders is to be found among this category than any of those previously discussed. The overall figure, taking all 19th-century circulated coins into account, would be under 10%. Yet among those in the upper ranges of price there is no doubt that the percentage would run somewhat higher. The explanation is essentially the same as given previously for uncirculated coins of the same time period. Those of the more common dates and types were not as frequently placed in cabinets and escaped cabinet friction. Most 19th-century split grade circulated coins are the rarer Bust dollars and Seated Liberty dollars. True splitting is not as common on Morgan dollars, but will be found fairly extensively on $10 and $20 gold pieces of the 19th century.

20th-Century Uncirculated Coins. True split grading on these is confined mostly to Morgan and Peace dollars and to gold coins, and is the result of one side ranking a little higher than MS-60 while the opposite side is a plain or straight MS-60. With 20th-century coins, cabinet friction is not the cause of split grading, even in circulated specimens, as the use of cabinets by domestic collectors was on the decline by 1900 and went totally out of fashion a few years before World War I. Split grading on 20th-century UNCs is ascribable to bag marks being more pronounced on one surface than the other. With earlier split graders you will note a pattern of the obverse (front or face of the coin) normally being in a higher grade of condition, due to cabinet storage. As split grade coins of the 20th century resulted from no such systematic procedure, but rather pure chance, the better side is just as likely to be the reverse.

20th-Century Circulated Coins. The number of split grade specimens is virtually nil, less than 1%. These coins received their wear in day-to-day circulation handling and tended to wear evenly on both sides. The methods by which 20th-century collectors have stored their coins have not contributed to the creation of split graders.

How should the smart collector deal with split grade coins? Should he buy them or avoid them? Should he be willing to pay premium prices for them, over and above the normal price for a specimen in the lower of the two grades?

As a general rule, split grade coins should be avoided unless you can place reasonable confidence in the person doing the grading. Many coin dealers are judicious in their use of split grading and apply such a designation only when it seems absolutely called for. Others are somewhat more frivolous with split grading, as you will quickly note by scanning the large display advertisements in numismatic newspapers and magazines. Checking these ads, including those offering coins you have no intention of buying, should be required for anyone interested in learning about the coin market. This can be most revealing. You will find, for example, ads in which 1,000 coins are separately listed and priced, and 200–300 of them are presented as split graders. That is simply too high a percentage to occur in the normal course of events, regardless of the type of coins involved. Few numismatists could objectively grade 1,000 coins and find 200–300 "splitters." When you encounter this sort of thing it is a fairly safe assumption that the advertiser is partial to split grading. He has a predisposition to it and wants to find cause for split grading in every coin he grades. In that he is not successful, as the majority of coins offer absolutely no basis for split grading. But he does much better in finding split grade coins than people who have no special leaning toward them. Of course we are talking about the coins he sells. When he buys, he will more than likely be extremely content to go with the lower grade. Any coin that he can split grade, in offering it for sale, becomes upgraded (though only marginally) over the condition in which it was acquired, with the potential for a somewhat greater profit margin. There is absolutely nothing wrong with this if he finds true split graders among the coins he has bought. All dealers, including the most reliable, will sometimes discover upon re-examining a purchase that the coin belongs in a different grade than they had originally believed. The more reputable conscientious dealers will regrade a coin *down* when that seems appropriate, so they can hardly be censured for grading up when that appears called for. The culprit is the maniacal split grader who seems to have an obsession with it. In any given advertisement showing a large proportion of the coins as split graders, there are apt to be additional indications that the advertiser is trying to pull his coins into more desirable grades. (Please understand that an advertiser is not necessarily a dealer; some ads are placed by private parties.) Ads with a preponderance of split graders are also likely to be above the normal in slider grades.

True split grade coins are a shade more desirable than if both surfaces fell into the lower of the two grades. If you have the opportunity to buy one for no more than the price of a straight specimen—say an AU-55/50 for the price of an AU-50—fine. You can hardly be making a mistake. But when you pay any kind of premium for a split grader, however slight, it is a questionable investment. The person who eventually buys it from you is likely to say, "I don't pay extra for split grades."

PUTTING YOUR COIN BUYING KNOWLEDGE TO WORK

General Suggestions (whether buying in person at a coin shop or by other means):

1. Deal with someone in whom you can have confidence. The fact that a dealer has been in the business a long period of time may not be an absolute guarantee of his reliability, but it is definitely a point in his favor. Is he a member of coin collector or coin dealer organizations? You do not have to ask about this to find out. If he does hold membership in good standing in any of the more prestigious organizations, that fact will be prominently displayed in his ads, his sales literature, and on the walls of his shop. The leading organization for coin dealers is the PNG, or Professional Numismatists' Guild. Its members are carefully screened and must, after gaining admittance, comply with its code of ethics. Complaints against PNG members *are* investigated. Those that cannot be easily resolved are brought before an arbitration panel. You are on the safest possible ground when dealing with a PNG member. As the PNG is rather a select group, however, your local dealer may not be a member. This in itself should not make him suspect. One of the requirements of PNG membership is to carry at least $100,000 retail value in coins and many dealers simply do not maintain that large an inventory. Is your dealer an American Numismatic Association member? Local Chamber of Commerce?

2. Don't expect the impossible, either in a dealer or his coins. The dealers are in business to make a profit and they could not do this by offering bargains on every coin they sell. Treat the dealers fairly. Look at things from their point of view. For example, a long "layaway" on an expensive coin may not be in the dealer's best interest. The dealers will go out of their way for established customers but, even then, they cannot be expected to place themselves at a disadvantage.

BUYING IN PERSON AT A COIN SHOP

1. Plan your visits in advance. Don't shop in a rush or on the spur of the moment. Give yourself time to look, think, examine, and decide.

2. Before entering the shop have a clear idea of the specific coins, or at least the type of coins, you want to see. If more than a few dates and mint marks are involved, do not trust it all to memory. Write a list.

3. Look at everything that interests you before deciding to buy anything.

4. When shopping for rarities, bring along your own magnifier. A small one with attached flashlight is the most serviceable. You may not be able to conduct really in-depth examinations in a shop, but you'll learn more with a magnifier than without one. Don't be reticent about using it. The dealers will not be insulted.

5. If the shop has more than one specimen of the coin that interests you, ask to see them all. Even if all are graded identically and priced identically, you may discover that one seems a shade nicer than the rest.

6. If this is your first visit to the shop, you will want to give some attention to whether or not the shop inspires confidence. An experienced collector tends to get different vibrations from each shop, to the point where he can form an opinion almost immediately—sometimes before entering. Some coin shops give the distinct impression of being more professional than others. And that impression is usually correct! There are various points on which this can be judged. Do all coins, with the exception of bullion items, have their prices marked on the holder? Is the price accompanied by a statement of condition grade? Are the holders, and the style of notations on them, fairly uniform from coin to coin? If the coins are housed in various different kinds of holders, with notations that seem to have been made by a dozen different people, they are most likely remnants from the stocks of other dealers or so-called "odd lots." Their condition grades should have been verified and they should have been transferred to uniform holders before being placed on sale. Since the shopkeeper failed to do this, he probably knows very little about their actual condition grades. He merely took the previous owners' word for it. Does the shopkeeper impress you as a person with intimate knowledge of coins? He need not love coins, as his business is selling them and not collecting them. But he should appear to regard them a little higher than "just merchandise." He ought to be appreciative of and perhaps even enthusiastic over the finer aspects of a rare coin. Under no circumstances should he treat coins as if he cares nothing about them, such as by handling them roughly or sloppily or touching their surfaces with his fingers.

7. Buying in person gives you an opportunity to converse with the dealer, and this can have its advantages. Upon expressing interest in a coin you may discover that the dealer offers a verbal discount from the market price—even without asking for one. If this does not occur, you do, of course, have the right to at least hint at the matter. Just a modest savings can often turn a borderline item into a sound purchase. Don't get a reputation of asking for a discount on every coin you buy. Let the circumstances guide you and be diplomatic. You are always in a better position to receive a discount when purchasing a number of coins at the same time. Dealers like volume buyers. Never say, "Will you take $300 for this?" or anything which could be construed as making the dealer an offer. The dealers make offers when they buy from the public and the right to make an offer is something they like to reserve for themselves. You can broach the subject in a more subtle fashion. Instead of mentioning what you would be willing to give for the coins, ask if there is a savings (savings is a much better word than discount) on large purchases. If you pay in cash, you have a better bargaining position as you're saving the dealer the time required in collecting the funds. That is the essence of reasonable discounts; playing fair, not becoming a nuisance, and being willing to accept a small consideration even if just 5%. At least with the small discounts you are, or should be, getting good coins. If anyone is willing to discount a coin by 50%, you can be virtually certain it is a problem item.

BUYING BY MAIL ORDER

There is no reason to shun mail orders. Most coin dealing is done by mail. There are at least a dozen mail-order coin dealers for every one who operates a shop. Your local shop may not specialize in your type of coins, but in dealing by mail you can reach any coin dealer in the country and obtain virtually any coin you may want.

Consider the following before doing any mail-order buying:

1. Compare ads and prices, compare descriptions, compare everything from one ad to another running in the same publication. Look for evidence of the advertiser's professional standing, such as PNG membership. Read his terms of sale. There should be an unqualified guarantee of authenticity plus a guarantee of satisfaction. If you are not satisfied with your purchase for any reason, you should have the option of returning it within a specific time period. This time period should be stated in the dealer's terms of sale. It will usually be ten days or two weeks. It should likewise be clearly stated that if you do choose to return the coins, you can receive a full refund or credit as *you* prefer (not as the dealer prefers). Full refund means the sum paid for the coins, with postage and registration fees deducted. Few dealers will refund postage charges. Consequently, when you return a shipment you are paying the postage both ways.

2. Send a small trial order if you haven't previously done business with the advertiser. This will give you an opportunity to judge his grading accuracy and see just what sort of coins he supplies. You will also discover how prompt and attentive he is. The results of this trial order should give a fairly good idea of what you can expect from that dealer when placing larger orders.

3. Do not Xerox an ad and circle numbers. Write out your order, simply and plainly. Mention the publication and issue date. The dealer probably has different ads running in different publications.

4. Give second choices only if this is necessary to qualify for a discount. Otherwise don't. Most dealers will send you your first choice if it's still available. Some will send the second choice, even if they do still have your first choice. This is called "stock balancing." If they have two remaining specimens of your first choice, and twenty of your second choice, they would much prefer sending you the second choice. Only a relatively small proportion of dealers will ignore your wishes in this manner, but our suggestion still applies: no second choices if you can avoid them. To speed things up, make payment by money order or credit card. A personal check may delay shipment by as much as three weeks.

5. Examine the coins as soon as possible upon receiving them. If a return is necessary, this must be done promptly to be fair to the dealer. Most likely you will not be permitted to remove a coin from its protective holder to examine it. The coins will be in clear mylar (an inert plastic) holders known as "flips" or "flipettes," with a staple at the top. The staple must be in place for a return to be honored. While this may seem harsh, it is necessary as a way for the dealer to protect himself against unscrupulous collectors who would switch coins on him. These individuals would replace a high-grade coin with one of a lower grade from their collection, and return the lower-grade specimen, asking for a refund.

In the unlikely event you receive a coin in a holder which does not permit satisfactory examination, the best course is to simply return it. In making your examination be fair to yourself and to the dealer. Should you have the least doubt about its authenticity, submit the coin to the American Numismatic Association for its opinion and inform the dealer of your action. If the ANA finds the coin to be fake or doctored, you can return it even if the grace period for returns has expired. Under these circumstances many dealers will reimburse you for the ANA's expertizing cost. Chances are, however, that you will never receive a suspect coin.

6. Do not file a complaint against the dealer unless he is clearly in violation of his printed "terms of sale." When it is absolutely necessary to do so, a report of the transaction may be forwarded to the organizations in which he maintains membership, as well as the publications in which he advertises. But even if you place hundreds of mail orders, it is unlikely that the need will ever arise to register a formal complaint against a dealer.

BUYING AT AUCTION SALES

The volume of collector coins sold at auction is enormous. Auction buying is preferred by many collectors, as the opportunity exists to buy coins at somewhat less than their book values.

Not everything sold by auction is a bargain, however, and the auction house's "terms of sale" allow you far less latitude in making returns. Still, auction buying in the present day entails considerably less risk than it traditionally did. A generation ago, or even more recently, everything sold at auction was strictly "as is." Nothing could be returned for any reason whatsoever, even if grossly misdescribed or counterfeit. Today, almost all coin auctioneers will take back a fake or doctored coin, and some will take returns of those that have been incorrectly graded or otherwise misdescribed. This varies somewhat from one auction firm to another.

There are two types of auction sales: mail sales, in which all bidding is conducted by mail or phone, and so-called "floor" sales, which have in-person bidding. Even at floor sales, however, one is permitted to make an absentee bid if he cannot personally attend. When an absentee bid is successful, the bidder is notified by mail.

You have just as good a chance of being successful with an absentee bid as if you were present. The reputable auction houses will not bill you for the full amount of your bid if there was weak bidding on the coin. If you placed a bid of

$500 and no one else offered more than $200, you would be billed only for an amount sufficient to beat the $200 bid. This would in most cases be $225. At some auctions, though, an automatic "buyer's premium" or surcharge in the amount of 10% is added to the price. In the example just given you would be paying a total of $247.50 plus charges for shipping. Sales at which bids are accepted exclusively by mail and phone do not, as a rule, utilize the buyer's premium. Check the terms of sale to be sure, as this obviously makes a difference in the amounts you should bid.

Whether the auction is a mail or floor sale, there will be a printed list of its contents available for those who may be interested in bidding. This list is circulated well in advance of the sale date to give everyone ample time to study it and plan their bidding. The list may appear as a full-page or multipage advertisement in one of the numismatic magazines or newspapers. It may be issued in the form of a handsome catalog with photos, sent to clients on the auctioneer's mailing list (and available to nonclients at a small charge). In any event, it will be accompanied by a set of regulations for those participating in the sale, and a bidsheet on which prospective buyers can enter their bids. The bidsheet will mention the sale's closing date. Bids received after the closing date, or after the start of vocal bidding in a floor sale, are ineligible.

Here is some advice for auction buying:

1. Find an auctioneer who specializes in your kind of coins and order a subscription to his catalogs. Regardless of the type of coins you collect, there are some auctioneers who handle them more regularly than others and these are the catalogs you should be receiving. Subscribing brings you the catalogs as early as possible and you also receive the list of "prices realized" following each sale. This in itself is extremely useful. It shows the prices actually paid for each coin, and it shows you the coins that failed to draw any bids or were removed from the sale for other reasons. You can utilize this information when placing bids in future sales conducted by the same auction house.

2. Read the entire catalog or list before filling out your bidsheet. Make a Xerox of the blank bidsheet in case you decide to make changes in your bids.

3. Determine whether the prices shown in the catalog are book values, estimated selling prices, or "minimum bids." In some sales you will encounter a mixture of all three, which can become confusing. Sometimes no prices at all will be shown. When estimated selling prices (sometimes called "estimated retail value") are used, you are usually safe in assuming that the majority will sell slightly below those figures. Some will sell for more and others for a good deal less, but most are likely to go for about 10% under the estimates. Once the buyer's premium is added, assuming one is used, they hit right around the auctioneer's estimate. This pattern maintains because a large number of bidders at any given auction will bid predictably by the percentage method. When the auctioneer states $100 as an estimated selling price or estimated retail value, they will bid $90. If the auctioneer states $200, many will bid $175 or some figure in that general neighborhood. This gives them the feeling of obtaining a bargain, though of course it hardly remains a bargain when the buyer's 10% surcharge is added. Such a bid is high enough in most instances to stand a very good chance of success. Those who bid 50% or 60% of the estimates are not really intent on being successful. They would rather lose a coin than pay anything near the normal retail price for it. Occasionally a few of their bids will come through if the sale turns out disappointingly. There will also be some bidders at every sale who bid above the estimate as a way of annihilating the competition. Needless to say, this can be an expensive way of acquiring coins.

If minimum bids are used, no bid lower than the sum stated will be entertained. In any sale in which all the lots are provided with minimum bids, a large number will sell right at the minimum or just fractionally above it, such as $55 for a lot carrying a $50 minimum bid. Minimum bid requirements tend to have a negative psychological influence on many bidders. They feel that if the stated price is satisfactory to the auctioneer and the coin's owner, the coin cannot be worth very much more. In actual fact, many lots with minimum bids are worth considerably more than the sums indicated, and you can sometimes get excellent buys at a "minimum bids" sale. It all depends on the specific nature of the sale and who is running it.

4. The auctioneers frequently stress advantages in bidding early, assuming you are placing an absentee bid. There is, in fact, more logic in bidding late, so long as you can be sure of making the deadline. An early bid is likely to be disclosed to other prospective bidders, who thereby have the opportunity to exceed it. A late bid may give competitors no time to react.

5. If you're interested in bidding on a coin which is not pictured in the catalog, ask the auction house for a photo of it. In most cases they will supply a photo if your request arrives early. There may be a token charge for the photo, but if you can get a photo, it's far preferable to bidding on a coin you have not seen. If you live close enough to the auction house, make a personal visit to examine any coins in the sale. In nearly all sales the coins will be available for inspection as soon as the catalog is circulated.

6. While the "terms of sale" will not vary too drastically from one auction house to the next, it is still advisable to read them thoroughly. If the words "all coins guaranteed genuine and may be returned for full refund if proven otherwise" are not included, this is not a sale in which you should be participating. In some mail sales—never in floor sales—you will find this statement: "no bids reduced." This means you pay the full amount of your bid if you win the coin, even if the next highest bid is considerably less. If you bid the fair market value or somewhat below, you can safely place bids in such a sale.

7. If the buyer's premium of 10% is being used, automatically reduce all your bids by 10%, but always bid in round numbers. A bid of $61 or $33.25 will not be accepted.

8. When bidding in person, always have your catalog open to the page showing the coin being sold at the moment. It is very easy to confuse one lot number with another and place a bid on the wrong coin. Once your bid has been acknowledged by the auctioneer, do not leave your hand up, as in the excitement this may be misinterpreted as a further bid—and you will be bidding against yourself. Always listen carefully to see if you have the high bid. Do not be led by the competitive spirit of a floor sale to bid higher than you had intended. Show no emotion whatsoever during bidding or at the conclusion of bidding. One of the basic strategies of auction bidding is to draw no attention to yourself.

The previous advice should help to better explain coin buying in its various phases. Space limitations have prevented us from covering some of the more specialized aspects of buying, and we have purposely refrained from mentioning things that should be apparent to everyone.

SELLING COINS TO A DEALER

All coin dealers buy from the public. They must replenish their stock and the public is a much more economical source of supply than buying from other dealers. Damaged, very worn, or common coins are worthless to a dealer. So, too, usually, are sets in which the "key" coins are missing. If you have a large collection or several valuable coins to sell, it might be wise to check the pages of coin publications for addresses of dealers handling major properties, rather than selling to a local shop.

Visit a coin show or convention. There you will find many dealers at one time and you will experience the thrill of an active trading market in coins. You will find schedules of conventions and meetings of regional coin clubs listed in various numismatic publications.

To find your local coin dealer, check the "Yellow Pages" under *"Coin Dealers."*

Coin collecting offers infinite possibilities as an enjoyable hobby or profitable investment. It need not be complex or problem-laden. But anyone who buys and sells coins—even for the most modest sums—owes it to himself to learn how to buy and sell wisely.

PUBLICATIONS

Coin World (weekly)
Amos Press
PO Box 150
Sidney, OH 45365-0150
1-800-253-4555
Subscription rates: U.S.—$36.95 for 52 weekly issues, $66.95 for 104 issues. Outside U.S.—Add $63 per year for postage (U.S. funds only).

COINage Magazine (monthly)
4880 Market Street
Ventura, CA 93003
(805) 644-3824
Subscription rates: In U.S.A. and possessions—$25 for one year (12 issues), $39.00 for two years, $60.00 for three years. Canada and all foreign countries—Add $14.00 per year postage.

COINS Magazine (monthly), *Numismatic News* (weekly), and *Coin Prices* (bi-monthly)
Krause Publications
700 East State Street
Iola, WI 54945-0001
Subscriber Services—1-800-258-0929; Krause Pub. Web Site—http.//www.krause.com; *Numismatic News* E-mail—numismatic_news@krause.com
Numismatic News is published weekly for $32.00 per year, $60.00 for 2 years.

First Strike (quarterly), and *The Numismatist* (monthly)
ANA
818 North Cascade Avenue
Colorado Springs, CO 80903-3729
(719) 632-2646; Fax (719) 634-4085

52

ERRORS AND VARIETIES

Freaks, FIDOs, and Oddities: If you were once active in the hobby this is what you once referred to mint errors and varieties as. If you are new to the hobby these are terms you are likely to think of when referring to perhaps the most fascinating and exciting segment of the hobby. No matter what the case, these terms are inaccurate but they do paint a rather accurate picture of what you are likely to encounter when exploring this arena of the hobby. Actually they are known as Mint Errors and Die Varieties, and there is no doubt in any hobby enthusiast's mind that this is unquestionably the fastest growing segment of the hobby today and may continue to be so for many years to come.

It is our belief that most readers of this section will be either novices or experienced collectors who desire to know more about this subject, so this chapter is being written in laymen's terms. Errors and varieties are, by far, the most complicated area of numismatics. Do not be discouraged. The learning curve is large and once you grasp the basic definitions of error and variety coinage causes and effects you will be well armed to begin your own search. We will even include a basic value table for most of the error types discussed, and many of the most popular varieties are listed throughout the book.

It is best to divide error and variety coinage into three primary categories: Planchet errors, die errors (or die varieties), and striking errors. This is known as the P-D-S System and was created by Alan Herbert of Krause Publications and the first Secretary of the Combined Organizations of Numismatic Error Collectors of America (CONECA), the only numismatic specialty club devoted exclusively to the study of error *and* variety coinage.

PLANCHET ERRORS

As the name suggests, planchet errors occur on or in a blank or a planchet. Until a planchet is struck, it is not a coin! Planchet errors occur *before* a coin is struck but can account for some very odd-looking struck coins.

Blank—Also known as a type I planchet. A blank is a round disk of metal punched from a long strip rolled for the proper thickness of an intended denomination. It will have a rough edge that appears to be sheared on the entire edge because it is! (Note: All coins have three sides: the obverse, the reverse and the edge.) Blanks are not intended to be struck, though they sometimes are.

Left: Lincoln cent blank.

Right: Lincoln cent planchet (planchet is smaller in diameter).

Planchet—Also known as a type II planchet. These are blanks that have gone through an upset mill which eliminates the rough edge and creates a raised rim to allow for a better design transfer from the die to the planchet and to protect the design from wear. It also makes coins easier to stack.

Improper Alloy Mix—An improper alloy mix is as the name suggests and appears as streaks on coins, such as yellow streaks on copper cents or entire coins of the wrong color. It can also appear as laminations (or flakes and peels on a coin's surface).

Partial Plated and Unplated—Beginning in 1982, the Lincoln cent composition was changed to a planchet primarily composed of zinc, with a copper plate. Planchets dated 1982 to date with only part of the copper plating are partial plated. Consequently, if no plating is present, they are "unplated."

1985D Lincoln cent partial plated.

Defective Planchet—Most often resembles a ragged clip planchet (see *Incomplete Planchets*) and sometimes appears as a broken or split planchet. This is caused by an improper alloy mix or bubbles and/or foreign materials trapped in the metal.

1967 Kennedy half dollar with lamination.

Lamination—Appears as flakes or peels on a coin's surface and is due to an improper alloy mix or debris and/or air trapped in the metal. This is very common on Wartime nickels and Wheat cents.

Shield Nickel broken planchet.

Split or Broken Planchet—Can be viewed as an advanced lamination. Split planchets are planchets split or broken through the center as in a clamshell or creme cookie, and broken planchets are those split in two pieces like a "lovers' heart" pendant. Broken planchets are ready to break before being struck but usually break after they are struck. More complete explanations of split planchets follow.

1945 Lincoln cent split planchet before strke.

Split Planchet Before Strike—In this case a planchet split in two before being struck, as the term would suggest. They are usually of normal diameter but are very thin. They are struck on both the obverse and reverse but much of the design is usually light with multitudes of striation lines visible on both sides.

Split Planchet After Strike—In this case a planchet was ready to split before it was struck but waited until after it was struck before splitting in two. These are usually of normal diameter; one side, however, will be fully struck showing no striations while the other side will have only a ghost of some design and be heavily striated. These are usually not as valuable as the Split Panchet Before Strike unless both pieces remain together as a set.

Split Planchet, Hinged—A normally struck coin that is ready to split but is still together on a small portion of the coin. These resemble open clamshells and are often affectionately referred to as "clamshell splits" or simply "clamshells."

Incomplete Planchets—More commonly referred to as "clipped planchets." There are several types of incomplete planchets and so, for simplicity's sake, they follow as independent definitions and will be referred to as "clips."

Rim Clip—Just a tiny portion of the planchet missing on the rim. May be straight or curved but is usually indistinguishable as to which.

1945 Lincoln cent curved clip.

Curved Clip—Larger than a simple rim clip, usually with 2% or more of the planchet missing from the rim inward forming an inward curve.

Straight Clip—Larger than a simple rim clip, usually with 2% or more of the planchet missing from the rim inward forming a straight or very straight outward bowed edge on the affected area.

Jefferson nickel with ragged clip.

Ragged Clip—A portion of the planchet from the rim inward missing, usually in a fairly straight line but having a very jagged edge on the affected area. If the line is very irregular in shape and comes significantly into the planchet it is known as a defective planchet rather than a ragged clip.

Crescent Clip—More than 50% (by weight) of the planchet missing from the rim inward forming a large crescent-shaped curve, much like the image found on old outhouse doors!

Incomplete Clip—This is somewhat more difficult to describe and more rare than any of the above clips. An incomplete clip is found on otherwise normal appearing coins forming long, rim-to-rim, incused curves in the same location on both the obverse and reverse of a planchet or coin. This

1968D Lincoln cent with incomplete clip.

is caused by an incomplete punch overlapping another punch from the metal strip when punching blanks.

1945P Jefferson nickel elliptical clip.

Elliptical Clip—A planchet or coin that appears oval in shape, much like a football. This is another rare type of clip and is created much like an incomplete clip except the overlapping punch was complete. A crescent clip and an elliptical clip are often formed at the same time when an incomplete clip finally breaks apart and both pieces are struck. If you have an incomplete clipped coin that appears ready to break apart do not break it apart thinking you will create an elliptical and a crescent clip. These pieces must separate before they are struck to qualify! If you do break apart an incomplete clip you have just damaged your valuable error coin, thereby diminishing its value significantly!

Disk Clip—This is a rim clip that usually goes undetected and, though they are minute as far as clips go, they are very scarce. For the most part they can only be positively identified on copper nickel clad coinage. For identification one must examine the edge of the coin where a *step* or *dip* will appear in the copper core. Look at all your copper nickel clad proof coins to try to find one of these; proof planchet and striking errors are rare as a general rule, and this may be your best opportunity to find a genuine, premium touting error on a proof coin.

1970 Lincoln cent with assay clip.

Assay Clip—Probably the most rare clip of them all. This is a clip that usually appears as if somebody cut a piece out of the coin. In effect that is what happened—it happened however, to a planchet before the coin was struck.

Corner Clip—Nearly as rare as assay clips, corner clips are literally the corner of a metal strip! It is only possible, therefore, to have four corner clips from a metal strip from which blanks are punched. Obviously few of these ever happen!

Incomplete Cladding—A copper nickel coin which for one reason or another was struck while missing some of the outer clad layer on either the obverse or reverse or both. These appear as having large copper areas on the surface(s). These should not be confused with sintered planchets (see next).

Sintered Planchets—Before planchets are struck they are given a bath. This bath takes place in a giant vat where thousands, even millions, of other planchets preceded them. In effect, a sintered planchet is a planchet that took a bath in dirty bath water! If a vat has typically been used to clean copper planchets, then a load of white metal coins is dumped in the same solution, the result is often one of the copper adhering to the surface of the white metal, much like electroplating. Genuine sintered planchets, though very scarce, command little premium as the effect is easily duplicated outside the mint and few people are able to authenticate them. A good example would be a Jefferson nickel, normal in all respects except that it looks like it was struck on a copper planchet.

Wrong Stock—A coin, usually copper nickel clad, that was struck on a planchet of normal diameter that was punched from metal strip rolled to the thickness intended for another denomination. These will appear normal in most respects but will either weigh too light or too heavy. The classic example of this is the 1970-D Washington quarter which was struck on dime stock, or planchets that were punched from metal strip that was rolled to the intended thickness of the Roosevelt dime.

Kennedy half struck on a nickel planchet. This is a "wrong metal" error.

Wrong Metal—A coin struck on a planchet created for another denomination or foreign planchet. These will almost never be perfectly round and are most desirable when the planchet used is of a different color than the intended planchet. For example, a Jefferson nickel struck on a cent planchet.

Those are among the most popular of all error types and command sharp premiums. Throughout the years the U.S. Mint has contracted to strike coins for many foreign nations and sometimes these foreign planchets get stuck in the "tote bins" which are used to transport planchets to the coining presses. The same thing happens with the wrong denominations for U.S. coins. On U.S. coins this can only occur on planchets that are smaller than the denomination being struck. For example: a nickel on a cent planchet, a cent on a dime planchet, a nickel on a quarter planchet, or a quarter on a dime planchet. These can also be classified as *striking errors*.

Fragments—A coin struck on an irregular-shaped piece (usually just a scrap) of metal. These pieces must be die

Susan B. Anthony dollar struck fragment.

struck on both sides. If struck on one side only they are simply laminations which peeled out of the surface of a coin. Fragments are quite rare and are usually found when turning a mint bag inside out and checking the bottom seam!

Jefferson nickel "Bowtie."

Bowtie—Actually a form of fragment but included because of its high premium and desirability. A bowtie is simply a piece of already punched metal strip (once punched it becomes known as webbing) that happens to find its way into the coining presses. They are roughly bowtie shaped, hence the name.

Lincoln cent thin planchet.

Thick or Thin Planchets—A coin or planchet that is unusually thick or thin. This is caused by the rolling machine that rolls each metal strip to its proper thickness. It is not enough that a coin *looks* thick or thin, it must weigh more or less than the Mint's tolerable weight.

STRIKING ERRORS

As the class designation suggests, striking errors occur during the actual minting (or striking) of a coin. Overall this group presents the most spectacular errors.

Washington quarter die trial strike.

Die Trial Strikes—Also known as die adjustment strikes and low pressure strikes. This may be a misnomer as there are several ways this could occur, the least common cause being that which the name implies. They can occur when a press is coming to a halt with a planchet seated between the dies, when adjusting the pressure of a strike to allow for proper design relief, when setting vertical and horizontal alignment, and, most often, when a planchet is intentionally left between dies to prevent clashing of the dies while maintenance, routine or otherwise, is being performed on the press. These can be identified as having very weak to no reeding, and very light to almost no design elements, with the strongest toward the center of the coin. As is the case with all errors and varieties, authentication by a specialist is highly recommended.

Strike Through—This occurs when any foreign substance gets struck into the surface of a coin. Debris composed of tiny metal shavings and thick grease or wax is the usual culprit but it could be anything from a piece of string to a piece of cloth or even a staple! The more bizarre the struck-through item the more desirable it becomes. Size of the strike through is also important. If the object or debris remains in place (is retained) the error usually commands a

Washington quarter struck
through cloth.

1978 Eisenhower dollar struck
through heavy debris.

higher premium. Struck-through debris and tiny pieces of lint are common and need to be impressive to command much of a premium.

1993 Lincoln cent broadstrike.

Broadstrike—A broadstrike is a coin that was struck without the retaining collar in place. The collar is actually the third die and it is what forms reeding on reeded edge coins. Broadstrikes are always larger in diameter than the coin was intended to be—sometimes just barely and sometimes much larger. The larger it is the more desirable. They are sometimes nearly round but they are usually slightly out of round. There are two types of broadstrikes: centered and uncentered. The centered broadstrikes are struck nearly perfectly in the center and, of course, the off-center broadstrikes are not centered. As long as all the design elements remain on the coin it is a broadstrike. If design elements (including the denticles) around the edge are missing, it is then considered an off-center strike.

Off-Center Strikes—As the name implies, these are coins which were struck off center and, naturally, out of collar. These are not to be confused with misaligned die strikes which are covered under die errors. Some of the obverse *and* reverse design elements (including denticles when

1920 off-center strike Buffalo nickel.

included as part of the design) must be missing. This usually occurs when a planchet does not rest in its proper position inside the press. The most desirable off-center strikes are those which are approximately 40–80% (measured by observing the unstruck portion of the planchet) off center and include a full date. Off-center strikes on obsolete series are very much in demand as well.

Double and Multiple Struck—A coin that is struck more than once. Because there are several types, for simplicity's sake they are listed individually below. "Double" and "multiple" are interchangeable on all, with multiple meaning anything more than two strikes. Also note that the most desirable of any of the following are the double or multiple strikes that exhibit more than one date. It may be the same year, but if it is there more than once it is more desirable.

Double Struck in Collar—A coin that was not ejected after having been struck or an already struck coin that found its way back into the coin press and was struck again. To positively identify this rare error type some rotation between strikes must take place.

Susan B. Anthony dollar double struck out of collar.

Double Struck Out of Collar—Usually a coin that was struck once normally, in collar, but did not eject properly, receiving a second strike off center. Both strikes can be off center as well.

Flip-over Double and Multiple Struck—All of the above rules apply with one exception; one of the strikes must have occurred after the coin flipped over in the coining press. This type of double strike exhibits an obverse and a reverse strike on both sides and is much more scarce than typical double and multiple strike coins. Also, a flip-over can occur in or out of collar.

Wrong Metal—Debatable as to whether this falls in this category or that of a planchet error. See the definition under "Planchet Errors."

Lincoln cent struck on an already struck Roosevelt dime.
This is a double denomination error.

Double Denomination—Unquestionably (as of the time of this writing) the most desirable of all error types. This, too, is debatable as to what heading it should fall under—planchet or striking error—but since it involves a previously struck and different denomination than that intended it is placed here. A double denomination is a coin that was struck with two different denomination dies! Of course that also means it is double struck. Examples are cents struck on already struck dimes, nickels struck on already struck cents, and Eisenhower dollars struck on already struck Kennedy halves! The same rule of planchet and die sizes for wrong metal strikes applies to double denominations. They are affectionately referred to as 6-cent, 11-cent, etc., pieces.

Indent—An indent is a depression in the surface of a struck coin caused by an overlapping planchet present during the strike. This depression is usually adjoining the rim and will have no design elements present in the depression. The coin will usually be almost perfectly round

1972 Lincoln cent with indent.

except at the outermost edges of the indent. A full indent is caused when one planchet is lying squarely on top of another at the time of the strike. In rare cases, coins may be fully indented with a planchet of smaller size intended for another denomination.

Lincoln cent brockage.   1990 Lincoln cent with partial brockage.

Brockage—Very similar to an indent with the difference being the coin was indented by an already struck coin as opposed to a planchet. As with the indent, brockages may be full or partial but the indent exhibits incused mirror images of the coin that caused the brockage. The larger the affected area the more desirable the brockage. Additionally, each subsequent strike spreads and weakens the brockage. Early strike brockages which show nearly perfect mirror images are by far the most desirable.

Lincoln cent counterbrockage.

Counterbrockage—Simply put, this is a brockage created by an already brockaged coin.

1975D Lincoln cent capped die strike.

Edge view of Lincoln cent capped die strike.

Die Cap—A coin stuck to a hammer die (the die which moves the most and is not below the collar) that has received several strikes and is spreading enough to creep up the sides of the hammer die. This often resembles a bottle cap (and is sometimes referred to as such) or a thimble. The image of a normally struck coin appears on the inside bottom while usually nothing appears on the outside bottom.

Capped Die Strike—This is actually a late-stage brockage but in order for it to be a late-stage brockage a capped die is created on the hammer die. In other words, this is yet another type of Strike Through error.

Clad Layer Errors—Like many other errors described in this chapter, clad layer errors have different causes and effects. Copper nickel planchets and coins that are missing one or both of the outer layers due to improper bonding to the copper core are clad layer errors. Again, for simplicity's sake, we will individually define the different types you may encounter. Also, again, it is debatable as to which classification these actually belong—striking or planchet.

Missing Clad Layer, Split Before Strike—These are coins that appear thin and are primarily nickel on one side and copper on the other, but exhibit an otherwise normal strike, though it may be a little weak.

Missing Clad Layer, After Strike—Coins that appear to be thin and primarily nickel on one side and copper on the other. The nickel side will appear normal. The copper side will have many striations and little to no design detail.

Washington quarter missing clad layer (the nickel layer itself).

Missing Clad Layer (the nickel layer itself)—These, too, can be struck before or after they split from the planchet. One that was struck before splitting will appear to be all nickel and will be normal on one side and striated with little detail on the other. Those struck after they split will be almost paper thin and weakly struck on both sides. These nickel layers struck on both sides are very rare as they are so delicate they rarely survive.

Edge Strike—A very rare and desirable striking error created when a planchet is standing rather than lying between the dies and is quickly ejected by the pressure of the strike before it can get folded. These coins display small struck areas on the edge directly opposite of one another and are usually slightly bent.

Lincoln cent fold-over strike.

Fold-over Strike—Rare, though not as rare as a true edge strike, but probably more desirable. Created when a planchet is standing rather than lying between dies while being struck. However, unlike an edge strike, they did not get ejected immediately and were subsequently folded over and struck. They are usually struck slightly off center with the fold itself being off center and very much resembling a piece of bread folded over for a sandwich.

Saddle Strike—This is basically a double-struck off-center coin with the following exception—it can only be produced in a dual or quad press, that is, a press with two or four die pairs and a single collar device with two or four holes corresponding to the die pairs. Differing from typical off-center double strikes, these are buckled in the middle and resemble an equestrian (horse) saddle, hence the name.

Edge view of a partial collar strike on a Jefferson nickel.

Partial Collar Strike—These occur when the anvil or bottom die fails to rise fully above the planchet, restricting outward metal flow. For that area of the coin above the collar the diameter will increase, giving the edge a flanged or "lipped" appearance. These may be full or tilted with the full partial collars bringing a slightly higher premium.

Lincoln cent mated pair.

Caution—Caution—Caution

Most of these planchet and striking errors are regularly fabricated either for the fun of it or intentionally to swindle innocent victims out of their hard-earned money. Some of them are quite good. Authentication should be considered mandatory on all of the more expensive and exotic error types!

DIE ERRORS

Die errors were not placed between the planchet and striking errors because they are really very different in that all planchet and striking errors are unique while die errors are recurring. From the moment the event causing the variety occurs each subsequent strike will show the same error until it is effaced in some way or the die is retired. In other words, this section could just as easily have been titled *Die Varieties* because that is what this section is all about. In the last several years die varieties have literally exploded in popularity and most collectors now collect varieties of some kind, be they doubled dies, repunched or over mint marks, or misplaced dates. Many collect all of them. With communications what they are today it has become much easier to locate all the pieces needed for completing a date and mint set of your favorite series, and in order to continue collecting in one's favorite series one naturally begins collecting by variety. With the explosion of information on die varieties collectors should be kept happy in their own series for many years! Besides, looking for die varieties, even in your pocket change, is, well, downright fun!

Before engaging in any dialogue regarding value, let us cover the basic definitions of the terms you are most likely to encounter when collecting die errors. Following you will find two sets of definitions. The first set is associated with true die errors and it is considered debatable as to what classification—striking or die—its entries belong. The second set of definitions is labeled *Die Varieties* and comprises those terms that specialists normally think of and refer to when discussing, writing about, researching, or lecturing on die varieties. Although both sets belong under the heading of *Die Errors*, we are separating the two because the entries in the first set, though they are recurring, tend to "grow" or get bigger or longer, which ever the case may be, with continued strikes.

True Die Errors

D Lincoln cent major die break (or "CUD").

Major Die Break (or "CUD")—This is exactly what it sounds like—a major break in the die. Not all dies are perfect and many do break with the repeated pressure applied during the striking process. When the most blatant major die breaks are encountered they resemble a cow's "cud," hence the most frequently encountered term for this highly collectible and prized error type. In order for a die break to qualify as a major die break the break must show definite separation taking place on the die. This may show as a piece of the die missing, in which case there will be a raised blank spot on the surface of the coin usually exhibiting weak design details in the same area on the opposite (opposite meaning obverse or reverse) side of the coin. It may also show as a portion of the coin being separated from the rest by a heavy line (die crack), with this separated portion being raised above the rest of the coin. This is known as a retained major die break or retained CUD. In almost all instances this major die break, full or retained, adjoins the rim and comes into the fields and design elements on the coin.

Split Die Strike—Actually another form of major die break but different because, rather than displaying a long curved break, it mostly splits the surface of the coin in two with a heavy, solid line down the middle of the surface. This is not to be confused with a rim-to-rim die crack, which is a very thin line with no rise in either half's surface. Split die strikes are quite rare and highly prized.

Die Crack—A thin raised line on the surface of a coin which is the result of the die beginning to break. With repeated strikes die cracks can and do eventually turn into major die breaks. However, die cracks are very common and usually

S Jefferson nickel with die crack.

command little or no premium. They are most often used as die markers to assist in identifying other known varieties.

Die Chip—Literally a chip out of a die or a tiny piece of a die broken out. They show as a small, raised area on the surface of a coin and this area usually has somewhat ragged looking boundaries. Die chips, much like die cracks, are often used as die markers in identifying other die varieties on the same coin. There are, however, several subclasses of die chips which are widely collected, though they do not command much of a premium. The perfect example would be "BIE" errors, which are nothing more than die chips located somewhere between the letters of "Liberty" on a Lincoln cent.

Die Gouge—This is actually damage to the die but shows on each struck coin after the damage occurred. It may be a sharp, angular, raised area on the surface of the coin. Depending on size and severity these can command a modest premium but, again, are usually used to identify other die varieties.

Shield nickel with clashed die.

Clashed Dies or Die Clash—This is the result of two dies coming together without a planchet between them. This transfers a partial impression from die to die. In other words, part of the reverse die images now show on the obverse and vice versa. The infamous "Prisoner cents" are a classic example of clashed dies. Prisoner cents are Lincoln Memorial cents that have the columns of the Memorial clashed both in front of Lincoln's face and behind his head, giving the impression of "prison bars." As a general rule clashed dies do not carry much of a premium. There are exceptions, however. The "Prisoner cents" carry a small premium and strong die clashes showing significant design transfers also carry a small premium. When the date also transfers, leaving a date on both the obverse and the reverse, they carry an even higher premium. Strong clashes on proof coins of the 20th century command a substantial premium.

Broken Collar Die Break—Also known as a collar break or collar cud. Keep in mind that the collar is actually the third die used in the modern minting process; therefore, they can break and exhibit similar properties to that of major die breaks on obverse and reverse dies. Of course there usually are no design elements involved (at least not on U.S. coins of the 20th century). These appear as normal coins except they will be out of round only on the affected area of the edge, which shows as a lump of extra metal on the edge. These are quite scarce and command a decent premium.

Rotated Die—This is the result of improperly installed dies or loose, moving dies. On U.S. coins the die alignment should be such that when you flip a coin vertically the design is supposed to be in the upright position. If it is not, then one or both of the dies is rotated from its normal position in the coining press. Rotated dies are quite common on pre-20th century U.S. coinage so they command little or no premium. Rotation is measured in degrees either clockwise or counterclockwise, and rotation of less than 15 degrees on 20th-century coinage is still common. However, there are some reported examples with significant rotation, such as the 1988-P Kennedy half dollar with 180-degree rotated dies, which are worth a decent and sometimes hefty premium.

Die Polish Errors—This is a very common type of die error encountered on virtually all denominations and design types. Sometimes it is necessary for the Mint to remove a die to "stone" (polish) off added undesirable elements such as a die clash. When this is done the polish lines appear as raised scratches on the surface of a coin and more often than not some of the intended design elements are missing. As previously mentioned these are very common and usually command no premium at all. With die-hard die variety enthusiasts they never command a premium. There are, however, exceptions which are noteworthy. The infamous 1937-D "3-legged Buffalo" is such an example. While hardcore die variety specialists do not acknowledge this as a major premium coin because they know what it is—die polishing—the hobby in general has embraced this coin largely because of its endearing nickname and the widespread publicity and marketing it has received. Other examples would be the "No FG" Kennedy half dollars and the "No V.D.B." (post-1917 only) Lincoln cent varieties. Again, because they are such common error types, hard-core specialists usually will pay no premium for such coins but the hobby in general often does. It pays to educate yourself.

Die Varieties

As previously stated, these are still die errors but have been separated here because they are the die error (die variety) types that are receiving all the hoopla in the hobby these days. These are the coins that often make headlines and are now dominating new research in the hobby. The doubled die is unquestionably the most popular and the most prominent of this group and will be cited last so that we may give you a brief explanation of the different classes of doubled dies immediately following the definition.

1941-S Winged Liberty (Mercury) dime with repunched mint mark (CONECA RPM #1). Photo courtesy of J. T. Stanton

1945-D Winged Liberty (Mercury) dime with repunched mint mark, though this one is normal over horizontal! Photo courtesy of J. T. Stanton

Repunched Mint Mark (RPM)—One of the hottest areas of the market because of the variety type desirability and the affordability of most RPMs. Until 1985 for proof coinage and 1990 for circulating coinage the mint mark was hand punched into all the working dies. More often than not a single blow of the punch did not result in sufficient relief so a second or more blows were necessary. If the punch was not placed in the perfect location for a second blow doubling of the mint mark was the result. In a few rare instances secondary mint marks are completely separate from the primary mint mark and these command substantially higher premiums than typical RPMs. Examples of this would be CONECA's 1956-D Lincoln cent RPM#8 which is completely separate way south of the primary mint mark, and CONECA's 1942-S Lincoln cent RPM#12 which is completely separate west of the primary mint mark.

Over Mint Mark (OMM)—The same as a repunched mint mark (RPM) only this involves two different punches with different mint marks. One mint mark is punched on a die and then a different mint mark is also punched on the same die. The most well-know examples would be the 1944-D/S Lincoln cent and the 1954-S/D Jefferson nickel. OMMs are very popular and typically command a substantial premium. Keep in mind that until 1996 all die preparation was done in Philadelphia so the mystery of "How could this happen?" is not so unimaginable.

Dual Mint Mark (DMM)—Many specialists are seeing this and asking "What?!!!" As of this writing this term and acronym are not widely accepted and, in fact, largely unheard of in the hobby. It is included here to alert you to a new and sure to be valuable variety type. This term was conceived by noted author and variety specialist Ken Potter, keeper of the Variety Coin Register, in late 1997 upon the discovery of a 1956 Lincoln cent that sports mint marks from both Denver and San Francisco. It is true! The variety appears to be a normal 1956-D Lincoln cent in every respect except it has an "S" mint mark punched below and between the "1" and the "9" of the date! This was a year when San Francisco produced no circulating coinage, yet the "S" mint mark is there! It differs from a typical OMM in that the mint marks are totally separate. In 1999 a 1980-D Lincoln cent was confirmed to have both a "D" and a separate "S" mint mark!

1844 Seated dime with an excellent repunched date.
Photo courtesy of J. T. Stanton

Repunched Date (RPD)—Repunched dates occur much the same way RPMs and OMMs do. Up to and including 1908 at least one digit (the last in the date) was punched into working dies by hand. This could involve a logo punch with one, two, three, or all four of the digits in the date. Again, in order for subsequent punches to be unnoticeable, perfect alignment was a must. This did not always happen with the result being some digits showing doubling or tripling or even more. Reds are quite common from the earliest days of the United States right up to and including 1908, appearing in most years from virtually every denomination. This does not mean, however, that they do not command a premium as most do. This premium can be small to exorbitant! The general rule of thumb is the more noticeable the repunching the more desirable the piece, therefore the higher the premium. Scarcity of certain reds is also a big factor when determining a value. Generally, the older the coin (from pre-1909) the more likely you are to encounter an RPD variety.

1868 Indian Head cent with digits in the denticles—an MPD.
Photo courtesy of J. T. Stanton

Misplaced Date (MPD)—These are, in effect, repunched dates, the major difference being they are digits punched in areas not normally associated with digit placement. In other words, digits punched in the die but not touching the date! Currently there are many hundreds of known MPD varieties and the list continues to grow almost daily! All the rules apply as those for RPDs but the digits may be found almost anywhere within a half inch or so of the date. Digits may be found in the denticles or on other design elements. Sometimes these digits are punched more than once. In fact, there is an 1870 Indian Head cent that has no less than 11 digits punched in the denticles—the exact number of visible digits is still being debated! This term was first coined by Larry Steve, noted author, specialist, and first president of the Flying Eagle and Indian Cent Collectors Society, in about 1990. The organization is affectionately referred to as "The Fly-In Club." Most MPDs command some kind of premium with many bringing substantial premiums. It is important to note that some MPDs are found on dates and denominations where only one die is known to have been used, therefore all the coins of that date and denomination display the variety; although these coins have no premium for the variety they are still likely to be valuable coins due to their low mintage. MPDs are extremely popular and widely sought, though in-depth research has really just begun.

Overdates—Overdates are just as the name applies— one date over or under another. These are probably the most desirable of die varieties across the board in numismatics and have been collected for a long time, even though until recently all the causes had not been understood. There are three ways this is known to occur. One digit may be

1849 Seated Liberty half dime overdate. Notice the 9 is punched over an 8 or a 6; specialists don't always agree as to which. Photo courtesy of J. T. Stanton

hand punched over another on a die. This is the most common type of overdate and many exist, especially from the early 19th century. Another way is by one gang punch, with all the digits placed in one punching device, punched over another date on a die. This is more scarce than the previous type of overdate but many examples do exist, mostly from the latter part of the 19th century. There are some known instances where both the above were created on dates in a series where only one die was used so, again, the variety itself commands no premium but the coin sure does due to its scarcity. The final cause for overdates leads us right into the hottest area of die variety collecting today—doubled dies. They are the result of Class III (design hub) doubling where a hub of one date received a hubbing of another date. These are rare instances that always bring substantial premiums. These are the cause of most, if not all, 20th-century overdates and will be discussed in more detail in the next section. Examples of this type of overdate are the 1943/2-P Jefferson nickel and the 1942/1 (both Philadelphia and Denver) Winged Liberty (Mercury) dimes.

Doubled Dies—The following definitions and descriptions are taken almost verbatim from a special four-page flyer written by Don Bonser and printed by J. T. Stanton Publishing. It is presented here because of the simplicity and brevity of the respective definitions and descriptions, as this is a very difficult area to grasp. Take the time to learn this as doubled die collecting is very rewarding and popular! Post-discussion and comments are by this chapter's author.

The result of an error in the hubbing process that causes doubling of some element(s) of a coin's design, doubled dies should not be confused with double strikes. A word of caution: do not confuse true doubled dies with common, virtually uncollectible machine doubling [also known as strike doubling and ejection doubling, as well as other similar terms]. True doubled dies show distinct, rounded doubled images most often with some separation and/or split serifs. Strike or machine doubling is caused [primarily] by a die being loose in the coining press and shows on struck coins as a flat, shelf-like doubling [with "sheer" lines usually visible under magnification on the "shelves"]. Doubled dies can range from fairly common to very rare. Each individual one [doubled die] is

1943 Lincoln cent with strong
Class VI doubled die obverse.
Photo courtesy of J. T. Stanton

1966 Washington quarter with
very strong doubled die reverse.
Photo courtesy of J. T. Stanton

1997 Doubled Ear Lincoln cent.
Is it a doubled die or not?
Specialists can't agree!

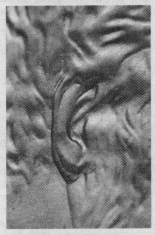

Close-up of the 1997
Doubled Ear Lincoln cent.
Photos courtesy of John A. Wexler

created under a separate circumstance. Most are scarce to very scarce. Following are the [most widely accepted] classes and causes of doubled dies.

Class I, Rotated Hub Doubling—This occurs when different hubbings result in a slight [to major] rotation about the center of the die being hubbed. Doubling is slight near the center of the die [and coins struck from it] and increases toward the edge. Doubling is more or less uniform. The best known examples are the major 1955 and 1972 doubled die cents.

Class II, Distorted Hub Doubling—This kind of doubling occurs when a hub that has been used to prepare a particular die is also employed for producing many other dies before being returned for use with the earlier one. During the interim while the hub is hubbing many more dies, its metal fatigues and, literally, "spreads out." Doubling results because the hub's design, when it is used to force its image into the die, is actually in a slightly different location each time. A simple analogy may help you to understand this better. What happens when a pencil eraser is pushed into a hard surface? It spreads out. The same occurs, although to a lesser degree, to a hub as it is used to prepare die after die.

Class III, Design Hub Doubling—This results from differing hub designs being used on the same die. This kind of doubling causes overdates, large over small dates, and small over large dates [to name a few]. It also caused the 1878 7 over 8 tailfeathers Morgan dollar varieties.

Class IV, Offset Hub Doubling—This is, by far, one of the rarest forms of doubling on United States coins. Out of over 2,000 listed doubled dies, under 30 are the result of this form of doubling. Ironically, though, both the well-known 1983 [doubled die reverse] and 1984 [doubled die obverse with doubled ear] Lincoln cent doubled dies are Class IV varieties. This kind of doubling occurs when a die, already having been hubbed properly, is hubbed again but is centered improperly under the hub. In other words, the die is somewhat displaced from its original position, but not rotated about this position. Doubling is offset in the same direction across the die and is uniform.

Class V, Pivoted Hub Doubling—This is very similar to rotated hub doubling [Class I] except the "pivot point" between hubbings is near the rim of the coin. Design elements farthest from the pivot point will be doubled most obviously, while those closer to it [the pivot point] will be doubled only slightly, if at all. The 1995 [Lincoln Cent—Die 1, still fresh in the mind of the entire hobby] is an example of pivoted hub doubling with the pivot point [area of least doubling] being around 3 o'clock on the obverse.

Class VI, Distended Hub Doubling—This form of doubling is unique in that there is little to no separation of images on coins produced by dies with this sort of doubling. As hubs are used, their raised design elements flatten out slightly. The design imparted by such a hub will not penetrate as far into a die and the die will produce coins showing designs that are thicker than normal. [The 1943 Lincoln cent with a super fat date is perhaps the most shining example of this form of doubling.]

Class VII, Modified Hub Doubling—This name arises from use of a hub that has had some undesirable part of design ground off, rather than wasting an otherwise useable hub. On occasion, the unwanted portion of design is not ground off completely and all dies prepared by this hub will produce coins showing doubling of a specific design element. Examples include 1970 cents of all mints with the remainder of a high or low 70 showing near the date [and a 1963-D cent which shows portions of a 3 whose design never was used, under the primary 3 in the date.]

Class VIII, Tilted Hub Doubling—This form of doubling is not included in the aforementioned flyer and is still hotly contested as to whether or not it is even another class of doubled die. However, most specialists agree that it is and, if so, it is the rarest known form of hub doubling as less than a handful of doubled dies are listed with this classification. It is included here because of the significance of those varieties listed with this classification.

This class is defined pretty much the way it sounds and supposedly involves a tilted hub. When we say tilted hub we mean tilted (either the the hub itself or the die being hubbed) in the hubbing press, not the coining press. Remember, the hubbing press is the press that "squeezes" the impression from the hubs to the dies, in effect striking the dies. Supposedly, again, the hub or die is tilted as the result of an uneven cut on the hub or die blank or from some debris or foreign object lodged in the hubbing press so as to not allow for firm, square seating of the die blank being "squeezed." Squeezing is the Mint's term for striking. Many specialists consider the rare 1891 doubled die obverse (Fivaz/Stanton #FS-010.87 and Snow #S-3) to be this class of doubled die as the doubling is easily visible on the word "Of" and slightly on the word "Liberty" but hardly anywhere else.

* * *

So there you have it—simple (as simple as can be anyway) and concise definitions of the types, causes, and classes of doubled dies normally accepted today. However, in 1996 the U.S. Mint introduced a new hubbing press which is supposed to bring about sufficient relief on working dies with just one squeeze, thereby eliminating the possibility of doubled dies. Prior to installation of these new hubbing presses one squeeze was never enough, which is why so many doubled dies are known to exist. This new single-squeeze hubbing press has already sparked controversy in the numismatic community with the discovery of a doubled ear 1997 Lincoln cent. First reported by Iowa collector Larry Philbrick, the coin remains mired in controversy as most specialists believe it to be a Class IV or VIII doubled die while some of the most respected specialists do not agree that it is a doubled die at all. And, indeed, the Mint itself has declared it not to be a doubled die, referring to it mostly as an unfinished die. The Mint claims the area in question (Lincoln's ear) is on all cent dies after the single squeeze and is always, except in this case, stoned or ground off before being used. Specialists who agree with it being a doubled die say, "Show me some other dies with this effect," while those who abide with the Mint's explanation still do not understand fully exactly what the Mint is trying to say! Needless to say, many specialists are lobbying for yet another classification of doubled dies, one that is created with a single hubbing! Stay tuned. . . .

As was stated at the beginning of this chapter, the study of error and variety coinage is very complex, requiring years of study to understand the causes and effects of certain anomalies in the die making and minting process. Obviously this chapter is greatly condensed and multitudes of fine references have been published on the subject—none of them, however, have been or will ever be complete! Also, because of the complexity of the subject and the length of time involved in fully explaining the die making and minting process, we have not even begun to explain the process. This requires a freestanding reference of which several are available and referenced as recommended reading at the end of this chapter.

Additionally, we have largely confined our discussion to those types most normally encountered on coins which have been manufactured using fairly modern equipment. This fairly modern equipment dates back to the mid-19th century but, hey, "If it ain't broke, why fix it?" as the saying goes. This is one area, in our opinion, where the government got it right a long time ago and only minor tweaking has been required since! For example, prior to the installation of this "modern" equipment, coins were hand struck using a giant, awkward screw press. Because each coin was handled by hand very few of the striking errors made it out of the Mint, so you are not as likely to encounter them as all the others discussed in this chapter. As for die varieties, the methods used to manufacture dies has changed as well and would require yet another chapter on the early die making practice. However, so you are aware of them, early die varieties have been cataloged for nearly as long as the coins themselves have been in existence, and most design types and denominations have excellent references available for the cataloging of their varieties. It was easy to do this with the early coinage as much fewer dies were produced. For example, there was but one original obverse die produced for the 1844 half cent, yet there was somewhere in the neighborhood of 9,000 obverse dies for the 1994-D Lincoln cent alone. Common sense should tell you it is much easier to catalog the half cent varieties than it is to catalog the Lincoln cent, yet collecting Lincoln cents by variety is easily one of the most active areas in the hobby today! Below are listed some of the design types not discussed (as well as many that were) in this chapter along with the name of the cataloging system(s) used and a sample number from each system; this way you may at least be familiar with what you are reading when you encounter them elsewhere.

Half Cents—Cohen, Munson & Munde—**CMM1**
   —Cohen—**Cohen 1, Cohen PO 1, SR 2,** etc.
   —Breen—**Breen 1**
Large Cents—Sheldon—**Sheldon 1**
   —Newcomb—**Newcomb 1**
Flying Eagle & Indian Cents—Snow—**S-1**
   —FINDERS Report (Larry Steve)—**FND-001**
Two Cents—Leone—**Leone 65P-3o1r**
   —Flynn—**KF-P12-RPD**
Half Dimes (Bust)—Valentine—**V-1**
   (Seated—Valentine—**V-1**
Shield Nickels—Fletcher—**F-01**
Liberty & Shield Nickels—Peters & Mohon—**PM 01.1**

s (Bust)—Davis—**Davis 1**
—Hilt—**Hilt 7F**
mes (Seated)—Ahwash—**Ahwash 1**
—Greer—**Greer No. 101**
Quarters (Bust)—Browning—**Browning 1**
Quarters (Seated)—Briggs—**Obverse 2-B**
Half Dollars (Flowing Hair & Bust)—Overton—**O-101**
Half Dollars (Seated)—Beistle—**Beistle 2-B**
Dollars (Flowing Hair & Bust)—Bolender-**B-1**
—Haseltine—**H-1**
—Bowers-Borckardt—**BB-251**
Dollars (Seated Liberty)—Breen—**Breen 5438**
—Bowers-Borckardt—**BB-1**
Dollars (Trade)—Breen—**Breen 5796**
—Bowers-Borckardt—**BB-1**
Dollars (Morgan & Peace)—Van Allen & Mallis—**VAM#1**
Gold (just about any)—Breen—**Breen 1B** or **Breen 6328**
20th-Century Die Varieties (some of which include those of
series for the 19th century as well):
Doubled Dies—CONECA—**CONECA DDO#1 & 1-O-I**
—Wexler—**Wexler DDO-001**
—Potter—**Potter VCR#1/DDO#1**
RPMs & OMMs—CONECA—**CONECA RPM#1**
—Wexler—**Wexler RPM-001**
—Potter—**Potter VCR#1/RPM**
Miscellaneous Varieties—
Fivaz/Stanton—**FS#023**

It should be noted here that the Wexler numbers are also
those of the National Collectors Association of Die Doubling
(NCADD).

THE COMBINED ORGANIZATIONS OF NUMISMATIC ERROR COLLECTORS OF AMERICA (CONECA)

In the early part of 1983 there were two significant national
error collecting clubs—Collectors of Numismatic Errors
(CONE) and Numismatic Error Collectors of America (NECA).
By mid-year the two organizations had merged forming
CONECA, the only numismatic specialty club devoted exclu-
sively to the study and advancement of error *and* variety

collecting. Since that time the organization has consistently forged the future of the error and variety hobby using its motto "Knowledge Through Education" as its guiding beacon.

The club supplies members with *Errorscope*, an award-winning publication, on a bi-monthly basis. *Errorscope* is full of educational and informative articles including splendid detailed photographs. Also included in each issue is an error and variety auction (in which only members participate) which often consists of more than 800 lots. The auctions offer one of the best sources available anywhere for members to add to their collections or sell their duplicates.

Also included with CONECA membership is perhaps the finest error and variety reference library in existence today. All members have to do to borrow from it is pay shipping both ways on what they borrow. As if that is not enough, the club also offers the fun and sometimes rewarding fundraiser known as Winner's Windfall where members have an opportunity to win error and variety coins worth sometimes in excess of $500!

For the last couple of years the club has been aggressively publishing photo attribution guides for die varieties on 20th-century coins. It is the goal of the club to not stop this trend until all 20th-century coinage is covered in these guides.

The club has always offered an authentication, examination, and attribution service but one in place today rivals anything ever available anywhere. For just $2.50 per coin for members ($5 for nonmembers), plus shipping and insurance, members receive confident, accurate attributions of their 20th-century die varieties. And, if a submission is a new listing (previously unreported die variety), the member also receives an $8\frac{1}{2} \times 11$ certificate, complete with photographs, the new number, and a complete description of the variety which is suitable for framing. All this for no extra charge!

The pinnacle of each calendar year, after having already been a force at many major coin shows throughout the year, is the group's annual Errorama, usually held in conjunction with the American Numismatic Association's Anniversary Convention. Errorama features many of the nation's top error and variety dealers; the majority of the finest researchers; educational and fellowship events; the club's annual business meeting where members are encouraged to attend; an annual cherrypicking contest; and the anxiously awaited, well-received, well-attended, and hottest party in town—The

Annual Awards Banquet. Here the club's most dedicated volunteers are recognized for their hard work amid camaraderie that is perhaps unrivaled in the hobby! The event is always casual and includes a fantastic dinner. CONECA believes hobbies are supposed to be fun so they also believe in having fun.

Membership is currently $25 per year for regular members and only $10 per year for YNs (under age 18). There is also a first-class mailing option which is highly recommended if you plan to actively participate in any club activities or events. This option costs $12.50 extra, with foreign postage extra as well. For more details and a membership application send a large, self-addressed, stamped envelope (LSASE) to: Send application and check/money order (payable to CONECA) to: Paul Funaiole 35 Leavitt Lane Glenburn, ME 04401-1013 or visit the club's Web site at http://conecaonline.org.

OTHER SPECIALTY CLUBS AND ORGANIZATIONS

Whereas CONECA may be the only specialty club devoted exclusively to the study of error *and* variety coinage, there are many clubs and organizations that specialize in a particular denomination and/or series of U.S. coinage that regularly feature error and variety articles in their publications also. Below is a partial list of them, their area of specialization, and an address you may write to for more information.

Barber Coin Collectors
Society (BCCS)
415 Ellen Drive
Brookhaven, MS 39601
All Barber Design Coinage

Early American Coppers
PO Box 15782
Cincinnati, OH 45215
Large & Half Cents

John Reich Collectors Society
PO Box 39541
Solon, OH 44139
U.S. Bust Coinage

Flying Eagle & Indian Cent
Collectors Society
(The Fly-In Club)
c/o Eagle Eye
PO Box 257
Seahurst, WA 98062
Flying Eagle & Indian Cents

Society of Silver Dollar
Collectors (SSDC)
PO Box 2123
North Hills, CA 91393
U.S. Silver Dollars

Bust Half Nut Club
PO Box 4875
Margate, FL 33063
Bust Halves

Liberty Seated Collectors Club
5718 King Arthur Drive
Kettering, OH 45429
Liberty Seated Coinage

RECOMMENDED ERROR- AND VARIETY-RELATED READING

As has been stated many times throughout this book and especially in this chapter, there is currently a wealth of information available to the error and variety enthusiast. Although it is impossible to list it all here, many of the best are given here for your consideration. Keep in mind that all of the specialty organizations listed previously publish excellent club journals which you should also consider. One should not forget *all* of the recommended publications listed elsewhere in this book as well. Each of them contains error- and variety-related articles and information in each issue, and most of them have regular error- and variety-related columns.

Periodicals

Cherrypickers' News
PO Box 15487
Savannah, GA 31416-2187
Published six times per year by Stanton Printing and Publishing and edited by Mike Ellis, President of CONECA; this publication is full of quality photographs of recent and not-so-recent finds. It also features the only variety price guide available today. This should be considered *must* reading by all variety enthusiasts.

Error Trends Coin Magazine
PO Box 158
Oceanside, NY 11572-0158
An excellent source of information on error coinage which usually includes some variety information as well. Each monthly issue also contains error coin pricing information.

Books

Cherrypickers' Guide to Rare Die Varieties, The, Fourth Edition, by Bill Fivaz, J. T. Stanton, and Mike Ellis. One of the best-selling books in the entire hobby! A must-have reference for all variety enthusiasts. 320+ pages and 1000+ photographs!

Error Coin Encyclopedia, The, Second Edition, by Arnold Margolis. One of the two best books available on the subject of error coinage. Loaded with photographs and pricing information, this book takes you through the entire minting process.

Modern Minting Process, The, and *U.S. Minting Errors and Varieties,* by Dr. James Wiles. Contains two correspondence courses from the ANA School of Numismatics with over 34 color photographs and hundreds more in black and white. Available only through the American Numismatic Association but one of the best references on the subject today!

Other

Note: All of the following, two of the preceding, and many more references are available through Stanton Printing and Publishing. For a complete catalog of books and supplies, write to Stanton Printing and Publishing, PO Box 15487, Savannah, GA 31416-2187 or request one via e-mail at sppmike@aol.com or visit the Web site at www.stanton printing.com.

Treasure Hunting Mercury Dimes, by John A. Wexler and Kevin Flynn.

Authoritative Reference on Three-Cent Nickels, The, by Kevin Flynn and Edward Fletcher.

Treasure Hunting Liberty Head Nickels, by Kevin Flynn and Bill Van Note.

Washington Quarter Dollar Book: An Attribution and Pricing Guide (1932–1941), The, by James Wiles, Ph.D.

Treasure Hunting Buffalo Nickels, by John A. Wexler, Ron Pope, and Kevin Flynn.

Complete Price Guide and Cross Reference to Lincoln Cent Mint Mark Varieties, The, by Brian Allen and John A. Wexler.

RPM Book, Second Edition: Lincoln Cents, The, by James Wiles, Ph.D.

Flying Eagle and Indian Cent Die Varieties, by Larry R. Steve and Kevin J. Flynn.

Fly-In Club Attribution Files, The, by Rick Snow.

Buyer's and Enthusiast's Guide to Flying Eagle and Indian Cents, A, by Q. David Bowers.

Complete Guide to Lincoln Cents, The, by David W. Lange.

Longacre's Two-Cent Piece—1864 Attribution Guide, by Frank Leone.

Shield Five Cent Series, The, by Edward L. Fletcher, Jr.

Complete Guide to Shield and Liberty Head Nickels, The, by Gloria Peters and Cindy Mohon.

Federal Half Dimes, by Russell J. Logan and John W. McCloskey.

Complete Guide to Liberty Seated Half Dimes, The, by Al Blythe.

Complete Guide to Liberty Seated Dimes, The, by Brian Greer.

Best of the Washington Quarter Doubled Dies, The, by John A. Wexler and Kevin Flynn.

Comprehensive Encyclopedia of United States Liberty Seated Quarters, The, by Larry Briggs.

Complete Guide to Barber Quarters, 2nd edition, The, by David Lawrence.

Complete Guide to Barber Halves, The, by David Lawrence.

Kennedy Half Dollar Book, The, by James Wiles, Ph.D.

Top 100 Morgan Dollar Varieties: The VAM Keys, The, by Michael S. Fey, Ph.D., and Jeff Oxman.

Comprehensive Catalog and Encyclopedia of Morgan and Peace Silver Dollars, 4th Edition, The, by Leroy C. Van Allen and A. George Mallis.

1878 Morgan Dollar 8-TF Attribution System, The, by Jeff Oxman and Les Hartnett.

1878 Morgan Dollar 7/8-TF Attribution Guide, The, by Jeff Oxman and Les Hartnett.

RPM Book,The, by John A. Wexler and Tom Miller.

Two Dates Are Better Than One: A Collector's Guide to Misplaced Dates, by Kevin Flynn.

Walter Breen's Encyclopedia of United States Half Cents—1793–1857, by Walter Breen.

Walter Breen's Complete Encyclopedia of U.S. and Colonial Coins, by Walter Breen.

Bill Fivaz's Counterfeit Detection Guide, by Bill Fivaz.

Encyclopedia of Doubled Dies, Volumes I and II, by John A. Wexler.

Cherrypickers' News 1996 Yearbook, by J. T. Stanton.

Cherrypickers' News 1997 Yearbook, by J. T. Stanton.

Cherrypickers' News 1998/99 Yearbook, by J. T. Stanton and Mike Ellis.

Joja Jemz Reprints, by J. T. Stanton and Bill Fivaz.

Lincoln Cent Doubled Die, The, by John A. Wexler.

WHERE TO BUY AND SELL ERROR AND VARIETY COINAGE

There are many good places to buy and sell error and variety coinage but it may be easiest to find one dealer who is honest, fair, friendly, and encouraging. If you locate that one dealer, even though he may not have what you are looking for nor want everything you have to offer, he can and usually will point you in the "right" direction. Good error and variety dealers enjoy their occupation as much as the collectors they are dealing with.

Currently, the best place to buy and sell error and variety coinage is through CONECA's auction or via the Internet. EBay has been a fantastic place to sell striking errors!

ERROR AND VARIETY VALUES

Error and variety coins are among the most difficult of all to assign value to. The number of variables involved in assigning value goes way beyond that of normal coins. Keep in mind that planchet and striking errors are unique—no two are ever just alike! Imagine the implications of that statement. Whereas it is possible to supply a very simple and basic generic error type value guide (which is provided beginning on the next page), it has been impossible, at least to date, to formulate such a price guide and maintain it with any accuracy. Many factors contribute to this dilemma. One of the largest obstacles is the fact that there are no known specific numbers of error types available. Error and variety collecting is a recent phenomena which is very much experiencing growing pains! One of the truly fascinating aspects governing the error and variety hobby is the fact that supply, demand, and desirability are the only governing aspects. In other words, most purchase a coin because they like the coin and not because they believe it will net them lots of money in the future (though at present most should buy for this reason because of the lack of availability!).

As for pricing of die varieties, the equation becomes only a little easier. There are thousands of well-documented, well-publicized die varieties, many of which have been actively sought and highly prized by collectors for years. Value information for these varieties is readily available in many price guides, including the guide found in this book. It is listed with all the normal coins. But what about the thousands more that are not listed anywhere? Again, availability and demand are the key factors. Hints as to relative scarcity and demand found in works about specific varieties or series may be used to formulate your own value. Additionally, specialists are regularly confronted with estimate requests and those who actively buy, sell, and trade these varieties should be considered the number one source for this information. However, don't rely on one, ask several. Then you may average out their estimates for a pretty good idea of what is fair for your coin. Several other factors must be considered also: demand, grade, and known availability are but a few.

The following values are for basic, no frills, 20th-century planchet and striking errors. As with all coin pricing guides, values are subject to change with market conditions. The values represented here are for super common and/or undated coins which are most often encountered. With the tremendous increase in popularity of these errors it would be ludicrous to establish prices here for the more glamorous error types as their value continues to spiral upward.

Basic Error Coin Prices

	BLANK OR PLANCHET	SMALL CLIP	OFF CENTER	BROAD-STRIKE	PARTIAL COLLAR
Lincoln Cent (CopperMem)	1.50	1.50	2.00	1.75	1.00
Lincoln Cent (Zinc)	1.00	1.50	1.50	1.75	1.00
Jefferson Nickel	2.00	1.50	2.00	2.00	2.00
Roosevelt Dime (Clad)	2.00	1.50	3.00	2.00	2.00
Washington Quarter (Clad)	5.00	2.00	9.00	6.50	5.00
Kennedy Half (Clad)	20.00	10.00	35.00	32.00	18.00
Eisenhower Dollar (Clad)	30.00	20.00	45.00	40.00	25.00
Susan B. Anthony Dollar	35.00	20.00	50.00	35.00	25.00

THE AMERICAN NUMISMATIC ASSOCIATION

HISTORY

Most of today's coin collectors probably know that there is an American Numismatic Association (ANA), the largest organization of "coin" collectors in the world. However, many may not realize that the Association is more than 100 years old.

DR. GEORGE F. HEATH, FOUNDER OF ANA.

AMERICAN NUMISMATIC ASSOCIATION HEADQUARTERS IN COLORADO SPRINGS FEATURES A MUSEUM AND A REFERENCE LIBRARY, BOTH OPEN TO THE PUBLIC AT NO CHARGE.

An educational, nonprofit organization, the American Numismatic Association invites and welcomes to membership all persons who have an interest in numismatics—whether they collect coins, paper money, tokens, or medals—whether advanced collectors or those noncollectors only generally interested in the subject. Members, located in every state of the Union and in many other countries, total nearly 30,000.

A factor that deterred the Association's development during its first three-quarters of a century was the geographic dispersal of its functional offices: the executive secretary was in Phoenix, Arizona; the treasurer in Washington, DC; the editor in Chicago, Illinois; and the librarian in Lincoln, Nebraska. None of the staff was full-time or received pay, and most operated out of their homes or private offices. Obviously, this situation limited and hampered communication and made for inefficient operation in general.

Since 1967 ANA operations have been centered in Colorado Springs, Colorado, and in 1982 the building was expanded to almost twice its original size. In 2001 the Money Museum and Library were expanded and completely renovated. Museum exhibits will soon be on line at www.money.org A board of governors, which establishes policy in determining all bylaws and regulations, is elected from the membership on a regular basis and serves without pay. Implementing established policy in Colorado Springs is a full-time salaried professional staff that includes an executive director, editor, librarian, curator, authenticator, and assistants and clerical staff.

The principal objectives of the Association are the advancement of numismatic knowledge and better relations among numismatists. Collectors will find the annual membership dues low compared to the tremendous value to be found in the prestige and services that membership offers.

The ANA does not buy or sell coins. Its revenue comes from membership dues and is supplemented by gifts, bequests, and contributions. It receives no operating funds from any governmental body. Any net income from various activities is used on behalf of its members and for the advancement of the hobby.

When the ANA was organized in October 1891, Dr. George F. Heath, the motivating force, was honored with membership No. 1. Member No. 1,000 was admitted in March 1908; No. 10,000 in March 1944; No. 50,000 in August 1963; and No. 100,000 in August 1979. Of course, the passing of time has taken its toll, and today's membership is slightly less than a third of the total number enrolled during the Association's more than ninety-nine years.

An important date in the history of ANA is May 9, 1912, when it was granted a federal charter by the U.S. Congress. Signed by President Taft, the act gave the charter a fifty-year life. A congressional amendment dated April 10, 1962, allowed for an increase in the number of ANA board members and perpetuated the charter indefinitely. One of very few such charters ever granted, it has given the Association prestige and has been a stabilizing influence on its management.

DUES

Collectors under the age of twenty-three are encouraged in the hobby by lower membership dues, special exhibit classes and programs at conventions, and other educational programs.

Classes of membership are as follows: **Regular**—adults twenty-three years of age and older (eligible for all benefits, including receipt of *Numismatist Magazine*); **Club**—nonprofit numismatic organizations (entitled to all benefits); **Student**—twenty-two years of age and younger (entitled to all benefits but cannot hold office); and **Life Member**—corresponding to Regular members but a one-time fee is paid for lifetime membership. Memberships are not transferrable from one person to another, and member numbers are never reassigned.

The amounts of dues and a few other details of membership follow:

Regular *(adult)*—U.S. only	$ 33.00
Regular *(adult)*—all other countries	43.00
Club—*any country*	29.00
Student *(twenty-two years old or younger)*	15.00
Senior *(65 years or older)*	29.00
Five-year individual or club	150.00
Life *(adult individual)*	750.00
Life *(senior)*	500.00
Life *(club)*	750.00
Nonmember annual subscription—*U.S. only*	35.00
Subscription—*all other countries*	45.00

NUMISMATIST

Numismatist, the Association's monthly magazine, is actually older than the ANA itself, having been started by Dr. Heath in 1888 (September–October) and published privately through 1910. It did, however, cooperate with and champion the cause of the Association—before and after its organization. In 1910 the vice president of ANA, W.W.C. Wilson of Montreal, purchased the magazine from publisher Farran Zerbe and gifted it to the Association, which has confirmed its publication without interruption.

Numismatist totally revamped with color images throughout the 112 page magazine continues to be the official publication and voice of the Association. It contains well-illustrated articles about various phases of collecting, identifying, and caring for coins, tokens, medals, and paper money. Included are news items regarding Association activities, new issues of coins, medals, and paper money, and developments within the hobby.

The advertising pages of the magazine are open only to ANA members, who must agree to abide by a strict "Code of Ethics." Members receive the magazine as one of the advantages of membership.

LIBRARY SERVICES

Aside from the magazine, one of the earliest services offered to ANA members was the use of a circulating numismatic library, which has grown to be the world's largest facility of its kind. The library houses more than 25,000 books and more than 22,000 periodicals and convention catalogs, the majority of which are loaned by mail to members and are available to non-members for use in the Colorado Springs headquarters.

The library's resource center maintains and loans numismatic videos and slide sets to members and clubs for their meeting programs. These sets cover many different phases of numismatics and are available without cost except for shipping charges.

ANA COLLECTOR SERVICES

CUSTOM PHOTOGRAPHY

Numismatic photography is an art in itself, as any collector or professional photographer can attest. ANA Collector Services is equipped to photograph all or part of your collection for audio-visual presentations, exhibits, publications, or insurance purposes. Those submitting material can request quality black-and-white prints (actual size or greatly enlarged) or 35mm color slides.

Searching for a photograph of a particular numismatic item? ANA Collector Services maintains a photographic archive of millions of coins, tokens, medals, paper money, and related material. Images of items in the ANA Money Museum cabinet also are available.

For additional information, contact: ANA Collector Services, 818 North Cascade Avenue, Colorado Springs, CO 80903-3279, telephone 800-467-5725, Fax 719-634-4085, e-mail: anamus@money.org.

VAULT STORAGE/INSURANCE

One of the primary concerns of hobbyists today is good security and insurance for their collections at a reasonable cost. Happily, both are available through ANA Collector Services. For a low rate, collectors can acquire "lock boxes" in vaults maintained at the ANA Money Museum. Your package will be opened and inventoried on videotape, and the contents evaluated. Subsequently, the package will be re-sealed and stored in climate-controlled vaults. (If desired, a videotape of the entire procedure can be provided.) All records of storage are private and confidential.

You can request return of your collection at any time. Collections under ANA custodial care are eligible for special, low-cost insurance rates.

NUMISMATIC CONSULTATION

ANA Collector Services' virtually limitless resources are at your disposal. For a reasonable fee, you can confer with experienced staff members about:

- Acquisition
- Appraisals
- Attribution
- Certification
- Charitable donations
- Consigning to an auction
- Estate assistance
- Identification
- Liquidation
- Preservation
- Research
- Storage

Items subsequently can be submitted to ANA Collector Services for further evaluation. Recommendations are based on this evaluation and the submitter's needs.

VIDEO DOCUMENTATION

An audio-visual record of your collection can be both valuable and versatile. Consider these advantages:

- **Enjoyment.** Share your collection with friends and fellow hobbyists without worry.
- **Security.** View your collection whenever you wish, knowing that actual specimens are securely locked away.

- **Sales.** Offer a preview of your items for sale or auction without risk.
- **Estate Assistance.** Prepare a copy of the video for the executor of your estate, complete with instructions for the disposition of your collection.
- **Insurance.** Record documentary evidence of ownership in the event of loss or damage.

THE UNITED STATES MINT

For sixteen years following the Declaration of Independence, this country still relied upon British and other foreign coinage. This was not only unsatisfactory but objectionable to many citizens, as Britain's coins bore the likeness of the not-too-popular George III. In 1791 Congress approved the establishment of a federal Mint. Presses for milling were purchased, designers and die-cutters hired. But the question remained whether to fashion U.S. coinage after Britain's or devise an entirely new series with different denominations. After much debate the latter plan was adopted, with the dollar (named for Thalers of the Dutch, who were not our enemies) as the chief currency unit and our coinage based upon divisions or multiples of it. The metal standard was fixed at 15 parts silver to one part gold. When finalized on April 2, 1792, the Mint Act provided for coins in values of $10, $5, $2.50, $1, 50¢, 25¢, 10¢, 5¢, 1¢, and ½¢. The 1¢ and ½¢ were of copper; other denominations, up to $1, silver; those over $1, gold. The $5 piece was regarded as the equivalent to Britain's pound sterling, the 25¢ to the British shilling, while the ½¢ was the counterpart to Britain's farthing or "fourthling" (¼ part of a British penny). It may seem odd that necessity was felt for a coin valued under one cent, but at this remote period even the penny had considerable buying power and fractional pricing of goods was common—apples at 1¢ each or 5½¢ per half dozen, for example. If such a coin was not available, the situation would have invited an onslaught of merchant tokens.

Philadelphia was selected as home for the first Mint building, whose cornerstone was laid July 21, 1792. George Washington, then serving as President, contributed silverware from which the first federal coins were struck—a few half dimes or half dismes as they were called (5¢ pieces). Proceeding cautiously, the Mint's first purchase of metal was six pounds of copper. This was used for cents and half cents, delivered to the Treasurer of the United States in 1793. The following year a deposit of $80,715.73$\frac{1}{2}$ worth of French silver coins was made to the Mint by the state of Maryland, to be melted down and used for coinage. They yielded a quantity of 1794-dated dollars and half dollars. Gold was not obtained until 1795 when a Boston merchant turned over $2,276.72 in ingots, which were quickly transformed (apparently along with gold from other sources) into 744 Half Eagles ($5 pieces). Later that year 400 Eagles ($10) were produced. By the close of the year 1800 the Mint had milled $2,534,000 worth of coins and succeeded in distributing them throughout the then-inhabited regions of the country, as far west as Michigan and Missouri.

HOW U.S. COINS
ARE MINTED

THE COIN ALLOY CONTENT

In the coinage process, the first step is to prepare the alloy to be used. Except for nickels and 1-cent pieces, the alloys formerly (1964 and earlier) used in the coining of U.S. coins were as follows:

Silver coins—90% silver and 10% copper

5-cent pieces—75% copper and 25% nickel

1-cent pieces—95% copper and 5% zinc

The cents of 1943 consisted of steel coated with zinc; and the nickels of 1942–45 consisted of 35% silver, 56% copper, and 9% manganese. In 1982 the cent was changed to a zinc interior with copper coating.

WHAT ARE THE NEW CLAD COINS MADE OF?

1971 to date—cupro-nickel dollars and half dollars

1965 to date—quarters and dimes; the outer surfaces are 75% copper and 25% nickel, and the inner core is 100% copper

1965–70—half dollars; the outer surface is 80% silver and 20% copper; the inner core is 21% silver and 79% copper; the overall silver content of the coin is 40%

When clad coinage was introduced in 1965, the designs then in use were retained: the Roosevelt dime, Washington quarter, and Kennedy half. (The United States was not at that time minting dollar coins.) The only alteration since then was for the special 1976 bicentennial designs.

Because of the ever-increasing demand for coinage, the Mint introduced new time-saving steps in its coin minting. Raw metal is cast into giant ingots eighteen feet long, sixteen inches wide, and six inches thick, weighing 6,600 pounds. Previously, they had weighed 400 pounds and were sixteen times smaller in measurement. The ingot is rolled red hot and scaled to remove imperfections. It's then ready for the coins to be stamped; no longer are blanks made and annealed (heated). The excess metal that's left behind is used to make new ingots in a continuous, never-ending process. The new coins are electronically scanned, counted, and automatically bagged. These facilities are in use at the new, ultra-modern Mint in Philadelphia. It has a production capacity of eight billion coins per year and is open to the public, featuring interesting displays and guided tours.

HOW PROOF COINS ARE MINTED

1. Perfect planchets are picked out.
2. They are washed with a solution of cream of tartar.
3. They are washed again and alcohol dipped.
4. The dies for making proof coins receive a special polishing for mirrorlike finish.
5. The planchets are then milled.
6. The coins are minted by special hydraulic presses at a much slower rate than regular coins. The fine lines are much more visible on a proof coin.

Minting: From Metal to Coins

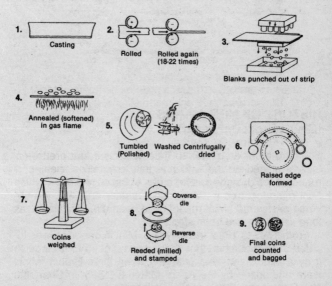

1. Casting
2. Rolled | Rolled again (18-22 times)
3. Blanks punched out of strip
4. Annealed (softened) in gas flame
5. Tumbled (Polished) | Washed | Centrifugally dried
6. Raised edge formed
7. Coins weighed
8. Obverse die | Reverse die | Reeded (milled) and stamped
9. Final coins counted and bagged

MINT MARKS

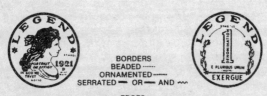

BORDERS
BEADED ······
ORNAMENTED ·······
SERRATED ── OR ── AND ∿∿

EDGES
MILLED • LETTERED • ORNAMENTED • VINE & BARS
• PLAIN • DIAGONALLY REEDED • ENGRAILED

HISTORY OF MINT MARKS
(Courtesy of *Coin World*)

A mint mark on a United States coin is a small letter (or letters) placed on the field (the flat, featureless areas surrounding the designs and lettering) of the coin to show which Mint manufactured it. [Mint marks appear on either the obverse or reverse.] Mint marks have been used for almost as long as coins have been struck.

From 1793 to 1838, the only U.S. Mint in operation was located at Philadelphia, thus there was no need to distinguish it by a mint mark. That changed when three Branch Mints were authorized by the Act of March 3, 1835: in Charlotte, NC; Dahlonega, GA; and New Orleans, LA.

In order to distinguish which Mint struck a particular coin, mint marks were introduced on coins struck at the Branch Mints. The Philadelphia Mint, however, continued to strike coins without mint marks.

As new Branch Mints were authorized and opened, new

104

mint marks were introduced. There have been eight different mint marks used since the United States began striking coins in 1792.

With one four-year exception, U.S. coins struck at the Philadelphia Mint bore no mint marks until 1979. A "P" mint mark was used on the Jefferson, Wartime 5-cent coins, struck from 1942 to 1945 in a silver alloy. The "P" mint mark on these issues was designed to distinguish the silver alloy issues from regular copper-nickel 5-cent coins.

In most cases, the mint marks were applied to the reverse sides of U.S. coins until 1968. There are a few exceptions, however, including 1838-O Capped Bust half dollars and 1916-D and 1916-S Walking Liberty half dollars.

Mint marks have not always been used, even at the Branch Mints. The Coinage Act of 1965, which authorized the replacement of silver coinage with copper-nickel clad coinage, also approved the dropping of mint marks. Mint marks were not used on coins dated 1965 through 1967. The move was designed to help alleviate a coin shortage by removing the distinction between coins struck at Branch Mints and those struck in Philadelphia so collectors could not determine which were the more limited strikes.

With the announcement on January 4, 1968, that mint marks would return to coins, Mint Director Eva Adams made a major change in mint mark application. To achieve uniformity, she directed that all mint marks be placed on the obverse. She continued the practice of not placing mint marks on coins struck at the Philadelphia Mint.

A coining facility was opened at the West Point Silver Bullion Depository in 1975, initially to strike cents (and in later years, quarter dollars). These coins are indistinguishable from Philadelphia Mint coins, since they bear no mint mark.

At the same time (mid-1970s into the 1980s), some coins struck at the San Francisco Assay Office were produced without mint marks, primarily to prevent collectors from hoarding the S-Mint coins.

Major changes were made in mint mark policy beginning in 1979. Anthony dollars struck at the Philadelphia Mint were given a P mint mark. The list of coins to bear the "P" mint mark grew in 1980, when all other Philadelphia denominations but the 1-cent coin received the new mint mark.

A new mint mark, "W," was belatedly established in September 1983, when the West Point Bullion Depository (now the West Point Mint) began striking 1984-dated $10 Gold Eagles commemorating the Los Angeles Olympic Games. As noted, the West Point facility had been striking coins for circulation without mint marks. Production of circulating coinage (strictly cents by this time) at West Point continued without the addition of a W mint mark.

The W mint mark has been used on various commemorative and bullion coins since then, as well as a 1996-W Roosevelt dime included in the 1996 Uncirculated Mint set as a commemoration of the 50th anniversary of the design. However, no coins struck for circulation have borne a W mint mark.

WHY ARE MINT MARKS IMPORTANT?

Collectors determine a coin's value by examining its date, mint mark, and condition. The most important criterion in determining a coin's value is its condition. However, determining the Mint that struck the coin is extremely important in arriving at its value. That's because the coin may be struck in large quantities at one Mint and very small quantities at another. Consider the 1914 and 1914-D Lincoln cents: more than 75 million examples were struck at Philadelphia (with no mint mark) but only 1.193 million have a little D mark below its date.

MINT MARKS TODAY

Let's examine our current pocket change or coins that collectors may find in today's circulating coinage.

Lincoln cents, 1909–96, have used two mint marks (but have been struck at four Mints). Collectors will find a little "D" for the Denver Mint or "S" for the San Francisco Mint, located directly beneath the date.

Jefferson 5-cent coins, 1938–96, have used three mint marks, in three different locations. Denver and San Francisco coins struck from 1938–42, and from 1946–64, feature the D or S on the reverse, to the right of the representation of Monticello. The mint marks were enlarged and moved to above the dome of Monticello on the wartime alloy coins of 1942–45, and as noted, a P mint mark was used for the first time. The D and S mint marks have appeared on the obverse, just below the last numeral of the date, since 1968, and the P mint mark has appeared in the same location since 1980.

Roosevelt dimes, 1946–96, have used four mint marks

since their introduction. The Denver and San Francisco dimes of 1946–64 bear a D or S mint mark on the reverse, to the lower left of the torch. The mint mark was moved to the obverse in 1968, to just above the last numeral in the date, where it remains today. The P was added in 1980, and the W was used on special 1996-W dimes sold to collectors.

Washington quarter dollars, 1932–96, have used three mint marks. Denver and San Francisco quarters struck from 1932–64 bear the D or S mint mark on the reverse, between the wreath and the denomination QUARTER DOLLAR. The mint marks were moved to the obverse in 1968, to behind Washington's queue. The P was added in 1980.

Kennedy half dollars, 1964–96, have used three mint marks. A D mint mark was used on the reverse of Denver Mint coins in 1964, just above the L in HALF. It's the only such Kennedy half dollar to bear a mint mark on the reverse. The D and S mint marks were moved to the obverse in 1968, right below the bust of Kennedy and above the date on the obverse side of the coin. The P was added in 1980.

MINTS AND THEIR MINT MARKS

By separate Acts of Congress, the government has established Mints in different parts of the country.

1. **"P"** **PHILADELPHIA,** *Pennsylvania*—1973 to date—No mint mark. Until 1973, coins minted at Philadelphia did not carry mint marks, except for the silver-content nickels of 1942–45.
2. **"C"** **CHARLOTTE,** *North Carolina*—gold coins only, 1838–61.
3. **"CC"** **CARSON CITY,** *Nevada*—1870–93.
4. **"D"** **DAHLONEGA,** *Georgia*—gold coins only, 1838–61.
5. **"D"** **DENVER,** *Colorado*—1906 to date.
6. **"O"** **NEW ORLEANS,** *Louisiana*—1838–61 and 1879–1909.
7. **"S"** **SAN FRANCISCO,** *California*—1854–1955 and 1968 to date.
8. **"W"** **WEST POINT,** *New York*—1976 to date, used for special issues only.

ABOUT THE PRICES IN THIS BOOK

Prices shown in this book represent the current *retail* selling prices at press time. In the first column of each listing, a current *average buying price* is also indicated. This is the price at which coin dealers are buying from the public. Readers should understand that the actual prices charged or paid by any given dealer (there are more than 12,000 coin dealers in the United States) can vary somewhat. Higher-grade coins will usually command a higher price based on a percentage of the value listed for the particular grade. Additional factors that will also affect what a dealer is willing to pay for a coin are: 1) how many other coins like yours the dealer has in his inventory; 2) how long it will take for the dealer to sell your coin; 3) whether or not the dealer is buying your coin for his own investment; 4) the rarity of the date or mint mark of your coin. Hence, the *Blackbook* is presented merely as a guide to the average buying and selling prices.

Prices are shown for each coin in various condition grades. It is of utmost importance that a coin be accurately graded before a value can be placed on it. So-called slider grades, such as MS-62, are not included in this book because of space limitations and the difficulties of gathering reliable information on their values. Nor are split-grade coins included (such as AU-55/MS-60), but with some simple mathematics their values can be estimated, based on the prices shown.

When a price is omitted, there is not enough reliable pricing information available. This is usually because the coin, in that particular condition grade, is seldom sold publicly. However, this should not lead to the assumption that all such coins are more valuable than those for which prices are indicated. This is not necessarily the case.

For some scarce coins which are not regularly sold, an example will be given of a specific auction sale result, along with the year in which the sale occurred. These are given purely in the interest of supplying some tangible pricing information, but *may not* (especially in the case of older prices) accurately reflect the price that would be obtained for the same coin if sold today.

When a coin is said to be "unique," this indicates that only one single specimen is recorded to exist. It does not preclude the possibility that other specimens, which have escaped the notice of numismatists, might exist.

Prices are given for the major or traditionally acknowledged die varieties, for coins on which die varieties occurred. Many additional die varieties will be noticed in dealers' and auctioneers' literature. The collector status of many of these "minor" die varieties—that is, whether they deserve to be recognized as separate varieties—is a point on which no general agreement has been, or is likely to be, reached. It is important, however, to note, whether discussing major or minor die varieties, that the market values of such coins are not automatically higher than those of the normal die type. Nor can it always be assumed that the variety is scarcer than the normal die type. However, make no mistake about it; many of these varieties do carry substantial premiums.

In the case of common date silver and gold coins of the late 19th and 20th centuries, it must be borne in mind that the values (for buying or selling) are influenced by the current value of the metal they contain. Most coin shops display the current "spot" prices for silver and gold bullion.

HOW TO USE THIS BOOK

Listings are provided in this book for all coins of the U.S. Mint plus colonial coins and several other groups of coins (please consult index).

Each listing carries the following information:

Denomination of coin.

Date (this is the date appearing on the coin, which is not necessarily the year in which it was actually manufactured).

Mintage (quantity manufactured by the Mint). In some cases this information is not available. In others, the totals announced by the Mint may not be entirely accurate. This is particularly true of coins dating before 1830.

Average Buying Price *(A.B.P.).* This is the price at which dealers are buying the coin in the first condition grade listed. Buying prices can vary somewhat from one dealer to another.

Current Retail Value, in various grades of condition, the price columns following the A.B.P. (or Average Buying Price) show retail prices being charged by dealers. Prices for each coin are given in various grades of condition. Check the column head, then refer to the Grading Guide if you have any doubt about the condition of your coin. Be sure you have correctly identified your coin and its condition. If the date is missing from your coin, it qualifies only as a "type filler" (that is, a "type" coin in low-grade condition), and its value will be lower than the price shown for a coin of that series.

OFFICIAL ANA GRADING SYSTEM

The descriptions of coin grades given in this book are intended for use in determining the relative condition of coins in various states of preservation. The terms and standards are based on the commonly accepted practices of experienced dealers and collectors. Use of these standards is recommended by the American Numismatic Association to avoid misunderstandings during transaction, cataloging, and advertising.

The method of grading described in this book should be referred to as the Official ANA Grading System. When grading by these standards, care must be taken to adhere to the standard wording, abbreviations, and numbers used in this text.

When a coin first begins to show signs of handling, abrasion, or light wear, only the highest parts of the design are affected. Evidence that such a coin is not Uncirculated can be seen by carefully examining the high spots for signs of a slight change in color, surface texture, or sharpness of fine details.

In early stages of wear the highest points of design become slightly rounded or flattened, and the very fine details begin to merge together in small spots.

After a coin has been in circulation for a short time, the entire design and surface will show light wear. Many of the high parts will lose their sharpness, and most of the original mint luster will begin to wear, except in recessed areas.

Further circulation will reduce the sharpness and relief of the entire design. High points then begin to merge with the next lower parts of the design.

After the protective rim is worn away the entire surface becomes flat, and most of the details blend together or become partially merged with the surface.

It should be understood that because of the nature of the minting process, some coins will be found which do not conform exactly with the standard definitions of wear as given in this text. Specific points of wear may vary slightly. Information given in the notes at the end of some sections does not cover all exceptions, but is a guide to the most frequently encountered varieties.

Also, the amount of mint luster (for the highest several grades) is intended more as a visual guide rather than a fixed quantity. The percentage of visible mint luster described in the text is the *minimum* allowance amount, and a higher percentage can usually be expected. Luster is not always brilliant and may be evident, although sometimes dull or discolored.

A *Choice* coin in any condition is one with an attractive, above average surface relatively free from nicks or bag marks. A *Typical* coin may have more noticeable minor surface blemishes.

In all cases, a coin in lower condition must be assumed to include all the wear features of the next higher grade in addition to its own distinguishing points of wear.

Remarks concerning the visibility of certain features refer to the *maximum* allowable amount of wear for those features.

Note: The official ANA Grading System used in this book is with the permission of the American Numismatic Association.

RECORD KEEPING

For your convenience, we suggest you use the following record-keeping system to note condition of your coin in the checklist box.

ABOUT GOOD ☒   FINE ☒ UNCIRCULATED ☒
GOOD ☒   VERY FINE ☒   PROOF ☒
VERY GOOD ☒ EXTREMELY FINE ☒

GRADING ABBREVIATIONS

Corresponding numbers may be used with any of these descriptions.

PROOF-70	Perfect Proof	Perf. Proof	Proof-70
PROOF-65	Choice Proof	Ch. Proof	Proof-65
PROOF-60	Proof	Proof	Proof-60
MS-70	Perfect Uncirculated	Perf. Unc.	Unc.-70
MS-65	Choice Uncirculated	Ch. Unc.	Unc.-65

MS-60	Uncirculated	Unc.	Unc.-60
AU-55	Choice About Uncirculated	Ch. Abt. Unc.	Ch. AU
AU-50	About Uncirculated	Abt. Unc.	AU
EF-45	Choice Extremely Fine	Ch. Ex. Fine	Ch. EF
EF-40	Extremely Fine	Ex. Fine	EF
VF-30	Choice Very Fine	Ch. V. Fine	Ch. VF
VF-20	Very Fine	V. Fine	VF
F-12	Fine	Fine	F
VG-8	Very Good	V. Good	VG
G-4	Good	Good	G
AG-3	About Good	Abt. Good	AG

PROOF COINS

The mirrorlike surface of a brilliant proof coin is much more susceptible to damage than are the surfaces of an Uncirculated coin. For this reason, proof coins which have been cleaned often show a series of fine hairlines or minute striations. (It should be noted that, when collecting coins, *under no circumstances should any effort be made to clean coins*. Their value is likely to be reduced by such an attempt.) Also, careless handling has resulted in certain proofs acquiring marks, nicks and scratches.

Some proofs, particularly 19th-century issues, have "lint marks." When a proof die was wiped with an oily rag, sometimes threads, bits of hair, lint, and so on would remain. When a coin was struck from such a die, an incuse or recessed impression of the debris would appear on the piece. Lint marks visible to the unaided eye should be specifically mentioned in a description.

Proofs are divided into the following classifications:

Proof-70 (Perfect Proof). A Proof-70 or Perfect Proof is a coin with no hairlines, handling marks, or other defects; in other words, a flawless coin. Such a coin may be brilliant or may have natural toning.

Proof-65 (Choice Proof). Proof-65 or Choice Proof refers to a proof which may show some fine hairlines, usually from friction-type cleaning or friction-type drying or rubbing after dipping. To the unaided eye, a Proof-65 or a Choice Proof will appear to be virtually perfect. However, $5\times$ magnification will reveal some minute lines. Such hairlines are best seen under strong incandescent light.

Proof-60 (Proof). Proof-60 refers to a proof with some scattered handling marks and hairlines which will be visible to the unaided eye.

Impaired Proofs; Other Comments. If a proof has been excessively cleaned, has any marks, scratches, dents, or other defects, it is described as an impaired proof. If the coin has seen extensive wear, then it will be graded one of the lesser grades—Proof-55, Proof-45, or whatever. It is not logical to describe a slightly worn proof as AU (Almost Uncirculated) for it never was "Uncirculated" to begin with, in the sense that Uncirculated describes a top-grade normal production strike. So, the term Impaired Proof is appropriate. It is best to describe fully such a coin, examples being: "Proof with extensive hairlines and scuffing," or "Proof with numerous nicks and scratches in the field," or "Proof-55, with light wear on the higher surfaces."

UNCIRCULATED COINS

The term "Uncirculated," interchangeable with "Mint State," refers to a coin that has never seen circulation. Such a piece has no wear of any kind. A coin as bright as the time it was minted or with very light natural toning can be described as "Brilliant Uncirculated." A coin which has natural toning can be described as "Toned Circulated." Except in the instance of copper coins, the presence or absence of light toning does not affect an Uncirculated coin's grade. Indeed, among silver coins, attractive natural toning often results in the coin bringing a premium price.

The quality of luster or "mint bloom" on an Uncirculated coin is an essential element in correctly grading the piece and has a bearing on its value. Luster may in time become dull, frosty, spotted, or discolored. Unattractive luster will normally lower the grade.

With the exception of certain Special Mint Sets made in recent years for collectors, Uncirculated or normal production strike coins were produced on high-speed presses, stored in bags together with other coins, run through counting machines, and in other ways handled without regard to numismatic posterity. As a result, it is the rule and not the exception for an Uncirculated coin to have bag marks and evidence of coin-to-coin contact, although the piece might not have seen actual commercial circulation. The amount of such marks will depend upon the coin's size. Differences in criteria in this regard are given in the individual sections under grading descriptions for different denominations and types.

Uncirculated coins can be divided into three major categories:

MS-70 (Perfect Uncirculated). MS-70 or Perfect Uncirculated is the finest quality available. Such a coin under 4× magnification will show no bag marks, lines, or other evidence of handling or contact with other coins.

A brilliant coin may be described as "MS-70 Brilliant" or "Perfect Brilliant Uncirculated." A lightly toned nickel or silver coin may be described as "MS-70 Toned" or "Perfect Toned Uncirculated." Or, in the case of particularly attractive or unusual toning, additional adjectives may be in order such as "Perfect Uncirculated with Attractive Iridescent Toning Around the Borders."

Copper and bronze coins: To qualify as MS-70 or Perfect Uncirculated, a copper or bronze coin must have its full luster and natural surface color, and may not be toned brown, olive, or any other color. (Coins with toned surfaces which are otherwise perfect should be described as MS-65, as the following text indicates.)

MS-65 (Choice Uncirculated). This refers to an above average Uncirculated coin which may be brilliant or toned (and described accordingly) and which has fewer bag marks than usual; scattered occasional bag marks on the surface or perhaps one or two very light rim marks.

MS-60 (Uncirculated). MS-60 or Uncirculated (typical Uncirculated without any other adjectives) refers to a coin which has a moderate number of bag marks on its surface. Also present may be a few minor edge nicks and marks, although not of a serious nature. Unusually deep bag marks, nicks, and the like must be described separately. A coin may be either brilliant or toned.

Striking and Minting Peculiarities on Uncirculated Coins

Certain early U.S. gold and silver coins have Mint-caused planchet or adjustment marks, a series of parallel striations. If these are visible to the naked eye, they should be described adjectivally in addition to the numerical or regular descriptive grade; for example: "MS-60 With Adjustment Marks," or "MS-65 With Adjustment Marks," or "Perfect Uncirculated With Very Light Adjustment Marks," or something similar.

If an Uncirculated coin exhibits weakness due to striking or die wear, or unusual (for the variety) die wear, this must be adjectivally mentioned in addition to the grade. Examples are: "MS-60 Lightly Struck," or "Choice Uncirculated Lightly Struck," and "MS-70 Lightly Struck."

CIRCULATED COINS

Once again, as a coin enters circulation it begins to show signs of wear. As time goes on the coin becomes more and more worn until, after a period of many decades, only a few features may be left.

Dr. William H. Sheldon devised a numerical scale to indicate degrees of wear. According to this scale, a coin in Condition 1, or "Basal State," is barely recognizable. At the opposite end, a coin touched by even the slightest trace of wear (below MS-60) cannot be called Uncirculated.

While numbers from 1 through 59 are continuous, it has been found practical to designate specific intermediate numbers to define grades. Hence, this text uses the following descriptions and their numerical equivalents:

AU-55 (Choice About Uncirculated). Only a small trace of wear is visible on the highest points of the coin. As is the case with the other grades here, specific information is listed in the following text under the various types, for wear often occurs in different spots on different designs.

AU-50 (About Uncirculated). With traces of wear on nearly all of the highest areas. At least half of the original mint luster is present.

EF-45 (Choice Extremely Fine). With light overall wear on the coin's highest points. All design details are very sharp. Mint luster is usually seen only in protected areas of the coin's surface such as between the star points and in the letter spaces.

EF-40 (Extremely Fine). With only slight wear but more extensive than the preceding, still with excellent sharpness. Traces of mint luster may still show.

VF-30 (Choice Very Fine). With light, even wear on the surface; design details on the highest points lightly worn, but with all lettering and major features sharp.

VF-20 (Very Fine). As preceding but with moderate wear on highest parts.

F-12 (Fine). Moderate to considerable even wear. Entire design is bold. All lettering, including the word LIBERTY (on coins with this feature on the shield or headband), visible, but with some weaknesses.

VG-8 (Very Good). Well worn. Most fine details such as hair strands, leaf details, and so on are worn nearly smooth.

The word LIBERTY, if on a shield or headband, is only partially visible.

G-4 (Good). Heavily worn. Major designs visible, but with faintness in areas. Head of Liberty, wreath, and other major features visible in outline form without center detail.

AG-3 (About Good). Very heavily worn with portions of the lettering, date, and legends being worn smooth. The date barely readable.

Note: The exact descriptions of circulated grades vary widely from issue to issue. It is essential to refer to the specific text when grading any coin.

SPLIT AND INTERMEDIATE GRADES

It is often the case that because of the peculiarities of striking or a coin's design, one side of the coin will grade differently from the other. When this is the case, a diagonal mark is used to separate the two. For example, a coin with an AU-50 obverse and a Choice Extremely Fine-45 reverse can be described as AU/EF or, alternately, 50/45.

The ANA standard numerical scale is divided into the following steps: 3, 4, 8, 12, 20, 30, 40, 45, 50, 60, 65, and 70. Most advanced collectors and dealers find that the gradations from AG-3 through Choice AU-55 are sufficient to describe nearly every coin showing wear. The use of intermediate grade levels such as EF-42, EF-43, and so on is not encouraged. Grading is not that precise, and using such finely split intermediate grades is imparting a degree of accuracy which probably will not be able to be verified by other numismatists. As such, it is discouraged.

A split or intermediate grade, such as that between VF-30 and EF-40, should be called Choice VF-35 rather than VF-EF or About EF.

An exception to intermediate grades can be found among Mint State coins, coins grading from MS-60 through MS-70. Among Mint State coins there are fewer variables. Wear is not a factor; the considerations are the amount of bag marks and surface blemishes. While it is good numismatic practice to adhere to the numerical classifications of 60, 65, and 70, it is permissible to use intermediate grades.

In all instances, the adjectival description must be of the next lower grade. For example, a standard grade for a coin is MS-60 or Uncirculated Typical. The next major category is MS-65 or Uncirculated Choice. A coin which is felt to grade, for example, MS-64, must be described as "MS-64 Uncirculated Typical." It may not be described as Choice Uncirculated, for the minimum definition of Choice Uncirculated is MS-65. Likewise, an MS-69 coin must be described as MS-69 Uncirculated Choice. It is not permissible to use Uncirculated Perfect for any coin which is any degree less than MS-70.

The ANA Grading System considers it to be good numismatic practice to adhere to the standard 60, 65, and 70 numerical designations. Experienced numismatists can generally agree on whether a given coin is MS-60 or MS-65. However, not even the most advanced numismatists can necessarily agree on whether a coin is MS-62 or MS-63; the distinction is simply too minute to permit accuracy. In all instances, it is recommended that intermediate grades be avoided, and if there is any doubt, the lowest standard grade should be used. The use of plus or minus signs is also not accepted practice.

SMALL CENTS—INDIAN HEAD 1859–1909

MINT STATE *(Absolutely no trace of wear.)*

MS-70 (Perfect Uncirculated)
A flawless coin exactly as it was minted, with no trace of wear or injury. Must have full mint luster and brilliance of light toning. Any unusual die or planchet traits must be described.

MS-65 (Choice Uncirculated)
No trace of wear; nearly as perfect as MS-70 except for some small blemish. Has full mint luster but may be unevenly toned or lightly fingermarked. A few barely noticeable nicks or marks may be present.

MS-60 (Uncirculated)
A strictly Uncirculated coin with no trace of wear, but with blemishes more obvious than for MS-65. May lack full mint luster, and surface may be dull or spotted. Check points for signs of abrasion: hair above ear; curl to right of ribbon; bow knot.

ABOUT UNCIRCULATED *(Small trace of wear visible on highest points.)*

AU-55 (Choice About Uncirculated)
OBVERSE: Only a trace of wear shows on the hair above the ear.
REVERSE: A trace of wear shows on the bow knot. Three-quarters of the mint luster is still present.

AU-50 (About Uncirculated)
OBVERSE: Traces of wear show on the hair above ear and curl to right of ribbon.
REVERSE: Traces of wear show on the leaves and bow knot. Half of the mint luster is still present.

EXTREMELY FINE *(Very light wear on only the highest points.)*

EF-45 (Choice Extremely Fine)
OBVERSE: Wear shows on hair above ear, curl to right of ribbon, and on the ribbon end. All of the diamond design and letters in LIBERTY are very plain.
REVERSE: High points of the leaves and bow are lightly worn. Traces of mint luster still show.

EF-40 (Extremely Fine)
OBVERSE: Feathers well defined and LIBERTY is bold. Wear shows on hair above ear, curl to right of ribbon, and on the ribbon end. Most of the diamond design shows plainly.
REVERSE: High points of the leaves and bow are worn.

VERY FINE *(Light to moderate even wear. All major features are sharp.)*

VF-30 (Choice Very Fine)
OBVERSE: Small flat spots of wear on tips of feathers, ribbons, and hair ends. Hair still shows half of details. LIBERTY slightly worn but all letters are sharp.
REVERSE: Leaves and bow worn but fully detailed.

VF-20 (Very Fine)
OBVERSE: Headdress shows considerable flatness. Nearly half of the details still show in hair and on ribbon. Head slightly worn but bold. LIBERTY is worn but all letters are complete.
REVERSE: Leaves and bow are almost fully detailed.

FINE *(Moderate to heavy even wear. Entire design clear and bold.)*

F-12 (Fine)
OBVERSE: One-quarter of details show in the hair. Ribbon is worn smooth. LIBERTY shows clearly with no letters missing.
REVERSE: Some details visible in the wreath and bow. Tops of leaves are worn smooth.

REVERSE
(without shield, 1859)
OBVERSE
REVERSE
(with shield, 1860–1909)

VERY GOOD *(Well worn. Design clear but flat and lacking details.)*

VG-8 (Very Good)
OBVERSE: Outline of feather ends shows but some are smooth. Legend and date are visible. At least three letters in LIBERTY show clearly, but any combination of two full letters and parts of two others are sufficient.
REVERSE: Slight detail in wreath shows, but the top is worn smooth. Very little outline showing in the bow.

GOOD *(Heavily worn. Design and legend visible but faint in spots.)*

G-4 (Good)
OBVERSE: Entire design well worn with very little detail remaining. Legend and date are weak but visible.
REVERSE: Wreath is worn flat but completely outlined. Bow merges with wreath.

ABOUT GOOD *(Outlined design. Parts of date and legend worn smooth.)*

AG-3 (About Good)
OBVERSE: Head is outlined with nearly all details worn away. Legend and date readable but very weak and merging into rim.
REVERSE: Entire design partially worn away. Bow is merged with the wreath.

SMALL CENTS—LINCOLN 1909 TO DATE

MINT STATE *(Absolutely no trace of wear.)*

MS-70 (Perfect Uncirculated)
A flawless coin exactly as it was minted, with no trace of wear or injury. Must have full mint luster and brilliance of light toning. Any unusual die or planchet traits must be described.

MS-65 (Choice Uncirculated)
No trace of wear; nearly as perfect as MS-70 except for some small blemish. Has full mint luster but may be unevenly toned or lightly fingermarked. A few barely noticeable nicks or marks may be present.

MS-60 (Uncirculated)
A strictly Uncirculated coin with no trace of wear, but with blemishes more obvious than for MS-65. May lack full mint luster, and surface may be dull or spotted. Check points for signs of abrasion: high points of cheek and jaw; tips of wheat stalks.

ABOUT UNCIRCULATED *(Small trace of wear visible on highest points.)*

AU-55 (Choice About Uncirculated)
OBVERSE: Only a trace of wear shows on the highest point of the jaw.
REVERSE: A trace of wear on the top of wheat stalks. Almost all of the mint luster is still present.

AU-50 (About Uncirculated)
OBVERSE: Traces of wear show on the cheek and jaw.
REVERSE: Traces of wear show on the wheat stalks. Three-quarters of the mint luster is still present.

EXTREMELY FINE *(Very light wear on only the highest points.)*

EF-45 (Choice Extremely Fine)
OBVERSE: Slight wear shows on hair above ear, on the cheek, and at the jaw.

REVERSE
(wheatline, 1909–1958)

OBVERSE

REVERSE
(memorial, 1959–date)

REVERSE: High points of wheat stalks are lightly worn, but each line is clearly defined. Half of the mint luster still shows.

EF-40 (Extremely Fine)
OBVERSE: Wear shows on hair above ear, on the cheek, and on the jaw.
REVERSE: High points of wheat stalks are worn, but each line is clearly defined. Traces of mint luster still show.

VERY FINE *(Light to moderate even wear. All major features are sharp.)*

VF-30 (Choice Very Fine)
OBVERSE: There are small flat spots of wear on cheek and jaw. Hair still shows details. Ear and bow tie slightly worn but show clearly.
REVERSE: Lines in wheat stalks are lightly worn but fully detailed.

VF-20 (Very Fine)
OBVERSE: Head shows considerable flatness. Nearly all the details still show in hair and on the face. Ear and bow tie worn but bold.
REVERSE: Lines in wheat stalks are worn but plain and without weak spots.

FINE *(Moderate to heavy even wear. Entire design clear and bold.)*

F-12 (Fine)
OBVERSE: Some details show in the hair. Cheek and jaw are worn nearly smooth. LIBERTY shows clearly with no letters missing. The ear and bow tie are visible.
REVERSE: Most details are visible in the stalks. Top wheat lines are worn but separated.

VERY GOOD *(Well worn. Design clear but flat and lacking details.)*

VG-8 (Very Good)
OBVERSE: Outline of hair shows but most details are smooth.

Cheek and jaw are smooth. More than half of bow tie is visible. Legend and date are clear.
REVERSE: Wheat shows some details and about half of the lines at the top.

GOOD *(Heavily worn. Design and legend visible but faint in spots.)*

G-4 (Good)
OBVERSE: Entire design well worn with very little detail remaining. Legend and date are weak but visible.
REVERSE: Wheat is worn nearly flat but is completely outlined. Some grains are visible.

ABOUT GOOD *(Outlined design. Parts of date and legend worn smooth.)*

AG-3 (About Good)
OBVERSE: Head is outlined with nearly all details worn away. Legend and date readable but very weak and merging into rim.
REVERSE: Entire design partially worn away. Parts of wheat and motto merged with the wreath.

Note: The Memorial cents from 1959 to date can be graded by using the obverse descriptions.

The following characteristic traits will assist in grading but must not be confused with actual wear on the coins:

Matte proof cents of 1909 through 1916 are often spotted or stained.

Branch Mint cents of the 1920s are usually not as sharply struck as later dates.

Many of the early dates of Lincoln cents are weakly struck either on the obverse or the reverse, especially the following dates: 1911D, 1914D, 1917D, 1918D, 1921, 1922D, 1923, 1924, 1927D, 1927S and 1929D.

1922 "plain" is weakly struck at the head, has a small I and joined RT in Liberty. Sometimes the wheat heads are weak on the reverse.

1924D usually has a weak mint mark.

1931S is sometimes unevenly struck.

1936 proof cents: early strikes are less brilliant than those made later that year.

1955 doubled die: hair details are less sharp than most cents of the period.

NICKEL FIVE CENTS— LIBERTY HEAD 1883–1912

MINT STATE *(Absolutely no trace of wear.)*

MS-70 (Perfect Uncirculated)
A flawless coin exactly as it was minted, with no trace of wear or injury. Must have full mint luster but this may range from brilliant to frosty. Any unusual die or striking traits must be described.

MS-65 (Choice Uncirculated)
No trace of wear; nearly as perfect as MS-70 except for some small weakness or blemish. Has full mint luster but may be unevenly toned, frosty, or lightly fingermarked. A few barely noticeable nicks or marks may be present.

MS-60 (Uncirculated)
A strictly Uncirculated coin with no trace of wear, but with blemishes more obvious than for MS-65. May lack full mint luster, and surface may be dull or spotted. Check points for signs of abrasion: high points of hair left of ear and at forehead, corn ears at bottom of wreath.

ABOUT UNCIRCULATED *(Small trace of wear visible on highest points.)*

AU-55 (Choice About Uncirculated)
OBVERSE: Only a trace of wear shows on the highest points of hair left of ear.
REVERSE: A trace of wear shows on corn ears. Half of the mint luster is still present.

AU-50 (About Uncirculated)
OBVERSE: Traces of wear show on hair left of ear and at forehead.
REVERSE: Traces of wear show on the wreath and on corn ears. Part of the mint luster is still present.

EXTREMELY FINE *(Very light wear on only the highest points.)*

EF-45 (Choice Extremely Fine)
OBVERSE: Slight wear shows on high points of hair from forehead to the ear.
REVERSE: High points of wreath are lightly worn. Lines in corn are clearly defined. Traces of mint luster may still show.

EF-40 (Extremely Fine)
OBVERSE: Wear shows on hair from forehead to ear, on the cheek, and on curls.
REVERSE: High points of wreath are worn, but each line is clearly defined. Corn shows some wear.

VERY FINE *(Light to moderate even wear. All major features are sharp.)*

VF-20 (Choice Very Fine)
OBVERSE: Three-quarters of hair details show. The coronet has full bold lettering.
REVERSE: Leaves are worn but most of the ribs are visible. Some of the lines in the corn are clear unless weakly struck.

VF-20 (Very Fine)
OBVERSE: Over half the details still show in hair and curls. Head worn but bold. Every letter on coronet is plainly visible.
REVERSE: Leaves are worn but some of the ribs are visible. Most details in the wreath are clear unless weakly struck.

FINE *(Moderate to heavy even wear. Entire design clear and bold.)*

F-12 (Fine)
OBVERSE: Some details show in curls and hair at top of head. All letters of LIBERTY are visible.
REVERSE: Some details visible in wreath. Letters in the motto are worn but clear.

VERY GOOD *(Well worn. Design clear but flat and lacking details.)*

VG-8 (Very Good)
OBVERSE: Bottom edge of coronet, and most hair details,

OBVERSE

"NO CENTS" REVERSE

REVERSE

are worn smooth. At least three letters in LIBERTY are clear. Rim is complete.
REVERSE: Wreath shows only bold outline. Some letters in the motto are very weak. Rim is complete.

GOOD *(Heavily worn. Design and legend visible but faint in spots.)*

G-4 (Good)
OBVERSE: Entire design well worn with very little detail remaining. Stars and date are weak but visible.
REVERSE: Wreath is worn flat and not completely outlined. Legend and motto are worn nearly smooth.

ABOUT GOOD *(Outlined design. Parts of date and legend worn smooth.)*

AG-3 (About Good)
OBVERSE: Head is outlined with nearly all details worn away. Date readable but very weak and merging into rim.
REVERSE: Entire design partially worn away.
Note: The 1912D, 1912S and 1883 "no cents" variety are often weakly struck.

NICKEL FIVE CENTS—
BUFFALO 1913–1938

MINT STATE *(Absolutely no trace of wear.)*

MS-70 (Perfect Uncirculated)
A flawless coin exactly as it was minted, with no trace of wear or injury. Must have full mint luster. Any unusual die or striking traits must be described.

MS-65 (Choice Uncirculated)
No trace of wear; nearly as perfect as MS-70 except for some small weakness or blemish. Has full mint luster but may be unevenly toned or lightly fingermarked. A few barely noticeable nicks or marks may be present.

NICKEL FIVE CENTS— BUFFALO 1913–1938

MS-60 (Uncirculated)
A strictly Uncirculated coin with no trace of wear, but with blemishes more obvious than for MS-65. May lack full mint luster and surface may be dull or spotted. Check points for signs of abrasion: high points of Indian's cheek; upper front leg, hip, tip of tail. Shallow or weak spots in the relief are usually caused by improper striking and not wear.

ABOUT UNCIRCULATED (*Small trace of wear visible on highest points.*)

AU-55 (Choice About Uncirculated)
OBVERSE: Only a trace of wear shows on high point of cheek.
REVERSE: A trace of wear shows on the hip. Half of the mint luster is still present.

AU-50 (About Uncirculated)
OBVERSE: Traces of wear show on hair above and to left of forehead, and at the cheek bone.
REVERSE: Traces of wear show on tail, hip, and hair above and around the horn. Traces of mint luster still show.

EXTREMELY FINE (*Very light wear on only the highest points.*)

EF-45 (Choice Extremely Fine)
OBVERSE: Slight wear shows on the hair above the braid. There is a trace of wear on the temple and hair near cheek bone.
REVERSE: High points of hip and thigh are lightly worn. The horn and tip of tail are sharp and nearly complete.

EF-40 (Extremely Fine)
OBVERSE: Hair and face are lightly worn but well defined and bold. Slight wear shows on lines of hair braid.
REVERSE: Horn and end of tail are worn but all details are visible.

VERY FINE (*Light to moderate even wear. All major features are sharp.*)

VF-30 (Choice Very Fine)
OBVERSE: Hair shows nearly full details. Feathers and braid are worn but sharp.
REVERSE: Head, front leg and hip are worn. Tail shows plainly. Horn is worn but full.

VF-20 (Very Fine)
OBVERSE: Hair and cheek show considerable flatness, but all details are clear. Feathers still show partial detail.
REVERSE: Hair on head is worn. Tail and point of horn are visible.

FINE (*Moderate to considerable even wear. Entire design clear and bold.*)

F-12 (Fine)
OBVERSE: Three-quarters of details show in hair and braid. LIBERTY is plain but merging with rim.
REVERSE: Major details visible along the back. Horn and tail are smooth but three-quarters visible.

VERY GOOD (*Well worn. Design clear but flat and lacking details.*)

VG-8 (Very Good)
OBVERSE: Outline of hair is visible at temple and near cheek bone. LIBERTY merges with rim. Date is clear.
REVERSE: Some detail shows in head. Lettering is all clear. Horn is worn nearly flat but is partially visible.

GOOD (*Heavily worn. Design and legend visible but faint in spots.*)

G-4 (Good)
OBVERSE: Entire design well worn with very little detail remaining in central part. LIBERTY is weak and merged with rim.
REVERSE: Buffalo is nearly flat but is well outlined. Horn does not show. Legend is weak but readable. Rim worn to tops of letters.

OBVERSE

REVERSE

ABOUT GOOD *(Outlined design. Parts of date and legend worn smooth.)*

AG-3 (About Good)
OBVERSE: Design is outlined with nearly all details worn away. Date and motto partially readable but very weak and merging into rim.
REVERSE: Entire design partially worn away. Rim is merged with the letters.

Note: Buffalo nickels were often weakly struck, and lack details even on Uncirculated specimens. The following dates are usually unevenly struck with weak spots in the details:
1913S I and II, 1917D, 1917S, 1918D, 1918S, 1919S, 1920D, 1920S, 1921S, 1923S, 1924D, 1924S, 1925D, 1925S, 1926D, 1926S, 1927D, 1927S, 1928D, 1928S, 1929D, 1931S, 1934D and 1935D.
1913 through 1916 matte proof coins are sometimes spotted or stained.

NICKEL FIVE CENTS— JEFFERSON 1938 TO DATE

MINT STATE *(Absolutely no trace of wear.)*

MS-70 (Perfect Uncirculated)
A flawless coin exactly as it was minted, with no trace of wear or injury. Must have full mint luster and brilliance. Any unusual striking or planchet traits must be described.

MS-65 (Choice Uncirculated)
No trace of wear; nearly as perfect as MS-70 except for some small weakness or blemish. Has full mint luster but may be unevenly toned or lightly fingermarked. A few barely noticeable nicks or marks may be present.

MS-60 (Uncirculated)
A strictly Uncirculated coin with no trace of wear, but with weaknesses and blemishes more obvious than for MS-65. May lack full mint luster, and surface may be dull or spotted. Check points for signs of abrasion: cheek bone and high points of hair, triangular roof above pillars. Shallow or weak

spots in the relief, particularly in the steps below pillars, are usually caused by improper striking and not wear.

ABOUT UNCIRCULATED *(Small trace of wear visible on highest points.)*

AU-55 (Choice About Uncirculated)
OBVERSE: Only a trace of wear shows on cheek bone.
REVERSE: A trace of wear shows on the beam above pillars. Three-quarters of the mint luster is still present.

AU-50 (About Uncirculated)
OBVERSE: Traces of wear show on cheek bone and high points of hair.
REVERSE: Traces of wear show on the beam and triangular roof above pillars. Half of the mint luster is still present.

EXTREMELY FINE *(Very light wear on only the highest points.)*

EF-45 (Choice Extremely Fine)
OBVERSE: Slight wear shows on cheek bone and central portion of hair. There is a trace of wear at bottom of the bust.
REVERSE: High points of the triangular roof and beam are lightly worn. Traces of mint luster still show.

EF-40 (Extremely Fine)
OBVERSE: Hair is lightly worn but well defined and bold. Slight wear shows on cheek bone and bottom of the bust. High points of hair are worn but show all details.
REVERSE: Triangular roof and beam are worn but all details are visible.

VERY FINE *(Light to moderate even wear. All major features are sharp.)*

VF-30 (Choice Very Fine)
OBVERSE: Hair worn but shows nearly full details. Cheek line and bottom of bust are worn but sharp.
REVERSE: Triangular roof and beam worn nearly flat. Most of the pillar lines show plainly.

OBVERSE　　　　"WARTIME"　　　　REVERSE
REVERSE 1942–1945

VF-20 (Very Fine)
OBVERSE: Cheek line shows considerable flatness. Over half the hair lines are clear. Parts of the details still show in collar.
REVERSE: Pillars are worn but clearly defined. Triangular roof is partially visible.

FINE *(Moderate to heavy even wear. Entire design clear and bold.)*

F-12 (Fine)
OBVERSE: Some details show in hair around face. Cheek line and collar plain but very weak.
REVERSE: Some details visible in pillars. Triangular roof is very smooth and indistinct.

VERY GOOD *(Well worn. Design clear but flat and lacking details.)*

VG-8 (Very Good)
OBVERSE: Cheek line is visible but parts are worn smooth. Collar is weak but visible. Only a few hair lines show separations.
REVERSE: Slight details show throughout building. The arch is worn away. Pillars are weak but visible.

GOOD *(Heavily worn. Design and legend visible but faint in spots.)*

G-4 (Good)
OBVERSE: Entire design well worn with very little detail remaining. Motto is weak and merged with rim.
REVERSE: Building is nearly flat but is well outlined. Pillars are worn flat. Rim worn to tops of letters.

ABOUT GOOD *(Outlined design. Parts of date and legend worn smooth.)*

AG-3 (About Good)
OBVERSE: Design is outlined with nearly all details worn away. Date and legend readable but very weak and merging into rim.
REVERSE: Entire design partially worn away. Rim is merged with the letters.

Note: Jefferson nickels are frequently seen weakly struck, and with the horizontal step lines joined even on Uncirculated specimens. Many of the 1950 and 1955 nickels are unevenly struck with weak spots in the details.

DIMES—BARBER 1892–1916

MINT STATE *(Absolutely no trace of wear.)*

MS-70 (Perfect Uncirculated)
A flawless coin exactly as it was minted, with no trace of wear or injury. Must have full mint luster and brilliance or light toning. Any unusual die or striking traits must be described.

MS-65 (Choice Uncirculated)
No trace of wear; nearly as perfect as MS-70 except for some small blemish. Has full mint luster but may be unevenly toned or lightly fingermarked. A few barely noticeable nicks or marks may be present.

MS-60 (Uncirculated)
A strictly Uncirculated coin with no trace of wear, but with blemishes more obvious than for MS-65. May lack full mint luster, and surface may be dull, spotted, or heavily toned. Check points for signs of abrasion: high points of cheek and hair below LIBERTY; ribbon bow and tips of leaves.

ABOUT UNCIRCULATED *(Small trace of wear visible on highest points.)*

AU-55 (Choice About Uncirculated)
OBVERSE: Only a trace of wear shows on highest points of hair below LIBERTY.
REVERSE: A trace of wear shows on ribbon bow, wheat grains, and leaf near O. Three-quarters of the mint luster is still present.

OBVERSE

REVERSE

AU-50 (About Uncirculated)
OBVERSE: Traces of wear show on cheek, top of forehead, and hair below LIBERTY.
REVERSE: Traces of wear show on ribbon bow, wheat grains, and tips of leaves. Half of the mint luster is still present.

EXTREMELY FINE *(Very light wear on only the highest points.)*

EF-45 (Choice Extremely Fine)
OBVERSE: Slight wear shows on high points of upper leaves, cheek, and hair above forehead. LIBERTY is sharp and band edges are bold.
REVERSE: High points of the wreath and bow lightly worn. Lines in leaves are clearly defined. Part of the mint luster is still present.

EF-40 (Extremely Fine)
OBVERSE: Light wear shows on leaves, cheek, cap, and hair above forehead. LIBERTY is sharp and band edges are clear.
REVERSE: High points of wreath and bow are worn, but all details are clearly defined. Traces of mint luster may still show.

VERY FINE *(Light to moderate even wear. All major features are sharp.)*

VF-30 (Choice Very Fine)
OBVERSE: Wear spots show on leaves, cap, hair, and cheek. Bottom row of leaves is weak but has some visible details. LIBERTY and band are complete.
REVERSE: Wear shows on the two bottom leaves but most details are visible. Nearly all the details in the ribbon bow and corn kernels are clear.

VF-20 (Very Fine)
OBVERSE: Over half the details still show in leaves. Hair worn but bold. Every letter in LIBERTY is visible.
REVERSE: The ribbon is worn, but some details are visible. Half the details in leaves are clear. Bottom leaves and upper stalks show wear spots.

FINE *(Moderate to heavy even wear. Entire design clear and bold.)*

F-12 (Fine)
OBVERSE: Some details show in hair, cap, and facial features. All letters in LIBERTY are weak but visible. Upper row of leaves is outlined, but bottom row is worn smooth.
REVERSE: Some details in the lower leaf clusters are plainly visible. Bow is outlined but flat. Letters in legend are worn but clear.

VERY GOOD *(Well worn. Design clear but flat and lacking details.)*

VG-8 (Very Good)
OBVERSE: Entire head weak, and most of the details in the face are worn smooth. Three letters in LIBERTY are clear. Rim is complete.
REVERSE: Wreath shows only a small amount of detail. Corn and grain are flat. Some of the bow is very weak.

GOOD *(Heavily worn. Design and legend visible but faint in spots.)*

G-4 (Good)
OBVERSE: Entire design well worn with very little detail remaining. Legend is weak but visible. LIBERTY is worn away.
REVERSE: Wreath is worn flat but is completely outlined. Corn and grains are worn nearly smooth.

ABOUT GOOD *(Outlined design. Parts of date and legend worn smooth.)*

AG-3 (About Good)
OBVERSE: Head is outlined with nearly all details worn away. Date readable but partially worn away. Legend merging into rim.
REVERSE: Entire wreath partially worn away and merging into rim.

DIMES—MERCURY 1916–1945

MINT STATE *(Absolutely no trace of wear.)*

MS-70 (Perfect Uncirculated)
A flawless coin exactly as it was minted, with no trace of wear or injury. Must have full mint luster and brilliance or light toning. Any unusual die or striking traits must be described.

MS-65 (Choice Uncirculated)
No trace of wear; nearly as perfect as MS-70 except for some small blemish. Has full mint luster but may be unevenly toned or lightly fingermarked. A few barely noticeable nicks or marks may be present.

MS-60 (Uncirculated)
A strictly Uncirculated coin with no trace of wear, but with blemishes more obvious than for MS-65. May lack full mint

OBVERSE

REVERSE

luster, and surface may be dull, spotted, or heavily toned. Check points for signs of abrasion: high points of hair and in front of ear, diagonal bands on fasces.

ABOUT UNCIRCULATED *(Small trace of wear visible on highest points.)*

AU-55 (Choice About Uncirculated)
OBVERSE: Only a trace of wear shows on highest points of hair above forehead and in front of ear.
REVERSE: A trace of wear shows on the horizontal and diagonal fasces bands. Three-quarters of the mint luster is still present.

AU-50 (About Uncirculated)
OBVERSE: Traces of wear show on hair along face, above forehead, and in front of ear.
REVERSE: Traces of wear show on the fasces bands but edges are sharply defined. Half of the mint luster is still present.

EXTREMELY FINE *(Very light wear on only the highest points.)*

EF-45 (Choice Extremely Fine)
OBVERSE: Slight wear shows on high points of feathers and at hair line. Hair along face is sharp and detailed.
REVERSE: High points of the diagonal fasces bands are lightly worn. Horizontal lines are clearly defined but not fully separated. Part of the mint luster is still present.

EF-40 (Extremely Fine)
OBVERSE: Wear shows on high points of feathers, hair, and at neck line.
REVERSE: High points of fasces bands are worn, but all details are clearly defined and partially separated. Traces of mint luster may still show.

VERY FINE *(Light to moderate even wear. All major features are sharp.)*

VF-30 (Choice Very Fine)
OBVERSE: Wear spots on hair along face, cheek, and neck line. Feathers are weak but have nearly full details.

REVERSE: Wear shows on the two diagonal bands but most details are visible. All vertical lines are sharp. All details in the branch are clear.

VF-20 (Very Fine)
OBVERSE: Three-quarters of the details still show in feathers. Hair worn but bold. Some details in hair braid are visible.
REVERSE: Wear shows on the two diagonal bands but most details are visible. All vertical lines are sharp. All details in the branch are clear.

FINE *(Moderate to considerable even wear. Entire design clear and bold.)*

F-12 (Fine)
OBVERSE: Some details show in hair. All feathers are weak but partially visible. Hair braid is nearly worn away.
REVERSE: Vertical lines are all visible but lack sharpness. Diagonal bands show on fasces but one is worn smooth at midpoint.

VERY GOOD *(Well worn. Design clear but flat and lacking details.)*

VG-8 (Very Good)
OBVERSE: Entire head is weak, and most details in the wing are worn smooth. All letters and date are clear. Rim is complete.
REVERSE: About half the vertical lines in the fasces are visible. Rim is complete.

GOOD *(Heavily worn. Design and legend visible but faint in spots.)*

G-4 (Good)
OBVERSE: Entire design well worn with very little detail remaining. Legend and date are weak but visible. Rim is visible.
REVERSE: Fasces is worn nearly flat but is completely outlined. Sticks and bands are worn smooth.

ABOUT GOOD *(Outlined design. Parts of date and legend worn smooth.)*

AG-3 (About Good)
OBVERSE: Head is outlined with nearly all details worn away. Date readable but worn. Legend merging into rim.
REVERSE: Entire design partially worn away. Rim worn half way into the legend.

Note: Coins of this design are sometimes weakly struck in spots, particularly in the lines and horizontal bands of the fasces.

The following dates are usually found poorly struck and lacking full details regardless of condition: 1916D, 1918S, 1921, 1921D, 1925D, 1925S, 1926S, 1927D and 1927S.

1920 and 1920D usually show the zero joined to the rim.

1921 usually has a weakly struck date, especially the last two digits.

1923 often has the bottom of the three weakly struck and joined to the rim.

1945 is rarely seen with full cross bands on the fasces.

DIMES—ROOSEVELT
1946 TO DATE

MINT STATE *(Absolutely no trace of wear.)*

MS-70 (Perfect Uncirculated)
A flawless coin exactly as it was minted, with no trace of wear or injury. Must have full mint luster and brilliance or light toning. Any unusual striking traits must be described.

MS-65 (Choice Uncirculated)
No trace of wear; nearly as perfect as MS-70 except for some small blemish. Has full mint luster but may be unevenly toned or lightly fingermarked. A few barely noticeable nicks or marks may be present.

MS-60 (Uncirculated)
A strictly Uncirculated coin with no trace of wear, but with blemishes more obvious than for MS-65. Has full mint luster, but surface may be dull, spotted, or toned. Check points for

OBVERSE

REVERSE

signs of abrasion: high points of cheek and hair above ear, tops of leaves and details in flame.

ABOUT UNCIRCULATED *(Small trace of wear visible on highest points.)*

AU-55 (Choice About Uncirculated)
OBVERSE: Only a trace of wear shows on highest points of hair above ear.
REVERSE: A trace of wear shows on highest spots of the flame. Three-quarters of the mint luster is still present.

AU-50 (About Uncirculated)
OBVERSE: Traces of wear show on hair above ear.
REVERSE: Traces of wear show on flame but details are sharply defined. Half of the mint luster is still present.

EXTREMELY FINE *(Very light wear on only the highest points.)*

EF-45 (Choice Extremely Fine)
OBVERSE: Slight wear shows on high points of hair above ear. Ear is sharp and detailed.
REVERSE: High points of flame are lightly worn. Torch lines are clearly defined and fully separated. Part of the mint luster is still present.

EF-40 (Extremely Fine)
OBVERSE: Wear shows on high points of hair and at cheek line. Ear shows slight wear on the upper tip.
REVERSE: High points of flame, torch and leaves are worn, but all details are clearly defined and partially separated. Traces of mint luster may still show.

VERY FINE *(Light to moderate even wear. All major features are sharp.)*

VF-30 (Choice Very Fine)
OBVERSE: Wear spots show on hair, ear, cheek, and chin. Hair lines are weak but have nearly full visible details.
REVERSE: Wear shows on flame but some details are visible. All vertical lines are plain. Most details in the torch and leaves are clear.

VF-20 (Very Fine)
OBVERSE: Three-quarters of the details still show in hair. Face worn but bold. Some details in the ear are visible.
REVERSE: Wear shows on the flame but a few lines are visible. All torch lines are worn but bold. Most details in leaves are clear.

FINE *(Moderate to heavy even wear. Entire design clear and bold.)*

F-12 (Fine)
OBVERSE: Half the details show in hair. All of the face is

weak but boldly visible. Half of inner edge of ear is worn away.
REVERSE: Vertical lines are all visible, but horizontal bands are worn smooth. Leaves show some detail. Flame is nearly smooth.

VERY GOOD *(Well worn. Design clear but flat and lacking details.)*

VG-8 (Very Good)
OBVERSE: Entire head is weak, and most of the details in hair and ear are worn smooth. All letters and date are clear. Rim is complete.
REVERSE: About half the outer vertical lines in torch are visible. Flame is only outlined. Leaves show very little detail. Rim is complete.

Good *(Heavily worn. Design and legend visible but faint in spots.)*

G-4 (Good)
OBVERSE: Entire design well worn with very little detail remaining. Ear is completely outlined. Legend and date are weak but visible. Rim is visible.
REVERSE: Torch is worn nearly flat but is completely outlined. Leaves are worn smooth. Legend is all visible.

ABOUT GOOD *(Outlined design. Parts of date and legend worn smooth.)*

AG-3 (About Good)
OBVERSE: Head is outlined with nearly all details worn away. Date readable but worn. Legend merging into rim.
REVERSE: Entire design partially worn away. Rim merges into the legend.

QUARTERS—BARBER
1892–1916

MINT STATE *(Absolutely no trace of wear.)*

MS-70 (Perfect Uncirculated)
A flawless coin exactly as it was minted, with no trace of

wear or injury. Must have full mint luster and brilliance or light toning. Any unusual die or striking traits must be described.

MS-65 (Choice Uncirculated)
No trace of wear; nearly as perfect as MS-70 except for some small blemishes. Has full mint luster but may be unevenly toned or lightly fingermarked. A few barely noticeable nicks or marks may be present.

MS-60 (Uncirculated)
A strictly Uncirculated coin with no trace of wear, but with blemishes more obvious than for MS-65. May lack full mint luster, and surface may be dull, spotted, or heavily toned. Check points for signs of abrasion: high points of cheek and hair below LIBERTY, eagle's head and tips of tail and wings.

ABOUT UNCIRCULATED *(Small trace of wear visible on highest points.)*

AU-55 (Choice About Uncirculated)
OBVERSE: Only a trace of wear shows on highest points of hair below BER in LIBERTY.
REVERSE: A trace of wear shows on head, tip of tail, and tips of wings. Three-quarters of the mint luster is still present.

AU-50 (About Uncirculated)
OBVERSE: Traces of wear show on cheek, tips of leaves, and hair below LIBERTY.
REVERSE: Traces of wear show on head, neck, tail, and tips of wings. Half of the mint luster is still present.

EXTREMELY FINE *(Very light wear on only the highest points.)*

EF-45 (Choice Extremely Fine)
OBVERSE: Slight wear shows on high points of upper leaves, cheek, and hair above forehead. LIBERTY is sharp and band edges are bold.
REVERSE: High points of head, neck, wings, and talons lightly worn. Lines in center tail feathers are clearly defined. Part of the mint luster is still present.

OBVERSE

REVERSE

EF-40 (Extremely Fine)
OBVERSE: Light wear shows on leaves, cheek, cap, and hair above forehead. LIBERTY is sharp and band edges are clear.
REVERSE: High points of head, neck, wings, and tail are lightly worn, but all details are clearly defined. Leaves show trace of wear at edges. Traces of mint luster may still show.

VERY FINE *(Light to moderate even wear. All major features are sharp.)*

VF-30 (Choice Very Fine)
OBVERSE: Wear spots show on leaves, cap, hair and cheek. Bottom row of leaves is weak but has some visible details. LIBERTY and band are complete. Folds in cap are distinct.
REVERSE: Wear shows on shield but all details are visible. Most of the details in neck and tail are clear. Motto is complete.

VF-20 (Very Fine)
OBVERSE: Over half the details still show in leaves. Hair and ribbon worn but bold. Every letter in LIBERTY is visible.
REVERSE: The shield is worn, but most details are visible. Half the details in feathers are clear. Wings and legs show wear spots. Motto is clear.

FINE *(Moderate to heavy even wear. Entire design clear and bold.)*

F-12 (Fine)
OBVERSE: Some details show in hair, cap, and facial features. All letters in LIBERTY are weak but visible. Upper row of leaves is outlined, but bottom row is worn nearly smooth. Rim is full and bold.
REVERSE: Half of the feathers are plainly visible. Wear spots show in center of neck, motto, and arrows. Horizontal shield lines are merged; vertical lines are separated. Letters in legend are worn but clear.

VERY GOOD *(Well worn. Design clear but flat and lacking details.)*

VG-8 (Very Good)
OBVERSE: Entire head weak, and most details in face are worn smooth. Three letters in LIBERTY are clear. Rim is complete.
REVERSE: Eagle shows only a small amount of detail. Arrows and leaves are flat. Most of the shield is very weak. Part of the eye is visible.

GOOD *(Heavily worn. Design and legend visible but faint in spots.)*

G-4 (Good)
OBVERSE: Entire design well worn with very little detail remaining. Legend is weak but visible. LIBERTY is worn away.
REVERSE: Eagle worn flat but is completely outlined. Ribbon worn nearly smooth. Legend weak but visible. Rim worn to tops of letters.

ABOUT GOOD (Outlined design. Parts of date and legend worn smooth.)

AG-3 (About Good)
OBVERSE: Head is outlined with nearly all details worn away. Date readable but partially worn away. Legend merging into rim.
REVERSE: Entire design partially worn away and legend merges with rim.

QUARTERS—LIBERTY STANDING, VARIETY I 1916–1917 LIBERTY STANDING, VARIETY II 1917–1924

MINT STATE (Absolutely no trace of wear.)

MS-70 (Perfect Uncirculated)
A flawless coin exactly as it was minted, with no trace of wear or injury. Must have full mint luster and brilliance or light toning. Head details* (see p. 148) are an important part of this grade and must be specifically designated. Any other unusual die or striking traits must be described.

MS-65 (Choice Uncirculated)
No trace of wear; nearly as perfect as MS-70 except for some small blemish. Has full mint luster but may be unevenly toned or lightly fingermarked, may be weakly struck in one small spot. A few barely noticeable nicks or marks may be present. Head details may be incomplete.

| OBVERSE | TYPE I REVERSE | TYPE II REVERSE |

MS-60 (Uncirculated)
A strictly Uncirculated coin with no trace of wear, but with blemishes more obvious than for MS-65. May lack full mint luster, and surface may be dull, spotted or heavily toned. One or two small spots may be weakly struck. Head details* (see p. 148) may be incomplete. Check points for signs of abrasion: mail covering breast, knee, high points of gown and shield; high points of eagle's breast and wings. Coins of this design frequently show weakly struck spots and usually lack full head details.

ABOUT UNCIRCULATED *(Small trace of wear visible on highest points.)*

AU-55 (Choice About Uncirculated)
OBVERSE: Only a trace of wear shows on highest points of mail covering breast, inner shield and right knee.
REVERSE: A trace of wear shows on breast and edges of wings. Three-quarters of the mint luster is still present.

AU-50 (About Uncirculated)
OBVERSE: Traces of wear show on breast, knee, and high points of inner shield.
REVERSE: Traces of wear show on edges of wings and at center of breast. All of the tail feathers are visible. Half of the mint luster is still present.

EXTREMELY FINE *(Very light wear on only the highest points.)*

EF-45 (Choice Extremely Fine)
OBVERSE: Light wear spots show on upper right leg and knee. Nearly all of the gown lines are clearly visible. Shield details are bold. Breast is lightly worn and may show small flat spot.
REVERSE: Small flat spots show on high points of breast and on front wing edges. Tail feathers have nearly full details. Part of the mint luster is still present.

EF-40 (Extremely Fine)
OBVERSE: Wear shows on breast and right leg above and below knee. Most of the gown lines are visible. Shield details are bold. Breast is well rounded but has small flat spot.
REVERSE: High points of eagle are lightly worn. Central part of edge on right wing is well worn. Traces of mint luster may still show.

VERY FINE (Light to moderate even wear. All major features are sharp.)

VF-30 (Choice Very Fine)
OBVERSE: Wear spots show on breast, shield, and leg. Right leg is rounded but worn from above knee to ankle. Gown line crossing thigh is partially visible. Half of mail covering breast can be seen. Circle around inner shield is complete.
REVERSE: Breast and leg are worn but clearly separated, with some feathers visible between them. Feather ends and folds are visible in right wing.

VF-20 (Very Fine)
OBVERSE: Right leg is worn flat in central parts. Wear spots show on head, breast, shield, and foot. Beads on outer shield are visible, but those next to body are weak. Inner circle of shield is complete.
REVERSE: Entire eagle is lightly worn but most major details are visible. Breast and edge of right wing are worn flat. Top tail feathers are complete.

FINE (Moderate to considerable even wear. Entire design clear and bold.)

F-12 (Fine)
OBVERSE: Gown details worn but show clearly across body. Left leg is lightly worn. Right leg nearly flat and toe is worn. Breast worn but some mail is visible. Date may show some weakness at top. Rim is full. Outer edge of shield is complete.
REVERSE: Breast is worn almost smooth. Half of the wing feathers are visible, although well worn in spots. The rim is full.

VERY GOOD (Well worn. Design clear but flat and lacking details.)

VG-8 (Very Good)
OBVERSE: Entire design is weak, and most details in gown are worn smooth. All letters and date are clear but tops of numerals may be flat. Rim is complete. Draper across breast is partially outlined.
REVERSE: About one-third of the feathers are visible and large feathers at ends of wings are well separated. Eye is visible. Rim is full and all letters are clear.

GOOD *(Heavily worn. Design and legend visible but faint in spots.)*
G-4 (Good)
OBVERSE: Entire design well worn with very little detail remaining. Legend and date are weak but visible. Top of date may be worn flat. Rim is complete.
REVERSE: Eagle worn nearly flat but is completely outlined. Lettering and stars worn but clearly visible. Rim worn to tops of legend.

ABOUT GOOD *(Outlined design. Parts of date and legend worn smooth.)*
AG-3 (About Good)
OBVERSE: Figure is outlined with nearly all details worn away. Legend visible but half worn away and may merge with rim. Date weak and readable.
REVERSE: Entire design partially worn away. Some letters merging into rim.

Note: Coins of this design are sometimes weakly struck in spots, particularly at Liberty's head, breast, knee, and shield and on the eagle's breast and wings.
   *Specimens with "full head" must show the following details: Three well-defined leaves in hair; complete hairline along brow and across face; small indentation at ear. Coins of any grade other than MS-70 can be assumed to lack full head details unless the amount of visible features is specifically designated.

QUARTERS—WASHINGTON 1932 TO DATE

MINT STATE *(Absolutely no trace of wear.)*
MS-70 (Perfect Uncirculated)
A flawless coin exactly as it was minted, with no trace of wear or injury. Must have full mint luster and brilliance or light toning. Any unusual striking traits must be described.

OBVERSE   REVERSE

MS-65 (Choice of Uncirculated)
No trace of wear; nearly as perfect as MS-70 except for some small blemishes. Has full mint luster but may be unevenly toned or lightly fingermarked. A few barely noticeable nicks or marks may be present.

MS-60 (Uncirculated)
A strictly Uncirculated coin with no trace of wear, but with blemishes more obvious than for MS-65. May lack full mint luster, and surface may be dull, spotted, or heavily toned. Check points for signs of abrasion: high points of cheek and hair in front and back of ear, tops of legs and details in breast feathers.

ABOUT UNCIRCULATED *(Small trace of wear visible on highest points.)*

AU-55 (Choice About Uncirculated)
OBVERSE: Only a trace of wear shows on highest points of hair in front and in back of ear.
REVERSE: A trace of wear shows on highest spots of breast feathers. Nearly all of the mint luster is still present.

AU-50 (About Uncirculated)
OBVERSE: Traces of wear show on hair in front and in back of ear.
REVERSE: Traces of wear show on legs and breast feathers. Three-quarters of the mint luster is still present.

EXTREMELY FINE *(Light wear on most of the highest points.)*

EF-45 (Choice Extremely Fine)
OBVERSE: Slight wear shows on high points of hair around ear and along hairline up to crown. Hairlines are sharp and detailed.
REVERSE: High points of legs are lightly worn. Breast feathers are worn but clearly defined and fully separated. Half of the mint luster is still present.

EF-40 (Extremely Fine)
OBVERSE: Wear shows on high points of hair around and at hairline up to crown.

REVERSE: High points of breast, legs, and claws are lightly worn, but all details are clearly defined and partially separated. Part of the mint luster is still present.

VERY FINE *(Light to moderate even wear. All major features are sharp.)*

VF-30 (Choice Very Fine)
OBVERSE: Wear spots show on hair at forehead and ear, cheek, and jaw. Hairlines are weak but have nearly full visible details.
REVERSE: Wear shows on breast but a few feathers are visible. Legs are worn smooth. Most details in the wings are clear.

FINE *(Moderate to considerable even wear. Entire design clear and bold.)*

F-12 (Fine)
OBVERSE: Details show only at back of hair. Motto is weak but clearly visible. Part of cheek edge is worn away.
REVERSE: Feathers in breast and legs are worn smooth. Leaves show some detail. Parts of wings are nearly smooth.

VERY GOOD *(Well worn. Design clear but flat and lacking details.)*

VG-8 (Very Good)
OBVERSE: Entire head is weak, and most details in hair are worn smooth. All letters and date are clear. Rim is complete.
REVERSE: About half of the wing feathers are visible. Breast and legs only outlined. Leaves show very little detail. Rim is complete.

GOOD *(Heavily worn. Design and legend visible but faint in spots.)*

G-4 (Good)
OBVERSE: Hair is well worn with very little detail remaining. Half of motto is readable. LIBERTY and date are weak but visible. Rim merges with letters.
REVERSE: Eagle is worn nearly flat but is completely outlined. Leaves, breast, and legs are worn smooth. Legend is all visible but merges with rim.

ABOUT GOOD *(Outlined design. Parts of date and legend worn smooth.)*

AG-3 (About Good)
OBVERSE: Head is outlined with nearly all details worn away. Date readable but worn. Traces of motto are visible. Legend merging into rim.
REVERSE: Entire design partially worn away. Rim merges into legend.

Note: The obverse motto is always weak on coins of 1932 and early issues of 1934.

The reverse rim and lettering has a tendency to be very weak particularly on coins dated 1934D, 1935D and S, 1936D and S, 1937D and S (especially), 1938D and S, 1939D and 1940D.

HALF DOLLARS—BARBER
1892–1915

MINT STATE *(Absolutely no trace of wear.)*

MS-70 (Perfect Uncirculated)
A flawless coin exactly as it was minted, with no trace of wear or injury. Must have full mint luster and brilliance or light toning. Any unusual die or striking traits must be described.

MS-65 (Choice Uncirculated)
No trace of wear; nearly as perfect as MS-70 except for some small blemish. Has full mint luster but may be unevenly toned or lightly fingermarked. A few barely noticeable nicks or marks may be present.

MS-60 (Uncirculated)
A strictly Uncirculated coin with no trace of wear, but with blemishes more obvious than for MS-65. May lack full mint luster, and surface may be dull, spotted, or heavily toned. Check points for signs of abrasion: high points of cheek and hair below LIBERTY, eagle's head and tips of tail and wings.

OBVERSE

REVERSE

ABOUT UNCIRCULATED *(Small trace of wear visible on highest points.)*

AU-55 (Choice About Uncirculated)
OBVERSE: Only a trace of wear shows on highest points of hair below BER in LIBERTY.
REVERSE: A trace of wear shows on head, tip of tail, and tips of wings. Three-quarters of the mint luster is still present.

AU-50 (About Uncirculated)
OBVERSE: Traces of wear show on cheek, tips of leaves, and hair below LIBERTY.
REVERSE: Traces of wear show on head, neck, tail, and tips of wings. Half of the mint luster is still present.

EXTREMELY FINE *(Very light wear on only the highest points.)*

EF-45 (Choice Extremely Fine)
OBVERSE: Slight wear shows on high points of upper leaves, cheek, and hair above forehead. LIBERTY is sharp and band edges are bold.
REVERSE: High points of head, neck, wings and talons lightly worn. Lines in reverse center tail feathers are clearly defined. Part of the mint luster is still present.

EF-40 (Extremely Fine)
OBVERSE: Light wear shows on leaves, cheek, cap, and hair above forehead. LIBERTY is sharp and band edges are clear.
REVERSE: High points of head, neck, wings, and tail are lightly worn, but all details are clearly defined. Leaves show trace of wear at edges. Traces of mint luster may still show.

VERY FINE *(Light to moderate even wear. All major features are sharp.)*

VF-30 (Choice Very Fine)
OBVERSE: Wear spots show on leaves, cap, hair, and cheek. Bottom row of leaves is weak but has some visible details. LIBERTY and band are complete. Folds in cap are distinct.
REVERSE: Wear shows on shield but all details are visible. Most of the details in neck and tail are clear. Motto is complete.

VF-20 (Very Fine)
OBVERSE: Over half the details still show in leaves. Hair and ribbon worn but bold. Every letter in LIBERTY is visible. Bottom folds in cap are full.
REVERSE: Shield is worn, but all details are visible. Half the details in feathers are clear. Wings, tail and legs show small wear spots. Motto is clear.

FINE *(Moderate to considerable even wear. Entire design clear and bold.)*

F-12 (Fine)
OBVERSE: Some details show in hair, cap, and facial features. All letters in LIBERTY are weak but visible. Upper row of leaves is outlined, but bottom row is worn nearly smooth. Rim is full and bold.
REVERSE: Half the feathers are plainly visible. Wear spots show in center of neck, motto and arrows. Horizontal shield lines are merged; vertical lines are separated. Letters in legend are worn but clear.

VERY GOOD *(Well worn. Design clear but flat and lacking details.)*

VG-8 (Very Good)
OBVERSE: Entire head weak, and most details in face are heavily worn. Three letters in LIBERTY are clear. Rim is complete.
REVERSE: Eagle shows only a small amount of detail. Arrows and leaves are flat. Most of shield is very weak. Parts of eye and motto visible.

GOOD *(Heavily worn. Design and legend visible but faint in spots.)*

G-4 (Good)
OBVERSE: Entire design well worn with very little detail remaining. Legend and date weak but visible. LIBERTY is worn away.
REVERSE: Eagle worn flat but is completely outlined. Ribbon worn nearly smooth. Legend weak but visible. Rim worn to tops of letters.

ABOUT GOOD *(Outlined design. Parts of date and legend worn smooth.)*

AG-3 (About Good)
OBVERSE: Head is outlined with nearly all details worn away. Date readable but partially worn away. Legend merging into rim.
REVERSE: Entire design partially worn away and legend merges with rim.

HALF DOLLARS—LIBERTY WALKING 1916–1947

MINT STATE *(Absolutely no trace of wear.)*

MS-70 (Perfect Uncirculated)
A flawless coin exactly as it was minted, with no trace of wear or injury. Must have full mint luster and brilliance or light toning. Any unusual die or striking traits must be described.

MS-65 (Choice Uncirculated)
No trace of wear; nearly as perfect as MS-70 except for some small blemishes. Has full mint luster but may be unevenly toned or lightly fingermarked. May be weakly struck in one or two small spots. A few minute nicks or marks may be present.

MS-60 (Uncirculated)
A strictly Uncirculated coin with no trace of wear, but with blemishes more obvious than for MS-65. May lack full mint luster, and surface may be dull, spotted, or heavily toned. A few small spots may be weakly struck. Check points for signs of abrasion: hair above temple, right arm, left breast; high points of eagle's head, breast, legs, and wings. Coins of this design frequently show weakly struck spots and usually lack full head and hand details.

ABOUT UNCIRCULATED *(Small trace of wear visible on highest points.)*

OBVERSE

REVERSE

AU-55 (Choice About Uncirculated)
OBVERSE: Only a trace of wear shows on highest points of head, breast, and right arm.
REVERSE: A trace of wear shows on left leg between breast and left wing. Three-quarters of the mint luster is still present.

AU-50 (About Uncirculated)
OBVERSE: Traces of wear show on head, breast, arms, and left leg.
REVERSE: Traces of wear show on high points of wings and at center of head. All leg feathers are visible. Half of the mint luster is still present.

EXTREMELY FINE *(Very light wear on only the highest points.)*

EF-45 (Choice Extremely Fine)
OBVERSE: Light wear spots show on head, breast, arms, left leg, and foot. Nearly all gown lines are clearly visible. Sandal details are bold and complete. Knee is lightly worn but full and rounded.
REVERSE: Small flat spots show on high points of breast and legs. Wing feathers have nearly full details. Part of the mint luster is still present.

EF-40 (Extremely Fine)
OBVERSE: Wear shows on head, breast, arms, and left leg. Nearly all gown lines are visible. Sandal details are complete. Breast and knee are nearly flat.
REVERSE: High points of eagle are lightly worn. Half the breast and leg feathers are visible. Central part of feathers below neck is well worn. Traces of mint luster may still show.

VERY FINE *(Light to moderate even wear. All major features are sharp.)*

VF-30 (Choice Very Fine)
OBVERSE: Wear spots on head, breast, arms, and legs. Left leg is rounded but worn from above knee to ankle. Gown line crossing body is partially visible. Knee is flat. Outline of breast can be seen.
REVERSE: Breast and legs are moderately worn but clearly separated, with some feathers visible in right wing. Pupil in eye is visible.

VF-20 (Very Fine)
OBVERSE: Left leg is worn nearly flat. Wear spots show on head, breast, arms and foot. Lines on skirt are visible, but may be weak on coins before 1921. Breast is outlined.
REVERSE: Entire eagle is lightly worn but most major details are visible. Breast, central part of legs and top edge of right wing are worn flat.

FINE *(Moderate to considerable even wear. Entire design clear and bold.)*

F-12 (Fine)
OBVERSE: Gown stripes worn but show clearly, except for coins before 1921, where only half are visible. Right leg is lightly worn. Left leg nearly flat and sandal is worn but visible. Center of body worn but some of the gown is visible. Outer edge of rim is complete.
REVERSE: Breast is worn smooth. Half the wing feathers are visible, although well worn in spots. Top two layers of feathers are visible in left wing. Rim is full.

VERY GOOD *(Well worn. Design clear but flat and lacking details.)*

VG-8 (Very Good)
OBVERSE: Entire design is weak; most details in gown are worn smooth except for coins after 1921, where half the stripes must show. All letters and date are clear but top of motto may be weak. Rim is complete. Drapery across body is partially visible.
REVERSE: About one-third of the feathers are visible, and large feathers at ends of wings are well separated. Eye is visible. Rim is full and all letters are clear.

GOOD *(Heavily worn. Design and legend visible but faint in spots.)*

G-4 (Good)
OBVERSE: Entire design well worn with very little detail remaining. Legend and date weak but visible. Top of date may be worn flat. Rim is flat but nearly complete.
REVERSE: Eagle worn nearly flat but is completely outlined. Lettering and motto worn but clearly visible.

ABOUT GOOD *(Outlined design. Parts of date and legend worn smooth.)*

AG-3 (About Good)
OBVERSE: Figure is outlined with nearly all details worn away. Legend visible but half worn away. Date weak but readable. Rim merges with lettering.
REVERSE: Entire design partially worn away. Letters merge with rim.

Note: Coins of this design are sometimes weakly struck in spots, particularly at Liberty's head, hand holding branch and drapery lines of dress, and on the eagle's leg feathers.

HALF DOLLARS—FRANKLIN
1948–1963

MINT STATE *(Absolutely no trace of wear.)*

MS-70 (Perfect Uncirculated)
A flawless coin exactly as it was minted, with no trace of wear or injury. Must have full mint luster and brilliance or light toning. Any unusual striking traits must be described.

MS-65 (Choice Uncirculated)
No trace of wear; nearly as perfect as MS-70 except for some small blemishes. Has full mint luster but may be unevenly toned or lightly fingermarked. A few barely noticeable nicks or marks may be present.

MS-60 (Uncirculated)
A strictly Uncirculated coin with no trace of wear, but with blemishes more obvious than for MS-65. May lack full mint luster, and surface may be dull, spotted, or heavily toned. Check points for signs of abrasion: high points of cheek, shoulder, and hair left of ear; straps around beam, lines, and lettering on bell.

ABOUT UNCIRCULATED *(Small trace of wear visible on highest points.)*

AU-55 (Choice About Uncirculated)
OBVERSE: Only a trace of wear shows on highest spots of cheek and hair left of ear.

OBVERSE

REVERSE

REVERSE: A trace of wear shows on highest points of lettering on bell. Nearly all of the mint luster is still present.

AU-50 (About Uncirculated)
OBVERSE: Traces of wear show on cheek and hair on shoulder and left of ear.
REVERSE: Traces of wear show on bell at lettering and along ridges at bottom. Three-quarters of the mint luster is still present.

EXTREMELY FINE *(Very light wear on only the highest points.)*

EF-45 (Choice Extremely Fine)
OBVERSE: Slight wear shows on cheek and high points of hair behind ear and along shoulder. Hairlines at back of head are sharp and detailed.
REVERSE: High points of straps on beam are lightly worn. Lines at bottom of bell are worn but clearly defined and separated. Lettering on bell is very weak at center. Half of the mint luster is still present.

EF-40 (Extremely Fine)
OBVERSE: Wear shows on high points of cheek and hair behind ear and at shoulder.
REVERSE: High points of beam straps and lines along bottom of bell are lightly worn, but details are clearly defined and partially separated. Lettering on bell is worn away at center. Part of the mint luster is still present.

VERY FINE *(Light to moderate even wear. All major features are sharp.)*

VF-30 (Choice Very Fine)
OBVERSE: Wear spots show on hair at shoulder and behind ear, on cheek and jaw. Hairlines are weak but have nearly full visible details.
REVERSE: Wear shows on bell lettering but some of the details are visible. Straps on beam are plain. Half of line details at bottom are worn smooth.

VF-20 (Very Fine)
OBVERSE: Three-quarters of the lines still show in hair. Cheek lightly worn but bold. Some hair details around the ear are visible.
REVERSE: Wear shows on beam but most details are visible. Bell is worn but bold. Lines across bottom of bell are flat near crack.

Fine *(Moderate to considerable even wear. Entire design clear and bold.)*

F-12 (Very Fine)
OBVERSE: Hair details show only at back and side of head. Designer's initials weak but clearly visible. Part of cheek is worn flat.
REVERSE: Most of lines at bottom of bell are worn smooth. Parts of straps on beam are nearly smooth. Rim is full.

VERY GOOD *(Well worn. Design clear but flat and lacking details.)*

VG-8 (Very Good)
OBVERSE: Entire head is weak, and most details in hair from temple to ear are worn smooth. All letters and date are bold. Ear and designer's initial are visible. Rim is complete.

HALF DOLLARS—KENNEDY 1964 TO DATE

MINT STATE *(Absolutely no trace of wear.)*

MS-70 (Perfect Uncirculated)
A flawless coin exactly as it was minted, with no trace of wear or injury. Must have full mint luster and brilliance or light toning. Any unusual striking traits must be described.

MS-65 (Choice Uncirculated)
No trace of wear; nearly as perfect as MS-70 except for some small blemish. Has full mint luster but may be unevenly toned or lightly fingermarked. A few barely noticeable nicks or marks may be present.

MS-60 (Uncirculated)
A strictly Uncirculated coin with no trace of wear, but with blemishes more obvious than for MS-65. Has full mint luster, but surface may be dull, spotted, or heavily toned. Check points for signs of abrasion: high points of cheek and jawbone, center of neck, hair below part, bundle of arrows, center tail feather, right wing tip.

OBVERSE   REVERSE

ABOUT UNCIRCULATED *(Small trace of wear visible on highest points.)*

AU-55 (Choice About Uncirculated)
OBVERSE: Only a trace of wear shows on highest points of cheek, jawbone, and hair below part.
REVERSE: A trace of wear shows on central tail feather. Nearly all of the mint luster is still present.

EXTREMELY FINE *(Very light wear on only the highest points.)*

EF-40 (Extremely Fine)
OBVERSE: Slight wear shows on cheek, along jawbone, and on high points of hair below part. Hairlines are sharp and detailed.
REVERSE: High points of arrows and right wing tip are lightly worn. Central tail feathers are worn but clearly defined and fully separated. Three-quarters of the mint luster is still present.

VERY FINE *(Light to moderate even wear. All major features are sharp.)*

VF-30 (Choice Very Fine)
OBVERSE: Wear spots show on hair below part and along cheek and jaw. Hairlines are weak but have nearly full visible details.
REVERSE: Wear shows on arrow points but some details are visible. All central tail feathers are plain. Wing tips are lightly worn.

DOLLARS—MORGAN
1878–1921

MINT STATE *(Absolutely no trace of wear.)*

MS-70 (Perfect Uncirculated)
A flawless coin exactly as it was minted, with no trace of wear or injury. Must have full mint luster and brilliance or light toning. Any unusual striking traits must be described.

MS-65 (Choice Uncirculated)
No trace of wear; nearly as perfect as MS-70 except for a few minute bag marks or surface marks. Has full mint luster but may be unevenly toned. Any unusual striking traits must be described.

MS-60 (Uncirculated)
A strictly Uncirculated coin with no trace of wear, but with bag marks and other abrasions more obvious than for MS-65. May have a few small rim marks and weakly struck spots. Has full mint luster but may lack brilliance, and surface may be spotted or heavily toned. For these coins, bag abrasions and scuff marks are considered different from circulation wear. Full mint luster and lack of any wear are necessary to distinguish MS-60 from AU-55. Check points for signs of wear: hair above eye and ear, edges of cotton leaves and blossoms, high upper fold of cap, high points of eagle's breast, and tops of legs. Weakly struck spots are common and should not be confused with actual wear.

ABOUT UNCIRCULATED *(Small trace of wear visible on highest points.)*

AU-55 (Choice About Uncirculated)
OBVERSE: Slight trace of wear shows on hair above ear and eye, edges of cotton leaves, and high upper fold of cap. Luster fading from cheek.
REVERSE: Slight trace of wear shows on breast, tops of legs,

OBVERSE   REVERSE

and talons. Most of the mint luster is still present, although marred by light bag marks and surface abrasions.

AU-50 (About Uncirculated)
OBVERSE: Traces of wear show on hair above eye and ear, edges of cotton leaves, and high upper fold of cap. Partial detail visible on tops of cotton blossoms. Luster gone from cheek.
REVERSE: There are traces of wear on breast, tops of legs, wing tips, and talons. Three-quarters of the mint luster is still present. Surface abrasions and bag marks are more noticeable than for AU-55.

EXTREMELY FINE *(Very light wear on only the highest points.)*

EF-45 (Choice Extremely Fine)
OBVERSE: Slight wear on hair above date, forehead, and ear. Lines in hair well detailed and sharp. Slight flat spots on edges of cotton leaves. Minute signs of wear on cheek.
REVERSE: High points of breast are lightly worn. Tops of legs and right wing tip show wear. Talons are slightly flat. Half of the mint luster is still present.

EF-40 (Extremely Fine)
OBVERSE: Wear shows on hair above date, forehead, and ear. Lines in hair well detailed. Flat spots visible on edges of cotton leaves. Cheek lightly worn.
REVERSE: Almost all feathers gone from breast. Tops of legs, wing tips, and feathers on head show wear. Talons are flat. Partial mint luster is visible.

VERY FINE *(Light to moderate even wear. All major features are sharp.)*

VF-30 (Choice Very Fine)
OBVERSE: Wear shows on high points of hair from forehead to ear. Some strands visible in hair above ear. There are smooth areas on cotton leaves and at top of cotton blossoms.
REVERSE: Wear shows on leaves of wreath and tips of wings. Only a few feathers visible on breast and head.

VF-20 (Very Fine)
OBVERSE: Smooth spots visible on hair from forehead to ear. Cotton leaves heavily worn but separated. Wheat grains show wear.
REVERSE: Some leaves on wreath are well worn. Breast is smooth, and only a few feathers show on head. Tips of wings are weak but lines are complete.

FINE *(Moderate to heavy even wear. Entire design clear and bold.)*

F-12 (Fine)
OBVERSE: Hairline along face is clearly defined. Lower two cotton leaves smooth but distinct from cap. Some wheat grains merging. Cotton blossoms flat but the two lines in each show clearly.
REVERSE: One-quarter of eagle's right wing and edge of left wing are smooth. Head, neck, and breast are flat and merging. Tail feathers slightly worn. Top leaves in wreath show heavy wear.

VERY GOOD *(Well worn. Design clear but flat and lacking details.)*

VG-8 (Very Good)
OBVERSE: Most details in hair are worn smooth. All letters and date are clear. Cotton blossoms flat and leaves merging in spots. Hair of eagle's right wing and one-third of left wing are smooth. All leaves in wreath are worn. Rim is complete.

GOOD *(Heavily worn. Design and legend visible but faint in spots.)*

G-4 (Good)
OBVERSE: Hair is well worn with very little detail remaining. Date, letters, and design clearly outlined. Rim is full.
REVERSE: Eagle is worn nearly flat but is completely outlined. Design elements smooth but visible. Legend is all visible; rim is full.

ABOUT GOOD *(Outlined design. Parts of date and legend worn smooth.)*

AG-3 (About Good)
OBVERSE: Head is outlined with nearly all details worn away. Date readable but worn. Legend merging into rim.
REVERSE: Entire design partially worn away. Rim merges into legend.

Note: Some of these dollars have a prooflike surface; this should be mentioned in any description of such pieces.

Portions of the design are often weakly struck, especially on the hair above the ear and on the eagle's breast.

DOLLARS—PEACE 1921–1935

MINT STATE *(Absolutely no trace of wear.)*

MS-70 (Perfect Uncirculated)
A flawless coin exactly as it was minted, with no trace of wear or injury. Must have full mint luster or light toning. Any unusual striking traits must be described.

MS-65 (Choice Uncirculated)
No trace of wear; nearly as perfect as MS-70 except for a few minute bag marks or surface marks. Has full mint luster but may be unevenly toned.

MS-60 (Uncirculated)
A strictly Uncirculated coin with no trace of wear, but with bag marks and other abrasions more obvious than for MS-65. May have a few small rim mars, and may be weakly struck. Has full mint luster but may lack brilliance, and surface may be spotted or heavily toned. For these coins, bag abrasions and scuff marks are considered different from circulation wear. Full mint luster and lack of any wear are necessary to distinguish MS-60 from AU-55. Check points for signs of wear: high points of cheek and hair, high points of feathers on right wing and leg. Weakly struck spots are common and should not be confused with actual wear.

ABOUT UNCIRCULATED *(Small trace of wear visible on highest points.)*

OBVERSE   REVERSE

AU-55 (Choice About Uncirculated)
OBVERSE: Trace of wear shows on hair over ear and above forehead. Slight wear visible on cheek.
REVERSE: High points of feathers on right wing show a trace of wear. Most of the mint luster is still present, although marred by light bag marks and surface abrasions.

AU-50 (About Uncirculated)
OBVERSE: Traces of wear visible on neck and hair over ear and above forehead. Cheek shows slight wear.
REVERSE: Traces of wear show on head and high points of feathers on right wing. Three-quarters of the mint luster is still present. Surface abrasions and bag marks are more noticeable than for AU-55.

EXTREMELY FINE *(Very light wear on only the highest points.)*

EF-45 (Choice Extremely Fine)
OBVERSE: Hair around face shows slight wear, but most hair strands are visible. Lower edge of neck lightly worn.
REVERSE: Top of neck and head behind eye show slight wear. Central wing and leg feathers lightly worn. Half of the mint luster is still present.

EF-40 (Extremely Fine)
OBVERSE: Slight flattening visible on high points of hair; most hair strands clearly separated. Entire face and lower edge of neck lightly worn.
REVERSE: Wear shows on head behind eye and top of neck. Some flat spots visible on central wing and leg feathers. Partial mint luster is visible.

DOLLARS—EISENHOWER
1971–1978

MINT STATE *(Absolutely no trace of wear.)*
MS-70 (Perfect Uncirculated)
A flawless coin exactly as it was minted, with no trace of

wear or injury. Must have full mint luster and brilliance or light toning. Any unusual striking traits must be described.

MS-65 (Choice Uncirculated)
No trace of wear; nearly as perfect as MS-70 except for some small blemish. Has full mint luster but may be unevenly toned or lightly fingermarked. A few minute nicks or marks may be present.

MS-60 (Uncirculated)
A strictly Uncirculated coin with no trace of wear, but with blemishes more obvious than for MS-65. Has full mint luster, but surface may be dull, spotted or heavily toned. Check points for signs of abrasion: high points of cheek and jawbone, center of neck, edge of bust, head, high points of ridges and feathers in wings and legs.

ABOUT UNCIRCULATED *(Small trace of wear visible on highest points.)*

AU-55 (Choice About Uncirculated)
OBVERSE: Only a trace of wear shows on highest points of jawbone and at center of neck.
REVERSE: A trace of wear shows on high points of feathers in wings and legs. Nearly all of the mint luster is still present.

EXTREMELY FINE *(Very light wear on only the highest points.)*

EF-45 (Choice Extremely Fine)
OBVERSE: Slight wear shows on cheek, along jawbone, and on high points at edge of bust. Hairlines are sharp and detailed.
REVERSE: High points of head, legs, and wing ridges are lightly worn. Central feathers are all clearly defined. Three-quarters of the mint luster is still present.

VERY FINE *(Light to moderate even wear. All major features are sharp.)*

VF-30 (Choice Very Fine)
OBVERSE: Wear spots show on hair below part and along cheek and jaw. Hairlines are weak but have nearly full visible details. Slight wear shows at center of neck and along edge of bust.

OBVERSE

REVERSE

REVERSE: Wear shows on head and feathers in wings and legs but all details are visible. All central tail feathers are plain. Wing and leg ridges are lightly worn.

GOLD DOLLARS—TYPE I
1849–1854

MINT STATE *(Absolutely no trace of wear.)*

MS-70 (Perfect Uncirculated)
A flawless coin exactly as it was minted, with no trace of wear or injury. Must have full mint luster and brilliance. Any unusual die or planchet traits must be described.

MS-65 (Choice Uncirculated)
No trace of wear; nearly as perfect as MS-70 except for some small blemish. Has full mint luster and brilliance but may show slight discoloration. A few barely noticeable nicks or marks may be present.

MS-60 (Uncirculated)
A strictly Uncirculated coin with no trace of wear, but with blemishes more obvious than for MS-65. May lack full mint luster and brilliance. Check points for signs of abrasion: hair near coronet; tips of leaves.

ABOUT UNCIRCULATED *(Small trace of wear visible on highest points.)*

AU-55 (Choice About Uncirculated)
OBVERSE: There is a trace of wear at upper hairline below coronet.
REVERSE: Trace of wear visible on tips of leaves. Three-quarters of the mint luster is still present.

AU-50 (About Uncirculated)
OBVERSE: There is a trace of wear on hairlines near coronet and below the ear.
REVERSE: Trace of wear visible on tips of leaves. Half of the mint luster is still present.

EXTREMELY FINE *(Very light wear on only the highest points.)*

OBVERSE

REVERSE

EF-45 (Choice Extremely Fine)
OBVERSE: Slight wear shows on highest wave of hair, hairline, and below ear. All major details are sharp. Beads at top of coronet are well defined.
REVERSE: Leaves show visible wear at tips, but central details are clearly defined. Traces of mint luster will show.

VERY FINE *(Light to moderate even wear. All major features are sharp.)*

VF-30 (Choice Very Fine)
OBVERSE: Beads on top of coronet are well defined. LIBERTY is complete. Hair around face and neck slightly worn but strands fully separated. Star centers show some details.
REVERSE: There is light even wear on legend and date. Some details show in center of leaves.

VF-20 (Very Fine)
OBVERSE: Beads at top of coronet are partially separated. LIBERTY is complete. Hair around face and neck noticeably worn but well outlined. Some star centers show details.
REVERSE: There is light even wear on legend and date. Only traces of leaf ribs are visible. Bow knot is flat on high point.

FINE *(Moderate to heavy even wear. Entire design clear and bold.)*

F-12 (Fine)
OBVERSE: LIBERTY is complete but weak. Ear lobe is visible. Hairlines and beads on coronet are worn smooth. Stars are clearly outlined, but centers are flat.
REVERSE: Legend within wreath is worn and weak in spots. Leaves and wreath are well outlined. Rim is full and edge beveled.

VERY GOOD *(Well worn. Design clear but flat and lacking details.)*

VG-8 (Very Good)
OBVERSE: Only the outline of hair is visible. Four letters in LIBERTY are clear.

REVERSE: Only the outline of leaves is visible. Legend and numeral are worn and very weak.

GOOD *(Heavily worn. Design and legend visible but faint in spots).*

G-4 (Good)
OBVERSE: Head is outlined with nearly all details worn away. Stars are weak. Full rim shows.
REVERSE: Date and legend well worn but readable. Leaves are outlined. Full rim shows.

Note: The gold dollars struck at Charlotte and Dahlonega are crude compared to those of the Philadelphia Mint. Frequently they have rough edges, and the die work appears to be generally inferior. In grading coins from these branch mints, consideration must be given to these factors.

QUARTER EAGLES— CORONET HEAD 1840–1907

MINT STATE *(Absolutely no trace of wear.)*

MS-70 (Perfect Uncirculated)
A flawless coin exactly as it was minted, with no trace of wear or injury. Must have full mint luster and brilliance. Any unusual die or planchet traits must be described.

MS-65 (Choice Uncirculated)
No trace of wear; nearly as perfect as MS-70 except for some small blemish. Has full mint luster and brilliance but may show slight discoloration. A few barely noticeable nicks or marks may be present.

MS-60 (Uncirculated)
A strictly Uncirculated coin with no trace of wear, but with blemishes more obvious than for MS-65. May lack full mint luster and brilliance. Check points for signs of abrasion: tip of coronet, hair wings, claws.

ABOUT UNCIRCULATED *(Small trace of wear visible on highest points.)*

OBVERSE   REVERSE

AU-55 (Choice About Uncirculated)
OBVERSE: There is a trace of wear on tip of coronet and above eye.
REVERSE: Trace of wear visible on wing tips. Three-quarters of the mint luster is still present.

AU-50 (About Uncirculated)
OBVERSE: There is a trace of wear on coronet and on hair above ear, eye, and forehead.
REVERSE: Trace of wear visible on wing tips, below eye, and on claw. Half of the mint luster is still present.

EXTREMELY FINE *(Very light wear on only the highest points.)*

EF-45 (Choice Extremely Fine)
OBVERSE: There is light wear on coronet, and on hair above ear, eye, forelocks, and top of head.
REVERSE: Light wear shows on edges and tips of wings, on neck, below eye, and on claws. Part of the mint luster is still present.

EF-40 (Extremely Fine)
OBVERSE: Light wear shows on coronet, hair above ear and eye, on forelocks, and on cheek. All major details sharp.
REVERSE: Light wear shows on edges and tips of wings, on neck, below eye, on feathers, and claws. Shield well defined. Traces of mint luster will show.

VERY FINE *(Light to moderate even wear. All major features are sharp.)*

VF-30 (Choice Very Fine)
OBVERSE: Light wear visible on coronet; hair is worn but shows considerable detail. Most stars show details. LIBERTY bold and clear.
REVERSE: Light wear shows on edges and tips of wings. Some detail shows on head and neck feathers. Vertical shield lines complete but some not separated; horizontal lines worn in center.

VF-20 (Very Fine)
OBVERSE: Hair outlined with very little detail. Only a few stars show any details. LIBERTY clear but not bold.
REVERSE: Half of wing feathers visible. Half of lines in shield are clear.

FINE *(Moderate to heavy even wear. Entire design clear and bold.)*

F-12 (Fine)
OBVERSE: Hair and cheek smooth. Stars outlined with no visible details. LIBERTY worn but visible.
REVERSE: Wings show very little detail. Head and one claw outlined only, with no details visible. Neck almost smooth. Most of shield lines merge.

Note: Coins of this type seldom appear in grades lower than Fine. Pieces made at Charlotte, Dahlonega and New Orleans are frequently found weakly struck. Those from San Francisco often lack feather details.

QUARTER EAGLES—INDIAN HEAD 1908–1929

MINT STATE *(Absolutely no trace of wear.)*

MS-70 (Perfect Uncirculated)
A flawless coin exactly as it was minted, with no trace of wear or injury. Must have full mint luster and brilliance. Any unusual die or planchet traits must be described.

MS-65 (Choice Uncirculated)
No trace of wear; nearly as perfect as MS-70 except for some small blemish. Has full mint luster and brilliance but may show slight discoloration. A few barely noticeable nicks or marks may be present.

MS-60 (Uncirculated)
A strictly Uncirculated coin with no trace of wear, but with blemishes more obvious than for MS-65. May lack full mint luster and brilliance. Checkpoints for signs of abrasion: cheek-

OBVERSE   REVERSE

bone, headdress, headband feathers, shoulder of eagle's left wing.

ABOUT UNCIRCULATED *(Small trace of wear visible on highest points.)*

AU-55 (Choice About Uncirculated)
OBVERSE: There is a trace of wear on cheekbone.
REVERSE: Trace of wear visible on shoulder of eagle's left wing. Three-quarters of the mint luster is still present.

AU-50 (About Uncirculated)
OBVERSE: There is a trace of wear on cheekbone and headdress.
REVERSE: Trace of wear visible on shoulder of wing, head, and breast. Half of the mint luster is still present.

EXTREMELY FINE *(Very light wear on only the highest points.)*

EF-45 (Choice Extremely Fine)
OBVERSE: There is light wear on cheekbone, headdress, and headband.
REVERSE: Light wear shows on upper portion of wing, head, neck, and breast.

EF-40 (Extremely Fine)
OBVERSE: Light wear shows on cheekbone, jaw, and headband. Slight wear visible on feathers of headdress. Stars sharp.
REVERSE: Light wear shows on wing, head, neck, and breast. Leg has full feather detail. Traces of mint luster will show.

VERY FINE *(Light to moderate even wear. All major features are sharp.)*

VF-30 (Choice Very Fine)
OBVERSE: Cheekbone shows flat spot. Small feathers clear; large feathers show some detail. Most of headband detail visible.
REVERSE: Wear shows on wing and neck. Some breast feathers show details. Most of leg feathers visible.

VF-20 (Very Fine)
OBVERSE: Cheekbone worn about halfway. Small feathers

clear but large feathers show a little detail. Hair cord knot is distinct. Headband shows some detail.
REVERSE: Little detail shows on breast and leg feathers. Top of wing and neck worn. Second layer of wing feathers shows.

FINE *(Moderate to heavy even wear. Entire design clear and bold.)*

F-12 (Fine)
OBVERSE: Cheekbone worn; all feathers worn with very little detail visible. Stars outlined, with no details visible. Hair cord knot is worn but visible.
REVERSE: Wing worn, with only partial feathers at bottom visible. All lettering worn but visible.

Note: Coins of this type are seldom collected in grades lower than Fine. Mint marks are often weakly struck.

HALF EAGLES—CORONET HEAD 1839–1908

MINT STATE *(Absolutely no trace of wear.)*

MS-70 (Perfect Uncirculated)
A flawless coin exactly as it was minted, with no trace of wear or injury. Must have full mint luster and brilliance. Any unusual die or planchet traits must be described.

OBVERSE

REVERSE

MS-65 (Choice Uncirculated)
No trace of wear; nearly as perfect as MS-70 except for some small blemishes. Has full mint luster and brilliance but may show slight discoloration. A few barely noticeable bag marks and surface abrasions may be present.

MS-60 (Uncirculated)
A strictly Uncirculated coin with no trace of wear, but with blemishes more obvious than for MS-65. Has full mint luster but may lack brilliance. Surface may be lightly marred by minor bag marks and abrasions. Check points for signs of wear: hair, coronet, wings.

ABOUT UNCIRCULATED *(Small trace of wear visible on highest points.)*

AU-55 (Choice About Uncirculated)
OBVERSE: There is a trace of wear on tip of coronet and hair above eye.
REVERSE: Trace of wear visible on wing tips. Three-quarters of the mint luster is still present.

AU-50 (About Uncirculated)
OBVERSE: There is a trace of wear on coronet, above ear and eye.
REVERSE: Trace of wear visible on wing tips, below eye and on claw. Half of the mint luster is still present.

EXTREMELY FINE *(Light wear on only the highest points.)*

EF-45 (Choice Extremely Fine)
OBVERSE: There is light wear on coronet, and on hair above ear, eye, forelocks, and top of head.
REVERSE: Light wear shows on edges and tips of wings, on neck, below eye, and on claws. Part of the mint luster is still present.

EF-40 (Extremely Fine)
OBVERSE: Light wear shows on coronet, on hair above ear and eye, on the forelock, on top of head, and on cheek. All major details are sharp.
REVERSE: Light wear visible on edges and tips of wings, on neck, below eye, on feathers, and claws. Shield is well defined. Traces of mint luster will show.

VERY FINE *(Light to moderate even wear. All major features are sharp.)*

VF-30 (Choice Very Fine)
OBVERSE: Light wear shows on coronet, hair, and stars but most details are visible. LIBERTY bold.
REVERSE: Light wear visible on edges and tips of wings. Head and neck feathers show some detail. Vertical lines in

shield complete but some not separated; horizontal lines worn in center.

VF-20 (Very Fine)
OBVERSE: Hair worn but major details visible. Top line of coronet broken. Some stars show partial detail. LIBERTY clear but not bold.
REVERSE: Half of wing feathers are visible. Half of lines in shield are clear.

FINE *(Moderate to heavy even wear. Entire design clear and bold.)*

F-12 (Fine)
OBVERSE: Hair and cheekbone smooth. Top line of coronet worn. LIBERTY worn but visible.
REVERSE: Wings show very little detail. Head and one claw outlined only, with no details visible. Neck almost smooth. Most of shield lines merge. (For the 1866 through 1908 group, the motto is worn but readable.)

Note: Coins of this type are seldom collected in grades lower than Fine.

HALF EAGLES—INDIAN HEAD
1908–1929

MINT STATE *(Absolutely no trace of wear.)*

MS-70 (Perfect Uncirculated)
A flawless coin exactly as it was minted, with no trace of wear or injury. Must have full mint luster and brilliance. Any unusual die or planchet traits must be described.

MS-65 (Choice Uncirculated)
No trace of wear; nearly as perfect as MS-70 except for some small blemish. Has full mint luster and brilliance but may show slight discoloration. A few barely noticeable bag marks and surface abrasions may be present.

MS-60 (Uncirculated)
A strictly Uncirculated coin with no trace of wear, but with

OBVERSE   REVERSE

blemishes more obvious than for MS-65. Has full mint luster but may lack brilliance. Surface may be lightly marred by minor bag marks and abrasions. Check points for signs of wear: cheekbone, headdress, headband feathers, shoulder of eagle's left wing.

ABOUT UNCIRCULATED *(Small trace of wear visible on highest points.)*

AU-55 (Choice About Uncirculated)
OBVERSE: There is a trace of wear on cheekbone.
REVERSE: Trace of wear visible on shoulder of eagle's left wing. Three-quarters of the mint luster is still present.

AU-50 (About Uncirculated)
OBVERSE: There is a trace of wear on cheekbone and headdress.
REVERSE: Trace of wear visible on shoulder of wing, head and breast. Half of the mint luster is still present.

EXTREMELY FINE *(Light wear on only the highest points.)*

EF-45 (Choice Extremely Fine)
OBVERSE: There is light wear on cheekbone, headdress and headband.
REVERSE: Light wear shows on upper portion of wing, head, neck, and breast. Part of mint luster is still present.

EF-40 (Extremely Fine)
OBVERSE: Light wear shows on cheekbone, jaw, and headband. Slight wear visible on feathers of headdress. Stars are sharp.
REVERSE: Light wear shows on wing, head, neck, and breast. Leg has full feather detail. Traces of mint luster will show.

VERY FINE *(Light to moderate even wear. All major features are sharp.)*

VF-30 (Choice Very Fine)
OBVERSE: Cheekbone worn, shows flat spot. Small feathers clear; large feathers show some details. Most of headband detail visible.

REVERSE: Wear shows on wing and neck. Some breast feathers show details. Most of leg feathers visible.

VF-30 (Very Fine)
OBVERSE: Cheekbone worn about half-way. Headdress feathers show some details. Hair cord knot is distinct. Headband shows only a little detail.
REVERSE: Little detail shows on breast and leg feathers. Top of wing and neck worn. Second layer of wing feathers shows.

FINE *(Moderate to heavy even wear. Entire design clear and bold.)*

F-12 (Fine)
OBVERSE: Cheekbone worn; all feathers worn with very little detail visible. Stars outlined with no details visible. Hair cord knot is worn but visible.
REVERSE: Wing worn, with only partial feathers at bottom visible. All lettering worn but visible.

Note: Coins of this type are seldom collected in grades lower than Fine. Mint marks are often very weakly struck.

EAGLES—CORONET HEAD
1838–1907

MINT STATE *(Absolutely no trace of wear.)*

MS-70 (Perfect Uncirculated)
A flawless coin exactly as it was minted, with no trace of wear or injury. Must have full mint luster and brilliance. Any unusual die or planchet traits must be described.

MS-65 (Choice Uncirculated)
No trace of wear; nearly as perfect as MS-70 except for some small blemishes. Has full mint luster and brilliance but may show slight discoloration. A few barely noticeable bag marks and surface abrasions may be present.

MS-60 (Uncirculated)
A strictly Uncirculated coin with no trace of wear, but with blemishes more obvious than for MS-65. Has full mint luster

OBVERSE   REVERSE

but may lack brilliance. Surface may be lightly marred by minor bag marks and abrasions. Check points for signs of wear: hair, coronet, wings.

ABOUT UNCIRCULATED *(Small trace of wear visible on highest points.)*

AU-55 (Choice About Uncirculated)
OBVERSE: There is a trace of wear on hair above eye and on coronet.
REVERSE· Trace of wear visible on wing tips. Three-quarters of the mint luster is still present.

AU-50 (About Uncirculated)
OBVERSE: There is a trace of wear on hair at ear and above eye, and on coronet.
REVERSE: Trace of wear visible on wing tips, below eye, and on claw. Half of the mint luster is still present.

EXTREMELY FINE *(Light wear on only the highest points.)*

EF-45 (Choice Extremely Fine)
OBVERSE: There is light wear on coronet, and on hair above ear, eye, forelocks, and top of head.
REVERSE: Light wear shows on edges and tips of wings, on neck, below eye, and on claws. Part of the mint luster is still present.

EF-40 (Extremely Fine)
OBVERSE: Light wear shows on coronet, hair, cheek, and stars. All major details sharp.
REVERSE: Light wear visible on wings, head, neck, and claws. Shield is well defined. Traces of mint luster will show.

VERY FINE *(Light to moderate even wear. All major features are sharp.)*

VF-30 (Choice Very Fine)
OBVERSE: There is light wear on coronet, hair, and stars, but most details are visible. There is a break on top line of coronet over two letters in LIBERTY. Cheek worn. LIBERTY bold.
REVERSE: Light wear visible on wings and head but some

details show. Vertical lines in shield complete but some are not separated; horizontal lines worn in center.

VF-20 (Very Fine)
OBVERSE: Hair worn but major details visible. Break on top line of coronet extends over at least three letters in LIBERTY. Cheek well worn. Stars worn but show most details. LIBERTY clear but shows wear.
REVERSE: About half of wing feathers are visible. Very little detail shows in head.

FINE *(Moderate to heavy even wear. Entire design clear and bold.)*

F-12 (Fine)
OBVERSE: Hair and cheekbone smooth. Top line of coronet worn. Some details show in stars. LIBERTY worn but visible.
REVERSE: Wings show very little detail. Head and one claw outlined only, with no details visible. Neck is almost smooth. Most of shield lines merge. (In the 1866 through 1907 group, the motto is worn but readable.)

Note: Coins of this type are seldom collected in grades lower than Fine.

EAGLES—INDIAN HEAD
1907–1933

MINT STATE *(Absolutely no trace of wear.)*

MS-70 (Perfect Uncirculated)
A flawless coin exactly as it was minted, with no trace of wear or injury. Must have full mint luster and brilliance. Any unusual die or planchet traits must be described.

MS-65 (Choice Uncirculated)
No trace of wear; nearly as perfect as MS-70 except for some small blemish. Has full mint luster and brilliance but may show some slight discoloration. A few minute bag marks and surface abrasions may be present.

MS-60 (Uncirculated)
A strictly Uncirculated coin with no trace of wear, but with blemishes more obvious than for MS-65. Has full mint luster but may lack brilliance. Surface may be lightly marred by minor bag marks and abrasions. Check points for signs of wear: above eye, cheek, wing.

ABOUT UNCIRCULATED *(Small trace of wear visible on highest points.)*

AU-55 (Choice About Uncirculated)
OBVERSE: There is a trace of wear above eye.
REVERSE: Trace of wear visible on wing. Three-quarters of the mint luster is still present.

AU-50 (About Uncirculated)
OBVERSE: There is a trace of wear on hair above eye and on forehead.
REVERSE: Trace of wear visible on wing. Half of the mint luster is still present.

EXTREMELY FINE *(Light wear on only the highest points.)*

EF-45 (Choice Extremely Fine)
OBVERSE: There is light wear on hair above eye and on forehead, and on cheekbone.
REVERSE: Light wear shows on wing and head. Part of the mint luster is still present.

EF-40 (Extremely Fine)
OBVERSE: Light wear shows on hair, cheekbone and feathers.
REVERSE: Light wear visible on wing and head. Traces of mint luster will show.

VERY FINE *(Light to moderate even wear. All major features are sharp.)*

VF-30 (Choice Very Fine)
OBVERSE: There is light wear along forehead, but most detail shows. Moderate wear visible on cheekbone. Light wear shows where feathers meet headband.
REVERSE: Left wing shows more than half the details. Some details in head are visible.

VF-20 (Very Fine)
OBVERSE: About half the hair detail is visible. Moderate wear shows on cheekbone. Some feathers do not touch headband.
REVERSE: There is moderate wear on left wing, which shows only about one-quarter detail. Head almost smooth. All lettering bold.

FINE *(Moderate to heavy even wear. Entire design clear and bold.)*

OBVERSE

REVERSE

F-12 (Fine)
OBVERSE: Hair smooth with no details; cheekbone almost smooth. No feathers touch headband but most feather details visible.
REVERSE: Left wing top and head are worn smooth. Lettering worn but visible.

Note: Coins of this type are seldom collected in grades lower than Fine.

DOUBLE EAGLES—LIBERTY HEAD 1850–1907

MINT STATE (Absolutely no trace of wear.)

MS-70 (Perfect Uncirculated)
A flawless coin exactly as it was minted, with no trace of wear or injury. Must have full mint luster and brilliance. Any unusual die or planchet traits must be described.

MS-65 (Choice Uncirculated)
No trace of wear; nearly as perfect as MS-70 except for some small blemishes. Has full mint luster and brilliance but may show slight discoloration. A few minute bag marks and surface abrasions are usually present.

MS-60 (Uncirculated)
A strictly Uncirculated coin with no trace of wear, but with blemishes more obvious than for MS-65. Has full mint luster but may lack brilliance. Surface is usually lightly marred by

OBVERSE   REVERSE

minor bag marks and abrasions. Check points for signs of wear: hair, coronet, eagle's neck and wing, top of shield.

ABOUT UNCIRCULATED *(Small trace of wear visible on highest points.)*

AU-55 (Choice About Uncirculated)
OBVERSE: There is a trace of wear on hair.
REVERSE: Trace of wear visible on wing tips and neck. Three-quarters of the mint luster is still present.

AU-50 (About Uncirculated)
OBVERSE: There is a trace of wear on hair at top and over eye, and on coronet.
REVERSE: Trace of wear visible on wing tips, neck, and at top of shield. Half of the mint luster is still present.

EXTREMELY FINE *(Light wear on only the highest points.)*

EF-45 (Choice Extremely Fine)
OBVERSE: There is light wear on hair and coronet prongs.
REVERSE: Light wear shows on edges and tips of wings, on head and neck, and on horizontal shield lines. Part of the mint luster is still present.

EF-40 (Extremely Fine)
OBVERSE: Light wear shows on hair, coronet prongs and cheek.
REVERSE: Light wear visible on wings, head, neck, horizontal shield lines, and tail. Traces of mint luster will show.

VERY FINE *(Light to moderate even wear. All major features are sharp.)*

VF-30 (Choice Very Fine)
OBVERSE: About one-quarter of hair detail below coronet visible; half the detail shows above coronet. Cheek and some coronet prongs worn. Stars show wear but all details visible.
REVERSE: Most of wing details visible. Top part of shield shows moderate wear. About half the details in tail visible.

VF-20 (Very Fine)
OBVERSE: Less than half the hair detail above coronet visible.

About half the coronet prongs are considerably worn. Stars are flat but show most details. LIBERTY shows wear but is very clear.
REVERSE: Some wing details visible. Shield shows very little detail at top. Tail is worn with very little detail.

FINE *(Moderate to heavy even wear. Entire design clear and bold.)*

F-12 (Fine)
OBVERSE: All hairlines are well worn with very little detail visible. And one-quarter of details within coronet visible. Stars show little detail. LIBERTY readable.
REVERSE: Wings show very little detail. Head and neck smooth. Eye visible. Tail and top of shield smooth.

Note: Coins of this type are seldom collected in grades lower than Fine. The hair curl under the ear is sometimes weakly struck.

In the group between 1866 and 1876, the reverse motto is sometimes weakly struck.

Pieces made at the Carson City Mint are usually found weakly struck and heavily bag marked.

DOUBLE EAGLES— SAINT-GAUDENS 1907–1932

MINT STATE *(Absolutely no trace of wear.)*

MS-70 (Perfect Uncirculated)
A flawless coin exactly as it was minted, with no trace of wear or injury. Must have full mint luster and brilliance. Any unusual die or planchet traits must be described.

MS-65 (Choice Uncirculated)
No trace of wear; nearly as perfect as MS-70 except for some small blemishes. Has full mint luster and brilliance but may show slight discoloration. A few minute bag marks and surface abrasions are usually present.

MS-60 (Uncirculated)
A strictly Uncirculated coin with no trace of wear, but with

blemishes more obvious than for MS-65. Has full mint luster but may lack brilliance. Surface is usually lightly marred by minor bag marks and abrasions. Check points for signs of wear: forehead, breast, knee, nose, eagle's wings and breast.

ABOUT UNCIRCULATED *(Small trace of wear visible on highest points.)*

AU-55 (Choice About Uncirculated)
OBVERSE: There is a trace of wear on left breast and left knee.
REVERSE: Trace of wear visible on high point of wing. Three-quarters of the mint luster is still present.

AU-50 (About Uncirculated)
OBVERSE: There is a trace of wear on nose, breast, and knee.
REVERSE: Trace of wear visible on wings. Half of the mint luster is still present.

EXTREMELY FINE *(Light wear on only the highest points.)*

EF-45 (Choice Extremely Fine)
OBVERSE: There is light wear on forehead, nose, breast and knee.
REVERSE: Light wear shows on wings and breast, but all feathers are bold. Part of the mint luster is still present.

EF-40 (Extremely Fine)
OBVERSE: Light wear shows on forehead, nose, breast, knee, and just below left knee. Drapery lines on chest visible.
REVERSE: Light wear visible on wings and breast but all feathers bold. Traces of mint luster will show.

VERY FINE *(Light to moderate even wear. All major features are sharp.)*

VF-30 (Choice Very Fine)
OBVERSE: There is light wear on all features, extending above and below left knee and along part of right leg. Some of garment lines on chest are visible.
REVERSE: Light wear visible on left wing and breast; feathers show but some are weak.

OBVERSE

REVERSE

VF-20 (Very Fine)
OBVERSE: Forehead moderately worn. Contours of breast worn. Only a few garment lines on chest are visible. Entire right leg shows moderate wear.
REVERSE: Half of feathers are visible in wings and breast.

FINE *(Moderate to heavy even wear. Entire design clear and bold.)*

F-12 (Fine)
OBVERSE: Forehead and garment smooth; breasts flat. Both legs worn with right bottom missing.
REVERSE: Less than half the wing details are visible. Only a little breast detail is visible.

Note: Coins of this type are seldom found in grades lower than Fine.

COLONIAL COINS, PATTERNS, AND TOKENS

HISTORY

The history of our coinage begins not with the first federal issues but with the coin used earlier by colonists. This period in American coin use, from the exploration of Florida and the first Virginia settlements up to 1792, spans 200 years and is considered one of the most fascinating specialties for collectors. It is rich in types, designs, and methods of production. While a great deal of colonial coinage is rare, some fall into the moderate price range. Here are historical objects of undisputed significance, purchasable in some cases for less than the cost of key-date modern coins. The celebrated Rosa Americana, circulated before George Washington was born, can be had in good condition for less than $100. Even some of the 17th-century "elephant tokens" sell for under $100, though this series also includes rarities of high price. The belief that colonial coinage is only for the wealthy just isn't so.

The story of this nation's beginnings is probably better told by its early money than by any other antiquities. Pilgrim settlers are often pictured as hunters and trappers living off the land. This is partly true, but even in the 1600s there were cities with shops and a real need existed for coinage. When nothing better was available the old barter system was resorted to, as used in ancient times, with goods traded for other goods of similar value. In Massachusetts, iron nails were accepted as legal tender, as well as Indian wampum (shells strung together on cords, each having a set value). As early as the 1640s, twenty years after the *Mayflower*, serious thought was given by the Bay Colony to striking its own money. In 1652 the Massachusetts General Court authorized experimental efforts in this direction, the first attempts being no more than rough metal discs stamped with small symbols. Compared to Europe's elaborate coinage they were meager but proved that this country had the ability to produce a medium of exchange. These were followed by improved domestic efforts as well as importation of coins from abroad, struck expressly for colonial use. These include the Lord Baltimore coins of Maryland and the Colonial Plantation token. By the 17th century's close, a variety of coins and pseudocoins circulated. Some were private or merchant tokens of British or Dutch manufacture. These were largely speculative issues brought to this country in large quantities by persons hoping to acquire vast land parcels. There was little confidence in the integrity of such coinage but it was nevertheless accepted on the basis of weight.

Coins of both England and Spain, brought over by immigrants and traders, circulated pretty freely. Other foreign coins were also met with. Rather than being changed at face value they were, in the early years, valued at metal content, every merchant having a scale to weigh coins brought to him. Spain's dollar or "piece of eight" became the most familiar coin in the colonies, replaced thereafter by the coins of Great Britain. By the time of the Revolution, probably as many as 90% of the coins in American circulation were of British mintage.

Because colonial coins and tokens were not issued by a central government and were produced under challenging conditions, standardization cannot be expected. Sizes, denominations, and quality of workmanship all vary, sometimes to an extreme degree. Included are crude pieces hardly recognizable as coins and works of considerable artistic merit. Some were not milled but hammered, struck by hammering the dies into metal blanks just as the Romans and Greeks made their coins 2,000 years ago. They also vary in scarcity. The collector should not be duped into paying inflated prices for coins merely on the grounds of their being pre-Revolutionary. This in itself is no assurance of rarity. Each issue has its own established value, as shown in the listings section of this book. Allowance must be made for the condition of hammered pieces (whose shape will be somewhat irregular) and for specimens of great rarity, as these are almost impossible to find in the kind of condition one would expect of later coins. On the whole, condition standards are less rigid for colonial than federal issues. On the other hand, the buyer should not accept badly damaged examples in the belief that nothing better can be found.

The most extensively circulated—and faithfully trusted—coin of early colonial America was the Spanish silver dollar or "piece of eight." Introduced to this country by the Spanish explorers and later imported in abundance by traders, it had a value of eight *reals*, each real or "bit" being worth $12\frac{1}{2}$ cents. Thus, the quarter or 25-cent piece came to be known as "two bits."

"Two-bits"

"Four-bits"

THE SPANISH MILLED DOLLAR
The "Piece of Eight"

The following pages contain descriptions and price valuations for most types of monies used in the American colonies, excluding foreign coins intended to serve currency needs abroad. Most can only be classed as tokens, as they either had no face value or were struck without government sanction. These include merchant pieces and other speculative issues. However, the colonists, being ever-resourceful, attempted from time to time to strike semiofficial or official coinage, and these will be found listed as well. Colonial coinage on the whole is not handsome. It was generally produced under conditions inferior to that of government-issued money, often designed and struck by persons who had little or no prior experience in such work. It is, nevertheless, of great interest from both a numismatic and historical point of view and much of it is extremely rare. As a general rule, the collector should be wary of counterfeits and reproductions, as the majority of these pieces have at one time or other been copied, either as legitimate souvenirs or fraudulently.

SOMMER ISLANDS (BERMUDA)

This so-called "hog money" is thought to be the first coinage of the American colonies. A hog is pictured on one side and a sailing vessel on the other. The workmanship is English. Hogs were not native to the islands but introduced around 1515 by the Spaniard Juan Bermudez, from whom Bermuda takes its name. They apparently increased and multiplied vastly within the next hundred years, serving as an important article of food for the inhabitants. The suggestion that the coins were intended to represent the market value of a hog, just as early Greek coins were sometimes stamped with a likeness of an animal whose price they equaled, is no longer given serious consideration. It was used merely as an emblem. These coins are of lightly silvered brass, inscribed SOMMER ISLANDS. The edges are, as to be expected, irregular, having been produced by the hammering technique rather than milling.

SHILLING

TYPE OF COIN	ABP	G-4 GOOD	EF-40 EX. FINE
☐ Shilling	1650.00	3350.00	8650.00

SIXPENCE

TYPE OF COIN	ABP	G-4 GOOD	EF-40 EX. FINE
☐ Twopence	1250.00	2400.00	8750.00
☐ Threepence			75000.00
☐ Sixpence	1250.00	2400.00	8000.00

MASSACHUSETTS—NEW ENGLAND COINAGE

This is the earliest coinage struck on the North American continent. This crude coinage may not be appealing aesthetically but its historical significance is as great, or greater, than any coins subsequently issued in this country. It was produced in limited quantities for local circulation in the Boston area and is extremely rare. When the decision was reached to attempt a native currency, the Massachusetts General Court appointed John Hull "mintmaster." The "mint" was an iron works operated by Joseph Jenks at Saugus, just north of Boston. These coins were made of silver by the ancient process of hammering—beating the designs into them by holding the die against the metal blank and striking it with a mallet. There was, in fact, no design at all. The coins were issued in three denominations—threepence, sixpence, and twelvepence (shilling)—and each carried the letters NE on one side and the value in Roman numerals on the other, most of the surface being blank. Variations in size, shape, and placement of the markings are common. They date to 1652, but no date appears upon them.

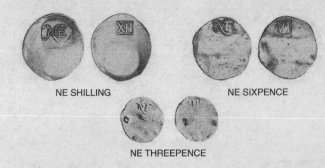

NE SHILLING   NE SIXPENCE

NE THREEPENCE

TYPE OF COIN	ABP	G-4 GOOD	EF-40 EX. FINE
☐ NE Shilling	10000.00	18500.00	42000.00
☐ NE Threepence (less than 3 known)		EXTREMELY RARE	
☐ NE Sixpence (less than 8 known)	10000.00	20000.00	46500.00

WILLOW TREE COINS

After about four months of circulation of the Massachu-setts–New England coinage, it was decided they were unsatis-factory. The legend and numeral of value were so simplistic that anyone possessing smith's tools could reproduce them. There was the further problem—not a new one, as it was faced by English Mints in the Middle Ages—that the large expanses of unstamped metal invited "clipping," a practice in which un-scrupulous persons trimmed down the edges and collected quantities of silver while still passing the coins at face value. It was impossible to improve the method of manufacture, there being no milling machines available. But the designs could be improved by the use of more fully engraved dies. This was accomplished with the so-called Willow Tree coinage, intro-duced in 1653. On the obverse appears a very abstract rendi-tion of a willow tree, surrounded by the place name, with the date and value designation on the reverse (III stood for three-pence, VI for sixpence, and XII for shilling). Although struck at odd moments from 1653–60 (there was no regular or continu-ous production), all specimens are dated 1652.

SHILLING   SIXPENCE

THREEPENCE

TYPE OF COIN	ABP	G-4 GOOD	EF-40 EX. FINE
☐ Willow Tree Shilling	6500.00	10000.00	42500.00
☐ Willow Tree Threepence		EXTREMELY RARE	
☐ Willow Tree Sixpence	10000.00	24000.00	56500.00

OAK TREE COINS

Successors to the Willow Tree coins, Oak Tree coins were likewise of Massachusetts origin and, like them, showed a tree on the obverse with the date and numeral of value on the reverse. They were introduced in 1660, the year of the English Restoration (the return of the Stuarts to the throne), an event of no small significance numismatically. While the previous regime, the Protectorate of Oliver Cromwell, was composed of politicians who supported the pilgrim cause, there was genuine fear that the new king—Charles II—might deal harshly with the colonists for being so bold as to strike coins. They attempted to camouflage this activity by retaining the old date, 1652, during the eight years that Oak Tree coins were struck; and, in fact, it remained unaltered for the sixteen years of their successors, Pine Tree coins. In terms of design, these Oak Tree coins were an improvement on their predecessors, being much sharper and bolder. Whether this can be attributed to more deeply engraved dies, more careful hammering, or (a usually overlooked possibility) better annealing or heating of the blanks, is uncertain. The mintmaster was still the same: John Hull. But this much is sure: the Oak Tree coins were turned out in far larger quantities than previous Massachusetts coins.

SHILLING

SIXPENCE

THREEPENCE

TYPE OF COIN	ABP	G-4 GOOD	F-12 FINE	EF-40 EX. FINE
☐ Shilling	300.00	500.00	2500.00	6250.00
☐ Twopence	525.00	1200.00	3200.00	5500.00
☐ Threepence	260.00	500.00	2200.00	5000.00
☐ Sixpence	200.00	375.00	2600.00	7000.00

PINE TREE COINS

The final version of the Bay Colony "tree" coin, the Pine Tree coin featured a much clearer, if not more botanically accurate, portrait of a tree. Though struck in the same three denominations as the earlier types, there is a Large Planchet and Small Planchet version of the shilling, the Large being slightly rare. Both are of the same weight; the metal was simply hammered thinner on the Large Planchet. It had been demonstrated, by the use of large planchets for the Willow and Oak Tree shillings, that the coin did not stand up well to handling and could be rendered sturdier by reducing its size and thereby increasing the thickness. It was also possible to strike the design more deeply with a thicker planchet. All coins from this series are dated 1652. They were actually struck from 1667–82, during the reign of Britain's Charles II. After 1682 the issuing of coinage was discontinued by the Bay Colony. Many varieties exist in this series.

SHILLING, Large Planchet   SHILLING, Small Planchet

SIXPENCE   THREEPENCE

TYPE OF COIN	ABP	G-4 GOOD	F-12 FINE	EF-40 EX. FINE
☐ Pine Tree Shilling, Small Planchet				
	275.00	450.00	1500.00	5500.00
☐ Pine Tree Shilling, Large Planchet				
	260.00	525.00	1750.00	5650.00
☐ Pine Tree Threepence	240.00	350.00	1000.00	3500.00
☐ Pine Tree Sixpence	240.00	400.00	1800.00	4650.00

MARYLAND

Maryland was the second colony, next to Massachusetts, to have coinage of its own. The origins of these coins bear little relation to those of the Bay Colony. While the Massachusetts pieces had been natively designed and struck, Maryland's coins were entirely a foreign product. They date from 1658. At this time Maryland was very sparsely inhabited, its only residents being small colonies of English immigrants, and could not have suffered too seriously from a shortage of coinage. Though not strictly classified as private issues they might well merit that designation. Maryland's first coins were the brainchild of Cecil Calvert, Lord Baltimore (for whom the colony's chief city was named). Calvert did not, as popularly supposed, "own Maryland." He did, however, possess large areas of its land and had the title of Lord Proprietor of Maryland. As an English lord with typical lordly pride, Calvert looked with disdain upon the prospect of Englishmen—his subjects, technically—trading with beads or iron or other objects of barter. So he ordered a batch of English-quality coins to be struck in Britain for use in the colony. They comprised a shilling, sixpence, fourpence or groat, and a penny. The first three were of silver, following the British tradition, the penny in copper. As a result of their production in an established, well-equipped Mint, these coins are considerably more professional in appearance than those of Massachusetts. Lord Calvert placed his own portrait upon them. There was no need to fear censure from the king for this brazen act, as the English Civil War had already swept the king (Charles I) from his throne and Britain was not again to be ruled by a king until 1660. The reverses of the silver pieces carry Calvert's heraldic insignia with the value in Roman numerals. The penny's obverse shows a regal crown surmounted by staffs and banners. There is no numeral of value on the penny but instead the word "denarium," the name of an ancient Roman coin from which the British penny evolved. (To this day the symbol for "penny" in Britain is the letter "d," meaning denarium. The cent sign, ¢, is never used.) Lord Calvert's portrait is a shoulder-length bust without crown, wreath of laurel, or other symbol of rulership. The penny is the scarcest of the denominations, as this is believed to have been a pattern only, not actually placed in use.

FOURPENCE   SHILLING

TYPE OF COIN	ABP	G-4 GOOD	EF-40 EX. FINE
☐ Maryland Shilling	600.00	1000.00	7500.00
☐ Maryland Fourpence	800.00	1500.00	6500.00
☐ Maryland Sixpence	700.00	1400.00	5500.00
☐ Maryland Denarium (Penny)		EXTREMELY RARE	

MARK NEWBY OR ST. PATRICK HALFPENCE

The coinage shortage in the early colonies, and the voraciousness with which anything resembling coinage was seized upon as a medium of exchange, is clearly demonstrated by the Newby or St. Patrick Halfpence. The coins are really misnamed, as they existed not only in halfpence but farthing denomination (in the British currency system, a farthing or "fourthling" was equal to one-quarter of a penny).

Mark Newby was neither an explorer nor royal governor but apparently a private Irish citizen who came from Dublin and settled in New Jersey in the year 1681. He brought with him a quantity of tokens—they could only very charitably be called coins—which are thought to have been struck at

Dublin about eight years earlier. These were coppers. On the obverse they depict a crowned king kneeling and playing a harp, almost certainly intended in art as the biblical King David, who is often represented in art as a harpist. St. Patrick, the legendary and patron saint of Ireland, appears on the reverse. On the halfpence he holds a crozier and cross (often mistaken for a clover) while giving benediction to a worshiper; on the farthing he is shown in a similar pose, driving the snakes out of Ireland, one of the many accomplishments with which this saint is credited. The obverse legend is FLOREAT REX, which can be translated as "Prosperity to the King." These are not at all bad-looking pieces and they feature an intriguing detail: the large crown on the obverse was inlaid in brass, to contrast in color with the copper and give the appearance of being golden. It is, however, sometimes lacking. The origin of this St. Patrick money is not clearly known. The possibility that it was struck for circulation in America seems very remote, as (a) there is no record of supportive legislation on either side of the Atlantic, and (b) the coins were apparently not brought to this country until long after striking, which hardly would have been the case had they been designed for use here. In any event, the General Assembly of the New Jersey Province authorized their use as legal tender in May 1682, and for some while thereafter they served as the common currency of New Jersey. The most logical conclusion to be drawn is that Newby was a commercial trader who sought to profit from the shortage of coinage in America, and that he settled in New Jersey because this area was virtually without money of any kind. If so, he would not have been the only colonist to do this. Silver and gold patterns of the farthing were struck, of which the silver is very rare and the gold unique. There may have been similar patterns of the halfpenny, but they have not been discovered. In their normal metal—copper—neither is a coin of extreme scarcity.

ST. PATRICK HALFPENCE   ST. PATRICK FARTHING

TYPE OF COIN	ABP	G-4 GOOD	EF-40 EX. FINE
☐ St. Patrick Halfpence	120.00	200.00	780.00
☐ St. Patrick Farthing (Brass Insert on Obverse)	60.00	175.00	500.00
☐ St. Patrick Farthing (Without Brass Insert)	60.00	100.00	240.00
☐ St. Patrick Farthing (Silver Pattern)	800.00	2000.00	3800.00
☐ St. Patrick Farthing (Gold Pattern)			UNIQUE

COLONIAL PLANTATION TOKEN

The so-called Plantation token was the first coinage authorized for use in the American colonies by the British government. Its history is of great interest. Throughout the middle 17th century it was well known in England that the American provinces, or "plantations" as they were called abroad (largely by persons unaware of the extent of population), suffered from a shortage of coinage. In 1688 an Englishman named John Holt petitioned the king (James II) for a patent or franchise for the striking of coinage for distribution in the colonies. In Britain at this time the system of "patents of exclusivity" was commonplace. Printers would pay a fee to have the exclusive right on putting out Bibles; merchants paid for a franchise to sell a particular product without fear of competition. The fee, which was considerable, had to be paid each year while the franchise was in force. Holt was convinced that the supply of coinage to America would be a very profitable endeavor. The government approved his request for a franchise and shortly thereafter he began to strike his coins, better called tokens. Large in size, they were made of tin and had the face value of one-quarter of a Spanish real or "piece of eight," say about fourpence. On their obverse they pictured an equestrian likeness of James II, regal-looking in this design but soon to be driven out of the country into exile. It is important to note that they were not intended for use in any special region but could be exchanged anywhere in the provinces; thus, they carry no place name. The original dies were preserved and restrikes made from them in the late 1820s; their appearance is quite similar to the original and could well be a cause of confusion to beginners. A very rare variety exists, in which the numeral "4" in the value legend on the reverse is positioned vertically instead of horizontally.

PLANTATION TOKEN

TYPE OF COIN	ABP	G-4 GOOD	F-12 FINE	EF-40 EX. FINE	MS-60 UNC.
☐ James II Plantation Token					
	140.00	225.00	475.00	1200.00	2750.00
Restrikes exist which are worth slightly less.					
☐ James II Plantation Token, Vertical "4"					RARE

ELEPHANT TOKEN

These extremely popular, intriguing pieces have been the subject of much study and debate. Their origins are only sketchily known. There are three specific types: London token, Carolina token, and New England token. All have the same obverse, a portrait of an elephant without legend or inscription of any kind. These pieces are coppers and were modeled as halfpennies, though they carry no indication of value. The extent to which they circulated in the American colonies is not established. Based on what little information is available, their history may be pieced together as follows.

First in the series was the London token, which on some specimens carries the wording GOD PRESERVE LONDON on the reverse, on others merely LONDON, accompanying a heraldic shield. The belief is that they were struck in 1664 when the population of that city was being decimated by an outbreak of bubonic plague, which apparently is the danger from which preservation was sought. So far this theory makes some historical sense, though it fails to explain the selection of an elephant as the obverse symbol. Could it be that this was a reference to "stamping out" the plague, and that the elephant, as the largest of creatures, would be best equipped to do so? That elephants were well known in London in the 1660s is well established. There were no zoos for the display of wild beasts but elephants and tigers (both from India) were kept in enclosed dungeons in the Tower of London for the amusement of visitors. Natural history drawing was still in an archaic state at that time, which explains why the elephant on Elephant tokens looks rather strange. For a long while thereafter there appears to have been no effort to revive the Elephant token, perhaps because the plague subsided. Then in 1694 it reappeared, in an edition bearing two different reverses: GOD PRESERVE CAROLINA AND THE LORD'S PROPRIETORS and GOD PRESERVE NEW ENGLAND. Just how these pieces came to be, what their intent was, and how they were circulated, is totally unknown. It may be presumed that GOD PRESERVE was used merely in the sense of "God Bless," after the fashion of the slogan "God Save the King," not as implication that either Carolina or New England suffered from any specific difficulty.

There is little doubt, based on physical evidence, that they were struck in England, as these tokens are handsomely milled (not hammered) and it is doubtful that such work could have been accomplished in the colonies. It has been said that the London variety was intended for circulation in Tangier, but even if that were so, there is no evidence of it being an official issue. The Carolina and New England pieces could have been entirely speculative. Their distribution may have been local (in England) with no intention of exporting or using them for actual currency in the colonies. This seems the logical answer, especially in view of the extremely small quantities struck. Of the London token there were considerably larger numbers struck, but to classify this as a piece designed for colonial use seems very presumptive. Some specimens undoubtedly reached the colonies at an early date but, if they did, it was only accidentally, in the baggage or pockets of immigrants or traders, just as almost everything else made abroad found its way across the Atlantic.

There are a number of types and varieties. The London token exists in both thin and thick planchet; with interlacing in the central portion of the shield; with sword in the second quarter of the shield (transposed from the first, where it is commonly found); and with the inscription LONDON rather than GOD PRESERVE LONDON. Of these, the transposed sword is the rarest. The chief variety of the Carolina issue is the alteration from PROPRIETERS to the more correct spelling, PROPRIETORS, accomplished not by the introduction of a fresh die but re-engraving the original. If closely inspected, the letter "E," or what remains of it, can be observed.

1694 NEW ENGLAND   1694 PROPRIETORS

1694 PROPRIETERS   1664 GOD PRESERVE LONDON

1664 GOD PRESERVE LONDON (SWORDS)   1664 LONDON

TYPE OF COIN	ABP	G-4 GOOD	EF-40 EX. FINE
☐ 1664 GOD PRESERVE LONDON (thin)	175.00	300.00	2600.00
☐ 1664 GOD PRESERVE LONDON (thick)	120.00	200.00	2200.00
☐ 1664 GOD PRESERVE LONDON (diag.)	215.00	425.00	3350.00
☐ 1664 GOD PRESERVE LONDON (swords)		EXTREMELY RARE	
☐ 1664 LONDON	340.00	575.00	6650.00
☐ 1694 NEW ENGLAND		18000.00	34000.00
☐ 1694 PROPRIETORS (overstrike)	1600.00	2750.00	7500.00
☐ 1694 PROPRIETERS		EXTREMELY RARE	

NEW YORKE TOKEN

The New York colony (referring to the state, not the city) had no coinage of its own in the 17th century. Though settled somewhat later than Massachusetts, the population of New York came close to equaling it by the century's close and the volume of business transacted was at least comparable. It is curious that tiny Maryland and equally tiny New Jersey had coins during the 17th century while New York did not. The closest it came to having one was the New Yorke token, but this can hardly be classed with the Massachusetts, Maryland, or even the New Jersey coinage, as there is no evidence it received official sanction. It was very likely nothing more than a merchant token. This is a smallish piece, roughly equal to our nickel, of which some were struck in brass and others in pewter. On the obverse it carries a rather scrawny eagle with an allegorical design (Cupid is one of the figures) on the reverse. The obverse legend reads NEW YORKE IN AMERICA. Of its origins practically nothing is known. The belief that this coin was struck in Holland is founded more upon assumption, because of New York's extensive Dutch population, than evidence. Its date has been the subject of controversy. The spelling of New York as "New Yorke" suggests a dating in the 17th century, but as this spelling lingered on into the 18th century it is quite possible that the coin or token is not as old as commonly presumed. It is very likely that even in the second quarter of the 18th century a European designing such a piece would have used the "New Yorke" spelling, even if it was no longer current in America. The likelihood that the New Yorke token was struck in Manhattan from dies prepared in Holland is a romantic but not convincing theory.

UNDATED BRASS

TYPE OF COIN	ABP	G-4 GOOD	EF-40 EX. FINE
☐ New Yorke Token, No Date: Brass	2200.00	4000.00	9200.00
☐ New Yorke Token, No Date: Tin (pewter)	2500.00	5000.00	9500.00

GLOUCESTER TOKEN

Very few specimens exist of this early amateur token and information about it is likewise scanty. It is apparently the first private token struck on American soil. The composition is brass, leading to the assumption that it might have been a pattern for a silver shilling that was never produced. Whether the brass pieces were intended to circulate is highly doubtful. The Gloucester token is thought to have been the work of Richard Dawson of Gloucester, Virginia. On one side appears a five-pointed star, with a building of modest design on the other. Known specimens are so thoroughly worn that the inscription surrounding this building is unreadable. The best guess is that it was intended to represent the Gloucester County Courthouse or some other public structure. It does not appear to be a place of worship. The Gloucester token dates to 1714.

SHILLING BRASS

TYPE OF COIN	ABP	G-4 GOOD	EF-40 EX. FINE
☐ Gloucester Shilling (brass)			45000.00*

*2000 Auction

ROSA AMERICANA

These extremely handsome coins, thoroughly European in appearance and workmanship, are often referred to as Wood tokens—not from being made of wood (their composition is copper, zinc, and silver) but from William Wood, the Englishman who originated them. Nearly forty years before their appearance, John Holt, another Englishman, had gained a patent from the then-king, James II, to strike coinage for circulation in the American colonies. Upon expiration of the Holt patent or franchise there had been little enthusiasm for its renewal, as Holt's coins—the so-called Plantation tokens—had not proved very successful. As time passed and the population of such cities as Boston, New York, and Philadelphia increased, the prospects for coinage seemed to brighten. William Wood, of whom there is not very much known, obtained a franchise from George I to supply coinage to America, as well as to Ireland. This resulted in the Rosa Americana tokens. These were struck in small denominations only, from a halfpence to twopence. The earliest, which apparently were struck in 1722, carried no date. Later a date was added and these pieces saw fairly large production in the years 1722, 1723, and 1724. After an interval of nearly ten years in which none were produced, a Rosa Americana pattern proof was struck off in 1733. As best as can be ascertained, the Wood patent had fallen into other hands, as Wood died in 1730. His successors probably toyed with the idea of reinstituting the Rosa Americana coins but never got beyond the stage of this single proof.

To judge by the relative commonness of the coin (except for certain varieties, which are rare), they must have been turned out at least in the hundreds and possibly the thousands. The obverses are all alike, picturing George I in profile facing the viewer's right (it was switched to the left on the 1733 trial proof). This is not the king against whom America went to war in the Revolution but the first English monarch of that name, a German who could speak but a few words of English. Surrounding the portrait is, generally, a legend giving the names of the countries over which the king ruled: Great Britain, France, and Hibernia (Ireland). The claim that he ruled France was a purely speculative one, a reference to the victories of Marlborough over Louis XIV's armies which had ended France's ambition to capture England but in no way gave England rulership over that nation. The reverse shows the rose, sometimes alone, sometimes surmounted by a crown. There is one variation (on the 1724 penny) where the rose is not pictured symbolically but as an actual flower growing up from the ground. These pieces gain their name from the reverse inscription, not present on all, reading ROSA AMERICANA UTILE DULCI, or, roughly, "American Rose, utility and pleasure." The rose had been a symbol of the Tudor kings and queens well before colonization of America. In their extent and variety the Rosa Americana coins are unmatched by any others intended for circulation in America. The opinion held of them today was not shared by colonists, however, who protested that the coins were short-weighted and refused to accept them.

1722 HALFPENNY "DEI GRATIA REX"   1723 PENNY

TYPE OF COIN	ABP	G-4 GOOD	F-12 FINE	EF-40 EX. FINE
☐ Twopence, No Date	80.00	160.00	350.00	1800.00
☐ Twopence, No Date, Motto Sans Label		EXTREMELY RARE		
☐ 1722 Halfpenny, D. G. REX	65.00	150.00	300.00	1500.00
☐ 1722 Halfpenny, DEI GRATIA REX	65.00	120.00	225.00	1250.00
☐ 1722 Halfpenny, VTILE DVLCI		395.00	800.00	2400.00
☐ 1722 Twopence, Period after REX	70.00	120.00	325.00	900.00
☐ 1722 Penny, UTILE DVLCI	42.00	80.00	210.00	1400.00
☐ 1722 Penny, VTILE DVLCI	60.00	125.00	250.00	1250.00
☐ 1722 Penny, GEORGIVS		EXTREMELY RARE		
☐ 1722 Twopence, No Period after Rex	80.00	135.00	275.00	1200.00
☐ 1723 Twopence	75.00	110.00	300.00	1500.00
☐ 1723 Halfpenny	65.00	100.00	135.00	1200.00
☐ 1723 Halfpenny, Rose Without Crown		EXTREMELY RARE		
☐ 1723 Penny	70.00	120.00	250.00	1150.00

TYPE OF COIN	ABP	G-4 GOOD	F-12 FINE	EF-40 EX. FINE
☐ 1724 Penny (Pattern)				EXTREMELY RARE
☐ 1724 Penny, No Date, ROSA: SINE: SPINA				EXTREMELY RARE
☐ 1724 Twopence (Pattern)				EXTREMELY RARE
☐ 1733 Twopence (Pattern Proof)				EXTREMELY RARE

WOOD'S COINAGE OR HIBERNIA

These coins, more properly called tokens, were issued under the patent granted to William Wood to strike coinage for America and Ireland (see Rosa Americana). Hibernia was the Latin name for Ireland. They are included here because these pieces proved unpopular in Ireland—just as did the Rosa Americanas in America—and Wood sought to recover his investment by circulating them in America. History does not record their fate on this side of the Atlantic but it is doubtful that they received a warm reception. They were struck in such enormous numbers, thanks to excessive overconfidence, that most types can be had inexpensively. George I appears on the obverse. There are two reverse types, both picturing a seated female with a harp representing Hibernia, the Irish equivalent of Britannia. There is no need to speculate on the reason for Type I being changed: the figure is portrayed in so ungainly a manner as to appear comical. Type II is only a slight improvement.

1723 OVER 22 HALFPENNY   1723 HALFPENNY

TYPE OF COIN	ABP	G-4 GOOD	F-12 FINE	EF-40 EX. FINE
☐ 1722 Farthing, D.G. REX	100.00	160.00	425.00	1400.00
☐ 1722 Halfpenny, Harp Facing Left	100.00	160.00	300.00	1200.00

TYPE OF COIN	ABP	G-4 GOOD	F-12 FINE	EF-40 EX. FINE
☐ 1722 Halfpenny, Harp Facing Right	40.00	75.00	150.00	750.00
☐ 1722 Halfpenny, D.G. REX		EXTREMELY RARE		
☐ 1723 Halfpenny	30.00	50.00	125.00	600.00
☐ 1723 Over 22 Halfpenny	40.00	75.00	110.00	1000.00
☐ 1723 Halfpenny, Silver (Pattern)		EXTREMELY RARE		
☐ 1723 Farthing, Silver (Pattern)	500.00	900.00	2000.00	4650.00
☐ 1723 Farthing, DEI, GRATIA REX	35.00	65.00	120.00	525.00
☐ 1723 Farthing, D.G. REX	45.00	85.00	160.00	750.00
☐ 1724 Halfpenny	40.00	100.00	130.00	1200.00
☐ 1724 Farthing	60.00	100.00	130.00	1200.00

HIGLEY COINAGE

The Higley or Granby tokens were entirely private issues. Had they been imported for circulation from abroad they might be of modest interest at best but these are, in fact, *the first privately produced tokens struck on American soil that actually reached circulation.* All are extremely rare. Dr. Samuel Higley, a Connecticut resident and graduate of Yale University, deplored the coinage shortage in his state and took matters into his own hands. Unsupported by legislation and unsponsored by government funds, Higley engraved his own dies and for coin metal used copper from a mine he owned located near Granby, Connecticut (hence the alternate title of these pieces). Considering their amateur origin, the designs and workmanship are of higher quality than might be expected. On the obverse appears a deer surrounded by inscription. There are two reverse types, one featuring a trio of small hammers, the other a broad-bladed cleaver. As originally issued in 1737 they carried the value of threepence, stated on the obverse legend. Though well received at first, protest was later raised by persons skeptical of their copper content. This inspired the ever-resourceful Higley to add the inscription, I AM GOOD COPPER. When this failed to silence critics, who persisted in their belief that the face value was too high and that Higley was gaining a profit from circulating them, the statement of value was replaced by the not-too-subtle suggestion to VALUE ME AS YOU PLEASE. Even so, the Roman numeral III remained. This placed them in the category of bartering pieces which could be exchanged on basis of weight. We are told that the local supply was numerous, but this is hardly reflected by their present rarity. It can only be assumed that many individuals hoarded the Higley tokens and melted them. The inscription on the second reverse type (the cleaver) states I CUT MY WAY THROUGH. The I is sometimes stated to be a J, but in fact was intended merely to represent an ornamental I with loop at the base.

The collector is cautioned that reproductions of the Higley Tokens exist, made by electrotyping and casting, and are of sufficient quality to confuse an inexperienced buyer.

1737 THREEPENCE "CONNECTICVT"

1737 VALVE.ME.AS.YOU.PLEASE
I.AM.GOOD.COPPER

1737 VALUE.ME.AS.YOU.PLEASE
I.CUT.MY.WAY.THROUGH

TYPE OF COIN	ABP	G-4 GOOD	EF-40 EX. FINE
☐ 1737 THE VALUE OF THREEPENCE (3 hammers, CONNECTICVT)	3500.00	5800.00	16000.00
☐ 1737 THE VALUE OF THREEPENCE (3 hammers, I AM GOOD COPPER)	4000.00	7000.00	20000.00
☐ 1737 VALUE ME AS YOU PLEASE (3 hammers, I AM GOOD COPPER)	3200.00	5500.00	15000.00
☐ 1737 VALUE ME AS YOU PLEASE (3 hammers, I AM GOOD COPPER)			EXTREMELY RARE

TYPE OF COIN	ABP	G-4 GOOD	EF-40 EX. FINE
☐ 1737 VALUE ME AS YOU PLEASE (broad axe, I CUT MY WAY THROUGH)	3500.00	6000.00	20000.00
☐ 1739 VALUE ME AS YOU PLEASE (broad axe, I CUT MY WAY THROUGH)	5000.00	8000.00	25000.00

VOCE POPULI COINAGE

These impressive pieces are exclusively private issues and not of American origin. They were struck in Dublin, Ireland, in 1760, by a firm whose chief occupation was the making of buttons for military uniforms. Its proprietor was named Roche. The 17th and 18th centuries both witnessed an inordinate quantity of private tokens and pseudomoney struck in Ireland, much of which reached America. It could all logically be included within the realm of Americana but the Voce Populi tokens have become special favorites of collectors, probably on strength of design more than anything else. The obverse features a classical-style portrait profile crowned with laurel wreath. It has traditionally been assumed to be George III but no actual evidence exists to support this belief. The inscription makes no reference to the king but merely carries the words VOCE POPULI, or "Voice of the People." Various interpretations (too lengthy to be discussed here) could be placed upon the use of this common slogan. The reverse pictures a female with harp, a standard Irish symbol, and the word HIBERNIA. This was the Latin name for Ireland. The date is shown in the exergue beneath the figure. It should always be 1760; however, on one occasion a defective die was used for the halfpenny, causing it to read 1700. That the token was actually struck in 1700 can easily be refuted on stylistic as well as other evidence. There is also a variety in which the inscription reads VOOE POPULI.

1760 "VOCE POPULI" HALFPENNY   1760 "VOCE POPULI" FARTHING

TYPE OF COIN	ABP	G-4 GOOD	EF-40 EX. FINE
☐ 1700 Halfpenny (die-cutter's error)		EXTREMELY RARE	
☐ 1760 Halfpenny	35.00	65.00	700.00
☐ 1760 Halfpenny, P Beneath Bust	60.00	150.00	1000.00
☐ 1760 Halfpenny, P Beside Face	100.00	200.00	1100.00
☐ 1760 Halfpenny, VOOE POPULI (die-cutter's error)			
	150.00	200.00	800.00
☐ 1760 Farthing	60.00	160.00	2500.00
☐ 1760 Farthing, Small Lettering	260.00	525.00	8500.00

PITT TOKENS

William Pitt, for whom Pittsburgh is named, is associated with these tokens only to the extent that his portrait appears on them. He apparently was connected in no way with their issuance. Two denominations were struck, or rather pieces in the *sizes* of two denominations (as they bear no value markings): farthing and halfpenny. They carry the date 1766. Just what their purpose was is not clear. The suggestion has been put forward that they were issued in the nature of medals as an honor to Pitt, who, for his stand against the British stamp tax, was held in high regard by agitators for self-government. The long-held popular belief that Pitt tokens were designed by Paul Revere would probably be best relegated to the ranks of numismatic folklore until some firm evidence is discovered. The similarly long-held belief that the engraver was Smithers of Philadelphia is more acceptable. The obverse has Pitt's likeness in profile with the legend NO STAMPS: THE RESTORE OF COMMERCE: 1766. The reverse shows a handsomely rendered sailing ship with the inscription THANKS TO THE FRIENDS OF LIBERTY AND TRADE. Next to the ship is the word AMERICA, which apparently suggests that the vessel is traveling from some foreign port with cargo for this country. "The Restore of Commerce" was a reference to the fact that British-imposed taxes were periling American commerce by rendering goods so costly that the public could not buy nearly as much as it wished to. The halfpenny is known to have been used briefly as coinage. No such use has been established for the farthing, which is much rarer.

1766 HALFPENNY   1766 FARTHING

TYPE OF COIN	ABP	G-4 GOOD	EF-40 EX. FINE
☐ 1766 Halfpenny	260.00	500.00	2500.00
☐ 1766 Farthing	1150.00	2500.00	16000.00

FRENCH COLONIES IN AMERICA

A number of coins were struck in France for use in that nation's colonies during the 18th century. These were non-geographical pieces that could be exchanged in any French province and carried inscriptions in French and Latin rather than in local languages. It is important to remember in collecting these coins that they were *not* expressly struck for use in America, though they did see use in areas such as Louisiana (named for Louis XIV).

1722 SOU   1767 SOU

COUNTERSTAMPED "RF"   1670 5 SOLS SILVER

TYPE OF COIN	ABP	G-4 GOOD	EF-40 EX. FINE
☐ 1670 5 Sols	320.00	600.00	3200.00
☐ 1670 15 Sols	3500.00	7000.00	28000.00
☐ 1709–1713 30 Deniers, mint mark AA	60.00	100.00	700.00
☐ 1709–1713 30 Deniers, mint mark D	60.00	100.00	700.00
☐ 1710–1713 15 Deniers	65.00	125.00	775.00
☐ 1738–1748 ½ Sou Marque	100.00	200.00	550.00
☐ 1738–1760 Sou Marque	50.00	80.00	420.00
☐ 1717 6 Deniers		EXTREMELY RARE	
☐ 1720 6 Deniers		EXTREMELY RARE	
☐ 1717 12 Deniers		EXTREMELY RARE	
☐ 1721 Sou, mint mark B for Rouen	45.00	80.00	450.00
☐ 1721 Sou, mint mark H for Rochelle	45.00	80.00	450.00
☐ 1722 Sou, mint mark H	75.00	175.00	350.00
☐ 1722 Over 1721	35.00	120.00	410.00
☐ 1767 Sou	55.00	100.00	750.00
☐ 1767 Sou, Counterstamped RF	55.00	100.00	400.00

VIRGINIA

Plagued by a coinage shortage, Virginia's colonists petitioned George III for supplies of trading pieces. He responded by authorizing the striking of a copper halfpenny, with his likeness on the obverse and the Virginia seal on its reverse. Proposals were also made for a penny and shilling, or coins which, to judge by the size of the few specimens struck, were intended for these denominations. They never reached circulation and are very rare. The halfpenny was struck in large quantities.

SHILLING

TYPE OF COIN	ABP	G-4 GOOD	EF-40 EX. FINE	MS-60 UNC.
☐ 1773 Halfpenny Period After GEORGIVS				
	60.00	120.00	350.00	800.00
☐ 1773 Halfpenny No Period After GEORGIVS				
	40.00	65.00	400.00	1200.00
☐ 1773 Penny	PROOF			8500.00
☐ 1774 Shilling Silver	PROOF			21500.00

STATE OF NEW HAMPSHIRE

New Hampshire has the distinction of being the first state to attempt a local coinage following the Declaration of Independence. In 1776 it authorized William Moulton to produce an experimental batch of copper pieces. The small numbers that have been traced indicate this coin never attained general circulation, though it probably circulated in a small way. The chief type has a tree on the obverse and a harp on the reverse. Other types are known but their status has not been positively established.

1776 PINE TREE   1776 WM COPPER

TYPE OF COIN	VG-8 VERY GOOD
☐ 1776 New Hampshire Copper	16500.00
☐ 1776 New Hampshire Copper, WM in center (Pattern Piece)	EXTREMELY RARE

STATE OF VERMONT

Vermont's postrevolutionary coinage, probably the best known for its designs of any regional pieces, was struck by Reuben Harmon of Rupert, Vermont, and some by Thomas Machin of Newburgh, New York. This extensive series most often employed portraits of George III but is best known for its "plough money," an obverse design picturing a farm plough in a field against a background of tree-laden mountains. This is sometimes referred to as the most original, creative, and authentically American design to be found on our colonial or federal-era coins. William Coley, a New York goldsmith, was the die-cutter for this design.

1785 VERMONTS   1786 VERMONTENSIUM

1787 BRITANNIA

TYPE OF COIN	ABP	G-4 GOOD	EF-40 EX. FINE
☐ 1785 Immune Colombia	2200.00	3500.00	6500.00
☐ 1785 VERMONTS	130.00	260.00	2000.00
☐ 1785 VERMONTIS	120.00	250.00	1800.00
☐ 1786 VERMONTENSIUM	130.00	235.00	1800.00
☐ 1786 Baby Head	170.00	300.00	2600.00
☐ 1786 Bust Faces Left	60.00	125.00	1750.00
☐ 1787 Bust Faces Right	65.00	150.00	850.00
☐ 1787 BRITANNIA reverse; it is thought that the reverse of the Brittania piece was struck from a worn, discarded die for a counterfeit British halfpenny	100.00	200.00	750.00
☐ 1788 Cent	150.00	400.00	2000.00
☐ 1788 ET LIB INDE	200.00	350.00	2600.00

TYPE OF COIN	ABP	G-4 GOOD	EF-40 EX. FINE
☐ 1788 VERMON AUCTORI, Reversed C	EXTREMELY RARE		
☐ 1788 GEORGIVS III REX	175.00	300.00	2800.00

STATE OF CONNECTICUT

Connecticut struck more coins in the period from the Revolution to the establishment of a federal currency than any other state. Or, it might be better put, more varieties, as they represent numerous variations of three basic issues. The Mint at which they were struck was established by authority of the state in 1785. It was located at New Haven. The chief die-cutters were Abel Buel and James Atlee.

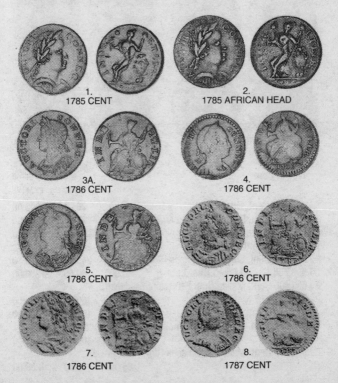

1.
1785 CENT

2.
1785 AFRICAN HEAD

3A.
1786 CENT

4.
1786 CENT

5.
1786 CENT

6.
1786 CENT

7.
1786 CENT

8.
1787 CENT

9.
1787 CENT

10.
1787 CENT

11a.
1787 CENT

12.
1787 CENT

13a.
1787 CENT

14.
1788 CENT

15a.
1788 CENT

16.
1788 CENT

TYPE OF COIN	ABP	G-4 GOOD	EF-40 EX. FINE
☐ 1. 1785 Cent, Bust Right	40.00	75.00	1500.00
☐ 2. 1785 Cent, Bust Right: African Head	80.00	125.00	2250.00
☐ 3. 1785 Cent, Bust Left	110.00	200.00	2000.00
☐ 3a. 1786 Cent, ET LIB INDE	125.00	245.00	1500.00
☐ 4. 1786 Cent, Large Bust Faces Right	115.00	245.00	1500.00
☐ 5. 1786 Cent, Mailed Bust Left	40.00	80.00	1200.00
☐ 6. 1786 Cent, Mailed Bust Left (Hercules Head)	100.00	180.00	1200.00
☐ 7. 1786 Cent, Draped Bust	65.00	100.00	1800.00
☐ 8. 1787 Cent, Mailed Bust, Small Head Faces Right, ET LIB INDE	85.00	160.00	1500.00
☐ 9. 1787 Cent, Mailed Bust Faces Right, INDE ET LIB	85.00	180.00	1200.00

TYPE OF COIN	ABP	G-4 GOOD	EF-40 EX. FINE
☐ 10. 1787 Cent, Muttonhead: INDE ET LIB	55.00	100.00	2000.00
☐ 11. 1787 Cent, Mailed Bust Faces Left	50.00	100.00	1200.00
☐ 11a. 1787 Cent, Horned Bust	50.00	100.00	1000.00
☐ 12. 1787 Cent, CONNECT	45.00	85.00	1200.00
☐ 13. 1787 Cent, Draped Bust Faces Left	40.00	85.00	800.00
☐ 13a. 1787 Cent, Bust Left, AUCIORI	40.00	100.00	1000.00
☐ 13b. 1787 Cent, AUCTOPI	40.00	100.00	1500.00
☐ 13c. 1787 Cent, AUCTOBI	40.00	90.00	1200.00
☐ 13d. 1787 Cent,CONNFC	35.00	65.00	850.00
☐ 13e. 1787 Cent, FNDE	50.00	100.00	1150.00
☐ 13f. 1787 Cent, ETLIR	35.00	80.00	1000.00
☐ 13g. 1787 Cent, ETIIB	35.00	80.00	900.00
☐ 14. 1788 Cent, Mailed Bust Faces Right	35.00	100.00	950.00
☐ 14a. 1788 Cent, Small Head	410.00	900.00	10500.00
☐ 15. 1788 Cent, Mailed Bust Faces Left	60.00	125.00	1000.00
☐ 15a. 1788 Cent, Mailed Bust Left, CONNLC	60.00	115.00	1400.00
☐ 16. 1788 Cent, Draped Bust Faces Left	35.00	65.00	850.00
☐ 16a. Same, CONNLC	115.00	200.00	1500.00
☐ 16b. 1788 Same, INDL ET LIB	120.00	200.00	1500.00

STATE OF NEW JERSEY

No coinage was struck for New Jersey in the colonial period (but *see* Mark Newby Halfpence). As the state's population increased, a serious coin shortage was experienced and, on June 1, 1786, its legislature authorized the striking of three million copper pieces, each to weigh "six pennyweight and six grains apiece." The contract for these tokens was awarded to Thomas Goadsby, Walter Mould, and Albion Cox. The full quantity was to be delivered by June 1788, with partial deliveries to be made in quarterly installments of 300,000 each. Soon after work had begun, Goadby and Cox requested and were granted permission to divide up the quantities and strike them separately, each operating his own facility. Mould set up at Morristown, New Jersey, Cox at Rahway. Goadsby's location is not established but is thought to also have been

Rahway. The obverses of all these tokens show a horse's head and a plough, symbolic of the state's economy being founded largely on agriculture. The legend NOVA CAESAREA is simply New Jersey in Latin. On the reverse is a U.S. shield and E PLURIBUS UNUM. A number of varieties are to be encountered.

TYPE OF COIN	ABP	G-4 GOOD	EF-40 EX. FINE
☐ 1. 1786 Date Under Plough Handle		EXTREMELY RARE	
☐ 2. 1786 Normal Legends	80.00	150.00	900.00
☐ 3. 1786 No Colter	120.00	200.00	3000.00
☐ 4. 1786 Bridle Variety (Not illus.)	40.00	85.00	1500.00
☐ 5. 1786 Narrow Shield (Not illus.)	55.00	100.00	1000.00
☐ 6. 1786 Wide Shield (Not illus.)	55.00	100.00	1600.00
☐ 7. 1787 Normal Legends (Not illus.)	60.00	120.00	1500.00
☐ 8. 1787 PLURIBS	55.00	110.00	2500.00
☐ 9. 1787 "Serpent Head" (Not illus.)	55.00	100.00	2600.00
☐ 10. 1788 Normal Legends (Not illus.)	40.00	80.00	850.00
☐ 11. 1788 Horse's Head Faces Right, Running Fox			
	65.00	140.00	3000.00
☐ 12. 1788 Horse's Head Left	135.00	300.00	5000.00

STATE OF NEW YORK

The history of New York's local coinage prior to the Revolution reveals only the supposed Dutch merchant token discussed previously and various coins and tokens struck for use elsewhere that, in the ordinary course of trade, found their way to the state. For more than 100 years it was without locally authorized coinage. This void was filled by Dutch, British, French, and, to a lesser extent, Spanish monies, which came to New York through its great port and disseminated throughout the region. Apparently no pressing need was felt for a local coinage because none was officially instituted, even after independence. However, quantities of privately struck money did circulate. Some were the work of Thomas Machin of Newburgh, New York (where Washington had a headquarters during the war), who operated what he surreptitiously called a "hardware manufactory." It was, in fact, a copper mill, whose chief products were tokens. Other New York coins were produced at Rupert, Vermont, by a team of millers (Reuben Harmon and William Coley) who also made coins for Vermont and Connecticut.

There is much yet to be learned about New York's federal-era coinage, but quite a good deal has already been determined. The theory, once popularly maintained, that coins bearing the inscription NOVA EBORAC are of foreign origin is now known to be false. "Nova Eborac" is not some sort of mysterious foreign term. It is simply New York in Latin. (If you wonder how there could be a Latin name for New York, when there are none for railroad and television and other things discovered after the Latin language died, the explanation is quite simple. The Romans did not know of New York but they certainly knew of *old* York in Britain, which they called Eborac. To change this into New York you need only add the Latin word for new—*nova*—and you have Nova Eborac.)

All the New York coins (or tokens) are coppers. They carry various designs, of which the portrait of George Clinton is most famous. There was also an Indian figure (not too impressively portrayed), a New York coat-of-arms, and profile bust pretty confidently believed to be George Washington. Though the designs are not very well drawn, the coins themselves are very professionally struck.

1.
1786

2.
1787

3.
1787

4.
1787

5.
1787

6c.
1787

TYPE OF COIN	ABP	G-4 GOOD	EF-40 EX. FINE
☐ 1. 1786 NON VI VIRTUTE VICI, Thought to be the head of George Washington	3200.00	5000.00	17500.00
☐ 2. 1787 EXCELSIOR, Eagle on Obverse Faces Left	800.00	1500.00	9500.00
☐ 3. 1787 EXCELSIOR, Eagle on Obverse Faces Right	1100.00	1800.00	10000.00
☐ 3a. 1787 EXCELSIOR, Large Eagle on Reverse (Not illus.)		EXTREMELY RARE	
☐ 3b. 1787 EXCELSIOR, George Clinton on Reverse (Not illus.)	3200.00	6500.00	25000.00
☐ 3c. 1787 EXCELSIOR, Indian Standing on Reverse (Not illus.)	1800.00	3500.00	16000.00
☐ 3d. 1787 EXCELSIOR, Indian Standing, Eagle on Globe (Not illus.)	3500.00	7000.00	30000.00
☐ 4. 1787 LIBERTATEM, Indian Standing, Eagle Faces Right		EXTREMELY RARE	
☐ 5. 1787 NOVA EBORAC, Reverse Seated Figure Faces Left	140.00	250.00	1200.00

TYPE OF COIN	ABP	G-4 GOOD	EF-40 EX. FINE
☐ 5a. 1787 NOVA EBORAC, Reverse Seated Figure Faces Right (Not illus.)	75.00	160.00	2200.00
☐ 5b. 1787 NOVA EBORAC, Small Head (Not illus.)	1800.00	3000.00	15000.00
☐ 6c. 1787 NOVA EBORAC, Large Head	250.00	550.00	4500.00

BRASHER DOUBLOONS

Perhaps the most celebrated, at any rate the most glamorized, U.S. colonial coin is the Brasher doubloon. Though traditionally referred to as colonial it should correctly be termed a federal-era piece, as it was struck after our independence had been gained. This is a private issue. Ephraim Brasher was a goldsmith from New York who became acquainted with George Washington when the latter resided there following the war. To classify this handsome gold piece as a speculative coin would be a mistake. Brasher, artist and patriot, appears to have manufactured it not for purposes of general circulation but as a memorial to the nation's independence and, possibly, a model from which federal coiners could gain inspiration. It dates to 1787, before the introduction of federal coinage but not before much speculation and debate on the matter. The Brasher doubloon, as the name suggests, was modeled after the Spanish coin of that name. It contained 408 grains of gold. As a goldsmith, Brasher would have encountered no difficulty securing the needed bullion for a small quantity of such pieces, but it is doubtful that he had either the resources or intention to strike this coin in large numbers. The obverse pictures the sun rising over a mountain, with the American eagle emblem on the back. The reverse bears the impressed letters E.B., the initials of Brasher's name. Obviously they were not clandestine issues or their origin would not have been so plainly identified. At the time of its issue the Brasher doubloon had a value of about $16. There was also a half doubloon worth $8. All are extremely rare, the variety in which the initials appear on the eagle's breast being preserved in a single specimen only.

EB Punch
on Wing

TYPE OF COIN

☐ 1787 (gold) Doubloon, EB Punch on Breast

ALL TYPES EXTREMELY RARE

☐ 1787 (gold) Doubloon, EB Punch on Wing

ALL TYPES EXTREMELY RARE

☐ 1787 (gold) Half Doubloon   ALL TYPES EXTREMELY RARE

STATE OF MASSACHUSETTS

Massachusetts, the first colony to strike its own coins in pre-revolutionary days, also had its own coinage in the period between independence and the establishment of the U.S. Mint. On October 17, 1786, the General Court of that state authorized the setting up of a Mint, "for the coinage of gold, silver, and copper." A stipulation was made that the design for coinage should employ the "figure of an Indian with bow and arrow and a star on one side with the word Commonwealth, on the reverse a spread eagle with the words Massachusetts 1787." The ambitiousness of this project was never fully realized. While coppers were struck in some quantities, a coinage of silver and gold never appeared. In 1789 the Mint was abandoned, having proven costly to operate.

1788 CENT   1788 HALF CENT

TYPE OF COIN	ABP	G-4 GOOD	EF-40 EX. FINE
☐ 1787 Cent, Arrows in Left Talon	65.00	150.00	1000.00
☐ 1787 Cent, Arrows in Right Talon	1500.00	4000.00	15000.00
☐ 1787 Cent, Horned Eagle (Die Break)	45.00	100.00	1100.00
☐ 1787 Half Cent	80.00	160.00	1500.00
☐ 1788 Cent	60.00	120.00	1150.00
☐ 1788 Half Cent	75.00	140.00	1150.00

MASSACHUSETTS PINE TREE COPPER

The origin of this unique coin is undetermined. Only one specimen is known, undoubtedly a pattern piece, and but for the greatest of good luck it would have been undiscovered. It turned up, buried beneath a Boston street, during an excavation in the 1800s, having probably been entombed nearly a century. Only the sharp eyes of a laborer prevented it from being discarded along with rubbish. Despite this imprisonment its condition is surprisingly good. It shows a pine tree on the obverse, obviously inspired by the Pine Tree Coinage of a century earlier, and a figure of Liberty posed as Britannia on the reverse, complete with globe and dog. The date 1776 appears beneath the reverse figure. Whether this was the year of striking or was used merely symbolically to denote our independence from Britain is unknown. The obverse inscription is MASSACHUSETTS STATE while the reverse reads LIBERTY AND VIRTUE. This unique item is owned today by the Massachusetts Historical Society. Reproductions exist.

1776 PINE TREE
(UNIQUE)

MASSACHUSETTS HALFPENNY

This intriguing coin, classical in appearance, is dated 1776 and is often referred to as the Janus Copper or Janus Halfpenny. This is a reference (though not quite historically accurate) to the obverse design, which shows a three-sided head with faces looking forward, left, and right. The mythological god Janus had only two faces, looking right and left (the month of January is named for him; one face looks to the old year, one to the new). On the reverse is a seated representation of Liberty. The Massachusetts Halfpenny is a unique pattern piece. The only known specimen sold for $40,000 in 1979.

MASSACHUSETTS
HALFPENNY

KENTUCKY TOKEN

This novel piece was not of American origin, but struck in England around the year 1792. It is thought to have been occasioned by admission of Kentucky into the Union. On the obverse is a hand holding a petition reading OUR CAUSE IS JUST surrounded by the wording UNANIMITY IS THE STRENGTH OF SOCIETY. The reverse is composed of a star in which are circular ornaments, each bearing the initial letter of a state. As K for Kentucky appears at the top, this piece is identified with that state. Some specimens have plain edges while others are stamped "Payable at Bedworth," "Payable in Lancaster," etc. It is vital to take note of these markings, as they have a great influence on the value.

1792 TOKEN

TYPE OF COIN	ABP	G-4 GOOD	EF-40 EX. FINE	MS-60 UNC.
☐ 1792 Token, Plain Edge	60.00	100.00	400.00	900.00
☐ 1792 Token, Engrailed Edge	50.00	115.00	675.00	2750.00
☐ 1792 Token, Lettered Edge, "Payable at I. Fielding," etc.				EXTREMELY RARE
☐ 1792 Token, Lettered Edge, "Payable at Bedworth," etc.				EXTREMELY RARE
☐ 1792 Token, Lettered Edge, "Payable at Lancaster, London, or Bristol"	55.00	100.00	600.00	1250.00

MARYLAND-CHALMERS

The Chalmers tokens were the second group of coins to be struck for circulation in Maryland, preceded by the Lord Baltimore money of a century earlier. Unlike these early pieces, which were of foreign manufacture, the Chalmers coins evolved locally. They were minted at Annapolis in 1783. Apparently they came into being because of the coinage shortage which then existed in Maryland and the hesitancy of that state's legislature to take official action. John Chalmers, their maker, was a goldsmith. He struck them in silver in denominations of threepence, sixpence, and one shilling (twelvepence). Their odd geometrical designs give them an almost cabalistic appearance. All are quite scarce but the majority are obtainable.

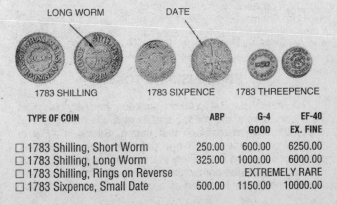

LONG WORM   DATE

1783 SHILLING   1783 SIXPENCE   1783 THREEPENCE

TYPE OF COIN	ABP	G-4 GOOD	EF-40 EX. FINE
☐ 1783 Shilling, Short Worm	250.00	600.00	6250.00
☐ 1783 Shilling, Long Worm	325.00	1000.00	6000.00
☐ 1783 Shilling, Rings on Reverse		EXTREMELY RARE	
☐ 1783 Sixpence, Small Date	500.00	1150.00	10000.00

TYPE OF COIN	ABP	G-4 GOOD	EF-40 EX. FINE
☐ 1783 Sixpence, Large Date	500.00	1000.00	8500.00
☐ 1783 Threepence	450.00	850.00	6500.00

BALTIMORE, MARYLAND OR STANDISH BARRY

Standish Barry was a private citizen of Baltimore who worked at various craft trades including watchmaking and silversmithing. In 1790 he struck, in very limited quantities, a silver threepenny token bearing a portrait on one side and the words THREE PENCE on the other. Due to the low face value and the fact of its being made of silver, the physical size is quite small, about comparable to our dime. Barry's motive is not known with certainty. That he wished to alleviate the shortage of small-denomination coinage in his neighborhood is a possibility, but he produced so few specimens that his goal, if such was his intent, could not have been achieved. A more likely suggestion is that the Barry token was intended chiefly as an advertising piece. This is supported by the appearance of his name, spelled out in full on the reverse, which commonly was done only with tradesmen's tokens. The obverse portrait is thought to have been intended as George Washington, which fails to resemble him only because of artistic inability. Not only the year but the month is stated and the day as well: JULY 4, 90. The whole appearance is crude and amateurish, but collectors treasure it.

TYPE OF COIN	ABP	G-4 GOOD	EF-40 EX. FINE
☐ 1790 Silver Threepence	1800.00	4250.00	12500.00

RHODE ISLAND TOKEN

The Rhode Island ship token has been variously classified as a coin, token, and medal, and its status is hardly clearer today than when research first began. Struck in 1778 or 1779 (the obverse carries one date, the reverse another), the piece is known in a variety of base metals: copper, brass, tin, and pewter, the composition having little influence on its value. That it was intended as a coin for ordinary circulation and exchange appears remote as it carries no mark of value and would have had to trade on the basis of weight. Being made of different metals, the weight varies and would have resulted in no small measure of confusion. The obverse shows a well-drawn ocean vessel. On the reverse is a complex scene representing the flight of Continental troops from Rhode Island. The inscriptions are in Dutch but the old belief that this production was of Dutch or Dutch-American origin is now given little support. Based upon the reverse theme it could well have been struck in England or by royalists in America. It should be kept in mind that the Revolutionary War had not yet ended in 1778–79 and coins or medals had a certain propaganda value. Reproductions are known to exist.

1778–1779 "VLUGTENDE"   1778–1779 WREATH

TYPE OF COIN	ABP	G-4 GOOD	EF-40 EX. FINE
☐ 1778–79 VLUGTENDE Below Ship		RARE	
☐ 1778–79 VLUGTENDE Removed	350.00	750.00	1500.00
☐ 1778–79 Wreath Below Ship	325.00	650.00	1350.00

1776 CONTINENTAL CURRENCY

The Continental dollar and its affiliates were struck as pattern pieces only, based upon the latest research, and never reached general circulation. They are believed to represent the first attempt at coinage by the Continental Congress, at any rate the first to achieve physical form. Upon declaring its independence from Britain, the United States was cut off from supplies of British currency and anticipated an extreme shortage within the coming months. Actually this shortage did not materialize to the degree feared. Continental currency is crown-size and struck in silver, pewter, and brass. Though the sizes are identical and the coins bear no indication of value, it is presumed the silver pieces were intended as dollars and the base metal varieties as divisions thereof. The exact history of their origin is not recorded, the documentation of it having apparently been swept away in the turbulent times of war. We know that the engraver bore the initials E.G. because he signed his work. An exhaustive search of goldsmiths, silversmiths, and other metalworkers active at that time, having the initials E.G., has led to the conclusion that the 1776 Continental currency was the work of Elisha Gallaudet of Philadelphia. If this is the case, they would undoubtedly have been struck in that city as well. Considering that it was headquarters of the Continental Congress, it seems to fit together historically. The legends include WE ARE ONE and MIND YOUR BUSINESS, the latter not, probably, having been directed toward the British but used merely as a piece of sage advice in the spirit of Ben Franklin. Copies exist, struck at the 1876 Centennial exposition.

1776
CURENCY
Brass, Pewter,
Silver

1776
CURRENCY
E. G. FECIT
Pewter, Silver

TYPE OF COIN	ABP	G-4 GOOD	EF-40 EX. FINE
☐ 1776 Currency, Brass		EXTREMELY RARE	
☐ 1776 Currency, Pewter	1500.00	3250.00	12000.00*
☐ 1776 Currency, Silver		EXTREMELY RARE	

*2000 Auction

TYPE OF COIN	ABP	G-4 GOOD	EF-40 EX. FINE
☐ 1776 Currency, E.G. FECIT, Pewter	800.00	1850.00	10000.00
☐ 1776 Currency, E.G. FECIT, Silver		EXTREMELY RARE	
☐ 1776 Currency, Pewter		EXTREMELY RARE	

NOVA CONSTELLATIO SILVER

These Nova Constellatio silvers are pattern pieces for a federal coinage, the first such pattern pieces of silver struck by the newly born government. They date from 1783, shortly after the War of Independence had been concluded. Supposedly the brainchild of Governor Morris, a signer of the Declaration of Independence and Assistant Financier of the Confederation, their designer was Benjamin Dudley. At this point the system of cents and dollars, later agreed upon, had not yet evolved; but there was no wish to continue use of the British pound standard. Morris evolved a currency system in which the chief denomination was a mark, consisting of 1,000 units. Division of this coin—also included among the Nova Constellatio patterns—were the quint, equal to 500 units or half a mark, and the bit, with a value of 100 units or a tenth of a mark. Further divisions could then supposedly be made of base metal, in fifty or ten units of whatever seemed practical. If we think of Morris' mark as the equivalent of the dollar (which in reality it was), then the 500 unit piece was the counterpart of 50¢ and the 100 unit piece of 10¢. Morris won little support for his currency proposals and the patterns were never approved for general circulation. Just one specimen is known to exist of each example; however, there are two types (and consequently two known specimens) of the 500-unit piece, one having an inscription on the obverse and the other bearing no inscription.

TYPE OF COIN

☐ 1783 MARK, 1000 Mills, Silver	ALL TYPES EXTREMELY RARE
☐ 1783 QUINT, 500 Mills, Silver	ALL TYPES EXTREMELY RARE
☐ 1783 QUINT, Second Variety, Silver	ALL TYPES EXTREMELY RARE
☐ 1783 Cent, 100 Mills, Silver	ALL TYPES EXTREMELY RARE
☐ 1783 "S" Copper	ALL TYPES EXTREMELY RARE

1783 QUINT

1783 MARK

1783 CENT

SECOND VARIETY

1783 QUINT

NOVA CONSTELLATIO COPPERS

Though their name and design are similar to the Nova Constellatio silver, it is important to note that these coins had quite different origins and purposes. The concept for both was that of Governor Morris, who, in addition to being a legislator, was also a prominent businessman in the late colonial/early federal age. While the silvers were pattern pieces for a proposed federal coinage, these coppers were struck as a personal speculative venture. It is quite likely that their place of origin was not America but Birmingham, England, and that their dies were engraved by an Englishman named Wyon. Upon importation to this country, Morris placed them into circulation as best he could. To judge from the fairly large quantities that exist of most types, their production must have reached the tens of thousands, if not higher.

CONSTELLATIO 1783 BLUNT RAYS

1785 CENT

TYPE OF COIN	ABP	G-4 GOOD	EF-40 EX. FINE
☐ 1783 Cent, CONSTELLATIO, Pointed Rays, Large U.S.	80.00	175.00	1000.00

TYPE OF COIN	ABP	G-4 GOOD	EF-40 EX. FINE
☐ 1783 Cent, CONSTELLATIO, Pointed Rays, Small U.S.	80.00	160.00	875.00
☐ 1783 Cent, CONSTELLATIO, Blunt Rays	60.00	125.00	950.00
☐ 1785 Cent, CONSTELLATIO, Blunt Rays	80.00	175.00	1000.00
☐ 1785 Cent, CONSTELLATIO, Pointed Rays	80.00	175.00	1000.00
☐ 1786 Cent, CONSTELLATIO, Pointed Rays		EXTREMELY RARE	

IMMUNE COLUMBIA

It is believed that these tokens, whose obverse designs are in some instances similar to those of the Nova Constellatio coppers, were struck from dies engraved by Thomas Wyon of Birmingham, England. Their history is otherwise shrouded in mystery. That they represent pattern pieces which did not actually circulate seems unquestionable, as they exist in extremely limited quantities. There are several varieties, chiefly in copper, but the piece does exist in silver. A single gold specimen, dated 1785, is included in the government's collection at Washington. It was obtained by trade with the collector Stickney, who accepted a duplicate 1804 silver dollar for it. A later version of the Immune Columbia token, date 1787, was struck from dies by James Atlee. Justice with scales is the reverse theme with a number of different obverses, including a portrait of the then not-too-popular George III.

OBVERSE 1785 IMMUNE COLUMBIA

1785 REVERSE "NOVA"

IMMUNIS COLUMBIA 1787

TYPE OF COIN	ABP	G-4 GOOD	EF-40 FINE
☐ 1785 Cent, Copper		EXTREMELY RARE	
☐ 1785 Cent, Silver		EXTREMELY RARE	
☐ 1785 Cent, Copper, Extra Star in Reverse		EXTREMELY RARE	

TYPE OF COIN	ABP	G-4 GOOD	EF-40 EX. FINE
☐ 1785 Cent, Copper, CONSTELLATIO, Blunt Rays		EXTREMELY RARE	
☐ 1785 Cent, VERMON AUCTORI	1100.00	2000.00	6250.00
☐ 1785 Cent, GEORGE III, Obverse	1000.00	1800.00	6000.00
☐ 1787 IMMUNIS COLUMBIA	1000.00	1800.00	5000.00

CONFEDERATIO

The Confederatio cent, also known as Confederatio copper, is a hybrid coin found with various obverse and reverse designs. Regardless of the designs these are all pattern pieces that never reached circulation and all are extremely rare. Identity of the die-cutters is not known but it is believed that at least some were the work of Thomas Wyon of Birmingham, England, and undoubtedly they were struck abroad. One of the obverse motifs features George Washington.

1785 CENT   1785 WASHINGTON

TYPE OF COIN	ABP	G-4 GOOD	EF-40 EX. FINE
☐ 1785 Cent, Stars in Small Circle		12000.00	20000.00
☐ 1785 Cent, Stars in Large Circle		10000.00	18000.00
☐ 1785 Cent, George Washington		EXTREMELY RARE	

SPECIMEN PATTERNS

A number of copper pattern pieces were struck in or about 1786 for possible use as token currency. Their history is not well established and all are extremely rare. The shield design and E PLURIBUS UNUM inscription on the reverse of some were subsequently used on New Jersey tokens, but the following patterns cannot be classified as belonging to any given locality.

TYPE OF COIN

☐ 1786 IMMUNIS COLUMBIA, Shield Reverse   EXTREMELY RARE
☐ 1786 IMMUNIS COLUMBIA, Eagle Reverse   EXTREMELY RARE
☐ 1786 Eagle on Obverse   EXTREMELY RARE
☐ 1786 Washington/Eagle   EXTREMELY RARE
☐ Undated, Washington Obverse   EXTREMELY RARE

NORTH AMERICAN TOKEN

This is a private piece, one of a number issued following the Revolution, that circulated in this country. Its origin is Irish, having been struck in Dublin. Undoubtedly it represented the effort of an Irish merchant or metalsmith to take advantage of America's coin shortage. The date shown is 1781 but belief is strong that it was actually produced at some later time, possibly in the late 1790s or early 1800s. The United States was experiencing a coin shortage during the presidency of Thomas Jefferson, so it could well date from that era. This situation was well known abroad, as foreigners melting down our coinage were chiefly responsible. On the obverse it pictures a sailing ship with the word COMMERCE and a seated likeness of Hibernia (symbol of Ireland) with her harp on the reverse, inscribed NORTH AMERICAN TOKEN. It may well be that the side of this token traditionally regarded as the obverse was intended as the reverse. Quantities in which the North American token were distributed in the United States are not known. The piece is far from rare. Its size is roughly equivalent to a quarter.

TYPE OF COIN	ABP	G-4 GOOD	EF-40 EX. FINE
☐ 1781 Token	80.00	150.00	675.00

MACHIN COPPERS

Thomas Machin operated a copper mill at Newburgh, New York. From 1786 to 1789 he was active in the production of tokens, some designed for use in the State of New York (*which see*) and others that were nothing but counterfeits of the British copper halfpenny. He attempted to profit by placing these counterfeits, of lighter than standard weight, into immense circulation. To avoid suspicion he used a variety of dates, going back as far as 1747. But the majority are dated in the early 1770s. The design is always the same: a portrait of the king on the obverse with Britannia on the reverse. As these pieces are not collected by date, their values are constant irrespective of date. They can easily be distinguished from genuine British halfpennies by their cruder die engraving. However, the Machin fakes were not the only ones made of this coin.

TYPE OF COIN	ABP	G-4 GOOD	EF-40 EX. FINE
☐ Halfpenny, various dates	85.00	175.00	2500.00

GEORGIUS TRIUMPHO TOKEN

This controversial coin, dating from 1783, is made of copper. On the obverse is a male portrait in profile with the inscription GEORGIUS TRIUMPHO, which cannot be translated in any other fashion but "George Has Triumphed." Considering that the War for Independence had recently ended with an American victory, the triumphal George should be Washington. But the portrait much more closely resembles George III, the British monarch who sought to preserve American colonization. Just how this George could be regarded to have triumphed at that moment is puzzling. Perhaps the explanation is that Washington was intended but the engraver, being unskilled and having no likeness at hand from which to copy, merely fashioned the portrait after that on English money. A similar situation prevailed at the time among illustrators who designed copperplate portraits for books, the likeness often being guessed at. As photography did not exist and few citizens actually saw celebrities in the flesh, it was not really known if such works were accurate. The reverse pictures Liberty holding an olive branch, and thirteen bars representing the confederation. Its inscription is VOCE POPOLI, an error for "Voce Populi" or "Voice of the People."

TYPE OF COIN	ABP	G-4 GOOD	EF-40 EX. FINE
☐ 1783 GEORGIUS TRIUMPHO	75.00	150.00	1000.00

AUCTORI PLEBIS TOKEN

Not much is known of this copper piece, other than the fact that it closely resembles the early coinage of Connecticut. It is thought to have been struck in England and may never have been intended for American circulation. It has, however, traditionally been included in American colonial and federal-era collections. It bears a date of 1787 and carries a male portrait profile on the obverse with a seated figure of Liberty on the reverse. The workmanship is not especially skilled.

TYPE OF COIN	ABP	G-4 GOOD	EF-40 EX. FINE
☐ 1787 AUCTORI PLEBIS Token	65.00	150.00	1000.00

MOTT TOKEN

An early trade token, this piece had no official sanction nor any legal value as money. Its issuers were William and John Mott, who operated a business on Water Street in the downtown area of Manhattan. Mott Street, now the central boulevard of New York's Chinatown, was named for this family. The Mott token is of copper, picturing on one side the American eagle emblem and (quite unusual) a shelf clock on the other. The clock served an advertising purpose, as the Motts dealt in goldware, silverware, and fancy goods including importations. This token dates from 1789. Of too high a quality for local production, it seems evident they were manufactured in England.

TYPE OF COIN	ABP	G-4 GOOD	EF-40 EX. FINE
☐ 1789 Mott Token, Thick Planchet	60.00	100.00	900.00
☐ 1789 Mott Token, Thin Planchet	75.00	150.00	1200.00
☐ 1789 Mott Token, Engrailed Edge	150.00	300.00	2000.00

BAR CENT

The Bar cent is a very simply designed coin whose name derives from the fact that its reverse design is composed of a grid containing thirteen bars (one for each state of the confederation). On the obverse are the letters USA in large size, intertwined. Beyond this there is no further ornament or inscription and the origin of this piece has proven a dilemma. It is almost surely a foreign product, made possibly by Wyon (of Nova Constellatio copper fame) of Birmingham, England. Its first public appearance was made in New York in late 1785. It may be presumed that the date of minting was either that year or possibly 1784. Reproductions, against which collectors are cautioned, were produced during the Civil War.

TYPE OF COIN	ABP	G-4 GOOD	EF-40 EX. FINE
☐ Undated, Bar Cent	375.00	600.00	3500.00

TALBOT, ALLUM, AND LEE CENTS

These are trade tokens, circulated by a firm of importers known as Talbot, Allum, and Lee, who were headquartered at 241 Pearl Street, New York, in what is now the financial district but then was given over largely to import/export because of its access to the Battery docks. There is no question but that they were struck in England. The corporation's name appears on one side, sometimes with and sometimes without its place of location. The earliest date is 1794 and at this point they carried a value legend of ONE CENT. In 1794 this was removed, possibly out of fear of government protest, and an inscription added to the edge: WE PROMISE TO PAY THE BEARER ONE CENT. There are, however, specimens of the 1795 edition with unlettered edge, which are considerably scarcer. This practice of issuing tokens redeemable at a certain place of business became widespread in the 19th century, especially during the small-change shortage of the Civil War.

1794 NEW YORK   1795 CENT

TYPE OF COIN	ABP	G-4 GOOD	EF-40 EX. FINE
☐ 1794 Cent, With NEW YORK	60.00	120.00	600.00
☐ 1794 Cent, Without NEW YORK	275.00	500.00	3500.00
☐ 1795 Cent	60.00	120.00	500.00

GEORGE WASHINGTON PIECES

Following the Revolution, George Washington became a national hero and idol to such a degree that he was virtually worshipped. Books were written on his life, engravers published pictures of him, and his likeness was set into snuff boxes, jewelry cases, and other fancy goods. It is only natural that Washington would also be the subject of numerous tokens and pseudocoins. These were issued beginning in 1783 and (for practical purposes) ceased about 1795, after official federal coinage began circulating. No exact date can be placed on their discontinuance, however, as tokens and medals honoring Washington appeared from time to time thereafter.

Those in the following listing are not strictly classed as commemoratives but might just as well be. They were primarily coppers and contained a cent's worth of that metal. They could, therefore, be used as money, but the extent to which this was done is not known and can be presumed to have been limited, as none were struck in large quantities. The best title for them might be "celebration pieces."

Building a complete collection is outside the realm of possibility because of the extreme scarcity of some issues. A fair assembly of them can, however, be made. Their origins are not well established. Some are believed to have been designed and struck in England. This would seem logical on the basis of workmanship. Those made abroad were surely not designed for circulation there, but for export and distribution within the United States. One of the Washington tokens—in half penny value—declares itself a Welsh product; it carries the inscription NORTH WALES on the reverse. Another was a London tradesman's token. As for their dates, the presumption is that some, at least, were struck subsequent to the year indicated, perhaps in the first decade of the 19th century or even later.

Most have distinctive reverses and are known chiefly by these reverse types. So far as the portraiture is concerned, there is a rich and interesting variety, differing not only in artistic quality but concept. On some, Washington is shown as a Roman-style emperor, wearing a laurel wreath. The majority portray him in military dress. Though a few coins of amateurish design are included in this group there are likewise several of the most skilled and impressive workmanship, which, if executed as sculptures, would be regarded as important works of art. The likelihood that Washington sat for any of the die-cutters is remote, but apparently they either had prior experience drawing or sculpting him or worked from some of the better oil pictures, such as those of Stuart. They could not have achieved such faithful portraiture merely from descriptions of his physical appearance.

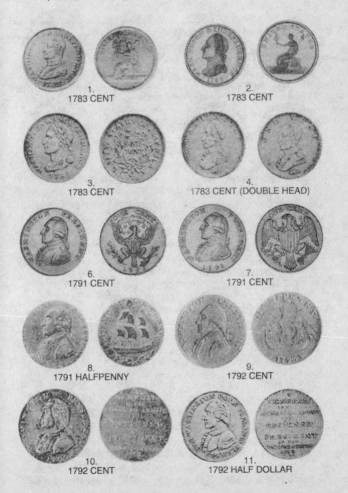

1.
1783 CENT

2.
1783 CENT

3.
1783 CENT

4.
1783 CENT (DOUBLE HEAD)

6.
1791 CENT

7.
1791 CENT

8.
1791 HALFPENNY

9.
1792 CENT

10.
1792 CENT

11.
1792 HALF DOLLAR

12.
1792 ROMAN HEAD

13.
1792 EAGLE

14.
1793 HALFPENNY

15.
1795 HALFPENNY

16.
1795 PENNY

17.
1795 HALFPENNY

18.
TOKEN

19.
TOKEN

20.
TOKEN

TYPE OF COIN	ABP	G-4 GOOD	EF-40 EX. FINE
☐ 1. 1783 Cent, Large Military Bust	60.00	120.00	425.00
☐ 1a. 1783 Cent, Small Military Bust (Not illus.)			
	60.00	120.00	500.00
☐ 1b. 1783 Cent, Small Military Bust, Engraved Edge (Not illus.)			
	55.00	110.00	600.00
☐ 2. 1783 Cent, Draped Bust	85.00	160.00	500.00

TYPE OF COIN	ABP	G-4 GOOD	EF-40 EX. FINE
☐ 2a. 1783 Cent, Draped Bust, Button on Cloak (Not illus.)			
	75.00	120.00	850.00
☐ 2b. 1783 Cent, Draped Bust (Not illus.)			
	ALL TYPES EXTREMELY RARE		
☐ 3. 1783 Cent, Draped Bust, UNITY STATES			
	55.00	100.00	450.00
☐ 4. 1783 Cent, Undated, Double Head	55.00	100.00	450.00
☐ 5. 1784 Ugly Head		EXTREMELY RARE	
☐ 6. 1791 Cent, Small Eagle	110.00	200.00	800.00
☐ 7. 1791 Cent, Large Eagle	110.00	200.00	700.00
☐ 8. 1791 Liverpool Halfpenny	325.00	600.00	3250.00
☐ 9. 1792 Cent, WASHINGTON PRESIDENT	1000.00	2000.00	8000.00
☐ 10. 1792 Cent, BORN VIRGINIA	650.00	1500.00	6000.00
☐ 11. 1792 Silver		EXTREMELY RARE	
☐ 11a. 1792 Copper		EXTREMELY RARE	
☐ 11b. 1792 Large Eagle		EXTREMELY RARE	
☐ 12. 1792 Roman Head		EXTREMELY RARE	
☐ 13. 1792 Eagle With Stars, Copper		EXTREMELY RARE	
☐ 13a. 1792 Eagle With Stars, Silver		EXTREMELY RARE	
☐ 13b. 1792 Eagle With Stars, Gold		EXTREMELY RARE	
☐ 14. 1793 Ship Halfpenny	80.00	200.00	1000.00
☐ 15. 1795 Halfpenny, Reeded Edge, GRATE, Small Buttons			
	75.00	125.00	500.00
☐ 15a. 1795 Halfpenny, Reeded Edge, GRATE, Large Buttons			
	75.00	125.00	500.00
☐ 15b. 1795 Halfpenny, Lettered Edge, GRATE, Large Buttons			
	175.00	350.00	850.00
☐ 16. 1795 Penny, Undated, LIBERTY AND SECURITY			
	60.00	100.00	700.00
☐ 17. 1795 Halfpenny, Dated, LIBERTY AND SECURITY, London			
	50.00	100.00	600.00
☐ 17a. 1795 Halfpenny, LIBERTY AND SECURITY, Birmingham			
	50.00	100.00	600.00
☐ 17b. 1795 Halfpenny, Dated, LIBERTY AND SECURITY, Asylum			
	100.00	275.00	1400.00
☐ 17c. 1795 Halfpenny, Dated, LIBERTY AND SECURITY, Plain Edge			
	40.00	65.00	500.00
☐ 18. Success Token, Small	50.00	100.00	1100.00
☐ 19. 1795 Halfpenny, NORTH WALES	80.00	150.00	800.00
☐ 20. Success Token, Large	120.00	200.00	875.00

FRANKLIN PRESS TOKEN

This copper token was struck in England as a merchant piece and its use apparently restricted there. Because of its connection with Benjamin Franklin it has interest for collectors of American coinage. The obverse pictures an old-fashioned screw press (driven by jerking a lever), with the words PAYABLE AT THE FRANKLIN PRESS LONDON on the opposite side. It carries a date of 1794. As Franklin died in 1790 he could not have seen this token. Reproductions exist.

TYPE OF COIN	ABP	G-4 GOOD	EF-40 EX. FINE
☐ 1794 Token	75.00	135.00	450.00

CASTORLAND

Royalists who fled France following the revolution's outbreak in 1791 scattered to many parts of the globe. A small colony settled in the New York State farmlands (near Carthage) and called the locality Castorland. The Castorland medal or token is said to be a pattern piece struck in France for a proposed currency. It never reached beyond the experimental stage and both varieties, in silver and copper, are extremely rare. They carry a date of 1796.

TYPE OF COIN

☐ 1796 Silver Original, Reeded Edge   EXTREMELY RARE

FUGIO CENTS

The Fugio cents, so called because that word is a component in the obverse inscription, were the first officially sanctioned U.S. federal coinage. It was resolved by Congress in 1787 that a contract be put out with a private miller, James Jarvis, for 300 tons of copper coins. The arrangement was for Jarvis to secure the metal himself and pay all expenses, then sell the coins to the government at face value—his profit arising from the difference between his cost and the total face value. It was a venture of enormous proportions, considering that the United States had not previously authorized any coins. The matter of designing was not left to the contractor. Congress specifically spelled out what these coins should look like: "thirteen circles linked together, a small circle in the middle with the words 'United States' around it, and in the center the words 'We are one'; on the other side of the same piece the following device, viz: a dial with the hours expressed on the face of it; a meridian sun above on one side of which is the word 'Fugio.'" *Fugio* is Latin for "flees." As the obverse carries the saying "Mind Your Business," often attributed to Benjamin Franklin, this is sometimes called the Franklin cent; such terminology is, however, misleading and confusing. The dies were produced by Abel Buel of New Haven, Connecticut, and most of the striking was apparently carried out in that city. Jarvis failed to deliver the agreed-on number of coins, was prosecuted for breach of contract, and imprisoned.

1787 CENT

TYPE OF COIN	ABP	G-4 GOOD	EF-40 EX. FINE
☐ 1787 Cent, Club Rays, Rounded Ends	325.00	600.00	2000.00
☐ 1787 Cent, Club Rays, Concave Ends, FUCIO (Not illus.)	1100.00	2400.00	10000.00

TYPE OF COIN	ABP	G-4 GOOD	EF-40 EX. FINE
☐ 1787 Cent, Club Rays, Concave Ends, FUGIO	1200.00	2600.00	10000.00
☐ 1787 Cent, Club Rays, STATES UNITED	EXTREMELY RARE		
☐ 1787 Cent, Pointed Rays, UNITED above, STATES below	EXTREMELY RARE		
☐ 1787 Cent, Pointed Rays, UNITED STATES at side of circle (Not illus.)	95.00	205.00	1200.00
☐ 1787 Cent, Pointed Rays, STATES UNITED at side of circle; Cinquefoils	100.00	200.00	1200.00
☐ 1787 Cent, Pointed Rays, STATES UNITED at sides, 8-pointed star on reverse band (Not illus.)	110.00	225.00	2000.00
☐ 1787 Cent, Pointed Rays, STATES UNITED, raised edge on reverse band	115.00	200.00	700.00
☐ 1787 Cents, Pointed Rays, UNITED STATES, No Cinquefoils	110.00	225.00	3500.00
☐ 1787 Cent, Pointed Rays, STATES UNITED, No Cinquefoils	220.00	450.00	3500.00
☐ 1787 Cent, AMERICAN CONGRESS, With Rays (Not illus.)	EXTREMELY RARE		

NEW HAVEN RESTRIKES

In 1858, C. Wyllys Betts found three sets of dies in New Haven. Restrikes in various metals were made. The restrikes were not made directly from these dies but copies fashioned from them.

1787 CENT

TYPE OF COIN	ABP	G-4 GOOD	EF-40 EX. FINE
☐ Copper	110.00	225.00	600.00
☐ Silver	175.00	375.00	1500.00
☐ Brass	100.00	200.00	600.00
☐ Gold		EXTREMELY RARE	

FIRST UNITED STATES OF AMERICA MINT ISSUES

1792 BIRCH CENT

The 1792 Birch cent was the first coin to be struck at the newly established U.S. Mint in Philadelphia and the first governmental issue struck by the government as opposed to private contractors. This coin was not circulated but produced as a trial piece only. Along with it were also trial or pattern pieces of half disme, disme, and quarter dollar denominations, all of which are extremely rare. A motion is said to have been made for placing George Washington's likeness on these pieces but that Washington, when informed of this plan, declined to be honored in such a manner. It was then decided to use a portrait of the Goddess of Liberty. The better-known version of the Birch cent is large in size and composed entirely of copper. A smaller cent was also produced, containing a droplet of silver at the center. This was done entirely as an experiment to determine whether a penny coin in small size might be publicly more acceptable than one made exclusively of base metal. The pattern quarter dollar has more the appearance of a medal than a coin. The Birch cent derives its name from Robert Birch, its designer. Birch is thought also to have been among the die-cutters for the half disme and disme.

TYPE OF COIN

☐ 1792 Disme (Silver)
☐ 1792 Disme (Copper)
☐ 1792 Half Disme (Silver)
☐ 1792 Birch Cent (Copper)

ALL COINS ARE RARE,
VERY RARE, OR UNIQUE

1792 BIRCH CENT

1792 HALF DISME

1792 HALF DISME

TYPE OF COIN

☐ 1792 Birch Cent (White Metal)   EXTREMELY RARE
☐ 1792 Quarter Dollar (Pattern, Copper)   EXTREMELY RARE
☐ 1792 Quarter Dollar (Pattern, White Metal)   EXTREMELY RARE

1792 SILVER CENTER CENT

TYPE OF COIN

☐ 1792 Silver Center Cent   ALL COINS ARE VERY RARE
☐ 1792 Cent, No Silver Center   OR UNIQUE

HALF CENTS, 1793–1857

That the lowly half cent survived into the second half of the 19th century is looked upon as remarkable today by persons not well acquainted with the economic conditions of that time. Despite its minute face value, and the grumblings of many citizens that it did little but clutter their pockets, it served an important function in trade. Many articles in shops were priced fractionally and, without the half cent, difficulty would have been encountered in making change for such purchases. Their availability was, however, frequently abused. Merchants, anxious to rid themselves of half cents, would often give them instead of pennies. As first introduced in 1793, the coin bore a portrait of Liberty facing left on its obverse and a wreathed reverse with the words HALF CENT and UNITED STATES OF AMERICA. The designer was Adam Eckfeldt. The original weight was 6.74 grams and the composition pure copper. The coin has a diameter of 22mm. and is stamped along the edge TWO HUNDRED FOR A DOLLAR. After being struck for a single year it was decided to redesign the coin (coin redesigning occurred frequently in the Mint's early days of operation), the new design being the work of Robert Scot. Liberty was switched round to face right, her features streamlined, and her cap (the "cap of liberty," a reference to caps worn by freed slaves in Roman times) enlarged. The reverse was restyled but not materially altered. Planchets were of the same weight but slightly larger physically, measuring $23^{1}/_{2}$mm. Another fresh version was placed into use in 1795, this one the work of John S. Gardner; its specifications were the same as its predecessor's. It was later concluded that the weight had been set too high. This ushered in the so-called "thin planchet" half cent, weighing 5.44 grams and still measuring 23.5mm. TWO HUNDRED FOR A DOLLAR was removed from the edge. The varieties of this Liberty Cap half cent are numerous, despite the brief period of its manufacture.

The Liberty Cap half cent was followed in 1800 by introduction of the Draped Bust design, after a period of two years in which coins of this denomination were not minted (they could hardly have been in short supply, as well over 200,000 had been circulated). Liberty's cap was removed and her hairstyle made somewhat more fashionable. The portrait was lengthened somewhat to include a suggestion of shoulders, over which a classical-style garment was placed. The designer was Robert Scot, who had done the 1794 version. Specifications remained the same as before. It was resolved to get these coins into very extensive circulation, resulting in a mintage quantity of more than one million in the year 1804 alone. By the end of 1808, the last year for this design, more than three million had been struck. The new half cent was the so-called Classic Head variety, designed by John Reich. Apparently this title was bestowed in the belief that Reich's Liberty more closely approximated Grecian sculpture than had the other types. The face, if stronger, became less physically attractive and more masculine. Stars were set at either side of the portrait and Liberty was given a band round her head with her name imprinted on it. The next design, and the last, was introduced in 1840 but used for proofs only, as the half cent did not return to general circulation until 1849. Christian Gobrecht was the designer and his rendition of Liberty has come to be known as the Braided Hair type. A sharp departure from the Reich approach, it pictured Liberty with a Roman nose and considerable loss of bulk. This could well be considered the most attractive design, portrait-wise, of the half-cent series.

HALF CENTS—LIBERTY CAP, 1793–1797

1793   1794 Pole to Cap

DATE	ABP	G-4 GOOD	F-12 FINE	VF-20 V. FINE
☐ 1793 Facing Left (34,534)				
	1100.00	1500.00	3500.00	5200.00
☐ 1794 Facing Right (81,600)				
	225.00	295.00	900.00	1400.00
☐ 1795 Plain Edge	175.00	225.00	650.00	1800.00
☐ 1795 Lettered Edge (125,600)				
	200.00	250.00	625.00	1250.00
☐ 1796 With Pole (5,090)	6000.00	8000.00	15000.00	22000.00
☐ 1796 No Pole			EXTREMELY RARE	
☐ 1797 Plain Edge	225.00	275.00	800.00	2000.00
☐ 1797 Lettered Edge (122,214)				
	650.00	1850.00	4000.00	7000.00
☐ 1797 1 Above 1	200.00	250.00	575.00	10000.00

HALF CENTS—DRAPED BUST, 1800–1808

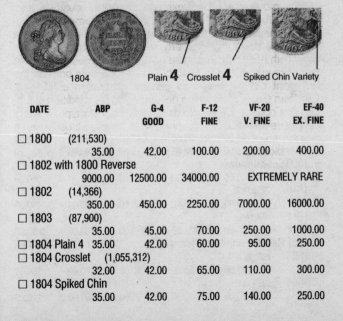

1804   Plain **4**   Crosslet **4**   Spiked Chin Variety

DATE	ABP	G-4 GOOD	F-12 FINE	VF-20 V. FINE	EF-40 EX. FINE
☐ 1800 (211,530)					
	35.00	42.00	100.00	200.00	400.00
☐ 1802 with 1800 Reverse					
	9000.00	12500.00	34000.00	EXTREMELY RARE	
☐ 1802 (14,366)					
	350.00	450.00	2250.00	7000.00	16000.00
☐ 1803 (87,900)					
	35.00	45.00	70.00	250.00	1000.00
☐ 1804 Plain 4	35.00	42.00	60.00	95.00	250.00
☐ 1804 Crosslet (1,055,312)					
	32.00	42.00	65.00	110.00	300.00
☐ 1804 Spiked Chin					
	35.00	42.00	75.00	140.00	250.00

DATE	ABP	G-4 GOOD	F-12 FINE	VF-20 V. FINE	EF-40 EX. FINE
☐ 1805 Small 5					
	375.00	600.00	2200.00	3250.00	7000.00
☐ 1805 Large 5 (814,464)					
	35.00	42.00	62.00	95.00	225.00
☐ 1806 (356,000)					
	32.00	40.00	70.00	100.00	250.00
☐ 1806 Small 6, Stems					
	125.00	185.00	600.00	1100.00	2200.00
☐ 1807 (476,000)					
	32.00	40.00	55.00	110.00	350.00
☐ 1808 (400,000)					
	30.00	38.00	70.00	1500.00	400.00
☐ 1808 Over 7	75.00	150.00	550.00	950.00	3200.00

HALF CENTS—TURBAN HEAD, 1809–1837

1837   1837 TOKEN

DATE	ABP	G-4 GOOD	F-12 FINE	VF-20 V. FINE	EF-40 EX. FINE
☐ 1809 (1,154,572)					
	25.00	30.00	48.00	65.00	140.00
☐ 1809 Over 6	25.00	32.00	75.00	90.00	175.00
☐ 1809 Circle Inside O					
	25.00	34.00	70.00	100.00	300.00
☐ 1810 (215,000)					
	25.00	36.00	80.00	180.00	400.00
☐ 1811 (63,140)					
	100.00	125.00	500.00	1150.00	4000.00
☐ 1811 Restrike with 1802 Reverse				EXTREMELY RARE	
☐ 1825 (63,000)					
	25.00	30.00	50.00	70.00	130.00
☐ 1826 (234,000)					
	25.00	30.00	45.00	60.00	110.00

DATE	ABP	G-4 GOOD	F-12 FINE	VF-20 V. FINE	EF-40 EX. FINE
☐ 1828 12 Stars (606,000)					
	25.00	32.00	45.00	80.00	170.00
☐ 1828 13 Stars	25.00	30.00	45.00	55.00	76.00
☐ 1829 (487,000)					
	25.00	30.00	45.00	62.00	98.00
☐ 1831, 8 Known (2,200)					
		Business	Strikes	Original	100000.00
☐ 1831 Small Berries	Proof Only		Restrike		100000.00
☐ 1831 Large Berries	Proof Only		Restrike		105000.00
☐ 1832 (154,000)					
	25.00	30.00	45.00	58.00	72.00
☐ 1833 (120,000)					
	25.00	30.00	45.00	58.00	72.00
☐ 1834 (141,000)					
	25.00	30.00	45.00	58.00	72.00
☐ 1835 (398,000)					
	25.00	30.00	46.00	55.00	72.00
☐ 1836	Proof Only	Original	18000.00	Restrike	10000.00
☐ 1837 Token, Pure Copper					
	30.00	35.00	50.00	110.00	150.00

HALF CENTS—BRAIDED HAIR, 1840–1857

DATE		ABP		PRF-65 PROOF
☐ 1840		7000.00	Proof Only	8600.00
☐ 1841		7000.00	Proof Only	8600.00
☐ 1842	ORIGINAL	7000.00	Proof Only	8600.00
☐ 1843	AND RESTRIKE	7000.00	Proof Only	8600.00
☐ 1844	PROOFS ONLY	7000.00	Proof Only	8600.00

DATE			ABP		PRF-65 PROOF
☐ 1845	1840–49		7000.00	Proof Only	8600.00
☐ 1846	NO MINTAGE		7000.00	Proof Only	8600.00
☐ 1847	RECORDS		7000.00	Proof Only	8600.00
☐ 1848			7000.00	Proof Only	8600.00
☐ 1849			7000.00	Proof Only	8600.00

DATE	ABP	G-4 GOOD	F-12 FINE	VF-20 V. FINE	EF-40 EX. FINE
☐ 1849	(39,864)				
	30.00	36.00	55.00	70.00	100.00
☐ 1850	(39,812)				
	25.00	32.00	55.00	66.00	115.00
☐ 1851	(147,672)				
	23.00	30.00	45.00	54.00	74.00
☐ 1852		Proofs Only—Original and Restrike: $9000.00			
☐ 1853	(129,964)				
	23.00	30.00	45.00	55.00	75.00
☐ 1854	(55,358)				
	23.00	30.00	45.00	55.00	75.00
☐ 1855	(56,500)				
	25.00	30.00	45.00	55.00	75.00
☐ 1856	(40,430)				
	23.00	30.00	45.00	80.00	85.00
☐ 1857	(35,180)				
	38.00	42.00	68.00	85.00	125.00

LARGE CENTS, 1793–1857

The shrinkage of the cent from its introduction in 1793 to its present size is ample evidence of inflation; the present Lincoln cent weighs only about one-third as much as its distant ancestor. But what the penny has lost in bulk and buying power has been compensated for, at least in part, by its greater convenience. The series began with the Flowing Hair/Chain Reverse type designed by Henry Voight. Its weight was set at 13.48 grams of pure copper, precisely twice that of the half cent. (The government set rigid standards of weight, fearing that without such regulations its coinage would not inspire confidence.) There were no long suspensions of production, as with the half cent. A quantity—varying, of course, in number—was minted each year from the coin's inception until conclusion of the Large Cent in 1857, with the single exception of 1815 because of a metal shortage.

The first design, aptly named Liberty, is shown with billowing hair that appears breeze-blown. Her features are delicate and the overall composition is pleasing. It will be noted that the reverse design bears very close resemblance to the Fugio cent or Franklin cent, struck in 1787. The diameter of this coin varies from 26–27mm. It is consequently not very much smaller than the present fifty-cent piece.

After three months of striking coins from these dies, during which time more than 36,000 were produced, a new design was introduced. The work of Adam Eckfeldt, designer of the first half cent, it retained the Flowing Hair portrait on the obverse but employed a wreath rather than the chained reverse, enclosing the words ONE CENT. Its weight was unchanged but the diameter varies from 26–28mm. or slightly larger than its predecessor. Along the edge is stamped the inscription ONE HUNDRED FOR A DOLLAR.

This design got somewhat further, resulting in a mintage of more than 60,000 pieces, but before the year was out another had taken its place. The Flowing Hair portrait, subjected to criticism in the press (to which the government seems to have been more sensitive than subsequently), was removed in favor of a Liberty Cap type, designed by Joseph Wright. Here the bust of Liberty is positioned somewhat to the right of center; over her left shoulder she balances a staff, on the tip of which rests a conical-shaped cap—the "cap of liberty," symbolic of freedom from slavery in Roman times. This version, too, was assailed, but minters were so weary of making alterations that they continued using it until 1796. The staff and cap looked like an Indian arrow in the opinion of some; others fancied that Liberty was wearing an oversized bow in her hair. The weight was retained but the planchet grew slightly larger, to 29mm.

In 1795, still using the same design, the weight was dropped to 10.89 grams, diameter remained 29mm., and new dies were engraved. The artist was John S. Gardner. His work is often said to be superior to other efforts. The Draped Bust type, first struck in mid-1796, was an effort to render more classicism to the portrait. Designed by Robert Scot, it deleted the much-maligned liberty cap and, while not materially altering Miss Liberty's facial features, gave her the appearance of chubbiness. Specifications remained as previously.

In 1808 the so-called Classic Head made its bow, designed by John Reich. Here Liberty wears a coronet with the word LIBERTY spelled out upon it and the bust is shortened with drapery removed. She grows chubbier still. The reverse is very close to that of a modern "wheat" cent: the words ONE CENT encircled in laurel, surrounded by the legend UNITED STATES OF AMERICA. There are numerous varieties, as enumerated in the listing that follows. The classic head survived until the copper shortage, which followed close upon the heels of the War of 1812, when production of Large Cents was temporarily halted. When resumed in 1816 the design was new. The work of Robert Scot, it was referred to as Matron Head, as Liberty appears to have taken on added years. She, in fact, was growing old with her coinage. A youth in 1792 when the series began, she had now advanced into middle age. The bust is shortened even further; stars now totally encircle it (except for the space containing the date), but the reverse remains the same.

In 1837 the last Large Cent design was put into production. The next two decades yielded many varieties of it, from die re-engravings. This is the Gobrecht version, basically a handsome portrait which returns the youthful goddess image to Liberty and slims her down. The weight was 10.89 grams (the penny was never to return to its old weight-standard), the diameter $27\frac{1}{2}$mm. Chief variations are the Silly Head and Booby Head, neither of which really merited such ridicule. There was also a Petite Head and Mature Head and ample differences in letter and numeral sizes.

LARGE CENTS—FLOWING HAIR, 1793

1793 Chain   1793 Wreath

DATE	ABP	G-4 GOOD	VG-8 V. GOOD	F-12 FINE	VF-20 V. FINE
☐ 1793 Chain AMERI	(36,103)				
	2850.00	3350.00	5000.00	6750.00	10000.00
☐ 1793 Chain AMERICA					
	2250.00	2750.00	4000.00	5400.00	9500.00
☐ 1793 Chain Type, Period after Date and LIBERTY					
	2350.00	2850.00	4750.00	7000.00	10000.00
☐ 1793 Wreath Type, Edge Has Vine and Bars		(63,353)			
	750.00	950.00	1350.00	2600.00	3850.00
☐ 1793 Wreath Type, Lettered Edge, 1 Leaf on Edge					
	800.00	1000.00	1500.00	2750.00	4000.00
☐ 1793 Wreath Type, Lettered Edge, Double Leaf on Edge					
					EXTREMELY RARE

LARGE CENTS—LIBERTY CAP, 1793–1796

1793 LIBERTY CAP   1795 JEFFERSON HEAD

ONE CENT
in Center of Wreath

ONE CENT
High in Wreath

DATE	ABP	G-4 GOOD	VG-8 V. GOOD	F-12 FINE	VF-20 V. FINE
☐ 1793 (11,056)					
	1400.00	2000.00	4000.00	5850.00	15000.00
☐ 1794	125.00	150.00	250.00	435.00	875.00
ALL KINDS					
☐ 1794*	700.00	1000.00	1850.00	3800.00	7600.00
☐ 1794**	135.00	170.00	260.00	450.00	800.00
☐ 1794*** (918,521)					
	140.00	165.00	250.00	385.00	850.00
☐ 1794****	6000.00	9000.00	17500.00	30000.00	42000.00
☐ 1795 Jefferson Head					
	3500.00	6800.00	12000.00	16000.00	34000.00

*Head of 1793 **Head of 1795 ***No Fraction Bar ****Stars on Back

☐1795† Lettered Edge*					
	165.00	200.00	350.00	700.00	1200.00
☐ 1795† Lettered Edge**					
	165.00	200.00	325.00	725.00	1200.00
☐ 1795†† Plain Edge*					
	160.00	190.00	250.00	375.00	775.00
☐ 1795†† Plain Edge**					
	145.00	175.00	240.00	410.00	750.00
☐ 1796††† Liberty Cap					
	165.00	210.00	300.00	650.00	1500.00

†Total Mintage: 82,000 ††Total Mintage: 456,500 †††Total Mintage: 109,825
*ONE CENT in Center of Wreath **ONE CENT High in Wreath

LARGE CENTS—DRAPED BUST, 1796–1800

Gripped or
Milled Edge ←

LIHERTY 1796 (error)

DATE	ABP	G-4 GOOD	VG-8 V. GOOD	F-12 FINE	VF-20 V. FINE
☐ 1796††	80.00	110.00	200.00	350.00	950.00
☐ 1796†† LIHERTY (error)	140.00	210.00	500.00	1000.00	2000.00
☐ 1796 † Stems on Wreath	70.00	70.00	150.00	250.00	900.00
☐ 1797†† Stemless Wreath	75.00	125.00	280.00	500.00	900.00
☐ 1797†† Stems on Wreath	55.00	70.00	120.00	240.00	400.00
☐ 1797†† Gripped	70.00	85.00	160.00	300.00	750.00
☐ 1797†† Plain Edge	70.00	80.00	200.00	350.00	750.00
☐ 1798††† over 97	85.00	110.00	175.00	300.00	950.00
☐ 1798††† Small Date	32.00	40.00	70.00	125.00	410.00
☐ 1798††† Large Date	32.00	38.00	65.00	130.00	330.00
☐ 1798†††*	50.00	75.00	150.00	325.00	875.00
☐ 1799* over 98	1000.00	1250.00	2350.00	5500.00	15000.00
☐ 1799** Normal Date	900.00	1150.00	2150.00	7000.00	13500.00
☐ 1800*** over 1798	35.00	45.00	75.00	210.00	550.00

†Total Mintage: 363,372 ††Total Mintage: 897,509 †††Total Mintage: 979,700
*Reverse of 96. Single leaf Reverse. Total Mintage: 904,584***Part of 2,822,170

LARGE CENTS—DRAPED BUST, 1800–1801

Normal Date—Normal Die

1800 Over 179

DATE	ABP	G-4 GOOD	VG-8 V. GOOD	F-12 FINE	VF-20 V. FINE
☐ 1800 over 79, Style I Hair	40.00	52.00	75.00	190.00	600.00
☐ 1800† over 79, Style II Hair	42.00	55.00	90.00	160.00	400.00
☐ 1800† Unfinished Cyphers	35.00	45.00	65.00	125.00	375.00
☐ 1800† Normal Date	35.00	42.00	80.00	140.00	400.00
☐ 1801†† Normal Dies, Blunt 1	30.00	40.00	50.00	125.00	320.00
☐ 1801†† First 1 Pointed	30.00	38.00	62.00	135.00	340.00
☐ 1801†† 3 Errors—1/1000, one stem, and UNITED	75.00	110.00	150.00	475.00	950.00

ERROR
1
100

OVER
1
100

1802- 1
100

DATE	ABP	G-4 GOOD	VG-8 V. GOOD	F-12 FINE	VF-20 V. FINE
☐ 1801†† 1/000	40.00	46.00	70.00	160.00	400.00
☐ 1801†† 1/100 over 1/000	45.00	62.00	80.00	170.00	450.00

†Total Mintage: 2,822,170 ††Total Mintage (all 1801 Varieties) 1,362,837

LARGE CENTS—DRAPED BUST, 1802–1804

DATE	ABP	G-4 GOOD	VG-8 V. GOOD	F-12 FINE	VF-20 V. FINE
☐ 1802††† Normal Dies	35.00	42.00	70.00	150.00	240.00
☐ 1802††† Stemless Wreath	32.00	43.00	800.00	150.00	260.00
☐ 1802††† Fraction 1/000	35.00	50.00	85.00	190.00	400.00
☐ 1803* Small Date, Small Fraction	30.00	42.00	64.00	110.00	230.00
☐ 1803* Small Date, Large Fraction	28.00	37.00	55.00	115.00	220.00
☐ 1803* Large Date, Small Fraction	3250.00	4000.00	8500.00	16000.00	36000.00
☐ 1803* Large Date, Large Fraction	40.00	80.00	90.00	300.00	850.00

Total Mintage: ††1,362,837 †††3,435,100 *2,471,350 .

"Mumps" Obverse   "Normal" Obverse

DATE	ABP	G-4 GOOD	VG-8 V. GOOD	F-12 FINE	VF-20 V. FINE
☐ 1803† Mumps Obverse	30.00	41.00	82.00	210.00	460.00
☐ 1803† Stemless Wreath	28.00	35.00	62.00	115.00	310.00
☐ 1803† 1/100 over 1/000	27.00	35.00	70.00	190.00	400.00
☐ 1804 Normal Dies (756,837)	375.00	500.00	1200.00	2000.00	3000.00
☐ 1804 Broken Obverse Die	380.00	480.00	900.00	1400.00	2100.00
☐ 1804 Broken Obverse and Reverse Die	400.00	475.00	900.00	1400.00	2200.00

†Part of 2,471,350

LARGE CENTS—DRAPED BUST, 1804–1807

1804
Normal Die

1804
Restruck
in 1860

Small Fraction   Large Fraction   Comet Variety, 1807

DATE	ABP	G-4 GOOD	VG-8 V. GOOD	F-12 FINE	VF-20 V. FINE
☐ 1805 Blunt 1 in Date (941,115)					
	34.00	42.00	65.00	140.00	300.00
☐ 1805 Pointed 1 in Date					
	34.00	42.00	68.00	150.00	350.00
☐ 1806 (348,000)					
	32.00	40.00	70.00	250.00	400.00
☐ 1807 over 6 Large 7					
	30.00	36.00	62.00	200.00	410.00
☐ 1807 over 6 Small 7					
	1000.00	2500.00	4400.00	8700.00	15000.00
☐ 1807 Small Fraction (727,000)					
	30.00	42.00	72.00	210.00	400.00
☐ 1807 Large Fraction					
	27.00	42.00	58.00	150.00	300.00
☐ 1807 Comet Variety					
	35.00	45.00	75.00	200.00	500.00

LARGE CENTS—TURBAN HEAD, 1808–1814

DATE	ABP	G-4 GOOD	VG-8 V. GOOD	F-12 FINE	VF-20 V. FINE
☐ 1808, 13 Stars	35.00	45.00	110.00	250.00	460.00
☐ 1808, 12 Stars	(1,109,000)				
	45.00	55.00	125.00	280.00	500.00
☐ 1809	(222,867)				
	70.00	100.00	200.00	400.00	875.00
☐ 1810 over 9	30.00	45.00	100.00	200.00	510.00
☐ 1810	(1,458,400)				
	32.00	44.00	80.00	200.00	525.00
☐ 1811 over 10	45.00	70.00	115.00	375.00	1000.00
☐ 1811	(218,025)				
	50.00	72.00	115.00	275.00	800.00
☐ 1812 Small Date					
	32.00	41.00	78.00	210.00	450.00
☐ 1812 Large Date	(1,075,500)				
	30.00	40.00	75.00	210.00	450.00
☐ 1813 Close Stars					
	30.00	50.00	90.00	200.00	510.00
☐ 1813 Distant Stars	(418,000)				
	28.00	42.00	82.00	210.00	475.00
☐ 1814 Plain 4	32.00	42.00	74.00	225.00	450.00
☐ 1814 Crosslet 4	(357,830)				
	30.00	42.00	70.00	200.00	465.00

LARGE CENTS—CORONET, 1816–1838

DATE	ABP	G-4 GOOD	VG-8 V. GOOD	F-12 FINE	VF-20 V. FINE	MS-60 UNC.
☐ 1816	(2,820,982)					
	10.00	13.00	22.00	35.00	85.00	475.00
☐ 1817 Wide Date						
	18.00	28.00	32.00	40.00	100.00	275.00

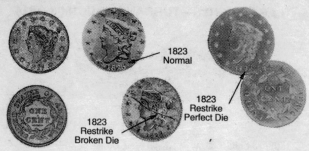

1823
Normal

1823
Restrike
Perfect Die

1823
Restrike
Broken Die

DATE	ABP	G-4 GOOD	VG-8 V. GOOD	F-12 FINE	VF-20 V. FINE	MS-60 UNC.
☐ 1817 13 Stars	(3,984,400)					
	10.00	13.00	22.00	23.00	60.00	270.00
☐ 1817 15 Stars						
	11.00	15.00	19.00	26.00	95.00	1400.00
☐ 1818	(3,167,000)					
	10.00	13.00	16.00	24.00	50.00	240.00
☐ 1819 over 18						
	10.00	12.00	17.00	29.00	65.00	550.00
☐ 1819 Large Date	(2,671,000)					
	10.00	12.00	16.00	27.00	62.00	265.00
☐ 1819 Small Date						
	10.00	13.00	16.00	27.00	62.00	265.00
☐ 1820 over 19						
	12.00	16.00	18.00	27.00	80.00	660.00
☐ 1820 Small Date	(4,407,550)					
	10.00	12.00	15.00	27.00	72.00	650.00
☐ 1820 Large Date						
	10.00	13.00	16.00	45.00	75.00	310.00
☐ 1821 Wide Date	(389,000)					
	20.00	25.00	42.00	125.00	410.00	6200.00
☐ 1821 Close Date	(389,000)					
	20.00	25.00	42.00	112.00	340.00	5900.00
☐ 1822 Wide Date	(2,075,339)					
	10.00	12.00	17.00	32.00	85.00	820.00
☐ 1822 Close Date						
	10.00	12.00	18.00	31.00	82.00	640.00
☐ 1823 over 22	(Part of 855,730)					
	45.00	55.00	120.00	275.00	500.00	11000.00

DATE	ABP	G-4 GOOD	VG-8 V. GOOD	F-12 FINE	VF-20 V. FINE	MS-60 UNC.
☐ 1823 Normal Date						
	45.00	75.00	120.00	310.00	525.00	1150.00
☐ 1823 Restrike from Broken Obverse Die						
				Uncirculated Only		900.00
☐ 1823 Restrike from Perfect Die (49 Known)					EXTREMELY RARE	
☐ 1824 over 22						
	12.00	17.00	27.00	58.00	240.00	3300.00
☐ 1824 Wide Date	(1,262,090)					
	10.00	12.50	19.00	35.00	135.00	860.00
☐ 1824 Close Date						
	10.00	12.50	20.00	38.00	114.00	875.00
☐ 1825 Small A's	(1,461,000)					
	10.00	14.00	19.00	36.00	110.00	950.00
☐ 1825 Large A's						
	10.00	14.00	18.00	37.00	120.00	950.00
☐ 1826 over 25						
	14.00	21.00	50.00	110.00	242.00	2100.00
☐ 1826 Wide Date	(1,517,422)					
	10.00	12.00	17.00	32.00	84.00	760.00
☐ 1826 Close Date						
	10.00	13.00	16.00	32.00	82.00	700.00
☐ 1827	(2,357,733)					
	10.00	12.00	17.00	33.00	86.00	400.00
☐ 1828 Small Date	(2,260,625)					
	10.00	12.00	15.00	27.00	70.00	640.00
☐ 1828 Large Date						
	10.00	12.00	15.00	45.00	120.00	450.00
☐ 1829 Small Letters	(1,414,500)					
	20.00	26.00	60.00	120.00	460.00	3800.00
☐ 1829 Large Letters	(1,414,500)					
	10.00	12.00	19.00	25.00	86.00	410.00
☐ 1830 Small Letters						
	15.00	20.00	31.00	82.00	250.00	3150.00
☐ 1830 Large Letters						
	10.00	12.00	16.00	24.00	64.00	385.00
☐ 1831 Small Letters	(3,359,260)					
	10.00	12.00	16.00	24.00	50.00	280.00
☐ 1831 Large Letters						
	10.00	12.00	16.00	24.00	50.00	280.00
☐ 1832 Small Letters	(2,362,000)					
	10.00	12.00	16.00	24.00	50.00	300.00

DATE	ABP	G-4 GOOD	VG-8 V. GOOD	F-12 FINE	VF-20 V. FINE	MS-60 UNC.
☐ 1832 Large Letters	(2,362,000)					
	10.00	12.00	16.00	24.00	50.00	320.00
☐ 1833 Small Letters	(2,739,000)					
	10.00	12.00	16.00	24.00	51.00	275.00
☐ 1833 Large Letters						
	10.00	12.00	16.00	21.00	46.00	260.00
☐ 1834*	10.00	12.00	17.00	20.00	50.00	810.00
☐ 1834**	(1,855,110)					
	10.00	13.00	17.00	23.00	52.00	1050.00
☐ 1834***	10.00	13.00	17.00	22.00	54.00	900.00
☐ 1835 Small Date, Small Stars						
	10.00	13.00	16.00	21.00	50.00	710.00
☐ 1835 Large Date, Large Stars	(3,878,397)					
	10.00	13.00	15.00	20.00	60.00	1100.00
☐ 1835 Type of 1836						
	10.00	13.00	16.00	21.00	52.00	385.00
☐ 1836	(2,111,000)					
	10.00	12.00	15.00	26.00	50.00	280.00
☐ 1837 Plain Hair Cord, Small Letters						
	10.00	12.00	16.00	21.00	51.00	510.00
☐ 1837 Plain Hair Cord, Large Letters	(5,558,301)					
	10.00	12.00	16.00	20.00	45.00	340.00
☐ 1837 Beaded Hair Cord, Small Letters						
	10.00	12.00	16.00	22.00	54.00	300.00
☐ 1838	(6,370,200)					
	10.00	11.00	16.00	21.00	52.00	240.00
☐ 1838 Line under CENT						
	12.00	15.00	18.00	24.00	45.00	260.00
☐ 1839 Silly Head (All Kinds)						
☐ 1839 No Center Dot						
	12.00	13.00	14.00	25.00	72.00	810.00
☐ 1839 Booby Head	(3,128,662)					
	10.00	12.00	15.00	24.00	72.00	850.00
☐ 1839 Petite Head						
	10.00	14.00	15.00	22.00	45.00	250.00
☐ 1839 over 36						
	150.00	180.00	400.00	850.00	2000.00	10000.00

*Large Date—Large Stars—Large Letters Reverse **Small Date—Small Stars—Small Letters Reverse ***Large Date—Small Stars—Small Letters Reverse.

LARGE CENTS—BRAIDED HAIR, 1839–1857

Booby Head

1856 Slants

DATE	ABP	G-4 GOOD	VG-8 V. GOOD	F-12 FINE	VF-20 V. FINE	MS-60 UNC.
☐ 1839 Type of 1840	10.00	12.00	14.00	18.00	36.00	310.00
☐ 1840 Small Date	10.00	12.00	13.00	21.00	37.00	250.00
☐ 1840 Large Date (2,462,700)	10.00	12.00	13.00	20.00	38.00	240.00
☐ 1841 (1,597,366)	9.00	11.00	14.50	17.00	36.00	240.00
☐ 1842 Small Date	10.00	12.50	15.00	15.00	29.00	270.00
☐ 1842 Large Date (2,383,390)	9.00	11.00	13.00	19.00	29.00	210.00
☐ 1843 Obverse and Reverse 1842	9.00	12.00	13.00	21.00	33.00	210.00
☐ 1843 Obverse 1842 Reverse 1844	9.00	12.00	15.00	22.00	30.00	210.00
☐ 1844	9.00	13.00	15.00	18.00	25.00	200.00
☐ 1844 over 81 (2,398,752)	12.00	15.00	20.00	36.00	72.00	740.00
☐ 1845 (3,894,805)	9.00	12.00	14.00	16.00	25.00	180.00
☐ 1846 Small Date	9.00	12.00	14.00	17.00	28.00	290.00

DATE	ABP	G-4 GOOD	VG-8 V. GOOD	F-12 FINE	VF-20 V. FINE	MS-60 UNC.
☐ 1846 Medium Date	(4,120,800)					
	9.00	11.00	13.00	16.00	28.00	185.00
☐ 1846 Tall Date						
	9.50	12.00	14.00	17.00	32.00	300.00
☐ 1847	9.00	11.00	14.00	16.00	30.00	165.00
☐ 1848	(6,320,680)					
	9.00	12.00	14.00	15.00	22.00	170.00
☐ 1849	(4,260,111)					
	9.00	12.00	13.00	16.00	22.00	190.00
☐ 1850	(4,426,844)					
	9.00	12.00	14.00	18.00	21.00	160.00
☐ 1851	9.00	12.00	13.00	16.00	21.00	160.00
☐ 1851 over 81	(9,899,700)					
	12.00	15.00	18.00	25.00	54.00	460.00
☐ 1852	(5,063,094)					
	9.00	11.00	13.00	16.50	21.00	150.00
☐ 1853	(6,641,131)					
	9.00	12.00	15.00	18.00	21.00	145.00
☐ 1854	(4,236,156)					
	9.00	12.00	14.00	16.50	22.00	150.00
☐ 1855 Upright 5's						
	10.00	12.00	14.00	16.00	36.00	210.00
☐ 1855 Slanting 5's	(1,574,829)					
	11.00	13.00	16.00	18.00	32.00	320.00
☐ 1855 Slanting 5's, Knob on Ear						
	10.00	12.00	16.50	18.00	38.00	280.00
☐ 1856 Upright 5	(2,690,465)					
	9.00	12.00	14.00	15.00	36.00	185.00
☐ 1856 Slanting 5						
	10.00	13.00	15.00	20.00	32.00	165.00
☐ 1857 Small Date	(333,456)					
	30.00	40.00	44.00	49.00	64.00	310.00
☐ 1857 Large Date						
	30.00	38.00	42.00	50.00	65.00	240.00

SMALL CENTS

SMALL CENTS—FLYING EAGLE, 1856–1858

It would be hard to find a coin in the standard U.S. series that proved so unpopular as the Flying Eagle cent—unpopular, that is, orginally. It has since become a favorite of collectors. During 1856, while the Large Cent continued in production, plans were under way to replace it with a smaller coin of the same value. A number of patterns of the Flying Eagle were struck that year at the Philadelphia Mint but were not circulated because the Large Cent was discontinued and minting switched over to this new piece, with a huge output in that one year of nearly 17,500,000 coins. The public balked, charging that the government was forcing the small cent on them. Not only didn't the public care much for that idea, they were also not too fond of the coin. Instead of being struck in pure copper and having the substantial appearance that a cent was supposed to have, its composition was 88% copper and 12% nickel, yielding a coin that was sufficiently pale in color to be called white. (If one wonders about the bickerings over coin sizes, designs, and compositions in the 18th and 19th centuries, it should be realized that far greater attention was focused upon money in those days, when few persons used checks and credit cards were unknown.)

The Flying Eagle cent was designed by James Longacre. Its weight was 4.67 grams and its diameter 19mm. As a designer, Longacre was not unskilled. He proved his abilities with the Indian Head cent, which replaced the Flying Eagle in 1859.

DATE	ABP	G-4 GOOD	F-12 FINE	EF-40 EX. FINE	MS-60 UNC.	PRF-65 PROOF
☐ 1856	(Approx. 1,000)					
	3500.00	4350.00	5350.00	6000.00	7900.00	21500.00
☐ 1857	(17,450,000)					
	13.00	18.00	26.00	125.00	270.00	22500.00
☐ 1858 Small Letters						
	13.00	18.00	26.00	125.00	265.00	20000.00
☐ 1858 Large Letters	(24,600,000)					
	13.00	18.00	26.00	130.00	265.00	18500.00

SMALL CENTS—INDIAN HEAD, 1859–1909

Probably the most famous of all U.S. coins (its only challenger for that honor being the Morgan dollar), the Indian Head cent remained in production without change in design for half a century. After the disaster of the Flying Eagle cent, rejected by the public because of its almost white color, the government knew that it must manufacture a cent whose appearance was that of good metal, even if it was not to return to the Large Cent. The question remained: would a small copper piece be accepted, when Large Cents, containing a much greater quantity of metal, were still widely circulating? The new cent had the same composition as its predecessor, 88% copper and 12% nickel. The first batch of Indian Heads, released in 1859, amounted to 36,400,000 pieces, more than had ever been coined of a single denomination in one year: $364,000 worth of pennies. Beginning in 1864 the copper content was increased to 95%, the nickel removed entirely and replaced with a 5% alloy of tin and zinc. This was so successfully absorbed into the copper that the resulting coin was hardly different in color than if copper alone were used.

Finally the problem was solved, and the Indian Head cent

was on the road to a long successful existence. Its designer was James Longacre. The weight was 4.67 grams and the diameter 19mm., these specifications being the same as the Flying Eagle cent. The portrait is that of an Indian maiden. As first designed, the reverse carried no shield but this was added in 1860, the second year of issue. The Indian Head became the first U.S. coin struck in a quantity of more than 100 million in a year, when 108 million specimens were turned out in 1907. This exceeded the country's population. It is interesting to note that the 1908 and 1909 editions, representing the last two years of this design, are the only dates to be found with mint marks.

The origin of the portrait has been for many years a matter of discussion. It was at one time thought that Longacre had taken it from life, using an Indian girl as his model. This was dismissed when the suggestion was advanced that the profile resembled Longacre's daughter. It is now generally believed that no live model sat for the likeness but that it was based upon classical statuary, of which Longacre was known to be a collector. The Indian Head cent portrait is neither as realistic nor impressive as that featured on the Buffalo nickel, but this is nevertheless an important coin whose design represented a bold innovation.

1901   1860–1864 Wreath on Shield

DATE	ABP	G-4 GOOD	F-12 FINE	EF-40 EX. FINE	MS-60 UNC.	PRF-65 PROOF
☐ 1859 Copper-Nickel	(36,400,000)					
	7.50	12.00	16.00	95.00	195.00	4300.00
☐ 1860 Copper-Nickel, Broad Bust	(20,566,000)					
	5.00	7.00	12.00	50.00	150.00	3150.00
☐ 1860 Copper-Nickel, Narrow Bust						
	10.00	14.00	20.00	85.00	275.00	
☐ 1861 Copper-Nickel	(10,100,000)					
	11.00	16.00	32.00	90.00	200.00	5750.00
☐ 1862 Copper-Nickel	(28,075,000)					
	4.50	6.50	14.00	28.00	92.00	1900.00
☐ 1863 Copper-Nickel	(49,840,000)					
	4.50	6.00	10.00	24.00	62.00	2650.00

DATE	ABP	G-4 GOOD	F-12 FINE	EF-40 EX. FINE	MS-60 UNC.	PRF-65 PROOF
☐ 1864 Copper-Nickel (13,740,000)						
	10.00	14.00	27.00	64.00	130.00	2650.00
☐ 1864 Bronze (39,233,714)						
	4.00	7.00	16.50	50.00	90.00	4250.00
☐ 1864 Bronze, L on Ribbon						
	35.00	50.00	100.00	190.00	325.00	67500.00
☐ 1865 Bronze (35,429,286)						
	4.00	5.00	18.00	32.00	80.00	1650.00
☐ 1866 Bronze (9,826,500)						
	28.00	33.00	55.00	160.00	220.00	775.00
☐ 1867 Bronze (9,821,000)						
	27.00	34.00	62.00	140.00	240.00	900.00
☐ 1867 Bronze, over 7						
	30.00	38.00	70.00	200.00	510.00	1850.00
☐ 1868 Bronze (10,266,500)						
	23.00	28.00	52.00	140.00	210.00	940.00
☐ 1869 Bronze (6,420,000)						
	35.00	45.00	200.00	270.00	425.00	900.00
☐ 1869 Bronze, over 9						
	80.00	95.00	210.00	360.00	510.00	
☐ 1870 Bronze (5,275,000)						
	28.00	40.00	160.00	285.00	400.00	1200.00
☐ 1871 Bronze (3,929,500)						
	40.00	50.00	195.00	285.00	400.00	1000.00
☐ 1872 Bronze (4,042,000)						
	52.00	65.00	265.00	320.00	410.00	1150.00
☐ 1873 Bronze, closed 3 (11,676,500)						
	12.00	15.00	45.00	140.00	360.00	700.00
☐ 1873 Bronze, open 3						
	12.50	14.00	40.00	120.00	160.00	
☐ 1873 Bronze, Doubled Liberty						
	75.00	100.00	500.00	1900.00	6100.00	
☐ 1874 Bronze (14,187,500)						
	9.00	12.00	28.00	84.00	160.00	700.00
☐ 1875 Bronze (13,528,000)						
	10.00	13.00	39.00	82.00	160.00	1450.00
☐ 1876 Bronze (7,944,000)						
	18.00	23.00	39.00	125.00	190.00	850.00
☐ 1877 Bronze (852,500)						
	365.00	435.00	750.00		1900.00	4500.00
☐ 1878 Bronze (5,799,850)						
	17.00	23.00	45.00	124.00	175.00	460.00

DATE	ABP	G-4 GOOD	F-12 FINE	EF-40 EX. FINE	MS-60 UNC.	PRF-65 PROOF
☐ 1879 Bronze (16,231,200)						
	4.00	5.50	13.00	60.00	71.00	420.00
☐ 1880 Bronze (38,964,955)						
	2.00	3.00	5.50	22.00	62.00	390.00
☐ 1881 Bronze (39,211,575)						
	2.00	3.00	5.50	17.00	40.00	390.00
☐ 1882 Bronze (38,581,100)						
	2.00	3.00	4.50	17.00	40.00	390.00
☐ 1883 Bronze (45,598,109)						
	1.50	2.50	4.00	18.00	40.00	410.00
☐ 1884 Bronze (23,261,742)						
	2.00	3.00	6.50	22.00	60.00	390.00
☐ 1885 Bronze (11,765,384)						
	4.00	6.00	11.00	48.00	95.00	385.00
☐ 1886 Bronze (17,654,290), I feather C						
	2.25	3.00	15.00	100.00	125.00	475.00
☐ 1886 Bronze, C Feather A						
	2.50	3.50	18.00	115.00	260.00	700.00
☐ 1887 Bronze (45,226,483)						
	1.00	1.50	3.00	16.00	41.00	460.00
☐ 1888 Bronze (37,494,414)						
	1.00	1.50	3.50	17.00	39.00	450.00
☐ 1888 Bronze, over 7						
	5.00	370.00	600.00	1000.00	5000.00	8000.00
☐ 1889 Bronze (48,868,361)						
	1.00	1.50	2.50	10.00	37.00	410.00
☐ 1890 Bronze (57,182,854)						
	1.00	1.50	2.15	10.00	38.00	470.00
☐ 1891 Bronze (47,072,350)						
	1.00	1.50	2.25	10.00	37.00	470.00
☐ 1892 Bronze (37,649,832)						
	1.00	1.50	2.25	12.00	37.00	460.00
☐ 1893 Bronze (46,642,195)						
	1.00	1.50	2.50	10.00	39.00	535.00
☐ 1894 Bronze (16,752,132)						
	2.00	3.00	11.00	38.00	58.00	480.00
☐ 1895 Bronze (38,343,636)						
	1.00	1.50	3.00	10.00	36.00	450.00
☐ 1896 Bronze (39,057,293)						
	1.00	1.50	2.75	9.00	32.00	400.00
☐ 1897 Bronze (50,466,330)						
	1.00	1.50	3.00	9.00	30.00	400.00

DATE	ABP	G-4 GOOD	F-12 FINE	EF-40 EX. FINE	MS-60 UNC.	PRF-65 PROOF
☐ 1898 Bronze	(49,923,079)					
	1.00	1.25	2.50	12.00	30.00	380.00
☐ 1899 Bronze	(53,600,031)					
	1.00	1.25	2.10	12.00	30.00	380.00
☐ 1900 Bronze	(66,833,764)					
	1.00	1.25	1.80	9.50	27.00	360.00
☐ 1901 Bronze	(79,611,143)					
	1.00	1.25	1.80	7.50	27.00	360.00
☐ 1902 Bronze	(87,376,722)					
	1.00	1.25	1.80	7.50	26.00	360.00
☐ 1903 Bronze	(85,094,493)					
	1.00	1.25	1.80	7.50	30.00	375.00
☐ 1904 Bronze	(61,328,015)					
	1.00	1.25	1.80	8.00	25.00	400.00
☐ 1905 Bronze	(80,719,163)					
	1.00	1.25	1.80	7.50	26.00	420.00
☐ 1906 Bronze	(96,022,255)					
	1.00	1.25	1.80	7.50	26.00	385.00
☐ 1907 Bronze	(108,138,618)					
	1.00	1.25	1.80	7.50	26.00	465.00
☐ 1908 Bronze	(32,327,987)					
	1.00	1.25	2.00	7.50	26.00	375.00
☐ 1908S Bronze	(1,115,000)					
	42.00	52.00	65.00	110.00	210.00	
☐ 1909 Bronze	(14,370,645)					
	1.00	1.50	3.00	14.00	32.00	450.00
☐ 1909S Bronze	(309,000)					
	200.00	240.00	310.00	410.00	500.00	

SMALL CENTS—LINCOLN HEAD, 1909 TO DATE

It is quite likely that, despite having remained in use for fifty years, the Indian Head design would have been retained for the cent beyond 1909 had not President Roosevelt pressed for its removal. The year 1909 marked the 100th anniversary of Abraham Lincoln's birth and Roosevelt (who, not coincidentally, was a member of the same political party) wished to memorialize the anniversary by placing a likeness of Lincoln on the penny. His suggestion was adopted, the result being a design that has survived in continuous use longer than any other in the Mint's history, with no indication that it will soon be replaced. The Indian Head cents were so popular that criticism was risked by their removal. Had they been abandoned in favor of any other design a public outcry might have ensued. But for Lincoln, allowances could be made. This was incidentally the first time an American citizen appeared on coinage of the Mint, as George Washington, though depicted on numerous coins and tokens, was never portrayed on an issue of the federal Mint.

Designer of the Lincoln cent was Victor D. Brenner. Rather than using a close-up profile, Brenner showed Lincoln in quarter-length, with beard, as he appeared in the last few years of his life. It is not known whether the likeness was adapted from a specific photograph, from statuary, or merely from a study of various photos and other artworks. As first struck, the coin carried Brenner's initials and this variety is known as the VDB cent. They were removed midway through production of the 1909 issue and not reinstated until 1918, when they were switched from the reverse to the obverse. Specimens of the 1909 coin with initials, especially those struck at San Francisco, where less than half a million were produced, eventually became favorite collectors' items. At the time little notice was taken of them.

Originally the reverse was composed of the wording ONE CENT—UNITED STATES OF AMERICA enshrouded by wheat sheaves. In 1959 a new reverse was introduced, on the occasion of the 150th anniversary of Lincoln's birth and the 50th of the coin's use. Designed by Frank Gasparro, it pictures the Lincoln Memorial building in Washington, D.C. From 1909–42 the Lincoln cent had a composition of 95% copper and 5% tin and zinc, with a weight of 3.11 grams and a diameter of 19mm.

In 1943 it was made of steel-coated zinc. From 1944–46 what are known as "shell case cents" were made from spent shell casings; their content was 95% copper and 5% tin and zinc, until September of 1962 when the tin was removed from the cent for the last time. The content of the cent from 1962 until 1981 was 95% copper and 5% zinc. Beginning in 1982, the cent has been made of a zinc core with copper coating. Thus, it is now another clad coin, leaving only the nickel as the lone nonclad U.S. coin.

1909　　　　　　　　　　No V.D.B.　　V.D.B. Restored

DATE	ABP	G-4 GOOD	F-12 FINE	VF-20 V. FINE	EF-40 EX. FINE	MS-60 UNC.	MS-65 CH. UNC.
(1909–1942 COMPOSITION-95% COPPER WITH 5% TIN AND ZINC)							
☐ 1909S V.D.B. (484,000)							
	350.00	425.00	535.00	625.00	675.00	825.00	3800.00
☐ 1909 V.D.B. (27,995,000)							
	2.50	3.10	4.00	4.50	5.00	9.00	100.00
☐ 1909 (72,702,618)							
	.85	1.25	2.00	2.50	3.00	13.00	68.00
☐ 1909S (1,825,000)							
	40.00	50.00	60.00	100.00	125.00	160.00	550.00
☐ 1909S over S							
	45.00	55.00	70.00	115.00	140.00	225.00	600.00
☐ 1910 (146,801,218)							
	.10	.20	.45	.65	3.00	15.00	120.00
☐ 1910S (6,045,000)							
	5.00	7.00	8.50	10.50	22.00	55.00	350.00
☐ 1911 (101,177,787)							
	.10	.20	1.10	1.60	3.50	18.00	160.00
☐ 1911D (12,672,000)							
	4.00	6.00	8.00	12.50	35.00	72.00	875.00
☐ 1911S (4,026,000)							
	10.00	14.00	18.00	24.00	42.00	135.00	1250.00
☐ 1912 (6,853,060)							
	1.00	1.50	1.50	4.50	8.75	30.00	285.00
☐ 1912D (10,411,000)							
	4.00	6.00	6.50	16.50	40.00	130.00	950.00
☐ 1912S (4,431,000)							
	7.00	10.00	14.00	17.00	42.00	100.00	1550.00
☐ 1913 (76,532,352)							
	.35	.50	1.50	2.75	12.50	25.00	250.00
☐ 1913D (15,804,000)							
	1.50	2.25	3.25	7.50	23.00	82.00	1175.00
☐ 1913S (6,101,000)							
	5.00	7.00	7.50	12.00	29.00	125.00	2400.00
☐ 1914 (75,238,432)							
	.25	.50	1.25	3.10	10.00	42.00	315.00
☐ 1914D (1,193,000)							
	75.00	90.00	175.00	235.00	450.00	975.00	9500.00
☐ 1914S (4,137,000)							
	6.00	9.00	13.00	22.00	45.00	240.00	7600.00
☐ 1915 (29,092,120)							
	1.00	1.40	4.00	9.50	34.00	80.00	550.00
☐ 1915D (22,050,000)							
	1.00	1.40	1.75	4.00	11.00	66.00	600.00

DATE	ABP	G-4 GOOD	F-12 FINE	VF-20 V. FINE	EF-40 EX. FINE	MS-60 UNC.	MS-65 CH. UNC.
☐ 1915S	(4,833,677)						
	4.00	6.00	9.00	12.00	33.00	125.00	2750.00
☐ 1916	(131,838,677)						
	.10	.20	.50	1.25	3.00	13.00	115.00
☐ 1916D	(35,956,000)						
	.20	.40	1.25	2.10	8.50	54.00	1700.00
☐ 1916S	(22,510,000)						
	.65	.95	1.60	2.50	9.50	60.00	3850.00
☐ 1917	(196,429,785)						
	.10	.20	.40	1.25	3.00	12.00	125.00
☐ 1917 Double Die							
	60.00	70.00	240.00	375.00	1000.00	1475.00	9000.00
☐ 1917D	(55,120,000)						
	.10	.25	1.00	2.00	10.00	60.00	1350.00
☐ 1917S	(32,620,000)						
	.30	.50	1.00	1.80	7.00	56.00	3850.00
☐ 1918	(288,104,634)						
	.10	.20	.45	1.00	3.50	12.00	190.00
☐ 1918D	(47,830,000)						
	.15	.30	.90	2.25	7.00	50.00	1550.00
☐ 1918S	(34,680,000)						
	.20	.40	.90	2.00	6.50	55.00	4500.00
☐ 1919	(392,021,000)						
	.07	.25	.46	.76	2.00	9.00	92.00
☐ 1919D	(57,154,000)						
	.15	.30	.50	1.00	4.25	43.00	1100.00
☐ 1919S	(139,760,000)						
	.10	.20	.46	1.25	2.70	32.00	2600.00
☐ 1920	(310,165,000)						
	.07	.16	.40	.65	1.80	8.50	95.00
☐ 1920D	(49,280,000)						
	.10	.25	.65	1.40	8.50	51.00	850.00
☐ 1920S	(46,220,000)						
	.15	.25	.85	1.30	6.50	75.00	4000.00
☐ 1921	(39,157,000)						
	.15	.25	.60	1.30	4.50	33.00	170.00
☐ 1921S	(15,274,000)						
	.85	1.25	1.40	3.10	16.00	86.00	3750.00
☐ 1922 Missing D, No Mint Mark*							
	250.00	300.00	465.00	550.00	1350.00	4600.00	
☐ 1922D	(7,160,000)						
	5.00	7.00	9.50	13.50	21.00	70.00	810.00

*Beware of removed mint mark

DATE	ABP	G-4 GOOD	F-12 FINE	VF-20 V. FINE	EF-40 EX. FINE	MS-60 UNC.	MS-65 CH. UNC.
☐ 1923	(74,723,000)						
	.07	.15	.40	.80	2.75	11.00	200.00
☐ 1923S	(8,700,000)						
	1.00	1.40	3.00	5.00	21.00	175.00	3850.00
☐ 1924	(75,178,000)						
	.07	.16	.35	.70	3.00	18.00	150.00
☐ 1924D	(2,520,000)						
	7.00	9.00	12.50	26.00	75.00	215.00	4200.00
☐ 1924S	(11,696,000)						
	.50	.75	1.40	3.00	21.00	120.00	6300.00
☐ 1925	(139,949,000)						
	.07	.15	.35	.60	2.50	8.00	90.00
☐ 1925D	(22,580,000)						
	.15	.20	.55	2.10	8.00	45.00	1600.00
☐ 1925S	(26,380,000)						
	.09	.15	.50	1.00	5.50	56.00	5200.00
☐ 1926	(157,088,000)						
	.05	.15	.40	.51	1.60	7.50	60.00
☐ 1926D	(28,022,022)						
	.10	.20	.65	1.35	6.00	50.00	1550.00
☐ 1926S	(4,550,000)						
	1.50	2.00	4.50	5.50	13.00	95.00	20000.00
☐ 1927	(144,440,000)						
	.05	.16	.30	.75	2.00	7.50	90.00
☐ 1927D	(27,170,000)						
	.10	.22		1.00	3.00	48.00	1175.00
☐ 1927S	(14,276,000)						
	.40	.65	1.30	2.50	8.50	60.00	3150.00
☐ 1928	(134,116,000)						
	.05	.14	.40	.65	1.50	7.00	85.00
☐ 1928D	(21,170,000)						
	.10	.20	.35	.80	3.00	26.00	500.00
☐ 1928S	(17,266,000)						
	.20	.35	.85	1.25	3.25	55.00	1500.00
☐ 1929	(185,262,000)						
	.05	.15	.30	.65	1.00	7.00	80.00
☐ 1929D	(41,730,000)						
	.05	.15	.40	.65	2.25	16.00	240.00
☐ 1929S	(50,148,000)						
	.05	.15	.40	.55	2.50	14.00	115.00
☐ 1930	(157,415,000)						
	.05	.12	.40	.50	1.25	6.00	40.00

DATE	ABP	G-4 GOOD	F-12 FINE	VF-20 V. FINE	EF-40 EX. FINE	MS-60 UNC.	MS-65 CH. UNC.
☐ 1930D	(40,100,000)						
	.05	.16	.40	.80	1.90	12.00	87.00
☐ 1930S	(24,286,000)						
	.10	.14	.35	.60	1.30	10.00	45.00
☐ 1931	(19,396,000)						
	.25	.45	.80	1.20	2.10	17.00	92.00
☐ 1931D	(4,480,000)						
	2.00	2.50	3.75	4.50	7.75	48.00	515.00
☐ 1931S	(866,000)						
	30.00	36.00	43.00	45.00	52.00	70.00	420.00
☐ 1932	(9,062,000)						
	.75	1.50	2.00	2.25	3.50	20.00	74.00
☐ 1932D*	(10,500,000)						
	.45	.80	1.25	1.90	2.50	14.00	75.00
☐ 1933	(14,360,000)						
	.75	1.00	1.30	1.80	2.60	18.00	66.00
☐ 1933D	(6,200,000)						
	1.00	1.60	2.30	3.10	5.00	18.00	60.00
☐ 1934	(219,080,000)						
	.05	.09	.20	.35	.65	3.50	30.00
☐ 1934D	(28,446,000)						
	.06	.13	.30	.50	4.75	15.00	55.00
☐ 1935	(245,388,000)						
	.05	.09	.20	.36	.50	1.65	17.00
☐ 1935D	(47,000,000)						
	.05	.09	.38	.47	.82	3.60	12.00
☐ 1935S	(38,702,000)						
	.05	.09	.75	1.50	2.60	7.75	46.00
☐ 1936	(309,637,569)						
	.05	.09	.18	.38	.72	1.10	5.75
☐ 1936D	(40,620,000)						
	.05	.09	.27	.40	.82	1.90	9.50
☐ 1936S	(29,130,000)						
	.05	.09	.27	.47	.96	2.80	10.50
☐ 1937	(309,179,320)						
	.04	.08	.21	.30	.50	.80	6.00
☐ 1937D	(50,430,000)						
	.04	.08	.21	.42	.60	2.25	8.10

*Note: More than 15,000 specimens of the 1932D cent were included in the Dr. Jerry Buss Collection, sold in 1985. This was the largest quantity ever sold at one time.

274 / SMALL CENTS

DATE	ABP	G-4 GOOD	F-12 FINE	VF-20 V. FINE	EF-40 EX. FINE	MS-60 UNC.	MS-65 CH. UNC
☐ 1937S	(35,500,000)						
	.04	.08	.24	.40	.65	2.00	6.50
☐ 1938	(156,696,734)						
	.04	.08	.22	.30	.60	1.65	5.50
☐ 1938D	(20,010,000)						
	.06	.13	.40	.64	.82	2.10	7.00
☐ 1938S	(15,180,000)						
	.06	.22	.44	.64	.72	2.10	8.00
☐ 1939	(316,479,520)						
	.04	.06	.15	.22	.30	.80	4.50
☐ 1939D	(15,160,000)						
	.15	.33	.54	.67	1.10	3.10	9.50
☐ 1939S	(52,070,000)						
	.05	.11	.21	.32	.60	1.70	11.00
☐ 1940	(586,825,872)						
	.03	.05	.20	.32	.40	1.10	4.30
☐ 1940D	(83,190,000)						
	.03	.07	.28	.45	.60	1.50	4.30
☐ 1940S	(112,940,000)						
	.04	.06	.28	.52	.60	1.65	5.10
☐ 1941	(887,039,100)						
	.03	.05	.22	.40	.50	.90	4.50
☐ 1941D	(128,700,000)						
	.03	.05	.40	.60	.90	2.10	6.60
☐ 1941S	(92,360,000)						
	.04	.06	.48	.70	.76	2.10	12.00
☐ 1942	(657,828,600)						
	.04	.06	.20	.30	.40	.75	3.50
☐ 1942D	(206,698,000)						
	.04	.06	.21	.40	.42	.82	4.00
☐ 1942S	(85,590,000)						
	.04	.09	.52	.72	.95	2.30	17.00

(1943 WARTIME STEEL COMPOSITION-STEEL COATED WITH ZINC)

DATE	ABP	G-4 GOOD	F-12 FINE	VF-20 V. FINE	EF-40 EX. FINE	MS-60 UNC.	MS-65 CH. UNC
☐ 1943	(684,628,670)						
	.10	.20	.30	.40	.55	1.25	5.00
☐ 1943D	(217,660,000)						
	.15	.25	.32	.46	.86	1.50	8.00
☐ 1943S	(191,550,000)						
	.20	.25	.46	.52	.92	2.15	12.00

(1944–1946 "SHELL CASE" COPPER COMPOSITION-95% COPPER AND 5% ZINC)

DATE	ABP	G-4 GOOD	F-12 FINE	VF-20 V. FINE	EF-40 EX. FINE	MS-60 UNC.	MS-65 CH. UNC
☐ 1944	(1,435,400,000)						
	.03			.11	.21	.52	2.00

DATE	ABP	VF-20 V. FINE	EF-40 EX. FINE	MS-60 UNC.	MS-65 CH. UNC.
☐ 1944D	(430,578,000)				
	.03	.20	.30	.52	2.10
☐ 1944D/S Variety 1					
	95.00	120.00	175.00	350.00	1600.00
☐ 1944D/S Variety 2					
	35.00	46.00	92.00	160.00	700.00
☐ 1944S	(282,760,000)				
	.03	.16	.21	.40	3.10
☐ 1945	(1,040,515,000)				
	.03	.09	.16	.52	2.75
☐ 1945D	(226,268,000)				
	.03	.10	.16	.52	1.50
☐ 1945S	(181,770,000)				
	.03	.12	.20	.52	4.25
☐ 1946	(991,655,000)				
	.03	.10	.16	.42	1.85
☐ 1946D	(315,690,000)				
	.05	.15	.16	.42	3.10
☐ 1946S	(198,100,000)				
	.03	.20	.26	.42	3.10
☐ 1946S/D				160.00	475.00

(1947–1962 COMPOSITION-95% COPPER AND 5% TIN AND ZINC)

DATE	ABP	VF-20 V. FINE	EF-40 EX. FINE	MS-60 UNC.	MS-65 CH. UNC.
☐ 1947	(190,555,000)				
	.03	.20	.41	.60	1.50
☐ 1947D	(194,750,000)				
	.03	.16	.22	.31	2.00
☐ 1947S	(99,000,000)				
	.03	.20	.25	.50	3.00
☐ 1948	(317,570,000)				
	.03	.20	.42	.51	2.10
☐ 1948D	(172,637,500)				
	.03	.20	.35	.46	2.30
☐ 1948S	(81,735,000)				
	.03	.38	.52	.85	4.50
☐ 1949	(217,490,000)				
	.03	.32	.40	.62	8.75
☐ 1949D	(154,370,500)				
	.03	.32	.50	.62	2.60
☐ 1949S	(64,290,000)				
	.03	.50	.62	1.00	5.50
☐ 1950	(272,686,386)				
	.03	.16	.22	.62	2.10

DATE	ABP	VF-20 V. FINE	EF-40 EX. FINE	MS-60 UNC.	MS-65 CH. UNC.
☐ 1950D	(334,950,000)				
	.03	.12	.19	.32	2.10
☐ 1950S	(118,505,000)				
	.03	.12	.19	.60	2.00
☐ 1951	(294,633,500)				
	.03	.12	.19	.58	1.80
☐ 1951D	(625,355,000)				
	.03	.09	.15	.30	1.60
☐ 1951S	(100,890,000)				
	.03	.18	.30	.56	2.85
☐ 1952	(186,856,980)				
	.03	.10	.22	.58	2.25
☐ 1952D	(746,130,000)				
	.03	.05	.14	.20	1.50
☐ 1952S	(137,800,004)				
	.03	.09	.22	.70	3.25
☐ 1953	(256,883,800)				
	.03	.06	.13	.14	2.50
☐ 1953D	(700,515,000)				
	.03	.06	.13	.16	1.25
☐ 1953S	(181,835,000)				
	.03	.10	.14	.30	1.50
☐ 1954	(71,873,350)				
	.03	.13	.17	.33	1.25
☐ 1954D	(251,552,500)				
	.03	.05	.10	.23	1.00
☐ 1954S	(96,190,000)				
	.03	.05	.08	.18	1.00
☐ 1955	(330,958,200)				
	.03	.05	.08	.10	1.50
☐ 1955 Double Die					
	350.00 425.00	485.00	525.00	1175.00	21500.00
☐ 1955D	(563,257,500)				
	.03	.05	.08	.20	.90
☐ 1955S	(44,610,000)				
	.10	.20	.30	.50	1.75
☐ 1956	(421,414,384)				
	.02	.04	.06	.10	.52
☐ 1956D	(1,098,201,100)				
	.02	.04	.06	.10	.52
☐ 1957	(283,787,952)				
	.02	.04	.06	.10	.52

DATE	ABP	VF-20 V. FINE	EF-40 EX. FINE	MS-60 UNC.	MS-65 CH. UNC.
☐ 1957D	(1,051,342,000)				
	.02	.04	.05	.11	.46
☐ 1958	(253,400,652)				
	.02	.04	.05	.11	.46
☐ 1958D	(800,953,000)				
	.02	.04	.05	.11	.46

SMALL CENTS—LINCOLN MEMORIAL DESIGN

LINCOLN MEMORIAL   1955 DOUBLE DIE   SMALL DATE   LARGE DATE

DATE	MINTAGE	MS-65 CH. UNC.	PRF-65 PROOF
☐ 1959	610,864,291	.35	1.75
☐ 1959D	1,279,760,000	.35	
☐ 1960 Small Date	588,096,602	6.00	17.00
☐ 1960 Large Date		.40	1.25
☐ 1960D Small Date	1,580,884,000	3.50	
☐ 1960D Large Date		.40	
☐ 1961	756,373,244	.40	.90
☐ 1961D	1,753,266,700	.40	
(SEPTEMBER 1961–1981 COMPOSITION-95% COPPER AND 5% ZINC)			
☐ 1962	609,263,019	.35	.90
☐ 1962D	1,793,148,400	.35	
☐ 1963	757,185,645	.35	.90
☐ 1963D	1,744,020,400	.35	
☐ 1964	2,652,525,762	.35	.90
☐ 1964D	3,799,071,500	.35	
☐ 1965	1,497,224,900	.35	
☐ 1966	2,188,147,783	.40	
☐ 1967	3,048,667,077	.35	
☐ 1968	1,707,880,965	.35	

DATE	MINTAGE	MS-65 CH. UNC.	PRF-65 PROOF
☐ 1968D	2,886,269,590	.40	
☐ 1968S	261,311,500	.45	1.00
☐ 1969	1,136,910,000	.75	
☐ 1969D	4,002,832,200	.40	
☐ 1969S	547,309,631	.40	1.00
☐ 1970	1,898,315,000	.50	
☐ 1970D	2,891,438,900	.45	
☐ 1970S	693,192,814	.45	
☐ 1970S Small Date		55.00	47.50
☐ 1970S Large Date		.45	1.35
☐ 1971	1,919,490,000	.70	
☐ 1971D	2,911,045,600	.55	
☐ 1971S	528,354,192	1.00	1.25
☐ 1972	2,933,255,000	.40	
☐ 1972 Double Die		375.00	
☐ 1972D	2,665,071,400	.40	
☐ 1972S	380,200,104	.40	1.25
☐ 1973	3,728,245,000	.40	
☐ 1973D	3,549,576,588	.40	
☐ 1973S	319,937,634	.40	1.00
☐ 1974	4,232,140,523	.40	
☐ 1974D	4,235,098,000	.40	
☐ 1974S	412,039,228	.45	1.00
☐ 1975	4,505,275,300	.40	
☐ 1975D	5,505,275,300	.40	
☐ 1975S Proof Only	2,909,369		3.75
☐ 1976	4,674,292,426	.30	
☐ 1976D	4,221,595,455	.30	
☐ 1976S Proof Only	4,149,945		3.00
☐ 1977	4,469,972,000	.30	
☐ 1977D	4,149,055,800	.30	
☐ 1977S Proof Only	3,250,895		2.80
☐ 1978	5,266,905,000	.30	
☐ 1978D	4,280,233,400	.30	
☐ 1978S Proof Only	3,127,781		2.75
☐ 1979P	6,018,515,201	.30	
☐ 1979D	4,139,357,000	.30	
☐ 1979S Proof Only, Filled S	3,677,200		2.60
☐ 1979S Proof Only, Clear S			3.25
☐ 1980	7,414,705,002	.30	
☐ 1980D	5,140,098,675	.30	
☐ 1980S Proof Only	3,547,130		.90

DATE	MINTAGE	MS-65 CH. UNC.	PRF-65 PROOF
☐ 1981	7,491,750,500	.30	
☐ 1981D	5,373,235,000	.30	
☐ 1981S Proof Only Type 1	4,065,000		2.25
☐ 1981S Proof Only Type 2			45.00
☐ 1982 Small Date	10,712,525,000	1.00	
☐ 1982 Large Date		.90	
☐ 1982D Large Date	6,012,979,368	.70	
(1982 COMPOSITION-COPPER-PLATED ZINC, 97% ZINC, 3% COPPER)			
☐ 1982 Small Date		1.50	
☐ 1982 Large Date		1.00	
☐ 1982D Small Date		.75	
☐ 1982D Large Date		1.00	
☐ 1982S Proof Only	3,857,480		3.00
☐ 1983	7,752,354,900	.35	
☐ 1983 Double Die Reverse		275.00	
☐ 1983D	6,468,000,000	.35	
☐ 1983S Proof Only	3,228,650		3.25
☐ 1984	8,183,657,000	.35	
☐ 1984D	5,570,000,000	.60	
☐ 1984S Proof Only			3.50
☐ 1985	5,842,628,000	.45	
☐ 1985D	5,329,742,000	.45	
☐ 1985S Proof Only	3,412,110		3.75
☐ 1986	4,622,410,712	.45	
☐ 1986D	4,287,870,420	.45	
☐ 1986S Proof Only	3,211,110		5.00
☐ 1987	4,427,867,241	.45	
☐ 1987D	4,782,420,670	.45	
☐ 1987S Proof Only			3.00
☐ 1988	6,180,720,000	.45	
☐ 1988D	5,151,621,120	.45	
☐ 1988S Proof Only			7.50
☐ 1989	7,321,462,111	.45	
☐ 1989D	5,362,174,181	.45	
☐ 1989S Proof Only			7.50
☐ 1990	6,927,491,004	.45	
☐ 1990D	4,921,800,542	.45	

Note: The 1982 cent was the first U.S. coin struck in a quantity of more than ten billion.

DATE	MINTAGE	MS-65 CH. UNC.	PRF-65 PROOF
☐ 1990S Proof Only	3,298,540		4.25
☐ 1991	5,165,920,000	.40	
☐ 1991D	4,158,440,218	.40	
☐ 1991S Proof Only	2,866,422		15.00
☐ 1992	4,648,904,000	.40	
☐ 1992D	4,448,672,250	.40	
☐ 1992S Proof Only	4,176,540		4.50
☐ 1993	5,684,705,000	.40	
☐ 1993D	6,426,650,571	.40	
☐ 1993S Proof Only	3,394,792		7.50
☐ 1994	6,500,850,000	.40	
☐ 1994D	7,131,765,000	.40	
☐ 1994S Proof Only	3,269,923		6.50
☐ 1995	6,411,440,000	.40	
☐ 1995 Double Die		23.00	
☐ 1995D	7,128,560,000	.40	
☐ 1995S Proof Only			7.50
☐ 1996	6,612,500,000	.40	
☐ 1996D	6,510,800,000	.40	
☐ 1996S Proof			4.25
☐ 1997	4,622,800,000	.20	
☐ 1997D	4,576,555,000	.20	
☐ 1997S Proof	1,975,000		7.50
☐ 1998	5,032,150,000	.20	
☐ 1998D	5,225,350,000	.20	
☐ 1998S Proof			6.00
☐ 1999	5,237,600,000	.20	
☐ 1999D	6,360,000,000	.20	
☐ 1999S Proof			3.50
☐ 2000	5,503,200,000	.20	
☐ 2000D	8,774,200,000	.20	
☐ 2000S Proof			3.50
☐ 2001	4,959,600,000	.20	
☐ 2001D	5,374,990,000	.20	
☐ 2001S Proof			3.50
☐ 2002P	3,260,800,000	.20	
☐ 2002D	4,028,055,000	.20	
☐ 2002S Proof			3.50

TWO-CENT PIECES (BRONZE), 1864–1873

The two-cent piece was a short-lived coin whose impact upon the world fell far short of its impact on modern numismatists. Small change was growing increasingly scarce during the Civil War, to the point where postage stamps, encased in holders, were being used for money. The government sought to alleviate this by increased production of the penny and introduced the two-cent piece to take the penny's place in areas where it might not be in sufficient supply. Enormous quantities were struck at the outset, approaching 20 million per year, the composition being the same as that of the penny—95% copper to 5% of tin and zinc. The diameter was 23mm. Designer of the two-cent piece was James Longacre, who did most of the Mint's designing at that time.

There is no portrait on the coin; it carries a U.S. shield on one side and a value statement on the other. The lack of portraiture was undoubtedly an effort to prevent this coin from being confused with the penny. Though larger by 4mm. in diameter than the penny, it must be remembered that Large Cents were still found in circulation in 1864—they had been discontinued less than ten years earlier—and one almost needed a scoreboard to keep track of the denominations of coins passing through one's hands. Production totals of the two-cent piece decreased each year of its minting, until only 65,000 were turned out in 1872, and nothing but proofs and restrikes the following year. It died a very silent death.

1864 Small Motto

First Coin to Bear the Motto IN GOD WE TRUST

1864 Large Motto

DATE	ABP	G-4 GOOD	F-12 FINE	EF-40 EX. FINE	MS-60 UNC.	PRF-65 PROOF
☐ 1864 Small Motto	(19,847,500)					
	50.00	65.00	125.00	350.00	600.00	60000.00
☐ 1864 Large Motto						
	9.00	12.00	20.00	32.00	80.00	3600.00
☐ 1865	(13,640,000)					
	9.00	12.00	22.00	32.00	85.00	2850.00
☐ 1866	(3,177,000)					
	9.00	12.00	22.00	32.00	85.00	1900.00
☐ 1867	(3,915,000)					
	10.00	12.50	22.00	31.00	100.00	2100.00
☐ 1867 Double Die				190.00	300.00	
☐ 1868	(3,252,000)					
	9.00	12.00	22.00	33.00	115.00	1800.00
☐ 1869	(1,546,500)					
	9.00	12.00	21.00	41.00	115.00	1775.00
☐ 1870	(861,250)					
	10.00	13.00	22.00	62.00	175.00	1775.00
☐ 1871	(721,250)					
	10.00	13.00	24.00	75.00	210.00	1775.00
☐ 1872	(65,000)					
	100.00	125.00	225.00	450.00	800.00	1950.00
☐ 1873 Closed 3, Proofs Only	(600)					2850.00
☐ 1873 Open 3 (Restrike), Proofs Only	(480)					5000.00

THREE-CENT PIECES

THREE CENT (SILVER), 1851–1873

America's burgeoning population, plus conditions brought about by the California gold strike, resulted in a shortage of small change during the mid 19th century. The decision was made to strike a coin in three-cents denomination and to have its composition of silver, alloyed with 25% copper. Because of its low face value and precious metal content the coin was extremely small physically. Its designer was James Longacre. Rather than portraiture, a symbolic obverse was used, consisting of a six-pointed star and shield. This was done to avoid confusion with the half dime, whose size and color were similar. On the reverse was the Roman numeral III enclosed within an ornamental letter C (for "cents") and surrounded by small stars. The weight was only $4/5$ of a gram—the lightest coin ever struck by the Mint—with a diameter of just 14mm. It was tiny, indeed. Undoubtedly the government expected that this coin, despite serving an important purpose, would not prove popular. It didn't. After striking about 35 million in the first three years of its production, quantities were sharply reduced thereafter. It was subsequently replaced by the "nickel" three-cent piece following the Civil War, which contained no silver whatever.

Though the basic design of the silver three-cent piece was maintained throughout its lifetime—they continued being struck until 1873, though were rarely circulated after 1862—some minor changes were introduced. In 1854 the obverse star was redrawn with a triple border. The final version, put into use in 1859, has a double border. As there are no great rarities among the circulating dates of this series, a complete

283

collection is well within the realm of possibility. In 1854 there was a change of composition to 90% silver/10% copper and the weight was brought down to $3/4$ of a gram. From then until conclusion of the series all minting was carried out in Philadelphia. Previously the manufacture of this coin had been divided between Philadelphia and New Orleans.

The Mint Mark "O" is on the Reverse to the Right of the III

DATE	ABP	G-4 GOOD	F-12 FINE	EF-40 EX. FINE	MS-60 UNC.	PRF-65 PROOF
☐ 1851 (5,447,400)						
	15.00	20.00	25.00	56.00	1455.00	
☐ 1851O (720,000)						
	20.00	25.00	34.00	110.00	305.00	
☐ 1852 (18,663,500)						
	15.00	22.00	25.00	57.00	140.00	
☐ 1853 (11,400,000)						
	15.00	22.00	25.00	56.00	140.00	
☐ 1854 (671,000)						
	15.00	21.00	25.00	92.00	320.00	32000.00
☐ 1855 (139,000)						
	18.00	23.00	49.00	150.00	510.00	14500.00
☐ 1856 (1,458,000)						
	15.00	22.00	28.00	82.00	285.00	14000.00
☐ 1857 (1,042,000)						
	15.00	22.00	26.00	85.00	280.00	10500.00
☐ 1858 (1,604,000)						
	15.00	21.00	26.00	85.00	250.00	7000.00
☐ 1859 (365,000)						
	13.00	18.00	25.00	62.00	150.00	2000.00
☐ 1860 (287,000)						
	14.00	20.00	25.00	65.00	160.00	3500.00
☐ 1861 (498,000)						
	13.00	18.00	25.00	62.00	160.00	1900.00
☐ 1862 (363,550)						
	13.00	17.00	25.00	62.00	155.00	1650.00

DATE	ABP	G-4 GOOD	F-12 FINE	EF-40 EX. FINE	MS-60 UNC.	PRF-65 PROOF
☐ 1862, 2 over 1						
	13.00	18.00	26.00	60.00	175.00	
☐ 1863	(21,460)					
	170.00	210.00	300.00	360.00	550.00	1400.00
☐ 1863, 3 over 2, Proofs Only						4600.00
☐ 1864	(470)					
	160.00	240.00	300.00	370.00	525.00	1350.00
☐ 1865	(8,500)					
	180.00	250.00	325.00	380.00	550.00	1350.00
☐ 1866	(22,725)					
	150.00	200.00	280.00	350.00	525.00	1350.00
☐ 1867	(4,625)					
	150.00	220.00	325.00	410.00	575.00	1420.00
☐ 1868	(4,100)					
	175.00	260.00	310.00	410.00	550.00	1450.00
☐ 1869	(5,100)					
	175.00	260.00	310.00	380.00	580.00	1420.00
☐ 1870	(4,000)					
	175.00	260.00	310.00	380.00	600.00	1410.00
☐ 1871	(4,260)					
	175.00	260.00	310.00	400.00	570.00	1350.00
☐ 1872	(1,950)					
	175.00	300.00	375.00	425.00	650.00	1350.00
☐ 1873 Proof Only	(600)					1500.00

THREE CENT (NICKEL), 1865–1889

For all practical purposes, the three-cent piece had been out of circulation during most of the Civil War. Upon the war's conclusion its manufacture was resumed, but no longer was the composition chiefly of silver. In fact, the new version contained no precious metal at all. It was composed of 75% copper and 25% nickel. What the three-cent piece lost metallically it gained physically: its weight more than doubled, rising to 1.94 grams, and its diameter increased to 17.0mm. It may be wondered why a coin containing 75% copper would be referred to as a "nickel" rather than a "copper." The explanation is that the term "copper" was already in use for the cent. Americans picked up this nickname from the British, who had long been calling their pennies "coppers." As the new three-cent coin represented the greatest use made of nickel by the Mint up to that time, the name "nickel" seemed appropriate. The coin was somewhat better received than its predecessor, as there was not as much danger of confusing it with another denomination. The fact that its life was not particularly long (it was discontinued in 1889) can be attributed more to inflation than any fault of its own. By 1889 there was simply no longer a pressing need for three-cent pieces. At least 20 million were in circulation at that time and this was deemed more than enough to meet whatever demand might exist. The five-cent piece, which began in 1866 to be composed of the same copper-nickel ratio as the three-cent, was adequately filling whatever need the three-cent had earlier satisfied.

The three-cent nickel carried a Liberty head on its obverse and a large Roman numeral III on the reverse. Like the silver version, it was designed by James Longacre. All were struck at Philadelphia. Throughout the quarter-century of production no changes occurred in its design.

In the following listing, note that ABP is for coins in Fine condition or better. Superbly struck, uncirculated coins bring proportionately more than the prices listed.

DATE	ABP	G-4 GOOD	F-12 FINE	EF-40 EX. FINE	MS-60 UNC.	PRF-65 PROOF
☐ 1865	(11,382,000)					
	8.00	11.00	14.00	21.00	82.00	5500.00
☐ 1866	(4,801,000)					
	8.00	10.00	15.00	21.00	82.00	1500.00
☐ 1867	(3,915,000)					
	8.00	11.00	15.00	21.00	82.00	1350.00
☐ 1868	(3,252,000)					
	8.00	10.00	15.00	21.00	83.00	1300.00
☐ 1869	(1,604,000)					
	8.00	10.00	15.00	21.00	95.00	1000.00

DATE	ABP	G-4 GOOD	F-12 FINE	EF-40 EX. FINE	MS-60 UNC.	PRF-65 PROOF
☐ 1870	(1,335,000)					
	8.50		15.00	23.00	110.00	1750.00
☐ 1871	(604,000)					
	8.50	11.00	15.00	23.00	115.00	1150.00
☐ 1872	(862,000)					
	8.50	11.00	15.00	23.00	110.00	1000.00
☐ 1873 Closed 3	(1,173,000)					
	8.50	11.00	15.00	33.00	135.00	1100.00
☐ 1873 Open 3						
	8.50	11.00	15.00	23.00	100.00	
☐ 1874	(790,000)					
	8.50	11.00	15.00	23.00	115.00	950.00
☐ 1875	(228,000)					
	8.50	11.00	15.00	31.00	135.00	1250.00
☐ 1876	(162,000)					
	9.00	12.00	18.00	38.00	170.00	1100.00
☐ 1877 Proofs Only	(510)					2000.00
☐ 1878 Proofs Only	(2,350)					650.00
☐ 1879	(41,200)					
	30.00	50.00	70.00	85.00	220.00	700.00
☐ 1880	(24,955)					
	40.00	65.00	90.00	130.00	240.00	750.00
☐ 1881	(1,080,575)					
	8.50	11.00	15.00	21.00	80.00	620.00
☐ 1882	(25,300)					
	40.00	70.00	72.00	110.00	250.00	620.00
☐ 1883	(10,609)					
	80.00	120.00	180.00	250.00	360.00	700.00
☐ 1884	(5,642)					
	180.00	260.00	350.00	400.00	475.00	800.00
☐ 1885	(4,790)					
	200.00	300.00	460.00	560.00	650.00	1500.00
☐ 1886 Proofs Only	(4,290)					650.00
☐ 1887	(7,961)					
	150.00	240.00	270.00	290.00	380.00	1000.00
☐ 1887 over 6, Proofs Only						675.00
☐ 1888	(41,083)					
	28.00	38.00	46.00	67.00	200.00	525.00
☐ 1889	(21,561)					
	40.00	62.00	90.00	100.00	240.00	550.00

NICKELS

NICKELS—SHIELD, 1866–1883

Though the silver half dime was still being struck in 1866, its production was too limited to serve as a general circulating coin. This noble old soldier, its origins dating back to the Mint's beginnings, was suffering the effects of general inflation and the bullion shortage of the Civil War, caused in part by a scarcity of laborers for the silver mines. Not knowing what the future might hold, the government had no wish to terminate the silver half dime but it wanted, at the same time, to introduce a coin of proportionate value made of base metal and attempt to popularize it. Thus was born the five-cent nickel or "true nickel," as opposed to the three-cent coin that was also called a nickel.

The five-cent nickel was authorized by Congress on May 16, 1866. It was to have a weight of 5 grams and be composed of three parts copper and one part nickel. The diameter was $20\frac{1}{2}$mm. James Longacre, chief engraver of the Mint, was called upon to design it and produced a portraitless coin consisting of a shielded obverse with Arabic numeral 5 on the reverse surrounded by stars and rays (or bars). IN GOD WE TRUST appears on the obverse above the shield. Nearly 15,000,000 pieces were struck in the first year of issue. In the following year, 1867, after production had continued briefly, the rays were removed from the reverse, resulting in a rarity of moderate proportions for the "with rays" type.

This is not, however, an expensive coin except in uncirculated condition. It may be asked why the 1867 variety With Rays and the standard 1866 date are valued almost equally, when only 2,019,000 of the former and 14,742,500 of the latter were struck, yielding a scarcity ratio of 7-to-1. The answer is simply that the 1866 would *not* be worth so much if it weren't the first date of its series. There are many collectors buying "first dates" who buy no other coins of the series. For this reason the first year of minting of *any* U.S. coin carries a premium over and above the quantity struck or available in the market. (Compare the 1866 value with that of the 1872, of which fewer than half as many were struck; the former is more common but worth more.)

1866–83

1866–67
With Rays

1867–83
Without Rays

DATE	ABP	G-4 GOOD	F-12 FINE	EF-40 EX. FINE	MS-60 UNC.	MS-65 CH. UNC
☐ 1866 With Rays (14,742,500)						
	15.00	20.00	28.00	100.00	225.00	2250.00
☐ 1867 With Rays (30,908,500)						
	15.00	20.00	29.00	130.00	300.00	3200.00
☐ 1867 No Rays						
	9.00	12.00	20.00	40.00	95.00	750.00
☐ 1868 (28,817,000)						
	9.00	12.00	20.00	40.00	95.00	700.00
☐ 1869 (16,395,000)						
	9.00	12.00	20.00	40.00	95.00	650.00
☐ 1870 (4,806,000)						
	9.00	12.00	20.00	40.00	115.00	1000.00
☐ 1871 (561,000)						
	27.00	38.00	48.00	120.00	235.00	1250.00
☐ 1872 (6,036,000)						
	9.00	12.00	17.00	38.00	120.00	850.00
☐ 1873 Closed 3 (4,550,000)						
	18.00	22.00	35.00	115.00	225.00	1000.00
☐ 1873 Open 3						
	10.00	13.00	18.00	45.00	145.00	950.00
☐ 1874 (3,538,000)						
	10.00	14.00	24.00	60.00	130.00	950.00
☐ 1875 (2,097,000)						
	11.00	15.00	28.00	68.00	160.00	1600.00

DATE	ABP	G-4 GOOD	F-12 FINE	EF-40 EX. FINE	MS-60 UNC.	MS-65 CH. UNC.
☐ 1876	(2,530,000)					
	12.00	15.00	26.00	62.00	135.00	850.00
☐ 1877 Proofs Only	(500)					2250.00
☐ 1878	(2,350)				PROOF—750.00	
☐ 1879	(29,100)					
	180.00	225.00	365.00	440.00	550.00	1400.00
☐ 1879 9 over 8					EXTREMELY RARE	
☐ 1880	(19,955)					
	200.00	260.00	365.00	550.00	950.00	5000.00
☐ 1881	(72,375)					
	110.00	140.00	235.00	350.00	550.00	1200.00
☐ 1882	(11,476,600)					
	9.00	12.00	17.00	34.00	110.00	600.00
☐ 1883	(1,456,919)					
	10.00	13.00	18.00	35.00	110.00	625.00
☐ 1883 over 2						
	50.00	65.00	130.00	215.00	390.00	3150.00

NICKEL—LIBERTY HEAD, 1883–1913

When production of the silver half dime picturing Liberty ceased in the 1870s, designers were free to transfer the likeness of this goddess to our nickel five-cent piece. This, however, was not immediately done and, when finally undertaken in 1883, the portrait was not the full figure used for half dimes but a profile bust. The new design was created by Charles E. Barber and gained for this piece the name "Barber nickel," which was once used commonly but seems to have lost popularity. Like its predecessor, it was made of 75% copper and 25% nickel and had a weight of 5 grams. The diameter was slightly larger, measuring 21.2mm., and striking was done at Philadelphia, Denver, and San Francisco.

An embarrassing difficulty occurred with this coin at the outset of production. As first designed, the reverse carried the Roman number V (for 5) without the word CENTS or any sign indicating that cents was intended. Very shortly, unscrupulous persons began gilding the coin with gold wash and passing it to foreigners and other uninformed individuals as a $5 gold piece. The government put a halt to this activity by having the die re-engraved and the word CENTS added.

From then until 1913, when a new design was introduced (the famous Buffalo/Indian), no changes were made in designing. The Liberty Head was struck in great quantities throughout almost its entire run of production, with the total output reaching well into the hundreds of millions. It could still be found in general circulation, though not with much frequency, as late as the 1940s. The 1913 Liberty Head, America's most valuable base-metal coin, has long proved an enigma. The Mint claims not to have struck any Liberty Heads that year, asserting that its production consisted entirely of the Buffalo/Indian. It is certainly believable that no regular production occurred, otherwise the total in existence would not be as small as just five specimens. Even assuming that minting for the year was started with the Liberty Head design and was switched off to the new type after a few days, thousands of coins would by that time have been struck. There seems no logical way in which just five pieces could have been manufactured. The likelihood— though it may slightly tarnish this rarity's appeal—is that 1913 dies were produced, then put aside when the change of design was authorized and used (possibly clandestinely) to strike just a few specimens by a person or persons unknown. This theory is supported by the fact that originally, when first brought to public light, *all five* were owned by the same individual: Colonel Edward H. R. Green of New York, a noted collector of coins, stamps, and art in the World War I era. If struck by the Mint and dispersed, it is almost beyond the realm of possibility that they could have been acquired by one collector within so short a period of time. (Colonel Green, incidentally, is equally noted for being the purchaser of the sheet of 24¢ inverted-center airmail stamps issued in 1918, which he *broke up and sold*; his approach to collecting was rather like that of a dealer or speculator, and one can only wonder at the reason for his association with the 1913 Liberty Head five-cent piece.)

1883   Without CENTS   1887 CENTS

DATE	ABP	G-4 GOOD	F-12 FINE	EF-40 EX. FINE	MS-60 UNC.	MS-65 CH. UNC.
☐ 1883 No CENTS	(5,479,519)					
	3.00	4.00	6.00	9.00	24.00	225.00
☐ 1883 With CENTS	(16,032,983)					
	6.00	8.00	13.50	47.00	90.00	485.00
☐ 1884	(11,273,942)					
	9.00	12.00	18.00	48.00	130.00	1250.00
☐ 1885	(1,476,490)					
	235.00	275.00	375.00	600.00	860.00	3000.00
☐ 1886	(3,330,290)					
	85.00	110.00	175.00	325.00	550.00	3150.00
☐ 1887	(15,263,652)					
	5.00	10.00	20.00	45.00	90.00	800.00
☐ 1888	(10,720,483)					
	10.00	13.00	22.00	60.00	165.00	1100.00
☐ 1889	(15,881,361)					
	3.50	6.00	17.00	40.00	90.00	700.00
☐ 1890	(16,259,272)					
	3.50	6.00	17.00	40.00	120.00	1200.00
☐ 1891	(16,834,350)					
	3.00	4.00	12.50	36.00	125.00	900.00
☐ 1892	(11,699,642)					
	3.00	4.00	15.00	35.00	110.00	1150.00
☐ 1893	(13,370,195)					
	3.00	3.50	12.50	35.00	92.00	950.00
☐ 1894	(5,413,132)					
	5.00	8.00	55.00	150.00	210.00	1050.00
☐ 1895	(9,979,884)					
	2.00	3.00	17.00	45.00	110.00	1350.00
☐ 1896	(8,842,920)					
	3.25	5.00	20.00	45.00	115.00	1300.00
☐ 1897	(20,428,735)					
	1.65	3.00	8.00	26.00	85.00	900.00
☐ 1898	(12,532,087)					
	1.25	1.75	8.00	29.00	115.00	975.00
☐ 1899	(26,029,031)					
	.85	1.60	6.00	26.00	87.00	525.00
☐ 1900	(27,255,995)					
	.85	1.25	4.50	23.00	72.00	525.00
☐ 1901	(26,480,213)					
	.85	1.25	5.00	23.00	72.00	525.00

DATE	ABP	G-4 GOOD	F-12 FINE	EF-40 EX. FINE	MS-60 UNC.	MS-65 CH. UNC.
☐ 1902	(31,480,579)					
	.85	1.25	4.50	23.00	70.00	525.00
☐ 1903	(28,006,725)					
	.85	1.25	4.50	23.00	62.00	525.00
☐ 1904	(21,404,984)					
	.85	1.25	4.50	24.00	62.00	525.00
☐ 1905	(29,827,276)					
	.85	1.25	4.50	23.00	62.00	525.00
☐ 1906	(38,613,725)					
	.85	1.25	4.50	23.00	62.00	525.00
☐ 1907	(39,214,800)					
	.85	1.25	4.50	23.00	62.00	850.00
☐ 1908	(22,686,177)					
	.85	1.25	4.50	23.00	62.00	800.00
☐ 1909	(11,590,526)					
	1.50	2.00	4.50	26.00	70.00	750.00
☐ 1910	(30,169,353)					
	.85	1.25	4.50	22.00	62.00	625.00
☐ 1911	(39,559,372)					
	.85	1.25	4.50	22.00	62.00	525.00
☐ 1912	(26,236,714)					
	.85	1.25	4.00	22.00	62.00	525.00
☐ 1912D	(8,474,000)					
	1.00	1.50	5.75	45.00	212.00	1000.00
☐ 1912S	(238,000)					
	50.00	70.00	120.00	500.00	950.00	3500.00

☐ 1913, Not a Regular Mint Issue, 5 Known

500,000.00–1,500,000.00 Bowers-Eliasberg Sale—1,800,000.00

NICKELS—BUFFALO OR INDIAN HEAD, 1913–1938

Undoubtedly the most dramatic, artistic, and original set of designs employed for a U.S. coin, the Buffalo/Indian Head nickel went into production in 1913. The composition was 75% copper and 25% nickel, with a weight of five grams. Its diameter was 21.2mm. James E. Fraser, the designer, was not one to go half way. He hired an Indian to sit for the obverse portrait and took his sketching gear to the Bronx Zoo to get a likeness of a buffalo in the flesh. The artwork of this coin is little short of superb: each motif fully fills the planchet ground and is unencumbered by large inscriptions or miscellaneous symbols. Unfortunately the rate of wear in handling was such that few individuals aside from collectors had the opportunity to see the coin at its best. Just like the noble animal it pictured, the American bison, this coin proved to be a rapidly disappearing species. Within only twenty years after its discontinuation in 1938 it had all but vanished from circulation, despite enormous production output.

Critics of the Buffalo/Indian Head nickel were few. Those who spoke against it raised the objection that the buffalo was in danger of extinction. So popular did the bison likeness become that the coin, unlike most others, came to be popularly known by its reverse rather than its obverse.

In 1916 a double-die error resulted on some specimens, producing a twin or ghost impression of the date. Of regularly struck pieces, those from the San Francisco Mint in the early and middle 1920s are scarcest.

Mint Mark
is on the
Reverse, Under
FIVE CENTS

1913–1938

1913–
Type I
Buffalo on High Mound

1913
Type 2
Buffalo on Level Ground

DATE	ABP	G-4 GOOD	F-12 FINE	EF-40 EX. FINE	MS-60 UNC.	MS-65 CH. UNC.
☐ 1913 Type 1 (30,993,520)						
	5.00	7.00	8.00	15.00	30.00	120.00
☐ 1913D Type 1 (5,337,000)						
	7.00	8.50	12.50	21.00	52.00	250.00
☐ 1913S Type 1 (2,105,000)						
	15.00	20.00	26.00	46.00	75.00	600.00
☐ 1913 Type 2 (29,858,700)						
	6.00	8.00	9.50	16.00	31.00	300.00
☐ 1913D Type 2 (4,156,000)						
	40.00	50.00	75.00	90.00	150.00	1200.00
☐ 1913S Type 2 (1,209,000)						
	110.00	135.00	225.00	265.00	340.00	3000.00

DATE	ABP	G-4 GOOD	F-12 FINE	EF-40 EX. FINE	MS-60 UNC.	MS-65 CH. UNC.
☐ 1914	(20,665,738)					
	10.00	13.00	15.00	20.00	40.00	375.00
☐ 1914 /3						
	85.00	125.00	350.00	860.00	2650.00	
☐ 1914D	(3,912,000)					
	40.00	50.00	70.00	135.00	225.00	1400.00
☐ 1914S	(3,470,000)					
	10.00	14.00	22.00	42.00	150.00	1750.00
☐ 1915	(20,987,270)					
	3.00	4.00	7.00	17.00	46.00	300.00
☐ 1915D	(7,569,500)					
	8.50	11.50	22.00	78.00	200.00	1950.00
☐ 1915S	(1,505,000)					
	13.00	17.00	46.00	150.00	470.00	2500.00
☐ 1916 Double Die Obverse						
	1200.00	1600.00	5500.00	11000.00	30000.00	
☐ 1916	(63,498,000)					
	2.00	3.00	4.00	6.00	51.00	250.00
☐ 1916D	(13,333,000)					
	6.00	8.50	15.00	60.00	150.00	1900.00
☐ 1916S	(11,860,000)					
	3.50	6.00	11.50	45.00	150.00	1950.00
☐ 1917	(51,424,029)					
	1.50	3.00	4.00	12.00	46.00	475.00
☐ 1917D	(9,910,800)					
	5.00	7.50	28.00	90.00	265.00	3250.00
☐ 1917S	(4,193,000)					
	10.00	15.00	35.00	115.00	335.00	3750.00
☐ 1918	(32,086,314)					
	1.50	3.00	5.00	27.00	80.00	1250.00
☐ 1918D	(8,362,000)					
	5.00	7.00	24.00	150.00	350.00	3850.00
☐ 1918D over 17						
	450.00	550.00	1500.00	5300.00	14000.00	
☐ 1918S	(4,882,000)					
	5.00	7.00	25.00	140.00	370.00	24000.00
☐ 1919	(60,868,000)					
	.75	1.00	1.75	9.50	42.00	485.00
☐ 1919D	(8,006,000)					
	6.00	9.00	32.00	175.00	440.00	5500.00

DATE	ABP	G-4 GOOD	F-12 FINE	EF-40 EX. FINE	MS-60 UNC.	MS-65 CH. UNC.
☐ 1919S	(7,521,000)					
	3.25	7.00	26.00	175.00	450.00	10500.00
☐ 1920	(63,093,000)					
	.60	.85	2.50	11.00	46.00	600.00
☐ 1920D	(9,418,000)					
	3.00	4.50	22.00	225.00	415.00	5750.00
☐ 1920S	(9,689,000)					
	1.50	2.50	15.00	150.00	415.00	18500.00
☐ 1921	(10,683,000)					
	.75	1.15	4.00	32.00	95.00	600.00
☐ 1921S	(1,557,000)					
	25.00	35.00	100.00	675.00	1300.00	5500.00
☐ 1923	(35,715,000)					
	.75	1.00	2.00	9.00	43.00	500.00
☐ 1923S	(6,142,000)					
	2.00	3.50	10.00	215.00	380.00	8250.00
☐ 1924	(21,620,000)					
	.50	1.00	2.00	12.00	62.00	750.00
☐ 1924D	(5,258,000)					
	2.00	3.50	15.00	165.00	310.00	4000.00
☐ 1924S	(1,437,000)					
	5.00	7.00	62.00	970.00	2100.00	9000.00
☐ 1925	(35,565,100)					
	1.00	1.50	2.10	8.50	40.00	475.00
☐ 1925D	(4,450,000)					
	3.50	5.50	28.00	135.00	375.00	4650.00
☐ 1925S	(6,256,000)					
	2.50	4.50	14.00	145.00	410.00	32500.00
☐ 1926	(44,693,000)					
	.40	.80	1.50	7.00	30.00	150.00
☐ 1926D	(5,638,000)					
	2.50	4.50	17.00	130.00	215.00	4400.00
☐ 1926S	(970,000)					
	8.50	11.00	48.00	675.00	3150.00	38500.00
☐ 1927	(37,981,000)					
	.40	.80	1.50	6.75	30.00	225.00
☐ 1927D	(5,730,000)					
	1.00	1.75	5.50	70.00	140.00	5750.00
☐ 1927S	(3,430,000)					
	.85	1.50	4.00	74.00	475.00	15000.00

DATE	ABP	G-4 GOOD	F-12 FINE	EF-40 EX. FINE	MS-60 UNC.	MS-65 CH. UNC.
☐ 1928	(23,411,000)					
	.40	.65	1.00	6.50	29.00	265.00
☐ 1928D	(6,436,000)					
	.75	1.00	3.25	33.00	45.00	750.00
☐ 1928S	(6,936,000)					
	1.00	1.50	2.15	20.00	190.00	4000.00
☐ 1929	(36,446,000)					
	.50	.65	1.00	6.10	28.00	275.00
☐ 1929D	(8,370,000)					
	.50	1.00	1.65	26.00	448.00	1600.00
☐ 1929S	(7,754,000)					
	.40	.65	1.00	11.00	48.00	385.00
☐ 1930	(22,849,000)					
	.40	.65	1.00	4.10	24.50	140.00
☐ 1930S	(5,435,000)					
	.40	.65	1.00	11.00	42.00	435.00
☐ 1931S	(1,200,000)					
	6.50	8.75	10.00	17.50	42.00	235.00
☐ 1934	(20,313,000)					
	.40	.65	.70	4.00	32.00	300.00
☐ 1934D	(7,480,000)					
	.40	.65	.75	12.50	55.00	750.00
☐ 1935	(58,264,000)					
	.40	.60	.70	2.10	21.00	90.00
☐ 1935 Double Die						
	30.00	35.00	75.00	360.00	2400.00	
☐ 1935D	(12,092,000)					
	.40	.65	2.00	12.00	50.00	400.00
☐ 1935S	(10,300,000)					
	.40	.65	.72	3.00	40.00	150.00
☐ 1936	(119,001,420)					
	.40	.65	.72	2.40	14.00	82.00
☐ 1936D	(24,418,000)					
	.40	.65	.72	3.00	28.00	96.00
☐ 1936S	(14,390,000)					
	.40	.65	.72	2.50	29.00	92.00
☐ 1937	(79,485,769)					
	.40	.65	.72	2.50	15.00	50.00
☐ 1937D	(17,826,000)					
	.50	.65	.72	2.00	20.00	55.00
☐ 1937D, 3-Legged Buffalo*						
	135.00	165.00	275.00	410.00	1300.00	18000.00

*Beware of altered coins

DATE	ABP	G-4 GOOD	F-12 FINE	EF-40 EX. FINE	MS-60 UNC.	MS-65 CH. UNC.
☐ 1937S	(5,635,000)					
	.40	.60	.90	2.60	22.00	60.00
☐ 1938D	(7,020,000)					
	1.00	1.40	2.10	3.10	17.50	40.00
☐ 1938D over S						
	3.00	4.50	8.50	12.00	42.00	190.00
☐ 1938D over D						
	1.50	2.50	3.00	5.00	25.00	60.00

NICKELS—JEFFERSON, 1938 TO DATE

In 1938 Thomas Jefferson became the third president to be pictured on an American coin (preceded by Lincoln and Washington) when his likeness was installed on the five-cent piece, replacing the Buffalo/Indian Head. When the decision was made to use Jefferson's portrait on this coin, a public competition was instituted to select the best design, accompanied by an award of $1,000. A total of 390 entries was received, the winning one being that of Felix Schlag.

Jefferson is shown in profile facing left on the obverse, with his home at Monticello pictured on the reverse. No alteration has ever been made in the design of this coin but some changes occurred in composition and modeling of the dies. In 1966 Schlag's initials were added, the feeling being that he deserved this honor as much as the designer of the Lincoln cent, whose initials were incorporated into the design.

The coin has always weighed five grams and measured 21.1mm. Originally its content was 75% copper and 25% nickel. Due to a shortage of nickel during World War II because of its use in military production, this metal was entirely removed from the coin in 1942 and substituted with a composition of 56% copper, 35% silver, and 9% manganese. Wartime nickels consequently carry a premium value because of their silver content, though the silver additive was so small that the premium is only minimal. In 1946 the pre-war composition was resumed and has since remained constant. Prior to 1968 the mint mark was on the reverse, to the right of the design. On wartime specimens (1942–45) it is considerably enlarged and placed above Monticello's dome. From 1968 on, it appears on the obverse between the date and portrait.

Mint Mark from 1968	Felix Schlag (after 1966)	1938–1942 1946 to 1968	1942–1945 Silver Content Type with Large Mint Mark over Dome

DATE	ABP	G-4 GOOD	F-12 FINE	EF-40 EX. FINE	MS-60 UNC.	PRF-65 PROOF
☐ 1938	(19,515,365)					
	.08	.15	.40	.70	2.60	70.00
☐ 1938D	(5,376,000)					
	.45	.70	.90	2.00	4.00	
☐ 1938S	(4,105,000)					
	1.00	1.50	2.10	2.60	4.50	
☐ 1939	(120,627,535)					
	.08	.15	.25	.60	1.30	72.00
☐ 1939 Double Die						
	15.00	26.00	50.00	72.00	175.00	
☐ 1939D	(3,514,000)					
	1.50	3.00	4.50	8.00	36.00	
☐ 1939S	(6,630,000)					
	.40	.70	1.25	3.50	17.00	
☐ 1940	(176,499,158)		.15	.35	.90	60.00
☐ 1940D	(43,540,000)		.25	.42	2.50	
☐ 1940S	(39,690,000)		.20	.42	2.00	
☐ 1941	(203,283,730)		.15	.25	.75	60.00
☐ 1941D	(53,432,000)		.15	.50	2.25	
☐ 1941S	(43,445,000)		.15	.65	3.00	
☐ 1942	(49,818,600)		.15	.45	1.50	60.00
☐ 1942D	(13,938,000)					
	.20	.30	.55	2.50	16.00	
☐ 1942D Horizontal D			42.00	90.00	475.00	
WARTIME SILVER NICKELS						
☐ 1942P	(57,900,600)					
	.20	.30	.70	1.40	5.00	150.00
☐ 1942S	(32,900,000)					
	.20	.30	.85	2.10	5.00	
☐ 1943P	(271,165,000)					
	.20	.30	.50	1.20	3.40	
☐ 1943/2P	25.00	32.00	42.00	90.00	260.00	
☐ 1943 Double Eye						
	15.00	18.00	28.00	50.00	140.00	
☐ 1943D	(15,294,000)					
	.25	.30	.65	1.50	3.00	

DATE	ABP	G-4 GOOD	F-12 FINE	EF-40 EX. FINE	MS-60 UNC.	PRF-65 PROOF
☐ 1943S	(104,060,000)					
	.25	.30	.70	1.20	3.10	
☐ 1944P	(119,150,000)					
	.25	.30	.60	1.20	3.10	
☐ 1944D	(32,309,000)					
	.20	.42	.80	1.60	6.50	
☐ 1944S	(21,640,000)					
	.20	.42	1.00	2.00	4.10	
☐ 1945P	(119,408,100)					
	.25	.32	.55	1.50	3.00	
☐ 1945P Double Eye						
	12.00	16.00	19.00	30.00	80.00	
☐ 1945D	(37,158,000)					
	.30	.42	.90	1.60	3.00	
☐ 1945S	(58,939,000)					
	.20	.30	.45	1.24	2.30	
REGULAR PRE-WAR TYPE						
☐ 1946	(161,116,000)		.10	.30	.62	
☐ 1946D	(45,292,200)		.12	.32	1.00	
☐ 1946D Horizontal D						
	30.00	40.00	76.00	200.00	300.00	
☐ 1946S	(13,560,000)		.24	.36	.45	
☐ 1947	(95,000,000)		.18	.27	.45	
☐ 1947D	(37,882,000)		.10	.37	.75	
☐ 1947S	(24,720,000)		.10	.34	.45	
☐ 1948	(89,348,000)		.10	.27	.45	
☐ 1948D	(44,734,000)		.10	.45	.75	
☐ 1948S	(11,300,000)		.19	.44	.60	
☐ 1949	(60,652,000)		.19	.30	.70	
☐ 1949D	(36,498,000)		.15	.42	.80	
☐ 1949, D over S			25.00	85.00	150.00	
☐ 1949S	(9,716,000)					
	.15	.28	.55	.82	1.60	
☐ 1950	(9,847,386)					
	.10	.17	.22	.47	.80	55.00
☐ 1950D	(2,530,000)					
	3.75	5.00	6.00	6.50	8.00	
☐ 1951	(28,689,500)		.15	.40	.75	40.00
☐ 1951D	(20,460,000)		.15	.40	.70	
☐ 1951S	(7,776,000)					
	.12	.20	.40	.70	1.75	
☐ 1952	(64,069,980)		.12	.15	.70	32.00

DATE	ABP	G-4 GOOD	F-12 FINE	EF-40 EX. FINE	MS-60 UNC.	PRF-65 PROOF
☐ 1952D	(30,638,000)		.10	.35	1.00	
☐ 1952S	(20,572,000)		.10	.25	.65	
☐ 1953	(46,772,800)		.10	.16	.25	32.00
☐ 1953D	(59,878,600)		.10	.16	.35	
☐ 1953S	(19,210,900)		.10	.24	.35	
☐ 1954	(47,917,350)		.10	.12	.22	19.00
☐ 1954D	(117,183,060)		.10	.12	.25	
☐ 1954S	(29,834,000)		.10	.12	.25	
☐ 1954, S over D				16.00	35.00	
☐ 1955	(8,266,200)	.20	.15	.40	.50	11.00
☐ 1955D	(74,464,110)	.08	.10	.12	.25	
☐ 1955, D over S				18.00	40.00	
☐ 1956	(35,885,374)		.10	.18	.22	3.50
☐ 1956D	(67,222,940)		.10	.18	.22	
☐ 1957	(39,655,952)		.10	.18	.22	2.50
☐ 1957D	(136,828,900)		.10	.19	.22	
☐ 1958	(17,963,653)		.10	.18	.22	2.75

Circulated coins of the following dates are not bought by dealers.

DATE	MINTAGE	MS-60 UNC.	PRF-65 PROOF
☐ 1958D	168,249,120	.15	
☐ 1959	28,397,291	.15	1.50
☐ 1959D	160,738,240	.15	
☐ 1960	57,107,602	.15	1.00
☐ 1960D	192,582,180	.15	1.00
☐ 1961	76,668,344	.15	1.00
☐ 1961D	229,342,760	.15	
☐ 1962	100,602,019	.15	1.00
☐ 1962D	280,195,720	.15	
☐ 1963	178,851,645	.15	1.00
☐ 1963D	276,829,460	.15	
☐ 1964	1,028,622,762	.15	1.00
☐ 1964D	1,787,297,160	.15	
☐ 1965	136,131,380	.12	
☐ 1966	156,208,283	.12	
☐ 1967	107,324,750	.12	
☐ 1968D	91,227,800	.12	
☐ 1968S	103,437,510	.12	.70
☐ 1969D	202,807,500	.12	
☐ 1969S	128,099,631	.12	.70
☐ 1970D	515,485,380	.12	
☐ 1970S	241,464,814	.12	.70
☐ 1971	108,884,000	.40	
☐ 1971D	316,144,800	.12	
☐ 1971S Proof Only	3,224,138		1.65

DATE	MINTAGE	MS-60 UNC.	PRF-65 PROOF
☐ 1972	202,036,000	.15	
☐ 1972D	351,694,600	.15	
☐ 1972S Proof Only	3,267,667		1.75
☐ 1973	384,396,000	.15	
☐ 1973D	261,405,400	.15	
☐ 1973S Proof Only	2,769,624		1.50
☐ 1974	601,752,000	.15	
☐ 1974D	277,373,000	.20	
☐ 1974S Proof Only	2,617,350		1.50
☐ 1975	181,772,000	.20	
☐ 1975D	401,875,300	.20	
☐ 1975S Proof Only	2,909,369		2.00
☐ 1976	376,124,000	.15	
☐ 1976D	563,964,147	.15	
☐ 1976S Proof Only	4,149,945		1.75
☐ 1977	585,175,250	.15	
☐ 1977D	297,325,618	.20	
☐ 1977S Proof Only	3,250,095		1.65
☐ 1978	391,308,000	.15	
☐ 1978D	313,092,780	.15	
☐ 1978S Proof Only	3,127,781		1.50
☐ 1979	463,188,123	.15	
☐ 1979D	325,867,600	.15	
☐ 1979S Proof Only, Filled S			1.40
☐ 1979S Proof Only, Open S			1.75
☐ 1980P	593,004,060	.15	
☐ 1980D	502,324,000	.15	
☐ 1980S Proof Only	3,554,800		.85
☐ 1981P	657,503,295	.15	
☐ 1981D	364,802,000	.15	
☐ 1981S Proof Only, Filled S			1.50
☐ 1981S Proof Only, Open S			1.85
☐ 1982P	292,350,000	.20	
☐ 1982D	373,725,500	.60	
☐ 1982S Proof Only			2.50
☐ 1983P	560,750,000	.25	
☐ 1983D	536,726,000	.25	
☐ 1983S Proof Only	3,228,537		2.85
☐ 1984P	750,000,000	.20	
☐ 1984D	518,000,000	.12	
☐ 1984S Proof Only			4.00
☐ 1985P	676,222,421	.12	
☐ 1985D	463,621,747	.12	
☐ 1985S Proof Only	3,241,412		2.25
☐ 1986P	572,842,600	.12	
☐ 1986D	382,610,212	.20	
☐ 1986S Proof Only	3,101,640		7.50
☐ 1987P	362,111,406	.12	
☐ 1987D	411,690,114	.12	

DATE	MINTAGE	MS-60 UNC.	PRF-65 PROOF
☐ 1987S Proof Only	39,821,745		2.75
☐ 1988P	770,350,000	.12	
☐ 1988D	672,700,640	.12	
☐ 1988S Proof Only	3,116,420		6.50
☐ 1989P	896,764,248	.12	
☐ 1989D	580,862,212	.12	
☐ 1989S Proof Only	3,184,776		3.50
☐ 1990P	652,720,114	.12	
☐ 1990D	646,111,042	.12	
☐ 1990S Proof Only	3,720,411		4.75
☐ 1991P	614,100,000	.25	
☐ 1991D	436,495,570	.25	
☐ 1991S Proof Only	2,867,677		4.00
☐ 1992P	399,550,210	.25	
☐ 1992D	450,568,100	.12	
☐ 1992S Proof Only	4,175,610		3.25
☐ 1993P	412,076,000	.12	
☐ 1993D	406,084,135	.12	
☐ 1993S Proof Only	3,394,792		3.25
☐ 1994P	772,160,000	.12	
☐ 1994P Matte Finish+			85.00
☐ 1994D	715,762,110	.12	
☐ 1994S Proof Only	3,269,923		3.00
☐ 1995P	774,156,000	.12	
☐ 1995D	888,112,000	.20	
☐ 1995S Proof Only			4.50
☐ 1996P	829,332,000	.15	
☐ 1996D	817,736,000	.15	
☐ 1996S Proof Only			3.00
☐ 1997P	470,972,000	.15	
☐ 1997D	466,640,000	.15	
☐ 1997S Proof Only	1,975,000		3.75
☐ 1997D Specimen Frosted Issued in 2-Piece Botanic Gardens + Jefferson $1.00 Sets.			190.00
☐ 1998P	640,776,000	.15	
☐ 1998D	612,920,000	.15	
☐ 1998S Proof Only			3.00
☐ 1999P	1,212,000,000	.15	
☐ 1999D	1,066,720,000	.15	
☐ 1999S Proof Only			2.50
☐ 2000P	846,220,000	.15	
☐ 2000D	1,509,520,000	.15	
☐ 2000S Proof Only			1.50
☐ 2001P	675,740,000	.15	
☐ 2001D	627,680,000	.15	
☐ 2001S Proof Only			1.75
☐ 2002P	539,280,000	.15	
☐ 2002D	691,200,000	.15	
☐ 2002S Proof			1.75

HALF DIMES, 1794–1873

The first half dimes did not technically reach manufacture until 1795 but carried a 1794 date, as the dies had been engraved that year and there was no desire to redo this work. The weight was 1.35 grams, the composition consisting of .8924 silver and .1076 copper; or, to speak in rounded figures, nine parts silver to one part copper. After more than forty years of being unchanged compositionally, the silver content was raised to a full nine parts in 1837, which necessitated a weight reduction to 1.34 grams.

The original obverse type was the Flowing Hair Liberty, similar to that of other silver coinage of the time. Its designer was Robert Scot. On the reverse appeared the standing eagle and legend UNITED STATES OF AMERICA. This was replaced by the Draped Bust type with similar reverse in 1796, and the shield eagle reverse in 1800. Beginning in 1829 the Capped Bust was introduced, along with a modified version of the shield eagle (wings downward instead of upturned). The sharpest departure occurred in 1837, with the introduction of a design that was to remain—with modifications—until the series closed out in 1873. This was the Seated Liberty, an attractive bit of classical portraiture but one to which some objection was voiced on the grounds that it closely resembled the figure of Britannia on British coins. The reverse carried the wording HALF DIME within an open wreath, encircled by UNITED STATES OF AMERICA. There was initially no decoration on the obverse beyond the figure of Liberty. In 1838 a series of stars was added as a half-frame to the portrait. Arrows were placed by the date in 1853. The chief revision came in 1860 when the words UNITED STATES OF AMERICA were removed from the reverse and placed on the obverse, supplanting the stars. The reverse wreath was redesigned and made larger and frillier to fill the vacancy.

304

HALF DIMES—LIBERTY WITH FLOWING HAIR, 1794–1795

DATE	MINTAGE	ABP	G-4 GOOD	F-12 FINE	VF-20 V. FINE
☐ 1794	86,416	650.00	750.00	1200.00	1900.00
☐ 1795		450.00	550.00	1000.00	1400.00

(Both the 1794 and 1795 were struck in 1795)

HALF DIMES—DRAPED BUST, SMALL EAGLE, 1796–1797

DATE	MINTAGE	ABP	G-4 GOOD	F-12 FINE	VF-20 V. FINE
☐ 1796 over 5		650.00	800.00	1500.00	2350.00
☐ 1796	10,230	550.00	650.00	1250.00	2100.00
☐ 1796 LIKERTY		575.00	675.00	1300.00	2100.00
☐ 1797 (13 stars)		550.00	725.00	1300.00	2300.00
☐ 1797 (15 stars)	44,527	550.00	675.00	1100.00	2100.00
☐ 1797 (16 stars)		575.00	675.00	1150.00	2200.00

HALF DIMES—DRAPED BUST, LARGE EAGLE, 1800–1805

DATE	MINTAGE	ABP	G-4 GOOD	F-12 FINE	VF-20 V. FINE
☐ 1800		300.00	425.00	750.00	1200.00
☐ 1800 LIBEKTY	24,000	300.00	425.00	950.00	1250.00
☐ 1801	33,910	400.00	500.00	975.00	1350.00
☐ 1802 VERY RARE	13,010	6500.00	8000.00	18000.00	32000.00
☐ 1803	37,850	400.00	450.00	850.00	1300.00
☐ 1805	15,600	510.00	650.00	950.00	1500.00

HALF DIMES—LIBERTY CAP, 1829–1837

DATE	ABP	G-4 GOOD	F-12 FINE	EF-40 EX. FINE	MS-63 UNC.
☐ 1829	(1,230,000)				
	15.00	20.00	34.00	115.00	575.00
☐ 1830	(1,240,000)				
	15.00	20.00	34.00	110.00	575.00
☐ 1831	(1,242,700)				
	15.00	20.00	28.00	110.00	575.00
☐ 1832	(965,000)				
	15.00	20.00	28.00	110.00	600.00
☐ 1833	(1,370,000)				
	15.00	20.00	28.00	110.00	580.00
☐ 1834	(1,480,000)				
	15.00	20.00	28.00	110.00	580.00
☐ 1835*	(2,760,000)				
	15.00	20.00	30.00	110.00	580.00
☐ 1836	(1,900,000)				
	15.00	20.00	34.00	110.00	650.00
☐ 1837 Large $.05	(2,276,000)				
	15.00	20.00	35.00	110.00	750.00
☐ 1837 Small $.05					
	20.00	22.00	45.00	150.00	1900.00

*Note: 1835 Large Date—Large $.05, Large Date—Small $.05, Same prices;
Small Date—Small $.05, Small Date—Large $.05, Same prices.

HALF DIMES—LIBERTY SEATED, 1837–1859

1837–1838O
No Stars

1838–1859
With Stars

1837–1859
Mint Mark is on the Reverse Under the Value

DATE	ABP	G-4 GOOD	F-12 FINE	EF-40 EX. FINE	MS-60 UNC.	MS-65 CH. UNC.
☐ 1837 Small Date, No Stars						
	20.00	26.00	52.00	180.00	600.00	3800.00
☐ 1837 Large Date, No Stars		(2,250,000)				
	20.00	26.00	50.00	175.00	600.00	3500.00
☐ 1838O No Stars (70,000)						
	50.00	75.00	180.00	575.00	2500.00	19500.00
☐ 1838 With Large Stars (2,255,000)						
	8.00	10.00	14.00	64.00	230.00	2000.00
☐ 1838 With Small Stars						
	12.00	18.00	46.00	140.00	610.00	4300.00
☐ 1839 (1,069,150)						
	8.00	11.00	14.00	50.00	275.00	1900.00
☐ 1839O (1,096,550)						
	9.00	13.00	18.00	72.00	475.00	5000.00
☐ 1839O With Large O						
	225.00	450.00	1000.00	2800.00		
☐ 1840 No Drapery (1,344,085)						
	8.00	10.00	15.00	50.00	275.00	2000.00
☐ 1840O No Drapery						
	9.00	12.00	18.00	72.00	525.00	12000.00
☐ 1840 Drapery						
	12.00		48.00	165.00	425.00	2500.00
☐ 1840O Drapery						
	20.00	27.00	85.00	36.00	2300.00	
☐ 1841 (1,500,000)						
	7.50	10.00	16.00	52.00	165.00	1200.00
☐ 1841O (815,000)						
	8.00	11.00	24.00	90.00	575.00	
☐ 1842 (815,000)						
	7.50	12.00	19.00	50.00	170.00	1550.00

DATE	ABP	G-4 GOOD	F-12 FINE	EF-40 EX. FINE	MS-60 UNC.	MS-65 CH. UNC.
☐ 1842O	(350,000)					
	18.00	25.00	47.00	450.00	925.00	13000.00
☐ 1843	(1,165,000)					
	7.50	10.00	16.00	50.00	175.00	1250.00
☐ 1844	(430,000)					
	8.50	12.00	14.00	58.00	190.00	1350.00
☐ 1844O	(220,000)					
	50.00	64.00	200.00	725.00	4700.00	17000.00
☐ 1844O Large O						
	55.00	74.00	160.00	800.00		
☐ 1845	(1,564,000)					
	7.50	10.00	14.00	43.00	145.00	1150.00
☐ 1846	(27,000)					
	125.00	165.00	415.00	1500.00	6350.00	
☐ 1847	(1,274,000)					
	7.50	10.00	15.00	46.00	165.00	1200.00
☐ 1848 Medium Date	(668,000)					
	7.50	10.00	15.00	46.00	185.00	2350.00
☐ 1848 Large Date						
	12.00	14.00	32.00	95.00	470.00	3350.00
☐ 1848O	(600,000)					
	10.00	14.00	27.00	82.00	340.00	1850.00
☐ 1849	(1,309,000)					
	7.50	11.00	16.00	52.00	150.00	1650.00
☐ 1849 over 46	(1,309,000)					
	9.00	12.00	22.00	87.00	370.00	6500.00
☐ 1849 over 48	(1,309,000)					
	10.00	13.50	27.00	90.00	380.00	2750.00
☐ 1849O	(140,000)					
	16.00	27.00	76.00	350.00	1700.00	12500.00
☐ 1850	(955,000)					
	7.50	10.00	15.00	46.00	160.00	1250.00
☐ 1850O	(690,000)					
	8.00	10.00	18.00	90.00	625.00	3800.00
☐ 1851	(781,000)					
	7.50	10.00	14.00	45.00	145.00	1250.00
☐ 1851O	(860,000)					
	7.50	10.00	18.00	85.00	410.00	3500.00
☐ 1852	(1,000,000)					
	7.50	9.50	16.00	50.00	160.00	1200.00
☐ 1852O	(260,000)					
	15.00	22.00	52.00	200.00	700.00	9000.00

DATE	ABP	G-4 GOOD	F-12 FINE	EF-40 EX. FINE	MS-60 UNC.	MS-65 CH. UNC.
☐ 1853 With Arrows (13,210,020)						
	8.00	10.00	11.00	42.00	160.00	1500.00
☐ 1853 No Arrows (135,000)						
	18.00	24.00	58.00	180.00	600.00	2850.00
☐ 1853O With Arrows (2,360,000)						
	7.50	10.00	13.00	52.00	180.00	3250.00
☐ 1853O No Arrows (160,000)						
	100.00	125.00	280.00	1100.00	5000.00	
☐ 1854 With Arrows (5,740,000)						
	7.50	10.00	16.00	44.00	180.00	1750.00
☐ 1854O With Arrows (1,560,000)						
	7.50	11.00	13.00	60.00	215.00	3850.00
☐ 1855 With Arrows (1,750,000)						
	7.50	11.00	13.00	45.00	182.00	1850.00
☐ 1855O With Arrows (600,000)						
	10.00	13.00	25.00	125.00	475.00	3750.00
☐ 1856 (4,880,000)						
	7.00	11.00	12.50	45.00	150.00	1450.00
☐ 1856O (1,100,000)						
	7.50	11.00	17.00	80.00	475.00	1800.00
☐ 1857 (7,280,000)						
	7.00	11.00	12.50	45.00	142.00	1350.00
☐ 1857O (1,380,000)						
	7.50	11.00	17.00	50.00	285.00	1650.00
☐ 1858 (3,500,000)						
	7.00	11.00	15.00	45.00	140.00	1150.00
☐ 1858 Over Inverted Date						
	18.00	27.00	54.00	180.00	500.00	2650.00
☐ 1858 Double Date						
	25.00	36.00	80.00	230.00	600.00	
☐ 1858O (1,660,000)						
	7.00	11.00	16.50	65.00	240.00	1600.00
☐ 1859* (340,000)						
	8.00	11.00	22.00	65.00	200.00	1400.00
☐ 1859O (560,000)						
	9.00	12.00	23.00	95.00	235.00	1700.00

*Note: There are two recognized patterns in this series: the transitional pieces of 1859 and 1860. 1859—proof: $9,500.00; 1860—unc: $4,100.00.

HALF DIMES—LIBERTY SEATED, 1860–1873
WITH "UNITED STATES OF AMERICA"
ON OBVERSE

Mint Marks are Under or Within Wreath on Reverse

DATE	ABP	G-4 GOOD	F-12 FINE	EF-40 EX. FINE	MS-60 UNC.	MS-65 CH. UNC.
☐ 1860	(799,000)					
	8.50	11.00	12.00	32.00	120.00	1050.00
☐ 1860O	(1,060,000)					
	7.00	10.00	16.00	42.00	150.00	1200.00
☐ 1861	(3,361,000)					
	7.00	10.00	12.00	32.00	115.00	950.00
☐ 1861 over O						
	15.00	21.00	47.00	210.00	480.00	3350.00
☐ 1862	(1,492,550)					
	7.50	10.00	12.00	31.00	120.00	1000.00
☐ 1863	(18,460)					
	100.00	120.00	200.00	350.00	550.00	1600.00
☐ 1863S	(100,000)					
	15.00	22.00	38.00	100.00	640.00	2100.00
☐ 1864	(48,470)					
	185.00	225.00	340.00	675.00	875.00	2250.00
☐ 1864S	(90,000)					
	30.00	40.00	72.00	200.00	610.00	3400.00
☐ 1865	(13,500)					
	175.00	190.00	340.00	480.00	700.00	1800.00
☐ 1865S	(120,000)					
	20.00	26.00	38.00	145.00	780.00	
☐ 1866	(10,725)					
	175.00	200.00	315.00	460.00	625.00	2750.00
☐ 1866S	(120,000)					
	15.00	200.00	35.00	125.00	410.00	4200.00
☐ 1867	(8,625)					
	275.00	300.00	410.00	575.00	750.00	2000.00
☐ 1867S	(120,000)					
	15.00	21.00	30.00	130.00	480.00	

DATE	ABP	G-4 GOOD	F-12 FINE	EF-40 EX. FINE	MS-60 UNC.	MS-65 CH. UNC.
☐ 1868	(89,200)					
	30.00	34.00	91.00	230.00	525.00	2000.00
☐ 1868S	(280,000)					
	8.00	10.00	21.00	42.00	260.00	3000.00
☐ 1869	(280,000)					
	8.00	10.00	15.00	38.00	175.00	1250.00
☐ 1869S	(230,000)					
	8.00	10.00	12.00	36.00	250.00	3600.00
☐ 1870*	(536,000)					
	7.50	9.00	12.00	32.00	125.00	1000.00
☐ 1871	(1,873,960)					
	7.50	9.00	12.00	32.00	115.00	1000.00
☐ 1871S	(161,000)					
	9.00	11.00	25.00	70.00	210.00	2250.00
☐ 1872	(2,947,950)					
	7.50	11.00	12.00	32.00	120.00	1000.00
☐ 1872S In Wreath	(837,000)					
	7.50	10.00	12.00	32.00	120.00	1000.00
☐ 1872S Below Wreath						
	7.50	11.00	12.00	32.00	120.00	1000.00
☐ 1873	(712,600)					
	7.50	11.00	13.50	32.00	120.00	1000.00
☐ 1873S	(324,000)					
	8.00	11.00	14.00	35.00	125.00	1050.00

*Note: 1870S is unique; only one known.

DIMES

EARLY DIMES, 1796–1891

A coin valued at one-tenth of a dollar was among the first to be authorized by the U.S. Mint, though production did not begin until 1796. Had the dime made its debut even just a year sooner, there is every likelihood it would have carried the Flowing Hair design, but by 1796 there was no longer much enthusiasm for this rendition of Liberty and so the coin got its start with the Draped Bust portrait. This version of Liberty, familiar on other silver pieces, lacks the "cap of liberty" and shows the goddess with a somewhat more fashionable hairdo. On the reverse was the standing eagle, encircled by branches and the inscription UNITED STATES OF AMERICA. Stars were placed in a circular pattern on the obverse, ranging in number from thirteen to sixteen. The designer was Robert Scot. The weight of this coin was 2.70 grams and its original composition was .8924 silver and .1076 copper, the same as that of the half dime (or, approximately, nine parts of silver to one part of copper). Its diameter was generally 19mm. but slight variations are observed.

In 1798 the standing eagle was replaced by the heraldic or shield eagle on the reverse, over which is a series of stars. Just like the stars on the original obverse, these too can vary in quantity from thirteen to sixteen. In 1809 the portrait was changed to the Capped Bust, whose chief characteristic (aside from Liberty's headgear) is that the profile is switched round to face left instead of right. The reverse type is now the eagle-on-branch, still bearing a shield but with its wings down instead of opened wide. The year 1837 witnessed the most significant alteration up to the time; a likeness of Liberty seated replaced the bust type and the eagle's place on the reverse was taken by the wording ONE DIME within a wreath, surrounded by UNITED STATES OF AMERICA. At first there were no stars on the obverse but these were added in 1838, and arrows were placed at the date in 1853. These, however, were of little duration as they disappeared in 1856.

DIMES—DRAPED BUST, 1796–1807
EAGLE ON REVERSE

1798–1807

1796–1797
Small Eagle

1798–1807
Large Eagle

DATE	MINTAGE	ABP	G-4 GOOD	F-12 FINE	VF-20 V. FINE
☐ 1796	22,135	750.00	900.00	1950.00	2850.00
☐ 1797 13 Stars		750.00	1000.00	1900.00	3000.00
☐ 1797 16 Stars	25,261	750.00	1050.00	1400.00	3000.00
☐ 1798		325.00	450.00	775.00	1100.00
☐ 1798 over 97 With 13 Stars on Reverse					
		800.00	1600.00	2850.00	4200.00
☐ 1798 Small 8	27,500	450.00	500.00	1000.00	1950.00
☐ 1798 over 97 With 16 Stars on Reverse					
		350.00	425.00	850.00	1050.00
☐ 1800	21,760	350.00	425.00	700.00	1050.00
☐ 1801	34,640	350.00	400.00	800.00	1500.00
☐ 1802	10,975	500.00	650.00	1300.00	2650.00
☐ 1803	33,040	300.00	450.00	800.00	1400.00
☐ 1804 With 13 Stars on Reverse					
	8,265	750.00	1000.00	2150.00	3850.00
☐ 1804 With 14 Stars on Reverse					
	8,265	850.00	1050.00	2750.00	5000.00
☐ 1805 With 4 Berries	120,780	250.00	400.00	600.00	750.00
☐ 1805 With 5 Berries	120,780	310.00	500.00	800.00	1200.00
☐ 1807	165,000	250.00	400.00	600.00	800.00

DIMES—LIBERTY CAP, 1809–1837

DATE	ABP	G-4 GOOD	F-12 FINE	EF-40 EX. FINE	MS-60 UNC.
☐ 1809 (44,710)					
	70.00	90.00	300.00	900.00	4000.00
☐ 1811 over 9 (65,180)					
	40.00	100.00	240.00	875.00	2400.00
☐ 1814 Small Date (421,500)					
	30.00	36.00	150.00	380.00	1700.00
☐ 1814 Large Date					
	20.00	26.00	50.00	350.00	900.00
☐ 1814 STATES OF AMERICA, No Breaks Between Words: Large Date					
	25.00	30.00	70.00	350.00	1000.00
☐ 1820 Small O					
	15.00	20.00	40.00	350.00	1000.00
☐ 1820 Large O (942,587)					
	15.00	22.00	40.00	300.00	875.00
☐ 1821 Small Date (1,186,512)					
	15.00	22.00	50.00	380.00	1150.00
☐ 1821 Large Date					
	15.00	22.00	40.00	340.00	900.00
☐ 1822 (100,000)					
	225.00	300.00	750.00	2000.00	8000.00
☐ 1823 over 22, Small E (440,000)					
	15.00	21.00	38.00	280.00	950.00
☐ 1824 over 22 Large E					
	15.00	22.00	75.00	475.00	1350.00
☐ 1824 over 22	15.00	20.00	45.00	450.00	1750.00
☐ 1825 (Mintage includes 1824) (510,000)					
	15.00	20.00	40.00	320.00	800.00
☐ 1827 (1,215,000)					
	15.00	18.00	36.00	290.00	800.00
☐ 1828 Large Date (125,000)					
	20.00	50.00	150.00	550.00	2000.00
☐ 1828 Small Date (125,000) (Reduced Beaded Borders)					
	20.00	25.00	65.00	310.00	900.00
☐ 1829 Small $.10 (770,000)					
	15.00	24.00	50.00	200.00	675.00

DATE	ABP	G-4 GOOD	F-12 FINE	EF-40 EX. FINE	MS-60 UNC.
☐ 1829 Medium Date					
	15.00	18.00	28.00	200.00	800.00
☐ 1829 Large $.10 (770,000)					
	16.00	21.00	75.00	300.00	1550.00
☐ 1830 Small $.10 (510,000)					
	15.00	18.00	27.00	185.00	700.00
☐ 1830 Large $.10					
	15.00	18.00	27.00	185.00	800.00
☐ 1830, 30 over 29					
	23.00	28.00	95.00	350.00	1000.00
☐ 1831 (771,350)					
	15.00	18.00	26.00	170.00	650.00
☐ 1832 (522,500)					
	15.00	18.00	26.00	170.00	575.00
☐ 1833 (485,000)					
	15.00	18.00	26.00	170.00	575.00
☐ 1834** Small 4 (635,000)					
	17.00	20.00	29.00	170.00	600.00
☐ 1834 Large 4					
	17.00	20.00	28.00	170.00	610.00
☐ 1835 (1,410,000)					
	15.00	18.00	26.00	170.00	575.00
☐ 1836 (1,190,000)					
	15.00	18.00	26.00	170.00	610.00
☐ 1837 ALL KINDS (359,500)					
	15.00	18.00	26.00	170.00	650.00

**1834—Small 4, 1834—Large 4: Same Price

DIMES—LIBERTY SEATED, 1837–1860

1837–38O
No Stars

1837–91

1838–60
With Stars

DATE	ABP	G-4 GOOD	F-12 FINE	EF-40 EX. FINE	MS-60 UNC.
☐ 1837 No Stars, Small Date (682,500)					
	25.00	.28	70.00	460.00	975.00

DATE	ABP	G-4 GOOD	F-12 FINE	EF-40 EX. FINE	MS-60 UNC.
☐ 1837 Large Date					
	18.00	27.00	66.00	425.00	950.00
☐ 1838O No Stars (402,404)					
	22.00	36.00	100.00	600.00	2400.00
☐ 1838 Small Stars No Drapery					
	14.00	17.00	45.00	145.00	600.00
☐ 1838 Large Stars (1,992,500)					
	10.00	14.00	16.00	65.00	340.00
☐ 1838 Partial Drapery					
	15.00	18.00	48.00	155.00	500.00
☐ 1839 (1,053,115)					
	10.00	13.00	15.00	67.00	290.00
☐ 1839O (1,243,272)					
	10.00	13.00	17.00	74.00	450.00
☐ 1839O Reverse 1838O					
	80.00	120.00	280.00	575.00	
☐ 1840 No Drape (1,358,580)					
	10.00	13.00	15.00	56.00	300.00
☐ 1840O No Drape (1,175,000)					
	10.00	13.00	20.00	80.00	850.00
☐ 1840 Drapery Added (377,541)					
	20.00	27.00	74.00	240.00	950.00
☐ 1841 (1,622,500)					
	7.00	10.00	15.00	42.00	290.00
☐ 1841O (2,007,500)					
	7.00	10.00	18.00	64.00	700.00
☐ 1841Large O Close Bud Reverse					
	450.00	600.00	1400.00		
☐ 1842 (1,887,500)					
	7.00	10.00	14.00	35.00	280.00
☐ 1842O (2,020,000)					
	8.00	11.00	18.00	175.00	2100.00

DATE	ABP	G-4 GOOD	F-12 FINE	EF-40 EX. FINE	MS-60 UNC.	MS-65 CH. UNC.
☐ 1843 (1,370,000)						
	7.00	9.00	15.00	42.00	270.00	
☐ 1843/1843						
	20.00	25.00	40.00	140.00	440.00	
☐ 1843O (150,000)						
	20.00	31.00	86.00	465.00	1700.00	
☐ 1844 (72,500)						
	140.00	175.00	390.00	910.00	2600.00	

DATE	ABP	G-4 GOOD	F-12 FINE	EF-40 EX. FINE	MS-60 UNC.	MS-65 CH. UNC.
☐ 1845	(1,755,000)					
	7.50	9.00	12.00	36.00	235.00	2750.00
☐ 1845/1845						
	15.00	20.00	28.00	140.00		
☐ 1845O	(230,000)					
	13.00	18.00	60.00	400.00	1500.00	
☐ 1846	(31,300)					
	42.00	65.00	125.00	700.00	3500.00	
☐ 1847	(245,000)					
	8.50	11.00	32.00	115.00	650.00	
☐ 1848	(451,000)					
	7.50	11.00	19.00	65.00	455.00	4400.00
☐ 1849	(839,000)					
	7.00	11.00	15.00	40.00	260.00	
☐ 1849O	(300,000)					
	8.00	11.00	35.00	225.00	2000.00	
☐ 1850	(1,931,500)					
	7.00	11.00	12.00	46.00	260.00	4500.00
☐ 1850O	(510,000)					
	7.00	11.00	21.00	87.00	860.00	
☐ 1851	(1,026,500)					
	7.00	11.00	14.00	35.00	285.00	4250.00
☐ 1851O	(400,000)					
	7.00	11.00	27.00	125.00	1750.00	
☐ 1852	(1,535,500)					
	7.00	11.00	14.00	36.00	2400.00	2500.00
☐ 1852O	(430,000)					
	10.00	15.00	32.00	200.00	1400.00	
☐ 1853 No Arrows	(95,000)					
	28.00	45.00	95.00	280.00	700.00	2700.00
☐ 1853 With Arrows	(12,173,010)					
	7.50	9.50	12.00	45.00	265.00	2600.00
☐ 1853O	(1,100,000)					
	7.50	9.50	16.00	80.00	900.00	7500.00
☐ 1854	(4,470,000)					
	7.50	9.50	14.00	40.00	280.00	2600.00
☐ 1854O	(1,770,000)					
	7.50	9.50	14.00	46.00	300.00	2800.00
☐ 1855	(2,075,000)					
	7.50	9.50	14.00	46.00	330.00	3000.00
☐ 1856 Small Date	(5,780,000)					
	7.00	9.00	14.00	37.00	240.00	2850.00

DATE	ABP	G-4 GOOD	F-12 FINE	EF-40 EX. FINE	MS-60 UNC.	MS-65 CH. UNC
☐ 1856 Large Date						
	8.00	11.00	15.00	45.00	260.00	3250.00
☐ 1856O	(1,180,000)					
	8.00	10.00	16.00	60.00	600.00	4750.00
☐ 1856S	(70,000)					
	65.00	84.00	220.00	710.00	2800.00	17500.00
☐ 1857	(5,580,000)					
	7.00	10.00	15.00	34.00	260.00	2600.00
☐ 1857O	(1,540,000)					
	7.00	10.00	15.00	46.00	375.00	2750.00
☐ 1858	(1,540,000)					
	7.00	10.00	15.00	32.00	250.00	2500.00
☐ 1858O	(290,000)					
	10.00	14.00	33.00	120.00	600.00	4000.00
☐ 1858S	(60,000)					
	55.00	71.00	150.00	500.00	2150.00	
☐ 1859*	(430,000)					
	7.00	11.00	15.00	45.00	250.00	2700.00
☐ 1859O	(480,000)					
	7.00	11.00	15.00	60.00	340.00	2600.00
☐ 1859S	(60,000)					
	50.00	75.00	165.00	700.00	3250.00	
☐ 1860S	(140,000)					
	20.00	27.00	50.00	240.00	2000.00	9000.00

*Note: There is a recognized pattern in this series—1859 Transitional Pattern Proof: $15,000

DIMES—LIBERTY SEATED, 1860–1891 WITH "UNITED STATES OF AMERICA" ON OBVERSE

Mint Marks Under or Within Wreath on Reverse

DATE	ABP	G-4 GOOD	F-12 FINE	EF-40 EX. FINE	MS-60 UNC.	MS-65 CH. UNC
☐ 1860	(607,000)					
	7.00	10.00	14.00	35.00	160.00	1300.00

DATE	ABP	G-4 GOOD	F-12 FINE	EF-40 EX. FINE	MS-60 UNC.	MS-65 CH. UNC
☐ 1860O	(40,000)					
	200.00	300.00	600.00	2600.00	1100.00	
☐ 1861	(1,924,000)					
	7.00	10.00	14.00	29.00	140.00	1250.00
☐ 1861S	(172,500)					
	24.00	30.00	82.00	260.00	1300.00	
☐ 1862	(847,550)					
	7.00	10.00	16.00	35.00	180.00	1350.00
☐ 1862S	(180,750)					
	23.00	34.00	62.00	200.00	1100.00	
☐ 1863	(14,460)					
	200.00	240.00	460.00	620.00	1050.00	3500.00
☐ 1863S	(157,000)					
	19.00	28.00	49.00	160.00	1000.00	
☐ 1864	(39,070)					
	140.00	190.00	340.00	625.00	940.00	2750.00
☐ 1864S	(230,000)					
	14.00	18.00	37.00	110.00	850.00	4500.00
☐ 1865	(10,500)					
	150.00	210.00	430.00	650.00	960.00	2850.00
☐ 1865S	(175,000)					
	14.00	21.00	46.00	180.00	1700.00	
☐ 1866	(8,725)					
	200.00	250.00	425.00	800.00	1150.00	2800.00
☐ 1866S	(135,000)					
	22.00	42.00	65.00	200.00	950.00	
☐ 1867	(6,625)					
	250.00	310.00	650.00	900.00	1250.00	2750.00
☐ 1867S	(140,000)					
	16.00	30.00	62.00	190.00	975.00	6100.00
☐ 1868	(466,250)					
	7.00	10.00	27.00	60.00	275.00	2850.00
☐ 1868S	(260,000)					
	9.00	15.00	27.00	110.00	375.00	4250.00
☐ 1869	(256,600)					
	9.00	14.00	30.00	72.00	475.00	3000.00
☐ 1869S	(450,000)					
	8.00	13.00	17.00	60.00	450.00	2750.00
☐ 1870	(471,500)					
	7.00	11.00	15.00	62.00	215.00	1750.00
☐ 1870S	(50,000)					
	150.00	185.00	275.00	600.00	1600.00	

DATE	ABP	G-4 GOOD	F-12 FINE	EF-40 EX. FINE	MS-60 UNC.	MS-65 CH. UNC
☐ 1871	(753,610)					
	8.00	10.00	12.00	40.00	310.00	1500.00
☐ 1871CC	(20,100)					
	650.00	750.00	1650.00	7000.00	21000.00	
☐ 1871S	(320,000)					
	15.00	21.00	34.00	150.00	475.00	
☐ 1872	(2,396,450)					
	7.00	10.00	13.00	27.00	150.00	1200.00
☐ 1872CC	(24,000)					
	225.00	300.00	950.00	4250.00	24000.00	
☐ 1872S	(190,000)					
	12.00	22.00	70.00	210.00	1000.00	
☐ 1873*	(2,378,500)					
	7.00	10.00	21.00	150.00	460.00	
☐ 1873** Open 3	(1,508,600)					
	12.00	18.00	43.00	130.00	460.00	
☐ 1873**Closed 3	(60,000)					
	7.00	10.00	12.00	37.00	140.00	1500.00
☐ 1873CC**	(12,400)	UNIQUE—ONLY ONE KNOWN—				
		BOWERS–ELIASBERG SALE 1999—632500.00				
☐ 1873CC*	(18,791)					
	450.00	800.00	2350.00	4600.00	18000.00	
☐ 1873S*	(455,000)					
	10.00	14.00	28.00	160.00	710.00	
☐ 1874 With Arrows	(2,940,000)					
	7.00	10.00	16.00	425.00	435.00	
☐ 1874CC With Arrows	(10,817)					
	800.00	2000.00	5000.00	16000.00		
☐ 1874S With Arrows	(240,000)					
	15.00	21.00	62.00	250.00	850.00	
☐ 1875	(10,350,000)					
	7.00	10.00	13.00	25.00	125.00	875.00
☐ 1875CC In Wreath						
	7.50	9.50	13.00	35.00	185.00	1650.00
☐ 1875CC Below Wreath	(4,645,000)					
	7.50	10.00	13.00	45.00	215.00	2000.00
☐ 1875S In Wreath						
	7.00	10.00	14.00	38.00	180.00	1100.00
☐ 1875S Below Wreath	(9,070,000)					
	7.50	9.50	14.00	22.00	170.00	1000.00
☐ 1876	(11,461,150)					
	7.00	10.00	13.00	22.00	160.00	875.00

*With Arrows **No Arrows

DATE	ABP	G-4 GOOD	F-12 FINE	EF-40 EX. FINE	MS-60 UNC.	MS-65 CH. UNC.
☐ 1876CC	(8,270,000)					
	7.00	10.00	13.00	32.00	180.00	1250.00
☐ 1876CC Double Obverse						
	15.00	20.00	41.00	210.00	460.00	
☐ 1876S	(10,420,000)					
	7.50	10.00	14.00	35.00	140.00	1650.00
☐ 1877	(7,310,510)					
	7.00	11.00	15.00	24.00	130.00	900.00
☐ 1877CC	(7,700,000)					
	7.00	11.00	14.00	29.00	160.00	950.00
☐ 1877S	(2,340,000)					
	8.00	11.00	15.00	36.00	140.00	1400.00
☐ 1878	(1,678,300)					
	7.00	9.00	14.00	23.00	155.00	975.00
☐ 1878CC	(200,000)					
	30.00	46.00	85.00	265.00	850.00	2300.00
☐ 1879	(15,100)					
	125.00	150.00	210.00	375.00	500.00	1050.00
☐ 1880	(37,355)					
	75.00	90.00	200.00	300.00	510.00	1250.00
☐ 1881	(24,975)					
	100.00	100.00	175.00	290.00	460.00	1500.00
☐ 1882	(3,911,100)					
	7.00	11.00	15.00	22.00	125.00	900.00
☐ 1883	(7,675,712)					
	7.00	11.00	12.00	22.00	130.00	875.00
☐ 1884	(3,366,380)					
	7.00	11.00	12.00	22.00	125.00	900.00
☐ 1884S	(564,969)					
	12.00	16.00	29.00	76.00	620.00	3750.00
☐ 1885	(2,533,427)					
	7.00	10.00	13.00	22.00	130.00	900.00
☐ 1885S	(43,690)					
	250.00	410.00	610.00	1800.00	4800.00	
☐ 1886	(6,377,570)					
	7.00	10.00	13.00	24.00	135.00	900.00
☐ 1886S	(206,524)					
	18.00	23.00	42.00	82.00	450.00	
☐ 1887	(11,283,939)					
	7.00	11.00	13.00	21.00	124.00	900.00
☐ 1887S	(4,454,450)					
	7.00	11.00	13.00	21.00	124.00	1050.00
☐ 1888	(5,496,487)					
	7.00	11.00	13.00	21.00	124.00	900.00

DATE	ABP	G-4 GOOD	F-12 FINE	EF-40 EX. FINE	MS-60 UNC.	MS-65 CH. UNC.
☐ 1888S	(1,720,000)					
	8.00	11.00	13.00	30.00	190.00	2500.00
☐ 1889	(7,380,711)					
	7.00	11.00	14.00	23.00	130.00	875.00
☐ 1889S	(972,678)					
	7.50	11.00	20.00	52.00	365.00	4000.00
☐ 1890	(9,911,541)					
	7.00	11.00	13.00	25.00	130.00	875.00
☐ 1890S	(1,423,076)					
	7.50	11.00	20.00	66.00	320.00	1750.00
☐ 1890S over S						
	15.00	24.00	38.00	124.00		
☐ 1891	(15,310,600)					
	7.00	11.00	13.00	24.00	140.00	875.00
☐ 1891O	(4,540,000)					
	7.00	11.00	13.00	23.00	150.00	1000.00
☐ 1891S	(3,196,116)					
	7.00	11.00	13.00	23.00	130.00	1300.00
☐ 1891O With Horizontal O						
	40.00	75.00	125.00	210.00		

DIMES—LIBERTY HEAD OR BARBER, 1892–1916

Mint Mark is Under Wreath on the Reverse

After many years of using a seated figure of Liberty on the dime, it was decided in 1892 to return to a facial portrait. The designer was Charles E. Barber, resulting in the coin coming to be popularly known among collectors as the "Barber dime." Liberty wears a wreath and is encircled by the inscription UNITED STATES OF AMERICA, with the date appearing below the portrait. The reverse is unchanged from that used earlier, the words ONE DIME enclosed in a wreath. This coin's weight was set at 2.5 grams. Its composition was nine parts silver to one part copper and its diameter 17.9mm. It was struck at Philadelphia, Denver, San Francisco, and New Orleans. The very rare 1894 San Francisco minting, of which only twenty-four were produced, is the stellar item of this series. In 1916 the Liberty Head design was replaced by the so-called Mercury Head.

DATE	ABP	G-4 GOOD	F-12 FINE	EF-40 EX. FINE	MS-60 UNC.	MS-65 CH. UNC
☐ 1892	(12,121,245)					
	2.00	4.00	16.00	25.00	94.00	700.00
☐ 1892O	(3,841,700)					
	5.00	7.00	25.00	50.00	142.00	1250.00
☐ 1892S	(990,710)					
	35.00	42.00	150.00	210.00	360.00	3250.00
☐ 1893	(3,340,792)					
	5.00	7.00	15.00	38.00	110.00	925.00
☐ 1893, 3 over 2						
	90.00	120.00	145.00	200.00	600.00	3800.00
☐ 1893O	(1,760,000)					
	20.00	25.00	100.00	150.00	275.00	2850.00
☐ 1893S	(2,491,401)					
	6.00	10.00	26.00	50.00	265.00	4000.00
☐ 1894	(1,330,972)					
	10.00	13.00	95.00	150.00	240.00	1200.00
☐ 1894O	(720,000)					
	35.00	45.00	175.00	310.00	1210.00	9250.00
☐ 1894S	EXTREMELY RARE—STACKS SALE OCT. 2000—431,250.00					
☐ 1895	(690,880)					
	45.00	60.00	275.00	440.00	600.00	2350.00
☐ 1895O	(440,000)					
	175.00	220.00	675.00	1750.00	4000.00	13500.00
☐ 1895S	(1,120,000)					
	25.00	35.00	110.00	180.00	475.00	7000.00
☐ 1896	(2,000,672)					
	5.00	7.00	45.00	72.00	180.00	1350.00
☐ 1896O	(610,000)					
	40.00	50.00	260.00	375.00	1100.00	8000.00
☐ 1896S	(575,056)					
	50.00	65.00	235.00	360.00	750.00	3500.00
☐ 1897	(10,869,264)					
	1.00	2.00	8.00	35.00	115.00	710.00
☐ 1897O	(666,000)					
	37.00	45.00	225.00	350.00	950.00	4000.00
☐ 1897S	(1,342,844)					
	10.00	15.00	90.00	125.00	450.00	3650.00

DATE	ABP	G-4 GOOD	F-12 FINE	EF-40 EX. FINE	MS-60 UNC.	MS-65 CH. UNC.
□ 1898	(16,320,735)					
	1.00	2.00	6.50	21.00	94.00	700.00
□ 1898O	(2,130,000)					
	5.00	7.00	72.00	140.00	410.00	3250.00
□ 1898S	(1,702,507)					
	3.50	5.00	24.00	52.00	360.00	3750.00
□ 1899	(19,580,846)					
	1.50	2.50	6.10	25.00	100.00	680.00
□ 1899O	(2,650,000)					
	3.50	5.00	60.00	115.00	380.00	4150.00
□ 1899S	(1,867,493)					
	4.00	7.00	18.00	40.00	275.00	4300.00
□ 1900	(17,600,912)					
	1.00	2.25	7.00	22.00	90.00	775.00
□ 1900O	(2,010,000)					
	10.00	13.00	85.00	185.00	540.00	5000.00
□ 1900S	(5,168,270)					
	2.00	3.00	9.50	24.00	165.00	1650.00
□ 1901	(18,860,478)					
	1.25	1.75	7.20	20.00	100.00	740.00
□ 1901O	(5,620,000)					
	1.75	3.00	13.00	47.00	375.00	2850.00
□ 1901S	(593,022)					
	45.00	55.00	290.00	400.00	900.00	4250.00
□ 1902	(21,380,777)					
	1.25	1.75	6.00	24.00	92.00	575.00
□ 1902O	(4,500,000)					
	1.80	3.00	13.00	42.00	335.00	4000.00
□ 1902S	(2,070,000)					
	3.50	6.00	45.00	85.00	350.00	2850.00
□ 1903	(19,500,755)					
	1.00	2.00	4.00	26.00	92.00	1000.00
□ 1903O	(8,180,000)					
	1.50	2.00	11.50	28.00	235.00	4350.00
□ 1903S	(613,300)					
	45.00	55.00	300.00	650.00	950.00	3000.00
□ 1904	(14,601,027)					
	1.00	2.00	7.00	18.00	115.00	1950.00
□ 1904S	(800,000)					
	22.00	30.00	120.00	235.00	660.00	3750.00
□ 1905	(14,552,350)					
	1.00	1.50	6.00	20.00	94.00	575.00

DATE	ABP	G-4 GOOD	F-12 FINE	EF-40 EX. FINE	MS-60 UNC.	MS-65 CH. UNC.
☐ 1905O	(3,400,000)					
	2.00	3.50	30.00	60.00	260.00	1700.00
☐ 1905O Micro O						
	12.00	21.00	72.00	150.00	775.00	5000.00
☐ 1905S	(6,855,199)					
	1.50	3.00	7.00	32.00	215.00	875.00
☐ 1906	(19,958,406)					
	1.00	3.00	4.00	24.00	86.00	575.00
☐ 1906D	(4,060,000)					
	1.50	2.50	7.00	31.00	150.00	1500.00
☐ 1906O	(2,610,000)					
	2.50	5.00	40.00	75.00	185.00	1200.00
☐ 1906S	(3,136,640)					
	1.25	2.50	12.00	38.00	220.00	1300.00
☐ 1907	(22,220,575)					
	1.00	2.00	4.00	20.00	86.00	575.00
☐ 1907D	(4,080,000)					
	1.25	3.00	7.00	42.00	250.00	3650.00
☐ 1907O	(5,058,000)					
	1.20	2.00	30.00	52.00	190.00	1150.00
☐ 1907S	(3,178,470)					
	1.50	3.00	10.00	44.00	335.00	2100.00
☐ 1908	(10,600,545)					
	1.00	1.50	4.50	20.00	86.00	575.00
☐ 1908D	(7,490,000)					
	1.20	2.00	4.50	24.00	120.00	900.00
☐ 1908O	(1,789,000)					
	3.00	5.00	40.00	72.00	265.00	1800.00
☐ 1908S	(3,220,000)					
	1.25	2.50	10.00	33.00	280.00	2350.00
☐ 1909	(10,240,650)					
	1.00	1.50	3.75	19.00	93.00	575.00
☐ 1909D	(954,000)					
	3.50	5.50	50.00	116.00	425.00	2650.00
☐ 1909O	(2,287,000)					
	1.25	2.75	9.00	30.00	180.00	1300.00
☐ 1909S	(2,000,000)					
	4.50	6.50	70.00	150.00	460.00	2750.00
☐ 1910	(11,520,551)					
	.90	1.50	4.00	18.00	90.00	575.00
☐ 1910D	(3,490,000)					
	1.25	2.00	7.00	42.00	200.00	1450.00

DATE	ABP	G-4 GOOD	F-12 FINE	EF-40 EX. FINE	MS-60 UNC.	MS-65 CH. UNC.
☐ 1910S	(1,240,000)					
	2.00	3.00	42.00	80.00	375.00	1900.00
☐ 1911	(18,870,543)					
	1.00	1.50	4.00	19.00	90.00	575.00
☐ 1911D	(11,209,000)					
	1.00	1.50	4.00	20.00	90.00	650.00
☐ 1911S	(3,530,000)					
	1.25	1.75	7.50	30.00	175.00	725.00
☐ 1912	(19,350,700)					
	1.00	1.50	4.00	20.00	90.00	575.00
☐ 1912D	(11,760,000)					
	1.00	1.50	4.00	18.00	92.00	575.00
☐ 1912S	(3,420,000)					
	1.00	1.50	5.00	28.00	135.00	900.00
☐ 1913	(19,760,000)					
	1.00	1.50	3.50	19.00	92.00	575.00
☐ 1913S	(510,000)					
	7.00	10.00	65.00	175.00	415.00	1100.00
☐ 1914	(17,670,655)					
	1.00	1.50	4.00	20.00	90.00	575.00
☐ 1914D	(11,908,000)					
	1.00	1.50	4.00	20.00	90.00	575.00
☐ 1914S	(2,100,000)					
	1.50	2.10	7.50	32.00	135.00	950.00
☐ 1915	(5,620,450)					
	1.00	1.65	4.00	20.00	92.00	575.00
☐ 1915S	(960,000)					
	2.50	4.00	28.00	55.00	230.00	1500.00
☐ 1916	(18,490,000)					
	1.00	1.50	4.00	20.00	92.00	575.00
☐ 1916S	(5,820,000)					
	1.00	1.50	4.50	19.00	92.00	750.00

DIMES—MERCURY DIMES, 1916–1945

The Mercury dime is misnamed. The likeness on its obverse is not that of Mercury (a male god) but Liberty, the same mythological figure who had graced dimes since their introduction in 1796. Confusion resulted from the attachment of small wings to Liberty's headdress, which, to students of Greek and Roman folklore, could only represent Mercury, the "quick messenger," whom the gods equipped with wings to better execute his duties. To give Liberty wings was a bit of poetic license; the intended meaning was "liberty of thought," but so vague was this concept that its purpose remained unserved. On the reverse was an object that caused only slightly less confusion—a vertical column of some kind that only the most astute observers could identify. This was designed as a bundle of fasces or sticks with an axe protruding. In Roman times, an imperial or senatorial procession was often accompanied by "fasces bearers" who carried these bundles of wood sticks throughout the streets. Their meaning was supposedly symbolic but they likewise served a practical function: when dusk fell they could be lighted to illuminate the path.

Designer of the Mercury dime was Adolph Weinman. Its specifications are the same as those of the Barber dime. The mint mark appears on the reverse, between the words ONE and DIME, to the left of the fasces. The Mercury dime was composed of 90% silver and 10% copper. It has a weight of 2.5 grams and diameter of 17.9mm.

Mint Mark is on Reverse at Bottom to Left of Branches

Enlargement Showing 1942 over 41 Dime

DATE	ABP	G-4 GOOD	F-12 FINE	VF-20 V. FINE	EF-40 EX. FINE	MS-60 UNC.
☐ 1916	(22,180,000)					
	2.00	3.00	6.00	6.00	12.00	28.00
☐ 1916D	(264,000)					
	450.00	550.00	1250.00	1600.00	2400.00	4500.00
☐ 1916S	(10,450,000)					
	2.50	4.00	7.50	11.00	17.00	36.00
☐ 1917	(55,230,000)					
	1.00	1.50	3.50	6.00	7.50	25.00
☐ 1917D	(9,402,000)					
	2.25	2.75	11.00	21.00	40.00	120.00
☐ 1917S	(27,330,000)					
	1.00	1.50	4.10	7.00	11.00	57.00

DATE	ABP	G-4 GOOD	F-12 FINE	VF-20 V. FINE	EF-40 EX. FINE	MS-60 UNC.
☐ 1918	(26,680,000)					
	1.25	2.00	5.00	11.00	24.00	65.00
☐ 1918D	(22,674,800)					
	2.00	3.00	4.50	11.00	21.00	95.00
☐ 1918S	(19,300,000)					
	1.25	1.75	4.00	10.00	15.00	86.00
☐ 1919	(35,740,000)					
	1.00	1.60	4.00	7.50	11.00	36.00
☐ 1919D	(9,939,000)					
	2.00	3.00	10.00	22.00	32.00	175.00
☐ 1919S	(8,850,000)					
	2.00	3.00	7.50	14.00	32.00	160.00
☐ 1920	(59,030,000)					
	.80	1.40	3.00	5.00	8.00	30.00
☐ 1920D	(19,171,000)					
	1.50	2.50	5.00	6.50	17.00	105.00
☐ 1920S	(13,820,000)					
	1.50	2.50	5.00	8.00	16.00	110.00
☐ 1921	(1,230,000)					
	20.00	26.00	78.00	170.00	440.00	950.00
☐ 1921D	(1,080,000)					
	30.00	38.00	122.00	220.00	470.00	1000.00
☐ 1923*	(50,130,000)					
	.75	1.40	2.35	4.10	8.00	28.00
☐ 1923S	(6,440,000)					
	1.25	1.75	6.50	13.00	52.00	150.00
☐ 1924	(24,010,000)					
	.70	1.25	2.50	5.50	11.50	40.00
☐ 1924D	(6,810,000)					
	1.75	2.75	6.00	15.00	42.00	145.00
☐ 1924S	(7,120,000)					
	1.50	2.50	4.10	9.10	42.00	160.00
☐ 1925	(25,610,000)					
	.70	1.10	2.60	5.00	8.10	26.00
☐ 1925D	(5,117,000)					
	2.50	3.00	11.00	36.00	95.00	350.00
☐ 1925S	(5,850,000)					
	1.50	2.50	6.00	12.00	60.00	165.00
☐ 1926	(32,160,000)					
	.65	1.10	1.75	3.10	5.10	26.00

*All dimes with 23D date are counterfeit

DATE	ABP	G-4 GOOD	F-12 FINE	VF-20 V. FINE	EF-40 EX. FINE	MS-60 UNC.
☐ 1926D	(6,828,000)					
	1.50	2.50	4.50	7.50	22.00	110.00
☐ 1926S	(1,520,000)					
	4.50	6.50	19.50	45.00	190.00	775.00
☐ 1927	(28,080,000)					
	.65	1.10	2.10	3.50	5.00	25.00
☐ 1927D	(4,812,000)					
	1.50	2.00	6.00	18.00	57.00	165.00

DATE	ABP	G-4 GOOD	F-12 FINE	VF-20 V. FINE	EF-40 EX. FINE	MS-60 UNC.	PRF-65 PROOF
☐ 1927S	(4,770,000)						
	1.25	1.75	4.50	7.00	21.00	250.00	
☐ 1928	(19,480,000)						
	.65	1.10	2.00	4.00	5.00	26.00	
☐ 1928D	(4,161,000)						
	1.75	2.25	7.50	17.00	41.00	150.00	
☐ 1928S	(7,400,000)						
	1.00	1.25	3.00	5.50	15.00	110.00	
☐ 1929	(25,970,000)						
	.65	1.25	2.50	3.50	5.50	19.00	
☐ 1929D	(5,034,000)						
	1.00	1.80	4.00	6.50	14.00	24.00	
☐ 1929S	(4,730,000)						
	1.00	1.25	2.50	4.10	6.50	30.00	
☐ 1930	(6,770,000)						
	.80	1.20	2.50	4.10	6.50	26.00	
☐ 1930S	(1,843,000)						
	1.50	2.50	4.00	6.50	14.00	65.00	
☐ 1931	(3,150,000)						
	1.50	2.00	3.00	6.00	9.00	32.00	
☐ 1931D	(1,260,000)						
	4.00	6.00	10.00	15.00	28.00	82.00	
☐ 1931S	(1,800,000)						
	2.00	2.75	4.25	7.00	12.00	75.00	
☐ 1934	(24,080,000)						
	.40	.65	1.50	2.25	3.75	18.00	
☐ 1934D	(6,772,000)						
	.60	.85	3.00	6.00	10.00	42.00	
☐ 1935	(58,830,000)						
	.40	.65	.90	1.20	1.60	9.00	

DATE	ABP	G-4 GOOD	F-12 FINE	VF-20 V. FINE	EF-40 EX. FINE	MS-60 UNC.	PRF-65 PROOF
☐ 1935D	(10,477,000)						
	1.00	1.10	2.35	4.25	7.50	32.00	
☐ 1935S	(15,840,000)						
	.85	1.00	1.60	1.80	3.50	22.00	
☐ 1936	(87,504,130)						
	.40	.60	.95	1.25	1.75	8.00	1750.00
☐ 1936D	(16,132,000)						
	1.00	1.10	1.50	2.60	5.00	25.00	
☐ 1936S	(9,210,000)						
	1.00	1.10	1.50	2.00	3.00	18.00	
☐ 1937	(56,865,756)						
	.40	.65	1.25	1.50	2.00	8.00	700.00
☐ 1937D	(14,146,000)						
	1.00	1.00	1.50	2.60	3.60	19.00	
☐ 1937S	(9,740,000)						
	1.00	1.00	1.50	2.60	4.25	21.00	
☐ 1938	(22,198,728)						
	.40	.55	.90	1.50	2.40	12.00	410.00
☐ 1938D	(5,537,000)						
	1.10	1.25	1.75	2.10	4.50	14.00	
☐ 1938S	(8,090,000)						
	.70	1.00	1.25	1.90	3.25	17.00	
☐ 1939	(67,749,321)						
	.40	.55	.90	1.10	1.20	8.00	400.00
☐ 1939D	(24,394,000)						
	.70	.90	1.16	1.35	1.50	7.00	
☐ 1939S	(10,540,000)						
	.70	1.00	1.45	2.10	3.50	18.00	
☐ 1940	(65,361,827)						
	.40	.50	.75	1.00	1.65	5.50	350.00
☐ 1940D	(21,198,000)						
	.40	.50	.75	1.10	1.85	7.50	
☐ 1940S	(21,560,000)						
	.40	.50	.90	1.10	1.60	8.00	
☐ 1941	(175,106,557)						
	.40	.50	.75	.90	1.25	5.50	325.00
☐ 1941D	(45,634,000)						
	.40	.50	.75	1.10	1.50	7.50	
☐ 1941S	(43,090,000)						
	.40	.50	1.10	1.30	1.50	7.50	

DATE	ABP	G-4 GOOD	F-12 FINE	VF-20 V. FINE	EF-40 EX. FINE	MS-60 UNC.	PRF-65 PROOF
☐ 1942	(205,432,329)						
	.40	.50	.75	1.00	1.35	5.00	325.00
☐ 1942 Part of Above over 41							
	250.00	325.00	385.00	400.00	500.00	1600.00	
☐ 1942/41D							
	200.00	225.00	350.00	375.00	490.00	1700.00	
☐ 1942D	(60,740,000)						
	.40	.50	.82	1.00	1.70	7.00	
☐ 1942S	(49,300,000)						
	.40	.50	.82	1.15	1.70	9.00	
☐ 1943	(191,710,000)						
	.40	.50	.80	.95	1.30	5.00	
☐ 1943D	(71,949,000)						
	.40	.50	.80	.90	1.45	6.50	
☐ 1943S	(60,400,000)						
	.40	.50	.85	1.00	1.65	7.50	
☐ 1944	(231,410,000)						
	.40	.50	.75	.90	1.35	5.00	
☐ 1944D	(62,224,000)						
	.40	.50	.80	1.15	1.40	6.50	
☐ 1944S	(49,490,000)						
	.40	.50	.85	1.15	1.40	6.50	
☐ 1945	(159,130,000)						
	.40	.50	.75	.85	1.25	5.10	
☐ 1945D	(40,245,000)						
	.40	.50	.80	1.20	1.50	5.10	
☐ 1945S	(41,920,000)						
	.40	.50	.80	1.20	1.35	6.50	
☐ 1945S Micro S							
	.80	1.10	2.10	2.75	5.50	23.00	

DIMES—ROOSEVELT, 1946 TO DATE

The Roosevelt dime series is significant for the change made to clad composition in 1965. Upon the death of President Roosevelt in 1945 there was considerable public sentiment to install his likeness on a coin. The penny, nickel, and quarter were not seriously considered, as they already carried portraits of former presidents. As no dollars were being struck, this left only the dime and half dollar, which both carried representations of Liberty, as suitable choices. The dime was selected, probably because of the much wider distribution of this coin. The designer was John Sinnock.

Roosevelt is shown in profile facing left, with the word LIB-ERTY and the inscription IN GOD WE TRUST. The bundle of fasces was retained as the central element for the reverse type, which was redrawn. Originally the mint mark appeared on the reverse, as it had on the Mercury dime, then was switched to the obverse on clad pieces. The weight was $2\frac{1}{2}$ grams. The composition of this coin, originally 90% silver and 10% copper, was altered in 1965 to three parts copper/one part nickel outer covering with an interior of pure copper, yielding a weight of 2.27 grams. The diameter remained 17.9mm.

In the first year of striking the clad dime, more pieces were manufactured than had ever been turned out of a ten-cent piece in the Mint's history, more than 1.6 billion. A serious shortage of dimes had resulted from spectators hoarding the silver coins and this abundant new supply was intended to replace those lost from circulation. A mintage figure of more than 2 billion was achieved in 1967, or more than $1 worth of dimes for every U.S. citizen.

  Mint Mark is on Reverse of Left, Bottom of Torch.

 From 1968 Mint Mark at Base of Neck.

DATE	MINTAGE	ABP	MS-60 UNC.	PRF-65 PROOF
☐ 1946	255,250,000	.60	1.00	
☐ 1946D	61,043,500	.75	1.25	
☐ 1946S	27,900,000	.85	1.50	
☐ 1947	121,500,000	.85	1.55	
☐ 1947D	46,835,000	1.50	2.25	
☐ 1947S	38,840,000	1.25	2.00	
☐ 1948	74,950,000	2.50	4.00	
☐ 1948D	52,841,000	1.75	2.75	
☐ 1948S	35,520,000	1.40	2.10	
☐ 1949	30,940,000	7.00	10.00	
☐ 1949D	26,034,000	2.50	3.75	
☐ 1949S	13,510,000	10.00	15.00	
☐ 1950	50,181,500	1.00	2.00	35.00
☐ 1950D	46,803,000	1.25	3.00	

DATE	MINTAGE	ABP	MS-60 UNC.	PRF-65 PROOF
☐ 1950S	20,440,000	6.00	10.00	
☐ 1951	103,937,602	.65	1.25	40.00
☐ 1951D	52,191,800	.70	1.50	
☐ 1951S	31,630,000	3.00	5.00	
☐ 1952	99,122,073	.85	1.75	27.00
☐ 1952D	122,100,000	.60	1.25	
☐ 1952S	44,419,500	2.50	4.00	
☐ 1953	53,618,920	.60	1.10	25.00
☐ 1953D	156,433,000	.60	1.00	
☐ 1953S	39,180,000	.50	.85	
☐ 1954	114,243,503	.45	.75	11.00
☐ 1954D	106,397,000	.45	.65	
☐ 1954S	22,860,000	.40	.60	
☐ 1955	12,828,381	.40	.70	9.25
☐ 1955D	13,959,000	.40	.70	
☐ 1955S	18,510,000	.40	.70	
☐ 1956	109,309,384	.40	.65	3.50
☐ 1956D	108,015,100	.40	.65	
☐ 1957	161,407,952	.40	.65	3.00
☐ 1957D	113,354,330	.40	.70	
☐ 1958	32,785,652	.40	.65	3.25
☐ 1958D	136,564,600	.40	.60	
☐ 1959	86,929,291	.40	.60	2.00
☐ 1959D	164,919,790	.40	.65	
☐ 1960	72,081,602	.35	.50	1.75
☐ 1960D	200,160,400	.35	.50	
☐ 1961	96,756,244	.35	.50	1.50
☐ 1961D	209,146,550	.35	.50	
☐ 1962	75,668,019	.35	.50	1.50
☐ 1962D	334,948,380	.35	.50	
☐ 1963	126,725,645	.35	.50	1.50
☐ 1963D	421,476,530	.35	.50	
☐ 1964	933,310,762	.35	.50	1.50
☐ 1964D	1,357,517,180	.35	.50	
☐ 1965 Clad Coinage Begins	1,652,140,570		.40	
☐ 1966	1,382,734,540		.40	
☐ 1967	2,244,077,300		.40	
☐ 1968	424,470,400		.40	
☐ 1968D	480,748,280		.40	
☐ 1968S Proof Only	3,041,508			1.00

DATE	MINTAGE	ABP	MS-60 UNC.	PRF-65 PROOF
☐ 1969	145,790,000		.85	
☐ 1969D	563,323,870		.40	
☐ 1969S Proof Only	2,934,631			1.25
☐ 1970	345,570,000		.40	
☐ 1970D	754,942,000		.40	
☐ 1970S Proof Only	2,632,810			1.25
☐ 1971	162,690,000		.45	
☐ 1971D	377,914,240		.40	
☐ 1971S Proof Only	3,244,138			1.25
☐ 1972	431,540,000		.40	
☐ 1972D	330,290,000		.40	
☐ 1972S Proof Only	3,267,667			1.25
☐ 1973	315,670,000		.40	
☐ 1973D	455,032,425		.40	
☐ 1973 Proof Only	2,769,624			1.25
☐ 1974	470,248,000		.40	
☐ 1974D	571,083,000		.40	
☐ 1974S Proof Only	2,617,350			1.40
☐ 1975	585,673,900		.45	
☐ 1975D	313,705,250		.35	
☐ 1975S Proof Only	2,909,369			2.00
☐ 1976	568,760,000		.45	
☐ 1976D	695,222,774		.45	
☐ 1976S Proof Only	4,149,945			1.40
☐ 1977	796,900,480		.35	
☐ 1977D	376,610,420		.35	
☐ 1977S Proof Only	3,250,895			1.75
☐ 1978	663,908,000		.35	
☐ 1978D	282,847,540		.35	
☐ 1978S Proof Only	3,127,781			1.50
☐ 1979	315,440,007		.35	
☐ 1979D	390,921,285		.35	
☐ 1979S Proof (I)	3,677,200			1.50
☐ 1979S Proof (II)				1.75
☐ 1980P	735,170,079		.35	
☐ 1980D	719,354,382		.35	
☐ 1980S Proof Only	3,547,130			1.50
☐ 1981P	676,000,000		.30	
☐ 1981D	712,285,000		.30	
☐ 1981S Proof Type I	4,063,080			1.50

DATE	MINTAGE	ABP	MS-60 UNC.	PRF-65 PROOF
☐ 1982P* 1981-S Type II	519,474,983		4.75	3.75
☐ 1982D	541,721,064		1.25	
☐ 1982S Proof Only	3,857,000			1.85
☐ 1983P	646,124,004		2.50	
☐ 1983D	730,130,000		.90	
☐ 1983S Proof Only	3,228,650			1.75
☐ 1984P	856,670,936		.50	
☐ 1984D	704,731,827		.55	
☐ 1984S Proof Only	3,000,210			2.00
☐ 1985P	712,182,461		.60	
☐ 1985D	589,641,000		.50	
☐ 1985S Proof Only	3,121,410			1.50
☐ 1986P	670,210,401		.90	
☐ 1986D	476,420,831		.85	
☐ 1986S Proof Only	3,110,120			3.25
☐ 1987P	774,621,460		.30	
☐ 1987D	676,294,210		.30	
☐ 1987S Proof Only	3,622,101			1.75
☐ 1988P	1,113,410,702		.35	
☐ 1988D	982,001,670		.30	
☐ 1988S Proof Only	3,124,683			2.75
☐ 1989P	1,301,640,121		.35	
☐ 1989D	898,421,711		.35	
☐ 1989S Proof Only	3,200,620			3.50
☐ 1990P	1,130,260,420		.35	
☐ 1990D	876,572,143		.35	
☐ 1990S Proof Only	3,726,456			2.00
☐ 1991P	927,200,110		.35	
☐ 1991D	601,245,110		.45	
☐ 1991S Proof Only	2,867,860			3.50
☐ 1992P	593,550,600		.35	
☐ 1992D	616,273,920		.35	
☐ 1992S Proof Only	2,858,970			3.75

*Note: In 1983, dimes dated 1982 and bearing no mint mark began to be discovered. At first they caused a furor as it was believed they might be great rarities (largely because a whole year had passed before any were noticed). During the first month or two of trading, prices on MS-65 specimens reached as high as $600. At that time it was thought that as few as 300 or 400 might exist. Later it was revealed that a Midwest source owned 4,000 and the existing total is now estimated at around 8,000. Prices on MS-65 specimens are in the $100 to $175 range. Beware of removed mint mark.

DATE	MINTAGE	ABP	MS-60 UNC.	PRF-65 PROOF
☐ 1992S Silver Proof	1,317,575			5.50
☐ 1993P	766,180,000		.35	
☐ 1993D	750,110,166		.35	
☐ 1993S Proof Only	2,633,439			6.50
☐ 1993S Silver Proof	761,350			7.50
☐ 1994P	1,189,000,000		.35	
☐ 1994D	1,303,268,110		.35	
☐ 1994S Proof Only	2,484,524			4.25
☐ 1994S Silver Proof	785,325			6.75
☐ 1995P	1,125,500,000		.35	
☐ 1995D	1,274,890,000		.40	
☐ 1995S Proof Only	2,010,284			20.00
☐ 1995S Silver Proof	838,950			23.00
☐ 1996P	1,421,160,000		.35	
☐ 1996D	1,400,300,000		.35	
☐ 1996S Proof Only				3.00
☐ 1996S Silver Proof				7.50
☐ 1996W			15.00	
☐ 1997P	991,640,000		.35	
☐ 1997D	979,810,000		.35	
☐ 1997S Proof Only	1,975,000			7.00
☐ 1997S Silver Proof				19.00
☐ 1998	1,163,000,000		.35	
☐ 1998D	1,172,250,000		.35	
☐ 1998S Proof				3.00
☐ 1998S Silver Proof				7.50
☐ 1999	2,164,000,000		.35	
☐ 1999D	1,397,444,000		.35	
☐ 1999S Proof				2.50
☐ 1999S Silver Proof				7.50
☐ 2000P	1,842,500,000		.20	
☐ 2000D	1,818,700,000		.20	
☐ 2000S Proof				2.00
☐ 2000S Silver Proof				5.75
☐ 2001P	1,369,590,000		.20	
☐ 2001D	1,412,800,000		.20	
☐ 2001S Proof				2.25
☐ 2001S Silver Proof				5.00
☐ 2002P	1,187,500,000		.20	
☐ 2002D	1,379,500,000		.20	
☐ 2002S Proof				2.50
☐ 2002S Silver Proof				3.75

TWENTY-CENT PIECES— LIBERTY SEATED, 1875–1878

The twenty-cent piece was the shortest-lived of any U.S. coin. Authorized by a Congressional Act on March 3, 1875, it was placed into production immediately thereafter, with manufacture divided among the Philadelphia, San Francisco, and Carson City Mints (Mints on the East and West Coasts being employed in hopes the coin would distribute more evenly in circulation than if released exclusively from a single source of production).

Designed by William Barber, it pictured a figure of the goddess Liberty seated on the obverse, framed by stars, with an eagle on the reverse. It was composed of nine-tenths silver and one-tenth copper, with a weight of five grams and a diameter of 22mm. Despite high hopes, the twenty-cent piece never achieved popularity, the chief reason for its rejection being the physical similarity to the quarter. Production was greatly cut back in 1876 and discontinued two years thereafter. All told, less than a million and a half were struck.

DATE	ABP	G-4 GOOD	F-12 FINE	EF-40 EX. FINE	MS-60 UNC.	PRF-65 PROOF
☐ 1875 (39,700)	45.00	52.00	75.00	180.00	540.00	8500.00
☐ 1875CC (133,290)	50.00	65.00	85.00	235.00	700.00	
☐ 1875S (1,155,000)	45.00	60.00	75.00	165.00	450.00	42000.00
☐ 1876 (15,900)	75.00	85.00	150.00	325.00	640.00	8500.00
☐ 1876CC (10,000)						
EXTREMELY RARE—ELIASBERG SALE APRIL 1997—148500.00						
☐ 1877 Proofs Only (510)						9250.00
☐ 1878 Proofs Only (600)						8750.00

337

QUARTERS

EARLY QUARTERS, 1796–1866

It became evident from a very early period that the quarter or twenty-five-cent piece would be the most significant division of the dollar in everyday commerce. However, the effect was not fully felt until the 19th century. Striking of the quarter dollar was authorized in 1792 along with other denominations, upon establishment of a national currency. No actual specimens came into circulation until 1796.

The earliest design was the Draped Bust portrait of Liberty, common to other silver coinage, with eagle reverse and the legend UNITED STATES OF AMERICA. Stars appeared alongside Liberty on the obverse and her name was affixed above the portrait, with the date below. The designer was Robert Scot. The original quarter dollar was composed of .8924 silver alloyed with .1076 copper, or roughly a nine-to-one ratio. Its weight was 6.74 grams and the diameter generally 27.5mm., with slight variations to be observed according to the flatness of the planchet. Only 6,146 pieces were struck in 1796 as a trial issue (influenced in some measure by a shortage of silver) and this date has become scarce, even in less than the best condition. Production of quarters was not resumed until 1804, when discontinuation of dollar coins increased the need for them. The Draped Bust type was retained but the reverse changed to the Heraldic or Shield Eagle design.

John Reich designed a new quarter dollar in 1815, identical in composition to its predecessors but having a slightly smaller diameter, 27mm. This was the Capped Bust type, with naturalistic shielded eagle on the reverse. Production got off to a small start but was rapidly expanded. No further change

338

occurred until 1831 when the coin was brought down in size to 24.3mm. and was made a bit thicker, retaining the old weight of 6.74 grams. The designer of this new twenty-five-cent piece was William Kneass (pronounced Niece) and all striking was done at Philadelphia. There is a Small Letters and Large Letters variety of this design, with little influence on value. The portrait is a somewhat streamlined Capped Liberty who appears more noble than previously. This design was of short duration, replaced by the Seated Liberty type in 1838. On the reverse was the shield eagle, beneath which appeared the words QUAR. DOL.. (The use of abbreviations did not fully meet the approval of artistic-minded persons.) There was an accompanying change in specifications as well. The silver content was slightly raised, to an even 90%; the copper dropped to an even 10%; and the weight went down to 6.68 grams. The diameter was the same as previously. Designer of this coin was Christian Gobrecht. It was struck at both Philadelphia and New Orleans.

A further reduction in weight was made to 6.22 grams in 1853; arrows were placed at the dates to remind users of the coin that it contained less silver than previously. Compositionally it was unaltered, with nine parts silver to one of copper. On the reverse, sunrays sprang from behind the eagle, an area of the design which previously had been blank. This addition was made for the same reason as the arrows.

QUARTERS—DRAPED BUST, 1796–1807

1796–1807

1796
Small Eagle

1804–1807
Large Eagle

DATE		ABP	G-4 GOOD	F-12 FINE	VF-20 V. FINE	MS-60 UNC.
☐ 1796	(5,894)	3000.00	3850.00	8000.00	10000.00	24000.00
☐ 1804	(6,738)	1250.00	1650.00	3300.00	3600.00	32000.00
☐ 1805	(121,394)	125.00	210.00	410.00	750.00	5000.00
☐ 1806	(206,124)	125.00	200.00	350.00	675.00	4000.00
☐ 1806 over 5		125.00	210.00	400.00	650.00	4000.00
☐ 1807	(220,643)	125.00	200.00	350.00	675.00	4100.00

QUARTERS—LIBERTY CAP, 1815–1838

1815–1838

1815–1828
Motto over Eagle

1831–1838
Without Motto

DATE	ABP	G-4 GOOD	F-12 FINE	VF-20 V. FINE	MS-60 UNC.	MS-65 CH. UNC.
☐ 1815 (89,235)						
	40.00	60.00	100.00	280.00	2100.00	21000.00
☐ 1818 (361,174)						
	40.00	52.00	110.00	270.00	1900.00	13000.00
☐ 1818 over 15 (361,174)						
	40.00	60.00	125.00	310.00	2200.00	20000.00
☐ 1819 Small 9 (144,000)						
	40.00	60.00	110.00	265.00	1850.00	17500.00
☐ 1819 Large 9						
	40.00	62.00	110.00	250.00	1850.00	
☐ 1820 Small O (127,440)						
	40.00	60.00	110.00	270.00	2700.00	23500.00
☐ 1820 Large O						
	40.00	60.00	100.00	270.00	1850.00	
☐ 1821 (216,850)						
	35.00	50.00	105.00	260.00	1850.00	14000.00
☐ 1822 (64,084)						
	42.00	60.00	150.00	310.00	2500.00	27500.00
☐ 1822 25 over $.50C						
	850.00	1150.00	3500.00	4800.00	17000.00	32500.00
☐ 1823 over 22 (17,821)						
	5500.00	8000.00	15000.00	23500.00		
☐ 1824	60.00	95.00	195.00	3000.00	4500.00	18500.00
☐ 1825 over Dates (168,000)						
	40.00	73.00	110.00	310.00	2150.00	13000.00
☐ 1827 (original) (4,000)		FEW PIECES KNOWN—EXTREMELY RARE				
☐ 1828 (102,000)						
	32.00	52.00	100.00	300.00	2400.00	19000.00
☐ 1828 25 over $.50 (102,000)						
	80.00	140.00	400.00	810.00	5500.00	

REDUCED SIZE—NO MOTTO ON REVERSE

Note: 1827 restrike proof 45,000

DATE	ABP	G-4 GOOD	F-12 FINE	VF-20 V. FINE	MS-60 UNC.	MS-65 CH. UNC.
☐ 1831 Small Letters	(398,000)					
	35.00	46.00	60.00	85.00	775.00	12000.00
☐ 1831 Large Letters						
	35.00	46.00	60.00	85.00	775.00	12000.00
☐ 1832	(320,000)					
	35.00	46.00	60.00	85.00	775.00	
☐ 1833	(156,000)					
	35.00	50.00	67.00	120.00	1250.00	
☐ 1834	(286,000)					
	35.00	47.00	62.00	95.00	780.00	
☐ 1835	(1,952,000)					
	35.00	47.00	62.00	80.00	780.00	
☐ 1836	(472,000)					
	35.00	47.00	62.00	95.00	780.00	
☐ 1837	(252,000)					
	35.00	47.00	62.00	80.00	780.00	
☐ 1838	(832,000)					
	35.00	47.00	65.00	96.00	800.00	

QUARTERS—LIBERTY SEATED, 1838–1865 NO MOTTO ABOVE EAGLE

1838–1865

1853 With Rays

Mint Mark is Below Eagle on Reverse 1838–1852 1854–1865 Without Rays

DATE	ABP	G-4 GOOD	F-12 FINE	EF-40 EX. FINE	MS-60 UNC.	MS-65 CH. UNC.
☐ 1838*	(832,000)					
	12.00	16.00	30.00	240.00	1000.00	23000.00
☐ 1839*	(491,146)					
	12.00	16.00	30.00	250.00	1000.00	25000.00
☐ 1840**	(188,127)					
	15.00	25.00	50.00	135.00	900.00	10500.00
☐ 18400*	12.00	16.00	55.00	325.00	1150.00	27500.00

*No Drapery **Drapery

DATE	ABP	G-4 GOOD	F-12 FINE	EF-40 EX. FINE	MS-60 UNC.	MS-65 CH. UNC.
☐ 18400**	(425,200)					
	15.00	22.00	60.00	190.00	875.00	
☐ 1841	(120,000)					
	30.00	45.00	85.00	250.00	900.00	
☐ 18410	(452,000)					
	12.00	16.00	45.00	140.00	600.00	
☐ 1842 Large Date	(88,000)					
	40.00	60.00	130.00	360.00	1000.00	
☐ 18420 Small Date						
	200.00	300.00	500.00	2150.00		
☐ 18420 Large Date	(769,000)					
	12.00	16.00	36.00	98.00	875.00	
☐ 1843	(645,000)					
	12.00	16.00	28.00	58.00	410.00	6000.00
☐ 18430 Small O	(968,000)					
	12.00	16.00	42.00	190.00	1650.00	
☐ 18430 Large O						
	14.00	17.00	43.00	195.00	1600.00	
☐ 1844	(421,000)					
	13.00	17.00	28.00	62.00	450.00	4500.00
☐ 18440	(740,000)					
	12.00	15.00	30.00	125.00	950.00	
☐ 1845	(922,000)					
	11.00	14.00	28.00	66.00	500.00	4150.00
☐ 1846	(510,000)					
	10.00	13.00	32.00	70.00	510.00	6500.00
☐ 1847	(734,000)					
	10.00	13.00	28.00	67.00	475.00	4300.00
☐ 18470	(368,000)					
	15.00	20.00	50.00	170.00	1600.00	
☐ 1848	(146,000)					
	15.00	25.00	52.00	170.00	900.00	
☐ 1849	(340,000)					
	12.00	16.00	42.00	120.00	775.00	
☐ 18490	(16,000)					
	250.00	325.00	700.00	2400.00		
☐ 1850	(190,800)					
	18.00	25.00	65.00	110.00	850.00	
☐ 18500	(412,000)					
	11.00	25.00	46.00	130.00	1250.00	

**Drapery

DATE	ABP	G-4 GOOD	F-12 FINE	EF-40 EX. FINE	MS-60 UNC.	MS-65 CH. UNC.
☐ 1851	(160,000)					
	25.00	30.00	70.00	175.00	800.00	
☐ 1851O	(88,000)					
	100.00	135.00	380.00	1000.00	4500.00	
☐ 1852	(177,060)					
	28.00	40.00	78.00	190.00	700.00	
☐ 1852O	(96,000)					
	100.00	140.00	325.00	1300.00	6250.00	
☐ 1853***	(15,210,020)					
	10.00	15.00	27.00	150.00	900.00	15000.00
☐ 1853/4	30.00	40.00	120.00	260.00	1350.00	
☐ 1853††	(44,200)					
	100.00	125.00	360.00	750.00	2900.00	
☐ 1853O***	(1,332,000)					
	12.00	15.00	30.00	240.00	2600.00	
☐ 1854†	(12,380,000)					
	12.00	15.00	28.00	75.00	500.00	6400.00
☐ 1854† O	(1,484,000)					
	12.00	15.00	28.00	85.00	750.00	
☐ 1854O Huge O						
	65.00	100.00	150.00	500.00		
☐ 1855†	(2,857,000)					
	12.00	15.00	26.00	80.00	525.00	7400.00
☐ 1855O†	(176,000)					
	24.00	40.00	75.00	375.00	2200.00	
☐ 1855S†	(396,400)					
	25.00	36.00	65.00	325.00	1800.00	
☐ 1856 No Arrows	(7,264,000)					
	10.00	13.00	24.00	60.00	310.00	4250.00
☐ 1856O	(968,000)					
	11.00	15.00	28.00	65.00	950.00	
☐ 1856S	24.00	40.00	78.00	350.00	1800.00	
☐ 1856S Over S	(286,000)					
	30.00	48.00	120.00	640.00		
☐ 1857	(9,644,000)					
	10.00	14.00	25.00	65.00	300.00	3400.00
☐ 1857O	(1,180,000)					
	10.00	14.00	29.00	80.00	850.00	

***W/Arrows and Rays †W/Arrows and no Rays ††Over 52, No Arrows

DATE	ABP	G-4 GOOD	F-12 FINE	EF-40 EX. FINE	MS-60 UNC.	MS-65 CH. UNC.
☐ 1857S	(82,000)					
	32.00	40.00	140.00	550.00	2600.00	
☐ 1858	(7,368,000)					
	10.00	13.00	28.00	50.00	290.00	3250.00
☐ 1858O	(520,000)					
	10.00	14.00	28.00	80.00	1250.00	
☐ 1858S	(121,000)					
	21.00	41.00	110.00	360.00		
☐ 1859	(1,344,000)					
	10.00	13.00	28.00	60.00	430.00	
☐ 1859O	(260,000)					
	10.00	15.00	40.00	95.00	1150.00	
☐ 1859S	(80,000)					
	55.00	75.00	150.00	700.00		
☐ 1860	(805,400)					
	10.00	13.00	25.00	60.00	475.00	8700.00
☐ 1860O	(388,000)					
	10.00	13.00	32.00	72.00	950.00	
☐ 1860S	(56,000)					
	85.00	110.00	325.00	1500.00		
☐ 1861	(4,854,000)					
	10.00	13.00	28.00	60.00	375.00	3300.00
☐ 1861S	(96,000)					
	34.00	50.00	150.00	700.00		
☐ 1862	(932,550)					
	10.00	14.00	30.00	60.00	350.00	3500.00
☐ 1862S	(67,000)					
	32.00	48.00	95.00	385.00	1850.00	
☐ 1863	(192,060)					
	20.00	27.00	55.00	125.00	610.00	3600.00
☐ 1864	(94,070)					
	40.00	60.00	90.00	190.00	670.00	3900.00
☐ 1864S	(20,000)					
	150.00	200.00	525.00	1450.00	5700.00	
☐ 1865	(59,300)					
	40.00	60.00	94.00	190.00	650.00	6250.00
☐ 1865S	(41,000)					
	50.00	70.00	130.00	450.00	1850.00	
☐ 1866	ONLY ONE PROOF KNOWN—HYDEMAN SALE 1961—24,500.00					

QUARTERS—LIBERTY SEATED, 1866–1891
MOTTO ABOVE EAGLE

In 1866 the words IN GOD WE TRUST were added to the reverse, on a banner between the eagle and the inscription UNITED STATES OF AMERICA. When the weight was changed slightly to 6.25 grams in 1873, the arrows were returned but no further use was made of sunrays on the reverse. The arrows were removed in 1875.

Motto Above Eagle

DATE	ABP	G-4 GOOD	F-12 FINE	EF-40 EX. FINE	MS-60 UNC.	MS-65 CH. UNC.
☐ 1866	(17,525)					
	200.00	280.00	460.00	850.00	1600.00	
☐ 1866S	(28,000)					
	100.00	150.00	400.00	950.00	2300.00	
☐ 1867	(20,625)					
	125.00	160.00	350.00	600.00	850.00	
☐ 1867S	(48,000)					
	75.00	110.00	290.00	600.00	2000.00	
☐ 1868	(30,000)					
	75.00	110.00	175.00	350.00	675.00	
☐ 1868S	(96,000)					
	50.00	72.00	140.00	465.00	1650.00	
☐ 1869	(16,600)					
	150.00	190.00	325.00	480.00	1050.00	
☐ 1869S	(76,000)					
	50.00	80.00	180.00	460.00	2000.00	
☐ 1870	(87,400)					
	35.00	65.00	94.00	210.00	675.00	
☐ 1870CC	(8,340)					
	1250.00	1450.00	5500.00	13000.00		
☐ 1871	(171,232)					
	20.00	30.00	46.00	140.00	500.00	
☐ 1871CC	(10,890)					
	900.00	1100.00	3400.00	15750.00		

DATE	ABP	G-4 GOOD	F-12 FINE	EF-40 EX. FINE	MS-60 UNC.	MS-65 CH. UNC.
☐ 1871S	(30,900)					
	150.00	220.00	375.00	900.00	2500.00	
☐ 1872	(182,950)					
	20.00	30.00	65.00	120.00	600.00	
☐ 1872CC	(9,100)					
	300.00	400.00	1100.00	3300.00		
☐ 1872S	(103,000)					
	450.00	550.00	775.00	1900.00	6250.00	
☐ 1873*	(1,263,700)					
	13.00	17.00	32.00	190.00	1000.00	4100.00
☐ 1873** Open 3	(220,600)					
	17.00	28.00	52.00	145.00	425.00	
☐ 1873** Closed 3						
	65.00	110.00	240.00	550.00	1600.00	
☐ 1873CC*	(12,462)					
	1000.00	1300.00	4000.00	13000.00	32000.00	
☐ 1873CC**	(4,000)		RARE—NORWEB 1998—MS64—209,000.00			
☐ 1873S*	(160,000)					
	14.00	24.00	50.00	240.00	950.00	
☐ 1874*	(471,900)					
	12.00	16.00	36.00	210.00	750.00	3900.00
☐ 1874S**	(392,000)					
	13.00	17.00	60.00	210.00	760.00	
Arrows Removed Starting 1875						
☐ 1875	(4,293,500)					
	11.00	14.00	28.00	55.00	260.00	1600.00
☐ 1875CC	(140,000)					
	40.00	55.00	150.00	435.00	1600.00	
☐ 1875S	(680,000)					
	20.00	28.00	62.00	185.00	640.00	2850.00
☐ 1876	(17,817,150)					
	12.00	15.00	30.00	60.00	250.00	1500.00
☐ 1876CC	(4,944,000)					
	12.00	15.00	35.00	70.00	350.00	3650.00
☐ 1876S	(8,596,000)					
	12.00	15.00	32.00	52.00	250.00	1750.00
☐ 1877	(10,911,710)					
	11.00	14.00	32.00	52.00	250.00	1500.00
☐ 1877CC	(4,192,000)					
	11.00	14.00	32.00	65.00	300.00	1500.00

*With Arrows **No Arrows

DATE	ABP	G-4 GOOD	F-12 FINE	EF-40 EX. FINE	MS-60 UNC.	MS-65 CH. UNC.
☐ 1877S	(8,996,000)					
	10.00	14.00	22.00	58.00	200.00	1450.00
☐ 1877 Horizontal S						
	20.00	32.00	72.00	210.00	650.00	
☐ 1878	(2,260,000)					
	11.00	14.00	32.00	60.00	230.00	2500.00
☐ 1878CC	(996,000)					
	15.00	20.00	50.00	125.00	550.00	2750.00
☐ 1878S	(140,000)					
	60.00	78.00	190.00	500.00	1000.00	
☐ 1879	(14,700)					
	85.00	135.00	175.00	260.00	475.00	1650.00
☐ 1880	(14,955)					
	85.00	130.00	185.00	290.00	480.00	1550.00
☐ 1881	(12,975)					
	100.00	140.00	210.00	285.00	475.00	1550.00
☐ 1882	(16,300)					
	85.00	135.00	180.00	280.00	600.00	1600.00
☐ 1883	(15,439)					
	80.00	135.00	190.00	300.00	520.00	2200.00
☐ 1884	(8,875)					
	140.00	185.00	285.00	400.00	600.00	1650.00
☐ 1885	(14,530)					
	80.00	115.00	190.00	350.00	600.00	2400.00
☐ 1886	(5,886)					
	200.00	270.00	400.00	600.00	750.00	2500.00
☐ 1887	(10,710)					
	140.00	175.00	300.00	420.00	600.00	1900.00
☐ 1888	(10,833)					
	110.00	150.00	300.00	450.00	600.00	1700.00
☐ 1888S	(1,216,000)					
	12.00	15.00	34.00	50.00	250.00	2500.00
☐ 1889	(12,711)					
	100.00	110.00	180.00	340.00	470.00	1500.00
☐ 1890	(80,590)					
	40.00	50.00	95.00	170.00	420.00	1500.00
☐ 1891	(3,920,600)					
	11.00	15.00	25.00	52.00	240.00	1500.00
☐ 1891O	(68,000)					
	85.00	110.00	235.00	500.00	2500.00	NO PRICE
						"O" MINT TOO RARE
☐ 1891S	(2,216,000)					
	12.00	15.00	26.00	56.00	250.00	1600.00

QUARTERS—BARBER OR LIBERTY HEAD, 1892–1916

The Barber or Liberty Head quarter, with its classical portrait bust, was introduced in 1892 after a design by Charles E. Barber. Liberty faces right and wears a cap and laurel wreath. On the reverse is a shield eagle holding arrows and branch with (at long last) the words QUARTER DOLLAR spelled out without abbreviation. This was without doubt the handsomest design in the quarter-dollar series and has become extremely popular with collectors. It was struck at Philadelphia, Denver, New Orleans, and San Francisco. The Barber quarter has a composition of 90% silver and 10% copper with a weight of 6.25 grams and a diameter of 24.3mm.

Mint Mark is Below the Eagle on Reverse

DATE	ABP	G-4 GOOD	F-12 FINE	EF-40 EX. FINE	MS-60 UNC.	MS-65 CH. UNC.
☐ 1892	(8,237,245)					
	3.00	4.00	24.00	70.00	300.00	1100.00
☐ 1892O	(2,640,000)					
	4.00	7.00	28.00	72.00	285.00	1450.00
☐ 1892S	(964,079)					
	10.00	14.00	55.00	115.00	400.00	4500.00
☐ 1893	(5,444,815)					
	3.00	4.00	24.00	70.00	225.00	1550.00
☐ 1893O	(3,396,000)					
	3.00	5.00	26.00	72.00	240.00	1750.00
☐ 1893S	(1,454,535)					
	5.00	7.00	45.00	100.00	410.00	6900.00
☐ 1894	(3,432,972)					
	3.00	5.00	27.00	72.00	230.00	1400.00
☐ 1894O	(2,852,000)					
	4.00	6.00	32.00	80.00	350.00	2000.00
☐ 1894S	(2,648,821)					
	4.25	6.00	28.00	80.00	290.00	3150.00
☐ 1895	(4,440,880)					
	3.00	4.50	23.00	70.00	210.00	1750.00

DATE	ABP	G-4 GOOD	F-12 FINE	EF-40 EX. FINE	MS-60 UNC.	MS-65 CH. UNC.
☐ 1895O	(2,816,000)					
	3.00	5.00	34.00	82.00	360.00	2350.00
☐ 1895S	(1,764,681)					
	6.00	9.00	38.00	80.00	350.00	3500.00
☐ 1896	(3,874,762)					
	3.00	5.00	24.00	65.00	260.00	1500.00
☐ 1896O	(1,484,000)					
	5.00	7.00	70.00	310.00	780.00	6600.00
☐ 1896S	(188,039)					
	250.00	285.00	750.00	2000.00	4500.00	19000.00
☐ 1897	(8,140,731)					
	3.00	4.00	21.00	75.00	170.00	1150.00
☐ 1897O	(1,414,800)					
	6.00	8.00	70.00	325.00	750.00	3500.00
☐ 1897S	(542,229)					
	17.00	22.00	160.00	300.00	875.00	5000.00
☐ 1898	(11,100,735)					
	3.00	4.00	22.00	74.00	175.00	1100.00
☐ 1898O	(1,868,000)					
	5.00	7.00	55.00	210.00	600.00	8750.00
☐ 1898S	(1,020,592)					
	3.50	6.00	40.00	72.00	400.00	6250.00
☐ 1899	(12,624,846)					
	2.50	4.00	20.00	86.00	165.00	1200.00
☐ 1899O	(2,644,000)					
	3.50	6.00	25.00	80.00	410.00	3350.00
☐ 1899S	(708,000)					
	7.00	10.00	55.00	120.00	400.00	3250.00
☐ 1900	(10,016,912)					
	2.50	3.00	19.00	70.00	175.00	1200.00
☐ 1900O	(3,416,000)					
	5.00	7.00	50.00	115.00	550.00	3250.00
☐ 1900S	(1,858,585)					
	4.00	6.00	34.00	65.00	350.00	4750.00
☐ 1901	(8,892,813)					
	4.00	5.00	21.00	65.00	180.00	2200.00
☐ 1901O	(1,612,000)					
	20.00	25.00	85.00	315.00	740.00	5400.00
☐ 1901S	(72,664)					
	1700.00	2100.00	5500.00	9250.00	15500.00	38000.00
☐ 1902	(12,197,744)					
	2.50	3.00	18.00	65.00	160.00	1100.00

DATE	ABP	G-4 GOOD	F-12 FINE	EF-40 EX. FINE	MS-60 UNC.	MS-65 CH. UNC.
☐ 1902O	(4,748,000)					
	4.00	5.50	35.00	95.00	375.00	4300.00
☐ 1902S	(1,524,612)					
	6.00	9.00	35.00	85.00	450.00	3400.00
☐ 1903	(9,670,064)					
	2.50	4.50	18.00	65.00	160.00	2300.00
☐ 1903O	(3,500,000)					
	3.50	5.00	35.00	90.00	365.00	5600.00
☐ 1903S	(1,036,000)					
	7.00	10.00	37.00	92.00	400.00	2500.00
☐ 1904	(9,588,813)					
	2.00	3.25	18.00	65.00	160.00	1300.00
☐ 1904O	(2,456,000)					
	4.00	5.50	42.00	150.00	675.00	2850.00
☐ 1905	(4,968,250)					
	2.50	5.00	20.00	65.00	175.00	1500.00
☐ 1905O	(1,230,000)					
	7.00	8.00	65.00	200.00	450.00	5500.00
☐ 1905S	(1,884,000)					
	4.50	7.00	32.00	100.00	300.00	3600.00
☐ 1906	(3,656,435)					
	2.00	3.50	18.00	65.00	160.00	1200.00
☐ 1906D	(3,280,000)					
	2.00	3.50	21.00	60.00	190.00	2100.00
☐ 1906O	(2,056,000)					
	2.00	3.50	32.00	75.00	275.00	1200.00
☐ 1907	(7,192,575)					
	2.00	2.75	18.00	65.00	170.00	1100.00
☐ 1907D	(2,484,000)					
	2.25	4.00	22.00	70.00	230.00	2350.00
☐ 1907O	(4,560,000)					
	2.25	4.50	15.00	70.00	200.00	2150.00
☐ 1907S	(1,360,000)					
	4.00	4.50	38.00	100.00	450.00	3100.00
☐ 1908	(4,232,545)					
	2.25	3.50	17.00	70.00	185.00	1200.00
☐ 1908D	(5,788,000)					
	2.25	3.50	16.00	65.00	210.00	1550.00
☐ 1908O	(6,244,000)					
	2.25	3.00	16.00	65.00	180.00	1100.00
☐ 1908S	(784,000)					
	8.00	12.00	63.00	215.00	625.00	4850.00
☐ 1909	(9,268,650)					
	2.25	4.00	18.00	65.00	185.00	1100.00

DATE	ABP	G-4 GOOD	F-12 FINE	EF-40 EX. FINE	MS-60 UNC.	MS-65 CH. UNC.
☐ 1909D	(5,114,000)					
	2.00	3.00	15.00	62.00	175.00	2000.00
☐ 1909O	(712,000)					
	9.00	14.00	75.00	275.00	750.00	7750.00
☐ 1909S	(1,348,000)					
	2.25	3.00	26.00	700.00	240.00	2350.00
☐ 1910	(2,244,551)					
	2.50	4.00	22.00	65.00	200.00	1200.00
☐ 1910D	(1,500,000)					
	4.00	6.00	38.00	95.00	320.00	2000.00
☐ 1911	(3,270,543)					
	2.25	4.00	15.00	68.00	165.00	1100.00
☐ 1911D	(933,600)					
	3.50	4.50	68.00	270.00	575.00	5000.00
☐ 1911S	(988,000)					
	3.00	4.50	40.00	125.00	325.00	1400.00
☐ 1912	(4,400,700)					
	3.00	5.00	16.00	65.00	165.00	1100.00
☐ 1912S	(708,000)					
	3.25	6.00	40.00	95.00	360.00	2700.00
☐ 1913	(484,613)					
	6.00	10.00	60.00	370.00	900.00	4000.00
☐ 1913D	(1,450,800)					
	4.00	6.00	32.00	75.00	260.00	1150.00
☐ 1913S	(40,000)					
	400.00	500.00	1750.00	3500.00	5000.00	12500.00
☐ 1914	(6,244,610)					
	2.25	3.00	20.00	60.00	160.00	1100.00
☐ 1914D	(3,046,000)					
	2.25	3.50	15.00	60.00	170.00	1200.00
☐ 1914S	(264,000)					
	45.00	65.00	135.00	375.00	800.00	3200.00
☐ 1915	(3,480,450)					
	2.25	4.00	16.00	60.00	160.00	1100.00
☐ 1915D	(3,694,000)					
	2.25	4.00	16.00	60.00	155.00	1100.00
☐ 1915S	(704,000)					
	3.00	5.00	22.00	90.00	250.00	1050.00
☐ 1916	(1,788,000)					
	2.25	4.50	15.00	60.00	160.00	1050.00
☐ 1916D	(6,540,000)					
	2.25	4.50	16.00	60.00	175.00	1050.00

QUARTERS—STANDING LIBERTY, 1916–1930

The Standing Liberty quarter was introduced in 1916 during World War I and its theme was intended to reflect the nation's sentiments at that time. The goddess is portrayed in full length holding a shield with which she, presumably, fends off the defilers of liberty. An eagle in flight is pictured on the reverse, with the words UNITED STATES OF AMERICA and E PLURIBUS UNUM. The designer was Herman A. MacNeil. Specifications are the same as for the Barber quarter.

This design carried so much fine detailing that very moderate handling resulted in obvious wear, making uncirculated specimens more valuable, proportionately, than in the case of most other coins. The chief point of vulnerability was the date, so small in size and positioned in such a way as to receive heavy wear, that many specimens lost their date after only a few years of circulation. The government wished to correct this fault without totally redesigning the obverse and in 1925 hit upon the plan of showing the date in incuse—that is, pressed into the coin rather than raised from its surface. While this did not totally prevent wear it helped keep the dates readable for a longer time.

A series of minor alterations was made in 1917, the second year of issue, including a dressing up of Liberty to satisfy public criticism that the figure was displaying a scandalous amount of flesh. Three stars were added beneath the eagle on the reverse.

Note: Prices listed for MS-60 specimens of Standing Liberty quarters are for ordinary strikes. Exceptional strikes with full head of Liberty in detail are scarcer and sell for higher sums. This is not a question of *wear*, but simply the quality of the coin as originally struck.

1916–30
Mint Mark is to
Left of Date on Obverse

1916–1917
Type I
No Stars Under Eagle

1917–1930
Type II
3 Stars Under Eagle

DATE	ABP	G-4 GOOD	VG-8 V. GOOD	F-12 FINE	EF-40 EX. FINE	MS-60 UNC.
☐ 1916	(52,000)					
	1200.00	1500.00	1900.00	2900.00	4650.00	6500.00
☐ 1917	(8,792,000)					
	14.00	18.00	27.00	40.00	65.00	160.00
☐ 1917D	(1,509,200)					
	15.00	20.00	27.00	40.00	95.00	185.00
☐ 1917S	(1,952,000)					
	17.00	22.00	29.00	40.00	125.00	200.00
STARS UNDER EAGLE						
☐ 1917	(13,880,000)					
	13.00	17.00	19.00	24.00	45.00	125.00
☐ 1917D	(6,224,400)					
	25.00	32.00	40.00	58.00	90.00	200.00
☐ 1917S	(5,552,000)					
	25.00	32.00	42.00	55.00	75.00	165.00
☐ 1918	(12,240,000)					
	10.00	12.00	20.00	30.00	50.00	110.00
☐ 1918D	(7,380,000)					
	17.00	21.00	30.00	40.00	80.00	200.00
☐ 1918S	(11,072,000)					
	12.00	17.00	20.00	30.00	50.00	175.00
☐ 1918S over 7						
	750.00	950.00	1350.00	1800.00	5000.00	10500.00
☐ 1919	(11,324,000)					
	25.00	32.00	38.00	48.00	70.00	130.00
☐ 1919D	(1,944,000)					
	52.00	65.00	90.00	130.00	300.00	550.00
☐ 1919S	(1,836,000)					
	50.00	62.00	85.00	140.00	400.00	625.00
☐ 1920	(27,860,000)					
	9.00	15.00	16.00	23.00	40.00	115.00
☐ 1920D	(3,586,400)					
	33.00	38.00	45.00	70.00	120.00	225.00
☐ 1920S	(6,380,000)					
	12.00	17.00	22.00	30.00	60.00	200.00
☐ 1921	(1,916,000)					
	80.00	110.00	125.00	160.00	285.00	460.00
☐ 1923	(9,716,000)					
	10.00	13.00	15.00	25.00	40.00	125.00
☐ 1923S*	(1,360,000)					
	175.00	210.00	300.00	365.00	475.00	700.00
☐ 1924	(10,920,000)					
	10.00	13.00	16.00	20.00	40.00	150.00

*Note: Check for altered date.

DATE	ABP	G-4 GOOD	VG-8 V. GOOD	F-12 FINE	EF-40 EX. FINE	MS-60 UNC.
☐ 1924D	(3,112,000)					
	35.00	42.00	55.00	65.00	90.00	140.00
☐ 1924S	(2,860,000)					
	20.00	25.00	27.00	35.00	90.00	250.00
☐ 1925	(12,280,000)					
	1.50	3.00	4.00	5.00	29.00	100.00
☐ 1926	(11,316,000)					
	1.50	3.00	4.00	7.00	29.00	100.00
☐ 1926D	(1,716,000)					
	3.50	4.00	7.50	14.00	50.00	140.00
☐ 1926S	(2,700,000)					
	2.00	4.00	5.00	12.00	95.00	310.00
☐ 1927	(11,912,000)					
	1.50	3.00	4.00	6.00	28.00	110.00
☐ 1927D	(976,400)					
	5.00	7.00	9.00	14.00	75.00	160.00
☐ 1927S	(396,000)					
	8.00	11.00	13.00	55.00	910.00	3500.00
☐ 1928	(6,336,000)					
	1.50	2.50	3.50	5.00	27.00	110.00
☐ 1928D	(1,627,600)					
	2.50	3.50	4.00	6.50	35.00	120.00
☐ 1928S	(2,644,000)					
	2.00	3.00	3.50	6.50	30.00	120.00
☐ 1929	(11,140,000)					
	1.50	3.00	5.00	6.00	27.00	100.00
☐ 1929D	(1,358,000)					
	2.50	4.00	5.00	6.00	30.00	120.00
☐ 1929S	(1,764,000)					
	1.50	2.30	5.00	6.50	30.00	125.00
☐ 1930	(5,632,000)					
	1.50	2.50	4.00	6.50	34.00	95.00
☐ 1930S	(1,556,000)					
	2.00	3.00	4.00	7.00	30.00	110.00

QUARTERS—WASHINGTON, 1932 TO DATE

DATE	ABP	G-4 GOOD	F-12 FINE	EF-40 EX. FINE	MS-60 UNC.	MS-65 CH. UNC.
☐ 1932	(5,404,000)					
	3.00	5.00	7.00	12.00	28.00	375.00
☐ 1932D	(436,800)					
	55.00	70.00	100.00	175.00	750.00	11000.00

1932–1967
Mint Mark is
on Reverse
Below Eagle

 1968 on—
Mint Mark
to Right of
Hair Ribbon

DATE	ABP	G-4 GOOD	F-12 FINE	EF-40 EX. FINE	MS-60 UNC.	MS-65 CH. UNC.
☐ 1932S	(408,000)					
	55.00	70.00	95.00	120.00	325.00	4500.00
☐ 1934	(31,912,052)					
	1.25	2.00	2.50	7.00	23.00	70.00
☐ 1934 Double Die						
	25.00	32.00	41.00	120.00	510.00	2500.00
☐ 1934D	(3,527,200)					
	2.75	3.75	7.00	17.00	210.00	1300.00
☐ 1935	(32,484,000)					
	1.10	2.00	2.50	5.00	21.00	100.00
☐ 1935D	(5,780,000)					
	1.25	3.00	4.50	20.00	225.00	750.00
☐ 1935S	(5,550,000)					
	1.25	2.10	6.00	13.00	80.00	265.00

DATE	MINTAGE	ABP	F-12 FINE	EF-40 EX. FINE	MS-60 UNC.	MS-65 CH. UNC.
☐ 1936	41,303,837	1.00	2.00	4.00	21.00	70.00
☐ 1936D	5,374,000	3.00	6.00	41.00	400.00	825.00
☐ 1936S	3,828,000	2.40	4.00	12.00	95.00	325.00
☐ 1937	19,701,542	2.00	3.00	6.00	22.00	85.00
☐ 1937D	7,189,600	2.00	4.00	11.00	55.00	120.00
☐ 1937S	1,652,000	3.00	5.00	20.00	100.00	240.00
☐ 1938	9,480,045	3.00	5.00	13.00	65.00	165.00
☐ 1938S	2,832,000	3.50	5.00	13.00	65.00	160.00
☐ 1939	33,548,795	1.25	3.00	4.00	14.00	65.00
☐ 1939D	7,092,000	2.00	4.00	8.00	32.00	80.00
☐ 1939S	2,628,000	3.00	4.50	14.00	70.00	200.00
☐ 1940	35,715,246	1.00	3.00	4.00	13.00	65.00
☐ 1940D	2,797,600	4.00	6.00	17.00	85.00	185.00
☐ 1940S	8,244,000	3.00	5.00	7.00	19.00	60.00
☐ 1941	79,047,287	1.10	2.50	4.00	6.00	42.00
☐ 1941D	16,714,800	1.10	2.50	4.00	20.00	65.00
☐ 1941S	16,080,000	1.10	2.50	3.50	19.00	70.00
☐ 1942	102,117,123	1.10	2.50	4.00	5.00	40.00
☐ 1942D	17,487,200	1.10	2.50	4.00	12.00	40.00

DATE	MINTAGE	ABP	F-12 FINE	EF-40 EX. FINE	MS-60 UNC.	MS-65 CH. UNC.
☐ 1942S	19,384,000	1.10	2.50	5.00	55.00	185.00
☐ 1943	99,700,000	1.10	2.25	4.00	4.00	42.00
☐ 1943D	16,095,600	1.10	2.25	4.00	20.00	45.00
☐ 1943S	21,700,000	1.10	2.25	4.00	27.00	50.00
☐ 1943S Double Die		70.00	90.00	180.00	300.00	1500.00
☐ 1944	104,956,000	1.00	2.25	3.00	5.00	43.00
☐ 1944D	14,600,000	1.00	2.25	3.00	13.00	43.00
☐ 1944S	12,560,000	1.00	2.25	3.25	14.00	43.00
☐ 1945	74,372,000	1.00	2.25	3.00	5.00	43.00
☐ 1945D	12,341,600	1.00	2.25	3.50	13.00	45.00
☐ 1945S	17,004,001	1.00	2.25	3.00	7.00	43.00
☐ 1946	53,436,000	1.00	2.25	3.00	5.00	40.00
☐ 1946D	9,072,800	1.00	2.25	3.00	3.50	42.00
☐ 1946S	4,204,000	1.00	2.25	3.00	3.50	42.00
☐ 1947	22,556,000	1.00	2.25	3.00	5.00	35.00
☐ 1947D	15,338,400	1.00	2.25	3.00	3.50	37.00
☐ 1947S	5,532,000	1.00	2.25	3.00	3.50	42.00
☐ 1948	35,196,000	1.00	2.25	3.00	3.50	38.00
☐ 1948D	16,768,800	1.00	2.25	3.00	3.50	38.00
☐ 1948S	15,960,000	1.00	2.25	3.50	5.00	40.00
☐ 1949	9,312,000	1.25	2.25	3.75	23.00	50.00
☐ 1949D	10,068,400	1.10	2.25	3.50	10.00	45.00
☐ 1950	24,971,512	1.00	2.25	2.75	3.00	20.00
☐ 1950D	21,075,600	1.00	2.25	2.75	4.00	20.00
☐ 1950D over S		25.00	40.00	165.00	350.00	675.00
☐ 1950S over D		25.00	40.00	190.00	425.00	750.00
☐ 1950S	10,284,004	1.00	2.25	2.50	5.50	27.00
☐ 1951	43,505,602	1.00	2.00	2.25	3.75	21.00
☐ 1951D	35,354,800	1.00	2.00	2.35	4.00	26.00
☐ 1951S	8,948,000	1.00	2.10	2.50	7.50	38.00
☐ 1952	38,862,073	1.00	1.75	2.00	4.00	20.00
☐ 1952D	49,795,200	1.00	2.00	2.25	4.00	25.00
☐ 1952S	13,707,800	1.00	2.10	2.25	7.00	35.00
☐ 1953	18,664,920	1.00	1.50	2.00	3.00	23.00
☐ 1953D	56,112,400	1.00	1.50	2.00	3.00	28.00
☐ 1953S	14,016,000	1.00	2.25	3.00	3.50	25.00
☐ 1954	54,654,503	1.00	1.40	1.65	3.00	22.00
☐ 1954D	46,305,500	1.00	1.40	1.65	3.00	24.00
☐ 1954S	11,834,722	1.00	1.75	2.00	3.00	20.00
☐ 1955	18,558,381	1.00	2.00	2.10	3.00	20.00
☐ 1955D	3,182,400	1.00	2.00	2.50	3.00	27.00
☐ 1956	44,813,384	1.00	1.35	1.65	3.00	15.00
☐ 1956D	32,334,500	1.00	1.50	1.85	3.00	18.00
☐ 1957	47,779,952	1.00	1.35	1.50	3.00	16.00
☐ 1957D	77,924,160	1.00	1.35	1.50	3.00	16.00
☐ 1958	7,235,652	1.00	1.50	1.70	3.00	16.00
☐ 1958D	78,124,900	1.00	1.35	1.50	3.00	16.00

DATE	MINTAGE	ABP	F-12 FINE	EF-40 EX. FINE	MS-60 UNC.	MS-65 CH. UNC.
☐ 1959	25,533,291	1.00	1.35	1.50	3.00	16.00
☐ 1959D	62,054,232	1.00	1.35	1.50	3.00	13.00
☐ 1960	30,855,602	1.00	1.35	1.50	3.00	12.00
☐ 1960D	63,000,324	1.00	1.35	1.50	1.80	10.00
☐ 1961	40,064,244	1.00	1.35	1.50	1.80	10.00
☐ 1961D	83,656,928	1.00	1.35	1.50	1.80	12.00
☐ 1962	39,374,019	1.00	1.35	1.50	1.80	10.00
☐ 1962D	127,554,756	1.00	1.35	1.50	1.80	10.00
☐ 1963	77,391,645	1.00	1.35	1.50	1.80	9.00
☐ 1963D	135,288,184	1.00	1.35	1.50	1.80	9.00
☐ 1964	564,341,347	1.00	1.35	1.50	1.80	7.00
☐ 1964D	704,135,528	1.00	1.35	1.50	1.80	7.00
☐ 1965	1,819,717,540				1.00	2.50
☐ 1966	821,101,500				1.00	2.50
☐ 1967	1,524,031,840				1.00	2.50
☐ 1968	220,731,500				1.00	2.50
☐ 1968D	101,534,000				1.00	2.50

DATE	MINTAGE	MS-60 UNC.	PRF-65 PROOF
☐ 1968S Proof Only	3,041,500		1.50
☐ 1969	176,212,000	.50	
☐ 1969D	114,372,000	.50	
☐ 1969S Proof Only	2,934,631		1.50
☐ 1970	136,420,000	.50	
☐ 1970D	417,341,364	.50	
☐ 1970S Proof Only	2,632,810		1.50
☐ 1971	109,284,000	.50	
☐ 1971D	258,634,428	.50	
☐ 1971S Proof Only	3,224,138		1.35
☐ 1972	215,048,000	.50	
☐ 1972D	311,067,732	.50	
☐ 1972S	3,267,667		1.35
☐ 1973	346,924,000	.50	
☐ 1973D	232,977,400	.60	
☐ 1973S Proof Only	2,796,624		1.25
☐ 1974	801,456,000	.50	
☐ 1974D	363,160,300	.50	
☐ 1974S Proof Only	2,612,568		1.25
☐ 1976 Copper-Nickel Clad	809,780,016	.55	
☐ 1976D Copper-Nickel Clad	860,108,836	.55	
☐ 1976S Copper-Nickel Clad Proof	7,055,099		1.25
☐ 1976S Silver Clad		.90	
☐ 1976S Silver Clad Proof			2.50
☐ 1977	468,556,900	.55	
☐ 1977D	256,524,078	.55	
☐ 1977S Proof Only	2,090,269		1.40
☐ 1978	521,452,000	.55	
☐ 1978D	287,373,152	.55	

DATE	MINTAGE	MS-60 UNC.	PRF-65 PROOF
☐ 1978S Proof Only	3,127,781		1.50
☐ 1979	515,709,000	.55	
☐ 1979D	489,790,020	.55	
☐ 1979S Proof, Variety I	3,677,200		1.50
☐ 1979S Proof, Variety II			2.00
☐ 1980P	635,832,101	.55	
☐ 1980D	518,327,444	.55	
☐ 1980S Proof	3,547,130		1.50
☐ 1981P	602,000,000	.55	
☐ 1981D	575,841,732	.55	
☐ 1981S Proof Only, Variety I	4,064,789		1.50
☐ 1981S Proof Only, Variety II			4.00
☐ 1982P	500,000,000	4.50	
☐ 1982D	490,665,000	1.75	
☐ 1982S Proof Only	3,856,941		2.00
☐ 1983P	674,000,000	12.00	
☐ 1983D	617,800,000	5.50	
☐ 1983S Proof Only	3,378,125		3.00
☐ 1984P	675,961,834	1.00	
☐ 1984D	550,000,000	1.00	
☐ 1984S Proof Only	3,164,210		2.50
☐ 1985P	780,201,621	1.50	
☐ 1985D	520,888,004	1.50	
☐ 1985S Proof Only	3,260,112		1.50
☐ 1986P	541,643,221	4.00	
☐ 1986D	502,121,106	6.50	
☐ 1986S Proof Only	3,006,420		4.00
☐ 1987P	572,286,210	.60	
☐ 1987D	642,873,921	.60	
☐ 1987S Proof Only	3,821,764		1.30
☐ 1988P	572,741,111	1.25	
☐ 1988D	586,710,461	.75	
☐ 1988S Proof Only	3,272,648		1.75
☐ 1989P	502,768,211	.50	
☐ 1989D	886,461,006	.50	
☐ 1989S Proof Only	3,164,718		1.75
☐ 1990P	632,464,118	.50	
☐ 1990D	964,720,107	.50	
☐ 1990S Proof Only	3,240,766		5.75
☐ 1991P	568,958,210	.50	
☐ 1991D	630,962,680	.50	
☐ 1991S Proof Only	2,867,710		3.75
☐ 1992P	384,760,100	.50	
☐ 1992D	389,764,222	.50	
☐ 1992S Proof Only	2,858,971		4.50
☐ 1992S Silver Proof	1,317,579		5.00
☐ 1993P	639,276,000	.50	
☐ 1993D	645,476,128	.50	
☐ 1993S Proof Only	2,633,439		7.00
☐ 1993S Silver Proof	761,353		9.00

DATE	MINTAGE	MS-60 UNC.	PRF-65 PROOF
☐ 1994P	825,600,000	.50	
☐ 1994D	880,034,000	.50	
☐ 1994S Proof Only	2,484,594		5.50
☐ 1994S Silver Proof	785,329		9.00
☐ 1995P	1,004,336,000	.50	
☐ 1995D	1,103,216,000	.50	
☐ 1995S Proof Only	2,010,000		20.00
☐ 1995S Silver Proof	838,950		21.50
☐ 1996P	925,040,000	.50	
☐ 1996D	908,868,000	.50	
☐ 1996S Proof			4.50
☐ 1996S Silver Proof			8.50
☐ 1997P	595,740,000	.40	
☐ 1997D	599,680,000	.40	
☐ 1997S Proof Only	1,975,000		7.50
☐ 1997S Silver Proof			16.50
☐ 1998P	896,268,000	.40	
☐ 1998D	821,000,000	.40	
☐ 1998S Proof Only			15.00
☐ 1998S Silver Proof			14.00
☐ 1999P DE	373,400,000	1.50	
☐ 1999D DE	401,424,000	1.75	
☐ 1999S DE			7.50
☐ 1999S DE Silver			17.50
☐ 1999P PA	349,000,000	1.75	
☐ 1999D PA	358,332,000	1.50	
☐ 1999S PA			5.00
☐ 1999S PA Silver			17.50
☐ 1999P NJ	363,200,000	1.00	
☐ 1999D NJ	299,028,000	1.25	
☐ 1999S NJ			5.00
☐ 1999S NJ Silver			15.00
☐ 1999P GA	451,188,000	.50	
☐ 1999D GA	488,744,000	.65	
☐ 1999S GA			5.00
☐ 1999S GA Silver			15.00
☐ 1999P CT	688,744,000	.50	
☐ 1999D CT	657,880,000	.60	
☐ 1999S CT			5.00
☐ 1999S CT Silver			15.00
☐ 2000P MA	628,600,000	.50	
☐ 2000D MA	535,184,000	.50	
☐ 2000S MA			3.50
☐ 2000S MA Silver			10.00
☐ 2000P MD	678,200,000	.50	
☐ 2000D MD	556,532,000	.50	
☐ 2000S MD			3.50
☐ 2000S MD Silver			10.00
☐ 2000P SC	742,756,000	.50	
☐ 2000D SC	566,208,000	.50	

DATE	MINTAGE	MS-60 UNC.	PRF-65 PROOF
☐ 2000S SC			3.50
☐ 2000S SC Silver			10.00
☐ 2000P NH	673,040,000	.50	
☐ 2000D NH	495,976,000	.50	
☐ 2000S NH			3.50
☐ 2000S NH Silver			10.00
☐ 2000P VA	943,000,000	.50	
☐ 2000D VA	651,616,000	.50	
☐ 2000S VA			3.50
☐ 2000S VA Silver			10.00
☐ 2001P NY	655,400,000	.50	
☐ 2001D NY	619,640,000	.50	
☐ 2001S NY			3.50
☐ 2001S NY Silver			11.00
☐ 2001P NC	627,600,000	.50	
☐ 2001D NC	427,876,000	.50	
☐ 2001S NC			3.50
☐ 2001S NC Silver			11.00
☐ 2001P RI	423,000,000	.50	
☐ 2001D RI	447,100,000	.50	
☐ 2001S RI			3.50
☐ 2001S RI Silver			11.00
☐ 2001P VT	423,400,000	.50	
☐ 2001D VT	459,404,000	.50	
☐ 2001S VT			3.50
☐ 2001S VT Silver			11.00
☐ 2001P KY	353,000,000	.50	
☐ 2001D KY	370,564,000	.50	
☐ 2001S KY			3.50
☐ 2001S KY Silver			11.00
☐ 2002P TN	361,600,000		
☐ 2002D TN	286,468,000	.50	
☐ 2002S TN		.50	3.25
☐ 2002S TN Silver			11.00
☐ 2002P OH	217,200,000	.85	
☐ 2002D OH	414,832,000	.50	
☐ 2002S OH			3.25
☐ 2002S OH Silver			11.00
☐ 2002P LA	362,000,000	.50	
☐ 2002D LA	401,804,000	.50	
☐ 2002S LA			3.25
☐ 2002S LA Silver			11.00
☐ 2002P IN	362,600,000	.50	
☐ 2002D IN	327,200,000	.50	
☐ 2002S IN			3.25
☐ 2002S IN Silver			11.00
☐ 2002P MS		.50	
☐ 2002D MS		.50	
☐ 2002S MS			3.25
☐ 2002S MS Silver			11.00

HALF DOLLARS

EARLY HALF DOLLARS, 1794–1838

As originally conceived, the half dollar was to contain precisely—to the grain—half as much metal as the dollar and was to be struck from metal of the same composition, .8924 silver alloyed with .1076 copper. It weighed 13.48 grams and was slightly larger in diameter than it subsequently became: 32.5mm. Its designer was Robert Scot and its obverse featured a profile portrait of Liberty facing right, the so-called Flowing Hair likeness used on other coins as well, backed by an eagle. Along the edge was stamped its value, as no statement of value appeared within the design (FIFTY CENTS OR HALF A DOLLAR,), the words set apart with small ornamental flourishes. Apparently the initial issue in 1794 was struck from just a single set of dies, but in the following year several dies were employed resulting in a number of minor varieties. This was the final appearance of the Flowing Hair fifty-cent piece. The design was replaced in 1796 by the Draped Bust version, to which the shielded eagle reverse was added in 1801.

Because of the trading significance of this coin, an effort was made to place as many half dollars as possible into circulation during its early years. It was temporarily discontinued in 1804 as a result of speculation along with the silver dollar; but unlike the latter, which did not return for more than thirty years, production of the half dollar was resumed in 1805. In that year more than 200,000 were struck, followed by a striking exceeding 800,000 in 1806.

The Capped Bust design was installed on the half dollar in 1807, as it was on other coins. Its designer was a German-

American named John Reich. The Capped Bust is sometimes referred to as Turban Head. The word LIBERTY appears on the cap or turban band. On either side of the portrait is a series of stars, with the date positioned beneath it. The reverse has a modified shielded eagle (or heraldic eagle) with the motto E PLURIBUS UNUM on a banner and 50 C. This coin weighs 13.48 grams and has the same metallic composition as its predecessors. Varieties of the Capped Bust half dollar are so numerous, despite being in use for only about thirty years, that a large collection can be built around this coin. And it is, indeed, an ideal target for specialization, as nearly all specimens fall within the low-to-moderate range of price. Christian Gobrecht redesigned the coin in 1836, retaining the same types but modifying them somewhat. The composition was changed to provide a slightly higher content of silver and a slightly lower content of copper, the ratio now being nine parts silver, one part copper. Its weight was 13.36 grams and the diameter reduced to 30mm. This design was replaced by Liberty Seated in 1839, which remained in use for more than fifty years.

HALF DOLLARS—FLOWING HAIR, 1794–1795

DATE	MINTAGE	ABP	G-4 GOOD	F-12 FINE	VF-20 V. FINE
☐ 1794	5,300	1000.00	1350.00	3850.00	5750.00
☐ 1795 2 Leaves		300.00	600.00	900.00	2000.00
☐ 1795 Recut Date	317,844	300.00	800.00	950.00	2100.00
☐ 1795*		600.00	900.00	3000.00	5000.00

*3 leaves under each wing

HALF DOLLARS—DRAPED BUST, SMALL EAGLE 1796–1797

DATE	MINTAGE	ABP	G-4 GOOD	F-12 FINE	VF-20 V. FINE
☐ 1796 15 Stars		8500.00	11000.00	17000.00	25000.00
☐ 1796 16 Stars		10500.00	14000.00	21000.00	32000.00
☐ 1797 15 Stars	3,918	8250.00	10000.00	18000.00	26500.00

HALF DOLLARS—DRAPED BUST, 1801–1807 EAGLE ON REVERSE

DATE	ABP	G-4 GOOD	VF-20 V. FINE	EF-40 EX. FINE	MS-60 UNC.
☐ 1801 (30,289)	150.00	200.00	825.00	2800.00	18000.00
☐ 1802 (29,890)	125.00	200.00	800.00	3000.00	15000.00
☐ 1803 Large 3	110.00	160.00	400.00	800.00	5750.00
☐ 1803 Small 3 (188,234)					
	110.00	160.00	500.00	900.00	6250.00
☐ 1805	100.00	135.00	350.00	875.00	5850.00
☐ 1805 over 4 (211,722)					
	125.00	225.00	650.00	1600.00	14500.00
☐ 1806	100.00	150.00	360.00	710.00	6000.00
☐ 1806 over 5 (839,576)					
	100.00	150.00	380.00	780.00	6100.00
☐ 1806 Inverted over 6					
	110.00	200.00	830.00	1600.00	9100.00

DATE	ABP	G-4 GOOD	VF-20 V. FINE	EF-40 EX. FINE	MS-60 UNC.
☐ 1806 Knobbed 6, Large Stars					
	100.00	130.00	340.00	650.00	5700.00
☐ 1806 Knobbed 6, Stem Not Through Claw				EXTREMELY RARE	
☐ 1807 (301,076)	100.00	130.00	420.00	650.00	5000.00

HALF DOLLARS—TURBAN HEAD OR "CAPPED BUST," 1807–1836

Motto Above Eagle, Lettered Edge, Large Size

DATE	ABP	G-4 GOOD	F-12 FINE	EF-40 EX. FINE	MS-60 UNC.
☐ 1807 Small Stars	40.00	60.00	180.00	700.00	3800.00
☐ 1807 Large Stars	(750,500)				
	35.00	50.00	160.00	800.00	4000.00
☐ 1807 .50 over .20C	30.00	50.00	100.00	450.00	3400.00
☐ 1808 (1,368,600)	30.00	42.00	65.00	275.00	1250.00
☐ 1808 over 7	30.00	50.00	75.00	275.00	1750.00
☐ 1809 (1,405,810)	30.00	42.00	65.00	200.00	1300.00
☐ 1810 (1,276,276)	30.00	38.00	65.00	160.00	1200.00
☐ 1811 (1,203,644)	30.00	35.00	60.00	135.00	750.00
☐ 1812 (1,628,059)	30.00	35.00	50.00	140.00	700.00
☐ 1812 over 11	30.00	42.00	90.00	250.00	2200.00
☐ 1813 (1,241,903)	30.00	40.00	70.00	150.00	900.00
☐ 1814 (1,039,075)	30.00	36.00	70.00	210.00	1500.00
☐ 1814 over 13	30.00	45.00	80.00	260.00	1750.00
☐ 1815 over 12 (47,150)					
	550.00	800.00	1300.00	2650.00	6750.00
☐ 1817 (1,215,567)	30.00	36.00		150.00	775.00
☐ 1817 over 13	60.00	90.00	170.00	710.00	3200.00
☐ 1818 (1,960,322)	30.00	35.00	52.00	140.00	820.00
☐ 1818 over 17	30.00	36.00	65.00	160.00	1200.00

DATE		ABP	G-4 GOOD	F-12 FINE	EF-40 EX. FINE	MS-60 UNC.
☐ 1819	(2,208,000)	30.00	35.00	60.00	200.00	800.00
☐ 1819 over 18 Large 9		32.00	40.00	65.00	160.00	1250.00
☐ 1820	(751,122)	30.00	40.00	75.00	200.00	975.00
☐ 1820 over 19		30.00	40.00	75.00	160.00	1350.00
☐ 1821	(1,305,797)	30.00	37.00	60.00	100.00	810.00
☐ 1822	(1,559,573)	30.00	37.00	50.00	85.00	6000.00
☐ 1822 over 21		40.00	60.00	90.00	250.00	800.00
☐ 1823	(1,694,200)	30.00	36.00	52.00	125.00	675.00
☐ 1823 Ugly 3		32.00	40.00	82.00	200.00	1000.00
☐ 1824	(3,504,954)	30.00	36.00	45.00	110.00	400.00
☐ 1824 over 21 and others						
		45.00	55.00	70.00	175.00	910.00
☐ 1825	(2,943,166)	30.00	35.00	45.00	85.00	410.00
☐ 1826	(4,044,180)	30.00	35.00	45.00	85.00	410.00
☐ 1827*	(5,493,400)	30.00	35.00	45.00	85.00	410.00
☐ 1827 over 6 Curled 2		30.00	40.00	60.00	100.00	900.00
☐ 1828	(3,075,200)	30.00	35.00	45.00	85.00	500.00
☐ 1829	(3,712,156)	30.00	35.00	48.00	85.00	450.00
☐ 1829 over 27		30.00	40.00	60.00	115.00	850.00
☐ 1830**	(4,764,800)	30.00	35.00	52.00	85.00	450.00
☐ 1831	(5,873,660)	30.00	35.00	52.00	85.00	450.00
☐ 1832***	(4,797,000)	30.00	35.00	60.00	100.00	450.00
☐ 1833	(5,206,000)	30.00	35.00	55.00	85.00	450.00
☐ 1834	(6,412,000)	30.00	35.00	55.00	85.00	450.00
☐ 1835	(5,352,006)	30.00	35.00	55.00	85.00	450.00
☐ 1836 All Kinds	(6,546,200)					
		30.00	35.00	50.00	85.00	450.00
☐ 1836 *Lettered edge 50 over 00						
		32.00	45.00	70.00	195.00	1500.00

*Square-Based 2. **Small O, in Date, Large O, in Date: Same Price
***Small Letters, Large Letters: Same Price

HALF DOLLARS—TURBAN HEAD OR "CAPPED BUST," 1836–1839, NO MOTTO ABOVE EAGLE, REEDED EDGE, REDUCED SIZE

DATE	ABP	G-4 GOOD	F-12 FINE	EF-40 EX. FINE	MS-60 UNC.	PRF-65 PROOF
☐ 1836 Reeded Edge						
	450.00	650.00	950.00	1800.00	6000.00	

1836–1837 50 CENTS

1838–1839 HALF DOL.

DATE	ABP	G-4 GOOD	F-12 FINE	EF-40 EX. FINE	MS-60 UNC.	PRF-65 PROOF
☐ 1837	(3,629,820)					
	32.00	42.00	55.00	160.00	725.00	
☐ 1838	(3,546,000)					
	32.00	42.00	62.00	150.00	725.00	
☐ 1838O	(Approx. 20)			EXTREMELY RARE—125000.00		
☐ 1839	(3,334,500)					
	32.00	42.00	62.00	175.00	950.00	
☐ 1839O	(179,000)					
	100.00	130.00	240.00	600.00	2350.00	

HALF DOLLARS—LIBERTY SEATED, 1839–1866 WITHOUT MOTTO ABOVE EAGLE

The Seated Liberty half dollar was based on the now-celebrated design of Christian Gobrecht. The goddess sits looking left, holding a shield on which the word LIBERTY appears and, in the other hand, a staff. The upper portion of the design is encircled by stars. On the reverse is a shield or heraldic eagle holding arrows and branch. Beneath the eagle are the words HALF DOL. After some minor modification of both the obverse and reverse design, the numerals used for giving the date were enlarged in 1846 and a major change occurred in 1853. Because the California gold strikes of 1849 had brought great quantities of this metal into circulation, public confidence in silver was gradually eroding. To inspire greater acceptance of silver coinage their composition was revised to include a higher proportion of bullion. The new ratio—not just for half dollars but silver pieces in general—was nine parts silver to one of copper, the one part of copper being necessary to give this durable metal a fair stability. The weight was 12.44 grams and the diameter 30.6mm. A pair of arrows was placed on the obverse beside the date as warning that the metal content had changed, and—in the event this was overlooked—sun rays were installed on the reverse, radiating from behind the eagle. These were discontinued in 1856.

Beginning in 1866, and probably not coincidentally because the Civil War had recently ended, the motto IN GOD WE TRUST was incorporated into the reverse design on a banner that flies above the eagle's head. When the weight was increased $^6/_{20}$ of a gram in 1873, resort was again made to arrows at the date, but no sunrays adorned the reverse. The arrows were removed in 1875. The Seated Liberty half dollar continued to be struck until 1891, though throughout the 1880s its output was very limited.

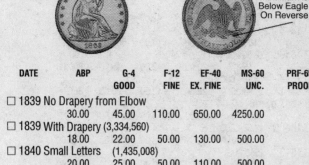

Mint Mark is Below Eagle On Reverse

DATE	ABP	G-4 GOOD	F-12 FINE	EF-40 EX. FINE	MS-60 UNC.	PRF-65 PROOF
☐ 1839 No Drapery from Elbow						
	30.00	45.00	110.00	650.00	4250.00	
☐ 1839 With Drapery (3,334,560)						
	18.00	22.00	50.00	130.00	500.00	
☐ 1840 Small Letters	(1,435,008)					
	20.00	25.00	50.00	110.00	500.00	
☐ 1840 Large Letters						
	80.00	100.00	210.00	500.00	2600.00	
☐ 1840O (855,100)						
	18.00	25.00	65.00	125.00	450.00	
☐ 1841 (310,000)						
	30.00	36.00	80.00	250.00	1150.00	
☐ 1841O (401,000)						
	15.00	22.00	45.00	115.00	600.00	
☐ 1842 Small Date	(2,012,764)					
	18.00	25.00	70.00	175.00	875.00	

DATE	ABP	G-4 GOOD	F-12 FINE	EF-40 EX. FINE	MS-60 UNC.	PRF-65 PROOF
☐ 1842 Large Date						
	14.00	20.00	50.00	95.00	1150.00	
☐ 1842O Small Date						
	400.00	575.00	1200.00	4000.00		
☐ 1842O Large Date						
	13.00	19.00	45.00	140.00	1100.00	
☐ 1843	(3,844,000)					
	13.00	19.00	45.00	90.00	410.00	
☐ 1843O	(2,268,000)					
	15.00	20.00	46.00	90.00	435.00	
☐ 1844	(1,766,000)					
	13.00	19.00	42.00	90.00	420.00	
☐ 1844O	(2,005,000)					
	13.00	19.00	42.00	85.00		
☐ 1844O Double Date						
	325.00	425.00	750.00	2100.00	7600.00	
☐ 1845	(589,000)					
	18.00	26.00	62.00	170.00	750.00	
☐ 1845O	(2,094,000)					
	14.00	18.00	42.00	90.00	490.00	
☐ 1846	(2,110,000)					
	14.00	18.00	42.00	85.00	460.00	
☐ 1846 over Horizontal 6						
	100.00	125.00	210.00	500.00	2850.00	
☐ 1846O	(2,304,000)					
	15.00	20.00	42.00	95.00	800.00	
☐ 1847	(1,156,000)					
	13.00	20.00	42.00	90.00	365.00	
☐ 1847 over 6						
	1000.00	1350.00	2850.00	5300.00		
☐ 1847O	(2,584,000)					
	13.00	16.00	38.00	90.00	525.00	
☐ 1848	(580,000)					
	25.00	35.00	82.00	210.00	900.00	
☐ 1848O	(3,180,000)					
	14.00	22.00	42.00	92.00	575.00	
☐ 1849	(1,252,000)					
	25.00	32.00	52.00	135.00	775.00	
☐ 1849O	(2,310,000)					
	15.00	23.00	50.00	92.00	650.00	
☐ 1850	(227,000)					
	140.00	175.00	390.00	575.00	1350.00	
☐ 1850O	(2,456,000)					
	14.00	18.00	45.00	95.00	450.00	

DATE	ABP	G-4 GOOD	F-12 FINE	EF-40 EX. FINE	MS-60 UNC.	PRF-65 PROOF
☐ 1851	(200,750)					
	185.00	240.00	385.00	575.00	1350.00	
☐ 1851O	(402,000)					
	15.00	18.00	55.00	150.00	500.00	
☐ 1852	(77,130)					
	250.00	310.00	525.00	900.00	1400.00	
☐ 1852O	(144,000)					
	35.00	50.00	165.00	425.00	1550.00	
☐ 1853**	(3,532,708)					
	14.00	23.00	42.00	200.00	1300.00	
☐ 1853O**	(1,328,000)					
	14.00	22.00	48.00	250.00	2200.00	
☐ 1853O No Arrows						
3 KNOWN—EXTREMELY RARE—AUCTION SALE 1997—155000.00						
☐ 1854***	(2,982,000)					
	13.00	17.00	44.00	110.00	525.00	
☐ 1854O***	(5,240,000)					
	13.00	17.00	44.00	115.00	525.00	
☐ 1855***	(759,500)					
	15.00	17.00	44.00	110.00	650.00	
☐ 1855O	(3,688,000)					
	13.00	18.00	40.00	110.00	550.00	
☐ 1855S***	(129,950)					
	200.00	280.00	610.00	2250.00	11000.00	
☐ 1856	(938,000)					
	13.00	18.00	45.00	90.00	410.00	12500.00
☐ 1856O	(2,658,000)					
	13.00	18.00	45.00	90.00	410.00	
☐ 1856S	(211,000)					
	30.00	38.00	85.00	375.00	2950.00	
☐ 1857	(1,988,000)					
	13.00	18.00	43.00	90.00	375.00	6750.00
☐ 1857O	(818,000)					
	15.00	24.00	43.00	90.00	800.00	
☐ 1857S	(158,000)					
	40.00	50.00	115.00	380.00	3300.00	
☐ 1858	(4,226,000)					
	13.00	18.00	43.00	85.00	420.00	6500.00
☐ 1858O	(7,294,000)					
	13.00	18.00	43.00	85.00	425.00	

**With Arrows and Rays ***With Arrows

DATE	ABP	G-4 GOOD	F-12 FINE	EF-40 EX. FINE	MS-60 UNC.	PRF-65 PROOF
☐ 1858S	(476,000)					
	15.00	20.00	48.00	175.00	760.00	
☐ 1859	(748,000)					
	18.00	25.00	62.00	120.00	450.00	5750.00
☐ 1859O	(2,834,000)					
	12.00	18.00	42.00	90.00	400.00	
☐ 1859S	(566,000)					
	16.00	22.00	47.00	150.00	600.00	
☐ 1860	(303,700)					
	17.00	25.00	40.00	90.00	650.00	5350.00
☐ 1860O	(1,290,000)					
	14.00	20.00	44.00	95.00	380.00	
☐ 1860S	(472,000)					
	18.00	24.00	42.00	95.00	660.00	
☐ 1861	(2,888,400)					
	12.00	16.00	45.00	90.00	400.00	5400.00
☐ 1861O	(330,000)					
	13.00	18.00	42.00	90.00	420.00	
☐ 1861S	(939,500)					
	15.00	19.00	42.00	95.00	500.00	
☐ 1862	(252,350)					
	16.00	30.00	65.00	142.00	575.00	5500.00
☐ 1862S	(1,352,000)					
	13.00	19.00	40.00	90.00	450.00	
☐ 1863	(503,660)					
	15.00	19.00	56.00	110.00	475.00	5800.00
☐ 1863S	(916,000)					
	12.00	18.00	42.00	90.00	425.00	
☐ 1864	(379,570)					
	20.00	28.00	52.00	150.00	500.00	5600.00
☐ 1864S	(658,000)					
	15.00	22.00	40.00	100.00	650.00	
☐ 1865	(511,900)					
	18.00	23.00	47.00	125.00	510.00	5250.00
☐ 1865S	(675,000)					
	15.00	22.00	42.00	90.00	650.00	
☐ 1866S*	50.00	80.00	160.00	600.00		

*Note: Part of total mintage: 1,054,000.

HALF DOLLARS—LIBERTY SEATED, 1866–1891 WITH MOTTO ON REVERSE

Arrows at Date   No Arrows at Date   Mint Mark is Below Eagle on Reverse

DATE	ABP	G-4 GOOD	F-12 FINE	EF-40 EX. FINE	MS-60 UNC.	PRF-65 PROOF
☐ 1866	(745,625)					
	14.00	20.00	42.00	110.00	380.00	3700.00
☐ 1866S*	14.00	19.00	41.00	82.00	500.00	
☐ 1867	(424,325)					
	20.00	26.00	50.00	150.00	385.00	3750.00
☐ 1867S	(1,196,000)					
	13.00	18.00	42.00	75.00	460.00	
☐ 1868	(378,000)					
	30.00	42.00	85.00	190.00	480.00	3850.00
☐ 1868S	(1,160,000)					
	15.00	21.00	46.00	95.00	465.00	
☐ 1869	(795,900)					
	18.00	27.00	45.00	96.00	360.00	3850.00
☐ 1869S	(656,000)					
	15.00	21.00	43.00	110.00	675.00	
☐ 1870	(600,900)					
	15.00	22.00	42.00	125.00	460.00	3850.00
☐ 1870CC	(54,617)					
	350.00	425.00	1250.00	6600.00	UNKNOWN IN BU	
☐ 1870S	(1,004,000)					
	15.00	20.00	47.00	115.00	725.00	
☐ 1871	(1,165,360)					
	14.00	20.00	40.00	75.00	370.00	3900.00
☐ 1871CC	(139,950)					
	85.00	115.00	325.00	1000.00	6400.00	
☐ 1871S	(2,178,000)					
	13.00	18.00	42.00	75.00	460.00	

*Part of total mintage: 1,054,000.

DATE	ABP	G-4 GOOD	F-12 FINE	EF-40 EX. FINE	MS-60 UNC.	PRF-65 PROOF
☐ 1872	(881,550)					
	13.00	21.00	45.00	75.00	425.00	3850.00
☐ 1872CC	(272,000)					
	50.00	65.00	150.00	550.00	3100.00	
☐ 1872S	(580,000)					
	20.00	32.00	56.00	175.00	900.00	
☐ 1873 With Arrows	(1,815,700)					
	14.00	20.00	45.00	190.00	910.00	9500.00
☐ 1873 No Arrows	(801,800)					
	18.00	25.00	60.00	135.00	600.00	3750.00
☐ 1873CC With Arrows	(214,560)					
	90.00	125.00	300.00	1160.00	6100.00	
☐ 1873CC No Arrows	(122,500)					
	100.00	130.00	275.00	875.00	7600.00	
☐ 1873S With Arrows	(288,000)					
	38.00	50.00	110.00	370.00	2400.00	
☐ 1873S No Arrows	(5,000)				NONE KNOWN TO EXIST	
☐ 1874 With Arrows	(2,360,300)					
	15.00	22.00	42.00	210.00	850.00	9600.00
☐ 1874CC With Arrows	(59,000)					
	180.00	220.00	675.00	1750.00	8500.00	
☐ 1874S With Arrows	(394,000)					
	21.00	32.00	77.00	310.00	1500.00	
☐ 1875	(6,027,500)					
	13.00	16.00	42.00	75.00	400.00	3350.00
☐ 1875CC	(1,008,000)					
	18.00	26.00	53.00	140.00	610.00	
☐ 1875S	(3,200,000)					
	13.00	18.00	42.00	90.00	350.00	
☐ 1876	(8,419,150)					
	13.00	18.00	40.00	75.00	350.00	3650.00
☐ 1876CC	(1,956,000)					
	14.00	21.00	46.00	125.00	610.00	
☐ 1876S	(4,528,000)					
	14.00	19.00	42.00	75.00	350.00	
☐ 1877	(8,304,510)					
	14.00	19.00	42.00	75.00	350.00	3750.00
☐ 1877CC	(1,420,000)					
	15.00	20.00	44.00	115.00	640.00	
☐ 1877S	(5,356,000)					
	14.00	19.00	40.00	75.00	350.00	

DATE	ABP	G-4 GOOD	F-12 FINE	EF-40 EX. FINE	MS-60 UNC.	PRF-65 PROOF
☐ 1878	(1,378,400)					
	18.00	26.00	50.00	110.00	460.00	3300.00
☐ 1878CC	(62,000)					
	215.00	265.00	450.00	1500.00	4100.00	
☐ 1878S	(12,000)					
	6500.00	8000.00	12000.00	16500.00	27000.00	
☐ 1879	(5,900)					
	175.00	225.00	275.00	450.00	600.00	2850.00
☐ 1880	(1,355)					
	150.00	200.00	250.00	300.00	650.00	2850.00
☐ 1881	(10,975)					
	150.00	190.00	220.00	300.00	650.00	2900.00
☐ 1882	(5,500)					
	150.00	250.00	290.00	360.00	660.00	2850.00
☐ 1883	(9,039)					
	150.00	210.00	240.00	380.00	660.00	2850.00
☐ 1884	(5,275)					
	180.00	265.00	310.00	350.00	610.00	2900.00
☐ 1885	(6,130)					
	160.00	200.00	250.00	400.00	610.00	2850.00
☐ 1886	(5,886)					
	200.00	280.00	400.00	475.00	760.00	3000.00
☐ 1887	(5,710)					
	275.00	350.00	460.00	650.00	800.00	2850.00
☐ 1888	(12,833)					
	100.00	165.00	210.00	330.00	600.00	3100.00
☐ 1889	(12,711)					
	140.00	210.00	240.00	320.00	650.00	3600.00
☐ 1890	(12,590)					
	140.00	200.00	225.00	340.00	625.00	3000.00
☐ 1891	(200,600)					
	28.00	43.00	90.00	140.00	410.00	3100.00

HALF DOLLARS—LIBERTY HEAD OR BARBER, 1892–1915

These coins, which resemble the Morgan dollar in portraiture, were prepared from designs by Charles E. Barber and really have no connection with the Morgan dollar aside from the possibility that Barber may have been inspired by it.

The face of Liberty, which faces right, is strong and classical, suggesting the portraiture of Greek coins of ancient time. The weight is somewhat greater than the final version of the Seated Liberty half, 12.5 grams, but its composition is the same, 90% silver and an alloy of 10% copper. The reverse has an attractive eagle with shield and wings spread wide; it holds the traditional arrows and branch. The mint mark appears directly beneath the eagle's tail feathers. Without question this was artistically the finest coin of the half dollar series. It was struck at Philadelphia, New Orleans, Denver, and San Francisco. Not a single rarity is to be found among the Barber halves, with the result that it offers splendid opportunities for completion—even if one wishes to include all the mint marks.

Mint Mark is Below Eagle on Reverse

DATE	ABP	G-4 GOOD	F-12 FINE	EF-40 EX. FINE	MS-60 UNC.	PRF-65 PROOF
☐ 1892	(935,245)					
	17.00	23.00	45.00	170.00	375.00	3000.00
☐ 1892O	(390,000)					
	120.00	160.00	290.00	375.00	800.00	
☐ 1892S	(1,029,028)					
	110.00	140.00	235.00	350.00	825.00	
☐ 1893	(1,826,792)					
	10.00	15.00	50.00	175.00	475.00	3000.00
☐ 1893O	(1,389,000)					
	15.00	24.00	78.00	280.00	575.00	
☐ 1893S	(740,000)					
	75.00	110.00	180.00	375.00	1150.00	
☐ 1894	(1,148,972)					
	14.00	19.00	70.00	225.00	475.00	3250.00
☐ 1894O	(2,138,000)					
	10.00	14.00	60.00	215.00	490.00	
☐ 1894S	(4,048,690)					
	9.00	14.00	52.00	200.00	550.00	

DATE	ABP	G-4 GOOD	F-12 FINE	EF-40 EX. FINE	MS-60 UNC.	PRF-65 PROOF
☐ 1895	(1,835,218)					
	7.00	12.00	50.00	180.00	525.00	3150.00
☐ 1895O	(1,766,000)					
	8.00	13.00	55.00	230.00	600.00	
☐ 1895S	(1,108,086)					
	14.00	21.00	70.00	260.00	700.00	
☐ 1896	(950,762)					
	14.00	20.00	60.00	210.00	550.00	3250.00
☐ 1896O	(924,000)					
	20.00	25.00	110.00	340.00	1100.00	
☐ 1896S	(1,140,948)					
	50.00	65.00	125.00	345.00	1100.00	
☐ 1897	(2,480,731)					
	6.00	9.00	32.00	145.00	470.00	3000.00
☐ 1897O	(632,000)					
	40.00	62.00	310.00	785.00	1400.00	
☐ 1897S	(933,900)					
	85.00	110.00	250.00	625.00	1200.00	
☐ 1898	(2,956,735)					
	5.00	9.00	29.00	142.00	420.00	3150.00
☐ 1898O	(874,000)					
	12.00	18.00	115.00	360.00	925.00	
☐ 1898S	(2,358,550)					
	6.00	11.00	43.00	200.00	810.00	
☐ 1899	(5,538,846)					
	5.00	8.00	27.00	130.00	460.00	3200.00
☐ 1899O	(1,724,000)					
	5.00	9.00	46.00	210.00	550.00	
☐ 1899S	(1,686,411)					
	8.00	12.00	45.00	210.00	700.00	
☐ 1900	(4,762,912)					
	5.00	8.00	28.00	135.00	375.00	3100.00
☐ 1900O	(2,744,000)					
	5.00	8.00	40.00	240.00	800.00	
☐ 1900S	(2,560,322)					
	6.00	9.00	41.00	190.00	675.00	
☐ 1901	(4,268,813)					
	5.00	9.00	27.00	135.00	410.00	3000.00
☐ 1901O	(1,124,000)					
	6.50	10.00	52.00	250.00	1100.00	

DATE	ABP	G-4 GOOD	F-12 FINE	EF-40 EX. FINE	MS-60 UNC.	PRF-65 PROOF
☐ 1901S	(847,044)					
	13.00	20.00	110.00	475.00	1400.00	
☐ 1902	(4,922,777)					
	5.00	9.00	28.00	140.00	510.00	3000.00
☐ 1902O	(2,526,000)					
	5.00	8.00	40.00	175.00	600.00	
☐ 1902S	(1,460,670)					
	5.00	9.00	48.00	210.00	600.00	
☐ 1903	(2,278,755)					
	5.00	8.00	38.00	185.00	475.00	3000.00
☐ 1903O	(2,100,000)					
	5.00	8.00	40.00	190.00	650.00	
☐ 1903S	(1,920,772)					
	5.00	8.00	40.00	210.00	600.00	
☐ 1904	(2,992,670)					
	5.00	8.00	29.00	140.00	500.00	3000.00
☐ 1904O	(1,117,600)					
	8.00	12.00	52.00	300.00	1000.00	
☐ 1904S	(553,038)					
	12.00	17.00	135.00	680.00	2350.00	
☐ 1905	(662,727)					
	8.00	13.00	50.00	215.00	600.00	3000.00
☐ 1905O	(505,000)					
	10.00	13.00	80.00	250.00	710.00	
☐ 1905S	(2,494,000)					
	5.00	8.00	36.00	185.00	660.00	
☐ 1906	(1,638,675)					
	5.00	8.00	27.00	155.00	390.00	3000.00
☐ 1906D	(4,028,000)					
	5.00	8.00	28.00	145.00	460.00	
☐ 1906O	(2,446,000)					
	5.00	8.00	36.00	160.00	560.00	
☐ 1906S	(1,740,154)					
	5.00	8.00	44.00	185.00	550.00	
☐ 1907	(2,598,575)					
	5.00	8.00	27.00	146.00	385.00	3000.00
☐ 1907D	(3,856,000)					
	5.00	8.00	27.00	140.00	400.00	
☐ 1907O	(3,946,600)					
	5.00	8.00	27.00	155.00	510.00	

DATE	ABP	G-4 GOOD	F-12 FINE	EF-40 EX. FINE	MS-60 UNC.	PRF-65 PROOF
☐ 1907S	(3,856,000)					
	5.00	8.00	70.00	300.00	1150.00	
☐ 1908	(1,354,545)					
	5.00	8.00	28.00	150.00	380.00	3000.00
☐ 1908D	(3,280,000)					
	5.00	8.00	27.00	160.00	385.00	
☐ 1908O	(5,360,000)					
	5.00	8.00	28.00	140.00	510.00	
☐ 1908S	(1,644,828)					
	5.00	8.00	45.00	210.00	700.00	
☐ 1909	(2,368,650)					
	5.00	8.00	27.00	145.00	415.00	3000.00
☐ 1909O	(925,400)					
	7.00	9.00	42.00	250.00	700.00	
☐ 1909S	(1,764,000)					
	5.00	8.00	32.00	185.00	610.00	
☐ 1910	(418,551)					
	8.00	11.00	65.00	260.00	550.00	3000.00
☐ 1910S	(1,948,000)					
	5.00	8.00	28.00	185.00	610.00	
☐ 1911	(1,406,543)					
	5.00	8.00	28.00	140.00	390.00	3000.00
☐ 1911D	(696,080)					
	5.00	8.00	33.00	180.00	610.00	
☐ 1911S	(1,272,000)					
	5.00	8.00	32.00	160.00	625.00	
☐ 1912	(1,550,700)					
	5.00	8.00	25.00	145.00	408.00	3100.00
☐ 1912D	(2,300,800)					
	5.00	8.00	26.00	140.00	460.00	
☐ 1912S	(1,370,000)					
	5.00	8.00	30.00	165.00	480.00	
☐ 1913	(188,627)					
	15.00	20.00	110.00	360.00	860.00	3000.00
☐ 1913D	(534,000)					
	5.50	9.00	34.00	180.00	400.00	
☐ 1913S	(604,000)					
	5.50	8.00	42.00	185.00	650.00	
☐ 1914	(124,610)					
	25.00	36.00	155.00	146.00	93.00	3000.00

DATE	ABP	G-4 GOOD	F-12 FINE	EF-40 EX. FINE	MS-60 UNC.	PRF-65 PROOF
☐ 1914S	(992,000)					
	5.00	8.00	33.00	150.00	400.00	
☐ 1915	(138,450)					
	15.00	21.00	84.00	390.00	800.00	3150.00
☐ 1915D	(1,170,400)					
	5.00	8.00	25.00	135.00	375.00	
☐ 1915S	(1,604,000)					
	5.00	8.00	26.00	135.00	400.00	

HALF DOLLARS—LIBERTY WALKING, 1916–1947

This attractive design, introduced in 1916, pictured a full-length representation of Liberty on the obverse, dressed in a diaphanous gown and strolling along a field, her right arm upraised as if in acknowledgment of the splendors of nature. In the distance the sun rises (or sets). The designer was A. Weinman, whose initials may be observed—if one has a coin with virtually no wear—on the reverse. His rendition of the eagle on the coin's reverse, a naturalistic type bearing little resemblance to the previously employed shield or heraldic eagle, is a noteworthy piece of art. Sadly, the Liberty Walking half dollar suffered a great deal from rubbing in circulation and much of its delicate linework wore down rapidly, resulting in a shortage of presentable specimens. The collector who wishes to build up a set would be well advised to seek the finest condition obtainable, and be prepared to give a slight premium for coins of the best quality, rather than collect "average" specimens which are, truly, mere shadows of their original selves. The Liberty Walking fifty-cent piece was struck at Philadelphia, San Francisco, and Denver. Its composition is 90% silver and 10% copper with a weight of 12.5 grams and a diameter of 30.6mm.

Note: The sale of Liberty Walking halves as silver bullion should be approached with care. While the majority of common dates in average condition are of no special numismatic value, this series, though modern, does include scarce dates and mint marks which deserve a better fate than the smelter's pot. The silver in these coins amounts to .36169 ounce, or slightly more than one-third of an ounce.

Mint Mark is Under IN
GOD WE TRUST on 1916
and Early 1917. Later Left of "H"
on Reverse

DATE	ABP	G-4 GOOD	F-12 FINE	EF-40 EX. FINE	MS-60 UNC.	MS-65 CH. UNC.
☐ 1916	(608,000)					
	20.00	29.00	56.00	150.00	260.00	1400.00
☐ 1916D on Obverse	(1,014,400)					
	17.00	22.00	35.00	130.00	250.00	1600.00
☐ 1916S on Obverse	(508,000)					
	65.00	90.00	130.00	460.00	900.00	4250.00
☐ 1917	(12,292,000)					
	2.00	5.00	10.00	27.00	100.00	825.00
☐ 1917D on Obverse	(765,400)					
	11.00	14.00	40.00	130.00	450.00	5500.00
☐ 1917D on Reverse	(1,940,000)					
	6.00	12.00	26.00	180.00	675.00	13000.00
☐ 1917S on Obverse	(952,000)					
	13.00	17.00	54.00	660.00	1950.00	14000.00
☐ 1917S on Reverse	(6,554,000)					
	3.50	6.00	15.00	46.00	300.00	9910.00
☐ 1918	(6,634,000)					
	2.50	5.00	16.00	124.00	552.00	3000.00
☐ 1918D	(3,853,040)					
	4.00	6.00	19.00	135.00	825.00	18000.00
☐ 1918S	(10,282,000)					
	2.50	4.00	13.00	53.00	425.00	14000.00
☐ 1919	(962,000)					
	12.00	16.00	40.00	375.00	960.00	5600.00
☐ 1919D	(1,165,000)					
	10.00	14.00	45.00	520.00	2800.00	85000.00
☐ 1919S	(1,552,000)					
	11.00	15.00	34.00	650.00	2150.00	12000.00
☐ 1920	(6,372,000)					
	2.50	4.10	12.00	62.00	290.00	5000.00
☐ 1920D	(1,551,000)					
	6.00	9.00	28.00	325.00	1000.00	8750.00

DATE	ABP	G-4 GOOD	F-12 FINE	EF-40 EX. FINE	MS-60 UNC.	MS-65 CH. UNC.
☐ 1920S	(4,624,000)					
	3.00	6.00	13.00	200.00	660.00	9250.00
☐ 1921	(246,000)					
	75.00	90.00	180.00	1300.00	2900.00	10500.00
☐ 1921D	(208,000)					
	120.00	150.00	265.00	1800.00	3000.00	12750.00
☐ 1921S	(548,000)					
	20.00	25.00	100.00	4250.00	9250.00	50000.00
☐ 1923S	(2,178,000)					
	6.00	10.00	20.00	235.00	1050.00	11000.00
☐ 1927S	(2,393,000)					
	2.75	6.00	10.00	85.00	650.00	7350.00
☐ 1928S	(1,940,000)					
	3.00	6.00	12.00	90.00	700.00	7250.00
☐ 1929D	(1,001,200)					
	4.00	7.00	12.00	72.00	310.00	1850.00
☐ 1929S	(1,902,000)					
	3.00	5.00	9.00	73.00	300.00	2000.00
☐ 1933S	(1,786,000)					
	5.00	7.00	11.00	47.00	490.00	2850.00
☐ 1934	(6,964,000)					
	2.00	5.00	7.00	8.75	65.00	400.00
☐ 1934D	(2,361,400)					
	2.50	5.00	7.00	24.00	150.00	775.00
☐ 1934S	(3,652,000)					
	2.00	5.00	7.00	25.00	325.00	3250.00
☐ 1935	(9,162,000)					
	2.00	3.00	5.00	7.50	46.00	325.00
☐ 1935D	(3,003,800)					
	2.25	4.00	6.00	25.00	130.00	1300.00
☐ 1935S	(2,854,000)					
	2.25	4.00	6.00	22.00	250.00	1750.00
☐ 1936	(12,617,901)					
	2.00	4.00	5.00	7.00	42.00	140.00
☐ 1936D	(4,252,400)					
	2.00	4.00	5.00	16.00	70.00	360.00
☐ 1936S	(3,884,000)					
	2.00	4.00	5.00	18.00	130.00	475.00
☐ 1937	(9,527,728)					
	2.00	4.00	5.00	7.00	42.00	185.00

DATE	ABP	G-4 GOOD	F-12 FINE	EF-40 EX. FINE	MS-60 UNC.	MS-65 CH. UNC.
☐ 1937D	(1,760,001)					
	4.00	5.00	7.50	27.00	185.00	450.00
☐ 1937S	(2,090,000)					
	2.50	4.00	7.50	18.00	150.00	410.00
☐ 1938	(4,118,152)					
	2.00	3.00	4.50	10.00	65.00	300.00
☐ 1938D	(491,600)					
	18.00	24.00	30.00	100.00	415.00	850.00
☐ 1939	(6,820,808)					
	2.00	3.00	4.25	6.50	42.00	131.00
☐ 1939D	(4,267,800)					
	2.00	4.00	6.00	9.00	41.00	145.00
☐ 1939S	(2,552,000)					
	2.50	5.00	6.50	12.00	115.00	185.00
☐ 1940	(9,167,279)					
	2.00	3.00	4.00	7.00	27.00	135.00
☐ 1940S	(4,550,000)					
	2.00	3.00	3.50	7.75	35.00	375.00
☐ 1941	(24,207,412)					
	2.00	3.00	3.50	7.00	30.00	110.00
☐ 1941D	(11,248,400)					
	2.00	3.00	3.50	6.25	36.00	150.00
☐ 1941S	(8,098,000)					
	2.25	3.50	4.00	7.50	72.00	1050.00
☐ 1942	(47,839,120)					
	2.00	3.00	4.00	6.00	29.00	110.00
☐ 1942D	(10,973,800)					
	2.00	3.00	4.00	6.25	40.00	250.00
☐ 1942S	(12,708,000)					
	2.00	3.00	4.00	6.25	38.00	625.00
☐ 1943	(53,190,000)					
	2.00	3.00	4.00	6.00	29.00	110.00
☐ 1943D	(11,346,000)					
	2.00	3.00	4.00	6.25	38.00	265.00
☐ 1943S	(13,450,000)					
	2.00	3.00	3.50	6.50	38.00	385.00
☐ 1944	(28,206,000)					
	2.00	3.00	4.00	6.00	29.00	150.00
☐ 1944D	(9,769,000)					
	2.00	3.00	4.00	6.25	32.00	130.00

DATE	ABP	G-4 GOOD	F-12 FINE	EF-40 EX. FINE	MS-60 UNC.	MS-65 CH. UNC.
☐ 1944S	(8,904,000)					
	2.00	3.10	4.00	6.25	37.00	600.00
☐ 1945	(31,502,000)					
	2.00	3.10	4.00	6.00	29.00	125.00
☐ 1945D	(9,966,500)					
	2.00	3.10	4.00	6.00	33.00	125.00
☐ 1945S	(10,156,000)					
	2.00	3.10	4.00	6.25	31.00	165.00
☐ 1946	(12,118,000)					
	2.00	3.10	4.00	6.00	31.00	190.00
☐ 1946D	(2,151,000)					
	3.00	4.50	5.50	9.50	37.00	95.00
☐ 1946S	(3,724,000)					
	2.50	3.50	4.00	6.00	32.00	125.00
☐ 1947	(4,094,000)					
	2.00	3.10	4.00	7.50	35.00	200.00
☐ 1947D	(3,900,000)					
	2.00	3.10	4.00	7.00	35.00	130.00

HALF DOLLARS—FRANKLIN OR LIBERTY BELL, 1948–1963

The likeness of Benjamin Franklin, which had not previously appeared on a U.S. coin, was installed on the half dollar in 1948. That he was not president can be accounted for by mere circumstance. Had the federal government been formed ten or twenty years sooner, before Franklin had advanced into old age, there is little doubt but that he would have attained the office. Like the Roosevelt dime, introduced two years earlier, this coin was designed by John R. Sinnock. On the reverse is a large representation of the Liberty Bell, adapted from the artwork on the 1926 Sesquicentennial medal celebrating the 150th anniversary of our Declaration of Independence. Franklin is shown in profile facing right. The mint mark is atop the Liberty Bell on the reverse, directly below the words UNITED STATES OF AMERICA. Composition is 90% silver, 10% copper, with a weight of 12.5 grams. The diameter is 30.6mm. It contains .36169 ounce of pure silver, or slightly more than one-third of an ounce.

Mint Mark
is Above
Liberty Bell
on Reverse

DATE	MINTAGE	ABP	F-12 FINE	EF-40 EX. FINE	MS-60 UNC.	MS-65 CH. UNC.
☐ 1948	3,006,184	2.25	3.00	4.30	14.00	85.00
☐ 1948D	4,028,600	2.25	3.00	5.00	11.00	125.00
☐ 1949	5,714,000	2.50	4.00	5.50	32.00	125.00
☐ 1949D	4,120,600	2.50	4.00	7.50	32.00	750.00
☐ 1949S	3,744,000	3.50	4.75	12.00	50.00	140.00
☐ 1950	7,793,509	2.00	3.00	3.75	22.00	100.00
☐ 1950D	8,031,600	2.00	3.25	4.25	18.00	385.00
☐ 1951	16,859,602	2.00	3.00	3.50	11.00	70.00
☐ 1951D	9,475,200	2.00	3.00	4.00	17.00	165.00
☐ 1951S	13,696,000	2.50	4.00	4.50	20.00	75.00
☐ 1952	21,274,074	2.00	3.00	3.60	7.00	65.00
☐ 1952D	25,394,600	2.00	3.00	3.60	7.00	135.00
☐ 1952S	5,526,000	2.00	3.00	4.50	32.00	65.00
☐ 1953	2,796,920	2.25	4.00	4.50	14.00	150.00
☐ 1953D	20,900,400	2.00	3.00	3.60	7.00	145.00
☐ 1953S	4,148,000	3.25	4.00	5.00	16.00	70.00
☐ 1954	13,421,503	2.00	3.00	3.60	6.00	70.00
☐ 1954D	25,445,580	2.00	3.00	3.60	6.00	100.00
☐ 1954S	4,993,400	2.00	3.00	4.00	6.50	40.00
☐ 1955	2,876,381	4.60	5.75	6.00	7.50	52.00
☐ 1956	4,701,384	1.70	3.00	3.75	6.25	38.00
☐ 1957	6,361,952	1.70	3.00	3.60	6.25	38.00
☐ 1957D	19,996,850	1.70	3.00	3.60	6.25	38.00
☐ 1958	4,917,652	1.70	2.60	3.60	6.25	38.00
☐ 1958D	23,962,412	1.70	2.25	2.50	5.10	38.00
☐ 1959	7,349,291	1.70	2.25	2.50	5.10	95.00
☐ 1959D	13,053,750	1.70	2.25	2.50	5.10	115.00
☐ 1960	7,715,602	1.70	2.25	2.50	5.10	120.00
☐ 1960D	18,215,812	1.70	2.25	2.50	5.10	435.00
☐ 1961	11,318,244	1.70	2.00	2.50	5.10	120.00
☐ 1961D	20,276,442	1.70	2.25	2.50	5.10	190.00
☐ 1962	12,932,019	1.70	2.25	2.50	5.10	140.00

DATE	MINTAGE	ABP	F-12 FINE	EF-40 EX. FINE	MS-60 UNC.	MS-65 CH. UNC.
☐ 1962D	35,473,281	1.75	2.25	3.00	4.00	195.00
☐ 1963	25,239,645	1.75	2.25	3.00	4.00	58.00
☐ 1963D	67,069,292	1.75	2.25	3.00	4.00	65.00

HALF DOLLARS—JOHN F. KENNEDY, 1964 TO DATE

Following the death of President Kennedy in 1963 there was considerable public sentiment for honoring his memory on coinage. As all coins except the half dollar already carried portraits of presidents, it was decided to install his likeness on this coin, even though its design had been changed as recently as 1948.

The portrait was designed by Gilroy Roberts and Frank Gasparro, the reverse featuring a shield eagle surrounded by stars. As introduced in 1964, the coin was of regular silver composition (90% silver, 10% copper, .36169 ounces of silver by weight) but was altered in 1965 to the clad standard, consisting of a 21% silver/79% copper interior covered with 80% silver/20% copper, total weight of silver being .14792 ounces. Its weight was 11.5 grams, down from 12.5. In 1971 the silver was removed from its core and a new composition used for the exterior, comprising three parts copper to one of nickel. The silver had been entirely replaced and the weight fell to 11.34 grams. The only alteration in design occurred in 1976 when a figure of Independence Hall in Philadelphia was added to the reverse, supplanting the eagle, as part of the Bicentennial program. On the obverse the date appeared as 1776–1976. In the following year the normal reverse was readopted. A quantity of silver-clad pieces were struck in 1976, the first (and last) in this series since 1970.

This has been termed a difficult coin on which to find the mint mark. As first issued, it may be observed on the reverse, above the L and F in the word HALF. In 1968 it was brought to the obverse, beneath the portrait and above the date.

The scarcest Kennedy half dollar is the 1993S silver proof, not minted for general circulation. The Kennedy half dollar has a diameter of 30.6mm.

Mint Mark 1964–1967

Mint Mark 1968 on

DATE	MINTAGE	ABP	EF-40 EX. FINE	MS-60 UNC.	PRF-65 PROOF
☐ 1964	277,254,766	1.50	2.25	3.00	10.00
☐ 1964D	156,205,446	1.50	2.25	3.00	
CLAD COINAGE					
☐ 1965	65,879,366			1.25	
☐ 1966	108,984,933			1.25	
☐ 1967	295,045,968			1.25	
☐ 1968D	246,951,930			1.25	
☐ 1968S Proof Only	3,041,508				4.00
☐ 1969D	129,881,800			1.25	
☐ 1969S Proof Only	2,934,631				4.00
☐ 1970D	2,150,000			11.00	
☐ 1970S Proof Only	2,632,810				12.00
☐ 1971	155,164,000			1.25	
☐ 1971D	302,097,424			1.25	
☐ 1971S Proof Only	3,224,138				3.25
☐ 1972	153,180,000			1.10	
☐ 1972D	141,890,000			1.10	
☐ 1972S Proof Only	3,224,138				3.25
☐ 1973	64,964,000			1.40	
☐ 1973D	83,171,400			1.25	
☐ 1973S Proof Only	2,769,624				2.50
☐ 1974	201,588,250			1.10	
☐ 1974D	79,088,210			1.25	
☐ 1974D Doubled Die				75.00	
☐ 1974S Proof Only	2,617,350				2.00
☐ 1976 Copper-Nickel Clad	234,318,200			1.00	
☐ 1976D Copper-Nickel Clad	287,565,290			1.00	
☐ 1976S Copper-Nickel Clad Proof Only	7,123,300				2.00
☐ 1976S Silver Clad	4,250,000			3.50	
☐ 1976S Silver Clad Proof	3,215,730				5.50
☐ 1977	43,569,000			1.35	
☐ 1977D	31,450,250			1.35	

DATE	MINTAGE	MS-60 UNC.	PRF-65 PROOF
☐ 1977S Proof Only	3,450,895		2.25
☐ 1978	14,350,000	1.40	
☐ 1978D	13,765,799	2.25	
☐ 1978S Proof Only	3,127,781		2.00
☐ 1979	68,311,400	1.35	
☐ 1979D	15,815,400	1.20	
☐ 1979S Proof Only (I)	3,677,200		2.00
☐ 1979S Proof Only (II)			11.00
☐ 1980P	29,500,000	1.10	
☐ 1980D	33,456,450	1.30	
☐ 1980S Proof Only	3,555,000		2.00
☐ 1981P	29,544,206	1.40	
☐ 1981D	27,839,525	1.30	
☐ 1981S Proof Only (I)	4,063,000		2.00
☐ 1981S Proof Only (II)			11.00
☐ 1982P	10,920,700	2.00	
☐ 1982D	13,150,000	2.25	
☐ 1982S Proof Only (I)	3,229,000		2.00
☐ 1983P	34,100,000	3.50	
☐ 1983D	32,475,000	3.25	
☐ 1983S Proof Only	3,228,621		3.75
☐ 1984P	26,031,084	1.60	
☐ 1984D	26,275,000	1.90	
☐ 1984S Proof Only			5.50
☐ 1985P	18,922,112	1.70	
☐ 1985D	19,911,760	1.70	
☐ 1985S Proof Only	3,372,220		4.00
☐ 1986P	12,110,530	7.50	
☐ 1986D	15,463,220	5.50	
☐ 1986S Proof Only	3,111,000		12.00
☐ 1987P	2,926,121	5.00	
☐ 1987D	2,926,121	4.00	
☐ 1987S Proof Only	3,820,764		4.00
☐ 1988P	12,979,642	4.00	
☐ 1988D	12,121,420	2.10	
☐ 1988S Proof Only	3,100,100		6.75
☐ 1989P	25,100,420	2.00	
☐ 1989D	23,006,111	1.75	
☐ 1989S Proof Only	3,115,720		6.50
☐ 1990P	22,368,400	1.50	
☐ 1990D	20,192,044	3.25	
☐ 1990S Proof Only	3,008,029		7.50
☐ 1991P	14,860,240	1.75	
☐ 1991D	15,156,667	4.00	
☐ 1991S Proof Only	2,877,789		14.00

DATE	MINTAGE	MS-60 UNC.	PRF-65 PROOF
☐ 1992P	17,658,310	1.10	
☐ 1992D	16,000,110	2.50	
☐ 1992S Proof Only	2,858,882		13.00
☐ 1992S Silver Proof Only	1,317,579		15.50
☐ 1993P	15,510,000	1.25	
☐ 1993D	15,000,000	1.25	
☐ 1993S Proof Only	2,633,439		14.00
☐ 1993S Silver Proof	761,353		25.00
☐ 1994P	23,718,000	1.15	
☐ 1994D	23,828,110	1.15	
☐ 1994S Proof Only	2,484,594		8.50
☐ 1994S Silver Proof	785,329		35.00
☐ 1995P	26,496,000	1.15	
☐ 1995D	26,288,000	1.15	
☐ 1995S Proof Only	2,010,000		25.00
☐ 1995S Silver Proof	838,950		80.00
☐ 1996P	24,442,000	1.15	
☐ 1996D	24,744,000	1.15	
☐ 1996S Proof Only			10.00
☐ 1996S Silver Proof			40.00
☐ 1997P	20,882,000	1.10	
☐ 1997D	19,876,000	2.50	
☐ 1997S Proof Only	1,975,000		19.00
☐ 1997 Silver Proof			75.00
☐ 1998P	15,646,000	1.10	
☐ 1998D	15,064,000	1.10	
☐ 1998S Proof Only			13.50
☐ 1998S Silver Proof			25.00
☐ 1998S Silver Matte Finish			190.00
☐ 1999P	8,900,000	2.00	
☐ 1999D	10,358,000	2.25	
☐ 1999S Proof			9.00
☐ 1999S Silver Proof			15.00
☐ 2000P	22,600,000	2.00	
☐ 2000D	19,466,000	2.25	
☐ 2000S Proof			7.50
☐ 2000S Silver Proof			12.50
☐ 2001P	21,200,000	2.00	
☐ 2001D	19,504,000	2.00	
☐ 2001S Proof			7.00
☐ 2001S Silver Proof			12.50
☐ 2002P Not Made for Circulation		4.75	
☐ 2002D Not Made for Circulation		4.75	
☐ 2002S Proof			7.00
☐ 2002S Silver Proof			10.00

SILVER DOLLARS

EARLY, 1794–1804; PATTERNS, 1836–1839; REGULAR ISSUE, 1840–1873

The silver dollar, probably the most significant U.S. coin of the 19th century, was authorized on April 2, 1792, and was intended as the chief currency piece or standard for other silver coinage. However, striking was not begun until 1794. The word "dollar" is a corruption of Taler or Thaler, a large silver coin widely distributed in Europe and well known to Colonial America. Prior to use of this term in domestic coinage it had become common to refer to Spain's "pieces of eight" as dollars, so it was natural that this crownlike silver piece should likewise be called a dollar.

The first design, the Flowing Hair variety, was executed by Robert Scot and may be observed on other coinage of that era. Its reverse was an eagle surrounded by the words UNITED STATES OF AMERICA. The composition was .8924 silver and .1076 copper, the addition of this roughly one-tenth part of base metal being needed to provide ruggedness. It weighed 26.96 grams and was the heaviest U.S. silver coin excepting the Trade dollar of much later vintage. Its diameter varies between 39 and 40mm. Along the edge is impressed the words HUNDRED CENTS ONE DOLLAR OR UNIT, interspersed with typographical ornament.

There was very limited striking of dollars in the initial year of their appearance, less than 2,000 being turned out. The following year, 1795, witnessed greatly increased production, but because of the surface softness of these coins and the extensive handling to which they were subjected, it is not easy finding specimens in the best grades of condition. "Average" examples can be had rather easily.

There are two reverse varieties of the 1795 Flowing Hair dollar, one in which three leaves appear beneath the eagle's wings on either side, another with two leaves. Toward the end of 1795 the Flowing Hair obverse was replaced by the Draped Bust, with the so-called "small eagle" reverse (the eagle's wings and body in general being scaled smaller than previously). The Draped Bust obverse is found with dates in small or large numerals, and with the legend UNITED STATES OF AMERICA in small or large letters on the reverse. There are also differences in the number of stars on the obverse. In 1798 the shield eagle reverse was introduced, still with the Draped Bust portrait. These types were continued until 1803 when the striking of silver dollars was suspended.

It was at one time believed that the Mint coined a few dollars in 1804 but it has now been established beyond reasonable doubt that silver dollars dated 1804 were struck in the 1830s for inclusion in proof sets. Apparently the die for an 1804 coin was prepared before any decision was reached to discontinue production and it was stored away at the Mint for those thirty years. In any case, the 1804 dollar is an extremely rare piece whose popularity (and price) has not suffered in the least by results of research into its origins. A handful of restrikes were later made in 1859. There is scarcely any difference in rarity or value between the 1830s proofs and the 1859 restrikes. Of all 1804 silver dollars (both types), fifteen exist.

In 1836 Christian Gobrecht prepared designs for a new silver dollar, which at first was struck in limited numbers to test public response. A seated figure of Liberty appeared on the obverse with a flying eagle reverse. The obverse carried no wording whatever. On the reverse were the words UNITED STATES OF AMERICA and ONE DOLLAR, the eagle set within a ground of stars. There are some varieties of this reverse containing no stars. Full-scale output of silver dollars was not resumed until 1840. For this issue, and for many years following, the shield or heraldic eagle was used for the reverse and the face value was abbreviated into ONE DOL. In 1866 the motto IN GOD WE TRUST was added to the reverse, on a banner flowing above the eagle. The mint mark is located below the eagle and above the statement of value. Striking of dollars in this design ceased in 1873.

SILVER DOLLARS—LIBERTY WITH FLOWING HAIR, 1794–1795

DATE	MINTAGE	ABP	G-4 GOOD	F-12 FINE	VF-20 V. FINE	MS-60 UNC.
☐ 1794	1,758	9000.00	11000.00	23000.00	47500.00	185000.00
☐ 1795*	160,295	575.00	800.00	1850.00	2800.00	20000.00

*Includes both 2 Leaf and 3 Leaf Varieties

SILVER DOLLARS—DRAPED BUST, 1795–1798 SMALL EAGLE ON REVERSE

DATE	MINTAGE	ABP	G-4 GOOD	F-12 FINE	VF-20 V. FINE	MS-60 UNC.
☐ 1795	42,738	550.00	700.00	1500.00	2350.00	20000.00
☐ 1796	72,920	500.00	700.00	1500.00	2350.00	21000.00
☐ 1796 Small Letters		500.00	700.00	1500.00	2350.00	21000.00
☐ 1796 Large Letters	7,776	500.00	700.00	1600.00	2350.00	21000.00
☐ 1797 9 Stars Left, 7 Right, Small Letters		900.00	1200.00	2400.00	4000.00	33000.00
☐ 1797 9 Stars Left, 7 Right, Large Letters		500.00	750.00	1500.00	2350.00	22000.00
☐ 1797 10 Stars Left, 6 Right		500.00	750.00	1500.00	2350.00	21000.00
☐ 1798 13 Stars	327,536	750.00	1000.00	1550.00	2500.00	23500.00

SILVER DOLLARS—DRAPED BUST, 1798–1804
LARGE EAGLE ON REVERSE

DATE	MINTAGE	ABP	G-4 GOOD	F-12 FINE	VF-20 V. FINE	MS-60 UNC.
☐ 1798		350.00	450.00	900.00	1500.00	11500.00
☐ 1799*	423,515	350.00	450.00	900.00	1500.00	10250.00
☐ 1800*	220,920	350.00	450.00	900.00	1500.00	10000.00
☐ 1801*	54,454	375.00	475.00	950.00	1600.00	17000.00
☐ 1802*	41,650	375.00	475.00	950.00	1600.00	12000.00
☐ 1802 over 1*		375.00	475.00	950.00	1600.00	12000.00
☐ 1803*	66,064	375.00	475.00	950.00	1600.00	12500.00

☐ 1804 One of the most valued coins in the world—less than 15 known. In March 1980, The Garrett Specimen was sold for $400,000.00. In 1993 the Reed Hawn specimen was sold by Sacks for $522,500.00. A 1997 auction specimen sold for $1,815,000 in proof condition. An AU PCGS graded specimen sold for over $800,000.00 by private treaty in 1998. In Dec. 2001 a Class III coin realized $874,000.00 at public auction.

*Includes all types

SILVER DOLLARS—LIBERTY SEATED
(GOBRECHT), 1836–1839
WITH FLYING EAGLE ON REVERSE

DATE	MINTAGE	VF-20 V. FINE	EF-40 EX. FINE	PRF-65 PROOF
☐ 1836	approx. 1,025	4850.00	5600.00	45000.00
☐ 1838	approx. 31		Proof Only	110000.00
☐ 1839	approx. 303		Proof Only	82000.00

SILVER DOLLARS—LIBERTY SEATED, 1840–1865
NO MOTTO OVER EAGLE

Mint Mark is Below Eagle on Reverse

DATE	ABP	G-4 GOOD	F-12 FINE	VF-20 V. FINE	MS-60 UNC.
☐ 1840	(61,005)				
	110.00	135.00	215.00	300.00	2500.00
☐ 1841	(173,000)				
	100.00	125.00	180.00	300.00	1500.00
☐ 1842	(184,618)				
	100.00	125.00	185.00	240.00	900.00
☐ 1843	(165,100)				
	100.00	125.00	185.00	240.00	1150.00
☐ 1844	(20,000)				
	125.00	170.00	310.00	440.00	2600.00
☐ 1845	(24,500)				
	175.00	210.00	250.00	360.00	4750.00
☐ 1846	(110,600)				
	100.00	125.00	220.00	260.00	1350.00
☐ 18460	(59,000)				
	110.00	130.00	230.00	310.00	2600.00
☐ 1847	(140,750)				
	100.00	125.00	215.00	260.00	900.00
☐ 1848	(15,000)				
	165.00	250.00	400.00	530.00	2750.00
☐ 1849	(62,600)				
	100.00	150.00	215.00	285.00	1650.00
☐ 1850	(7,500)				
	250.00	380.00	550.00	770.00	4250.00
☐ 18500	(40,000)				
	150.00	215.00	330.00	640.00	6500.00
☐ 1851	(1,300)				
	1750.00	2250.00	2900.00	4000.00	22500.00
☐ 1852	(1,100)				
	1300.00	1700.00	2100.00	3000.00	21500.00

DATE	ABP	G-4 GOOD	F-12 FINE	VF-20 V. FINE	MS-60 UNC.
☐ 1853	(46,110)				
	125.00	200.00	250.00	340.00	2150.00
☐ 1854	(33,140)				
	700.00	920.00	1650.00	2100.00	6250.00
☐ 1855	(26,000)				
	525.00	710.00	1200.00	1775.00	6350.00
☐ 1856	(63,500)				
	160.00	210.00	415.00	600.00	3200.00
☐ 1857	(94,000)				
	180.00	250.00	450.00	600.00	2200.00
☐ 1858 Proofs Only (80)				Proof 63—8500.00	
☐ 1859	(256,500)				
	125.00	230.00	310.00	460.00	1250.00
☐ 1859O	(360,000)				
	100.00	125.00	175.00	225.00	810.00
☐ 1859S	(20,000)				
	140.00	215.00	375.00	575.00	6750.00
☐ 1860	(218,930)				
	125.00	175.00	260.00	410.00	925.00
☐ 1860O	(515,000)				
	100.00	125.00	175.00	230.00	920.00
☐ 1861	(78,500)				
	300.00	350.00	625.00	815.00	2500.00
☐ 1862	(12,090)				
	250.00	320.00	610.00	760.00	2200.00
☐ 1863	(27,660)				
	140.00	270.00	365.00	510.00	2200.00
☐ 1864	(31,170)				
	140.00	180.00	275.00	400.00	2100.00
☐ 1865	(47,000)				
	120.00	175.00	280.00	450.00	1850.00
☐ 1866 No Motto, 2 Known				Proof—375000.00	

SILVER DOLLARS—LIBERTY SEATED, 1866–1873
MOTTO "IN GOD WE TRUST" ADDED

DATE	ABP	G-4 GOOD	F-12 FINE	EF-40 EX. FINE	MS-60 UNC.
☐ 1866	(49,625)				
	130.00	185.00	270.00	470.00	1350.00
☐ 1867	(47,525)				
	125.00	160.00	300.00	435.00	1250.00
☐ 1868	(162,700)				
	100.00	131.00	230.00	400.00	1300.00
☐ 1869	(424,300)				
	100.00	130.00	200.00	360.00	1300.00
☐ 1870	(416,000)				
	115.00	150.00	185.00	325.00	1150.00
☐ 1870CC	(12,462)				
	200.00	250.00	425.00	1150.00	8500.00
☐ 1870S				EXTREMELY RARE	
☐ 1871	(1,074,760)				
	100.00	130.00	210.00	325.00	800.00
☐ 1871CC	(1,376)				
	900.00	1200.00	2950.00	7500.00	37500.00
☐ 1872	(1,106,450)				
	100.00	130.00	185.00	325.00	875.00
☐ 1872CC	(3,150)				
	650.00	900.00	1650.00	3200.00	16000.00
☐ 1872S	(9,000)				
	150.00	180.00	410.00	875.00	7600.00
☐ 1873	(193,600)				
	100.00	140.00	210.00	330.00	1050.00
☐ 1873CC	(2,300)				
	2400.00	2750.00	5510.00	11300.00	60000.00
☐ 1873S	(700)		UNKNOWN IN ANY COLLECTION		

SILVER DOLLARS—TRADE, 1873–1885

In the early 1870s there was mounting pressure to increase the silver dollar's weight, as American commerce with Japan was being hindered by the fact that our silver dollar was somewhat smaller than European crowns. It was decided to strike a special coin, known as the "Trade dollar," to weigh 27.22 grains and be composed of nine parts silver to one part copper. Much agitation to retain the silver dollar as a domestic circulating coin resulted in the government authorizing this new enlarged version to pass as legal tender (for its $1 face value) in transactions of $5 or less. This caused confusion and dissatisfaction, and in 1878 striking of a separate domestic silver dollar, based upon the pre–Trade dollar standard, was resumed. For a while they were issued simultaneously until the Trade dollar died a gradual death, its final year of striking being 1885. The last year in which they were struck in numbers that could be termed sufficient for free circulation was 1878.

The Trade dollar has sometimes been called one of the handsomest U.S. coins of that denomination. True enough, the design is well drawn, but striking of circulating specimens was in such low relief that the slightest handling all but obliterated the more attractive detailing. Only when seen in proof state can the Trade dollar's beauty be recognized. The designer was William Barber. On the obverse is a seated figure of Liberty, with an eagle reverse. The wording TRADE DOLLAR appears at the foot of the reverse. This is the only U.S. coin to proclaim its composition; the reverse is inscribed 420 GRAINS, 900 FINE meaning, of course, .900 silver to .100 base metal.

Beginning in 1876 the Trade dollar was no longer legal for domestic use. The Treasury Department (assailed from all sides in those days) left itself open to sharp criticism by not offering to redeem Trade dollars until 1887, eleven years later. In diameter the Trade dollar was no larger than the normal issues, 38.1mm., but somewhat thicker. It was the heaviest U.S. silver coin ever minted. Only recently has it come into what might be termed popularity among collectors. In terms of mintage totals vs. regular dollars it is still rather underpriced.

In the following listing, note that superbly struck pieces bring proportionately more than the prices shown.

Mint Mark
is Below Eagle
in Reverse

DATE	ABP	G-4 GOOD	F-12 FINE	EF-40 EX. FINE	MS-60 UNC.
☐ 1873 (397,500)					
	50.00	75.00	115.00	185.00	465.00
☐ 1873CC (124,500)					
	60.00	90.00	160.00	500.00	2250.00
☐ 1873S (703,000)					
	55.00	80.00	100.00	180.00	775.00
☐ 1874 (987,800)					
	50.00	65.00	96.00	160.00	425.00
☐ 1874CC (1,373,200)					
	60.00	85.00	100.00	200.00	950.00
☐ 1874S (2,549,000)					
	50.00	68.00	95.00	150.00	400.00
☐ 1875 (218,000)					
	70.00	120.00	270.00	400.00	1500.00
☐ 1875CC (1,573,700)					
	60.00	85.00	115.00	200.00	675.00
☐ 1875S (4,487,000)					
	50.00	70.00	90.00	140.00	400.00
☐ 1875S over CC (155,000)					
	120.00	200.00	280.00	670.00	2150.00
☐ 1876 (456,150)					
	50.00	70.00	90.00	145.00	400.00
☐ 1876CC (509,000)					
	65.00	92.00	100.00	250.00	2100.00
☐ 1876S (5,227,000)					
	50.00	70.00	110.00	125.00	400.00
☐ 1877 (3,039,710)					
	50.00	70.00	90.00	145.00	435.00
☐ 1877CC (534,000)					
	65.00	100.00	175.00	400.00	800.00

DATE	ABP	G-4 GOOD	F-12 FINE	EF-40 EX. FINE	MS-60 UNC.	PRF-63 PROOF
☐ 1877S	(9,519,000)					
	50.00	70.00	95.00	155.00	400.00	
☐ 1878 Proofs Only	(900)					2250.00
☐ 1878CC	(97,000)					
	200.00	275.00	600.00	1450.00	8000.00	
☐ 1878S	(4,162,000)					
	50.00	70.00	95.00	150.00	410.00	
☐ 1879 Proofs Only	(1,541)					2100.00
☐ 1880 Proofs Only	(1,987)					2100.00
☐ 1881 Proofs Only	(960)					2150.00
☐ 1882 Proofs Only	(1,097)					2100.00
☐ 1883 Proofs Only	(979)					2200.00
☐ 1884 Proofs Only	(10)					100000.00
☐ 1885 Proofs Only	(5)			EXTREMELY RARE—375000.00		

SILVER DOLLARS—LIBERTY HEAD OR MORGAN, 1878–1904 and 1921

For the resumption of the standard silver dollar series a new design was chosen. The work of George T. Morgan, and thereby popularly called the Morgan dollar, it showed a profile head of Liberty backed with an eagle holding arrows and branch. The motto IN GOD WE TRUST was installed above the eagle in Old English Gothic lettering. On the obverse appeared the slogan E PLURIBUS UNUM. For many years the Morgan dollar was the best known and probably most respected silver "crown" in the world. Artistically the work is superb, rendered all the more impressive by the fact that its detailing did not become easily effaced with use. Morgan's goal was to fashion for this country a coin which, if it did not carry the financial power of ancient Greek silver pieces, might be regarded as their equal in design.

The Morgan dollar remained unchanged in weight and composition throughout its history. It was comprised of nine parts silver to one part copper and weighed 412.5 grains. The diameter is 38.1mm. After having been struck in large quantities for two and a half decades, production sometimes exceeding 30 million pieces annually, it was suspended in 1904 because of a shortage of silver. Striking was resumed in 1921, but only briefly, as the new Peace dollar was introduced that same year. However there were more Morgan dollars coined in 1921—over 80 million—than in any previous year. The mint mark is placed below the eagle on the reverse. The Morgan dollar contains .77344 ounce of silver, or slightly more than three-quarters of an ounce.

In the following listing, note that superbly struck specimens with few bag marks bring substantially more than the prices listed.

Mint Mark is Below Eagle on Reverse

DATE	ABP	F-12 FINE	EF-40 EX. FINE	MS-60 UNC.	MS-65 CH. UNC.
☐ 1878, 8 Tail Feathers, (750,000)					
	14.00	21.00	28.00	110.00	1150.00
☐ 1878, 7 Tail Feathers (416,000)					
	11.00	15.00	22.00	45.00	1100.00
☐ 1878, 1879 Reverse					
	11.00	18.00	22.00	52.00	2250.00
☐ 1878, 7 over 8 Tail Feathers					
	13.00	17.00	25.00	120.00	2650.00
☐ 1878CC (2,212,000)					
	40.00	50.00	60.00	165.00	1100.00
☐ 1878S (9,774,000)					
	12.00	16.00	18.50	40.00	250.00
☐ 1879 (14,807,100)					
	9.50	14.00	16.00	23.00	850.00
☐ 1879CC (756,000)					
	60.00	86.00	360.00	1500.00	17000.00
☐ 1879CC over CC					
	55.00	75.00	290.00	1300.00	20000.00
☐ 1879O (2,887,000)					
	10.00	13.00	17.00	68.00	2850.00
☐ 1879S, 1878 Reverse (9,110,000)					
	10.00	14.00	18.00	95.00	6500.00
☐ 1879S, 1879 Reverse					
	10.00	12.50	16.00	28.00	90.00

DATE	ABP	F-12 FINE	EF-40 EX. FINE	MS-60 UNC.	MS-65 CH. UNC.
☐ 1880 (12,601,355)	10.00	12.00	15.00	24.00	650.00
☐ 1880CC (591,000)	75.00	90.00	165.00	315.00	750.00
☐ 1880CC,1878 Reverse	75.00	90.00	160.00	315.00	1950.00
☐ 1880 over 79CC	75.00	90.00	170.00	325.00	2000.00
☐ 1880O (5,305,000)	10.00	12.00	18.00	52.00	14750.00
☐ 1880S (8,900,000)	10.00	12.00	18.00	25.00	94.00
☐ 1881 (9,163,975)	10.00	13.00	18.00	28.00	750.00
☐ 1881CC (206,000)	135.00	165.00	225.00	300.00	550.00
☐ 1881O (5,708,000)	10.00	12.00	17.00	23.00	1450.00
☐ 1881S (12,760,000)	10.00	12.00	17.00	25.00	85.00
☐ 1882 (11,101,000)	10.00	12.00	17.00	23.00	425.00
☐ 1882CC (1,133,000)	40.00	50.00	62.00	125.00	365.00
☐ 1882O (6,090,000)	10.00	12.00	15.00	23.00	675.00
☐ 1882O, O over S	12.00	15.00	19.00	160.00	25000.00
☐ 1882S (9,250,000)	10.00	12.00	15.00	26.00	90.00
☐ 1883 (12,191,039)	10.00	12.00	16.00	24.00	150.00
☐ 1883CC (1,204,000)	45.00	57.00	62.00	120.00	290.00
☐ 1883O (8,725,000)	10.00	12.00	16.00	24.00	90.00
☐ 1883S (6,250,000)	11.00	14.00	27.00	425.00	19500.00
☐ 1884 (14,070,875)	10.00	11.00	16.00	23.00	250.00
☐ 1884CC (1,136,000)	45.00	57.00	70.00	120.00	290.00
☐ 1884O (9,730,000)	10.00	13.00	15.00	23.00	90.00
☐ 1884S (3,200,000)	11.00	14.00	40.00	3100.00	145000.00
☐ 1885 (17,787,767)	10.00	13.00	15.00	23.00	90.00

DATE	ABP	F-12 FINE	EF-40 EX. FINE	MS-60 UNC.	MS-65 CH. UNC.
☐ 1885CC	(228,000)				
	200.00	240.00	275.00	325.00	700.00
☐ 1885O	(9,185,000)				
	10.00	12.00	16.00	24.00	90.00
☐ 1885S	(1,497,000)				
	12.00	15.00	22.00	165.00	1750.00
☐ 1886	(19,963,886)				
	10.00	13.00	14.00	23.00	90.00
☐ 1886O	(10,710,000)				
	10.00	16.00	19.00	365.00	185000.00
☐ 1886S	(750,000)				
	18.00	24.00	49.00	210.00	3000.00
☐ 1887	(20,290,710)				
	10.00	11.00	17.00	25.00	90.00
☐ 1887 over 6					
	15.00	20.00	40.00	210.00	3850.00
☐ 1887O	(11,550,000)				
	10.00	12.00	17.00	50.00	3500.00
☐ 1887O over 6					
	15.00	21.00	46.00	330.00	25000.00
☐ 1887S	(1,771,000)				
	11.00	13.00	21.00	95.00	3250.00
☐ 1888	(19,183,833)				
	10.00	13.00	15.00	24.00	190.00
☐ 1888O	(12,150,000)				
	10.00	13.00	15.00	27.00	385.00
☐ 1888S	(657,000)				
	28.00	40.00	52.00	200.00	3350.00
☐ 1889	(21,726,811)				
	10.00	12.00	15.00	24.00	300.00
☐ 1889CC	(350,000)				
	275.00	350.00	1300.00	7500.00	225000.00
☐ 1889O	(11,875,000)				
	10.00	12.50	15.00	125.00	5000.00
☐ 1889S	(700,000)				
	19.00	26.00	35.00	165.00	1875.00
☐ 1890	(16,802,590)				
	10.00	13.00	16.00	25.00	2250.00
☐ 1890CC	(2,309,041)				
	45.00	58.00	65.00	300.00	4750.00
☐ 1890O	(10,701,000)				
	10.00	14.00	17.00	42.00	1750.00
☐ 1890S	(8,230,373)				
	10.00	14.00	14.00	50.00	900.00

DATE	ABP	F-12 FINE	EF-40 EX. FINE	MS-60 UNC.	MS-65 CH. UNC.
☐ 1891	(8,694,206)				
	10.00	14.00	15.00	48.00	7000.00
☐ 1891CC	(1,618,000)				
	50.00	63.00	70.00	310.00	3000.00
☐ 1891O	(7,954,529)				
	10.00	12.00	16.00	125.00	7750.00
☐ 1891S	(5,296,000)				
	10.00	12.00	21.00	58.00	1250.00
☐ 1892	(1,037,245)				
	12.00	16.00	28.00	140.00	4000.00
☐ 1892CC	(1,352,000)				
	50.00	63.00	150.00	600.00	5900.00
☐ 1892O	(2,744,000)				
	11.00	15.00	28.00	125.00	5500.00
☐ 1892S	(1,200,000)				
	14.00	19.00	160.00	14500.00	115000.00
☐ 1893	(378,792)				
	65.00	90.00	170.00	420.00	7000.00
☐ 1893CC	(667,000)				
	110.00	140.00	585.00	1800.00	45000.00
☐ 1893O	(300,000)				
	75.00	100.00	215.00	1250.00	150000.00
☐ 1893S	(100,000)				
	1100.00	1300.00	4350.00	40000.00	225000.00
☐ 1894	(110,972)				
	325.00	410.00	525.00	1200.00	18500.00
☐ 1894O	(1,723,000)				
	18.00	24.00	64.00	510.00	41000.00
☐ 1894S	(1,260,000)				
	28.00	35.00	115.00	425.00	5000.00
☐ 1895*	(12,880)				
	12000.00			19000.00	29000.00
☐ 1895O	(450,000)				
	85.00	115.00	262.00	9500.00	190000.00
☐ 1895S	(400,000)				
	150.00	200.00	425.00	1700.00	16500.00
☐ 1896	(9,976,762)				
	10.00	12.00	16.00	26.00	145.00
☐ 1896O	(4,900,000)				
	11.00	13.50	22.00	700.00	125000.00
☐ 1896S	(5,000,000)				
	18.00	26.00	160.00	760.00	13000.00
☐ 1897	(2,822,731)				
	10.00	14.00	16.00	24.00	225.00

*Check carefully for removed mint mark.

DATE	ABP	F-12 FINE	EF-40 EX. FINE	MS-60 UNC.	MS-65 CH. UNC.
☐ 1897O	(4,004,000)				
	11.00	13.00	23.00	570.00	45000.00
☐ 1897S	(5,825,000)				
	11.00	14.00	17.00	62.00	500.00
☐ 1898	(5,884,725)				
	12.00	15.00	16.00	24.00	225.00
☐ 1898O	(4,440,000)				
	10.00	13.00	16.00	27.00	115.00
☐ 1898S	(4,102,000)				
	12.00	15.00	29.00	210.00	2150.00
☐ 1899	(330,846)				
	25.00	30.00	50.00	96.00	575.00
☐ 1899O	(12,290,000)				
	10.00	13.00	16.00	28.00	110.00
☐ 1899S	(2,562,000)				
	12.00	16.00	34.00	250.00	1800.00
☐ 1900	(8,830,912)				
	11.00	15.00	16.00	30.00	165.00
☐ 1900O	(12,590,000)				
	11.00	15.00	17.00	32.00	125.00
☐ 1900O over CC					
	18.00	25.00	46.00	185.00	1300.00
☐ 1900S	(3,540,000)				
	12.00	16.00	34.00	215.00	1300.00
☐ 1901	(6,962,813)				
	15.00	20.00	55.00	1450.00	160000.00
☐ 1901O	(13,320,000)				
	10.00	16.00	17.00	28.00	170.00
☐ 1901S	(2,284,000)				
	13.00	16.00	47.00	290.00	3500.00
☐ 1902	(7,994,777)				
	11.00	14.00	16.00	38.00	450.00
☐ 1902O	(8,636,000)				
	11.00	14.00	17.00	26.00	140.00
☐ 1902S	(1,530,000)				
	30.00	37.00	96.00	250.00	2800.00
☐ 1903	(4,652,755)				
	20.00	25.00	35.00	48.00	190.00
☐ 1903O	(4,450,000)				
	125.00	150.00	200.00	325.00	435.00
☐ 1903S	(1,241,000)				
	25.00	32.00	270.00	2600.00	6750.00

DATE	ABP	F-12 FINE	EF-40 EX. FINE	MS-60 UNC.	MS-65 CH. UNC.
☐ 1904	(2,788,650)				
	10.00	14.00	18.00	70.00	4000.00
☐ 1904O	(3,720,000)				
	10.00	14.00	17.00	24.00	95.00
☐ 1904S	(2,304,000)				
	18.00	22.00	185.00	900.00	5650.00
☐ 1921	(44,690,000)				
	7.50	10.00	16.00	18.00	130.00
☐ 1921D	(20,345,000)				
	7.50	10.00	12.00	35.00	250.00
☐ 1921S	(21,695,000)				
	7.50	10.00	11.50	25.00	1450.00

SILVER DOLLARS—PEACE, 1921–1935; 1964

It was decided, following the Armistice of 1918, to issue a coin commemorating world peace, and to make this a circulating coin rather than a limited issue. As production of silver dollars was being resumed in 1921, this was the logical denomination. This coin, known as the Peace dollar, was designed by Anthony DeFrancisci, who had some reputation as a designer of medals. Its obverse pictured a profile head of Liberty, quite different in character from those on other coins, and a standing eagle (perched on a mound) on its reverse. The word "Peace" was incorporated into the reverse.

As originally engraved, the dies were similar in nature to those of a medal, intended to strike in high relief. The following year modified dies were introduced. Coining of silver dollars was halted in 1935 and never resumed, the subsequent Ike and Anthony dollars being of a different metallic composition. Mint mark appears beneath the word ONE in ONE DOLLAR on the reverse. The Peace dollar is composed of 90% silver and 10% copper and has a weight of 412.5 grains. The diameter is 38.1mm. and the silver content is .77344 of an ounce.

Note: In 1964 it was decided to resume striking silver dollars after a nearly 30-year lapse. The Peace design was used and production was at the Denver Mint. Before the coins reached circulation, the "silver controversy" of the year culminated in the Mint's decision to switch to clad coinage.

Production of the 1964D silver dollar was halted and the un-released total of 316,000 was ordered melted. In the inter-vening years a number of rumors have circulated about specimens which escaped melting, but there is no proven evidence of any in existence. Technically this coin, if it did exist, would be illegal to own and subject to confiscation.

Mint Mark—Below ONE and to Left of Wingtip

DATE	MINTAGE	ABP	F-12 FINE	EF-40 EX. FINE	MS-60 UNC.
☐ 1921	1,006,473	30.00	38.00	48.00	150.00
☐ 1922	51,737,000	6.50	8.50	10.00	16.00
☐ 1922D	15,063,000	6.50	8.50	10.00	23.00
☐ 1922S	17,475,000	6.50	8.50	10.00	20.00
☐ 1923	30,800,000	6.50	8.50	9.00	16.00
☐ 1923D	6,811,000	7.50	9.00	11.00	50.00
☐ 1923S	19,020,000	7.50	9.00	10.00	25.00
☐ 1924	11,811,000	6.50	8.50	9.00	16.00
☐ 1924S	1,728,000	8.00	11.00	23.00	175.00
☐ 1925	10,198,000	6.50	8.50	9.50	15.00
☐ 1925S	1,610,000	7.50	9.50	13.00	60.00
☐ 1926	1,939,000	8.00	10.00	13.00	28.00
☐ 1926D	2,348,700	8.00	10.00	15.00	52.00
☐ 1926S	6,980,000	7.50	10.00	12.00	32.00
☐ 1927	848,000	14.00	18.00	25.00	60.00
☐ 1927D	1,268,900	11.00	14.00	23.00	135.00
☐ 1927S	866,000	11.00	14.00	23.00	125.00
☐ 1928	360,649	125.00	150.00	175.00	215.00
☐ 1928S	1,632,000	11.00	14.00	21.00	125.00
☐ 1934	954,057	10.00	13.50	20.00	75.00
☐ 1934D	1,569,500	10.00	13.50	18.00	80.00
☐ 1934S	1,011,000	10.00	15.00	135.00	1350.00
☐ 1935	1,576,000	10.00	13.00	18.00	55.00
☐ 1935S	1,964,000	10.00	13.00	23.00	145.00
☐ 1964D	316,000			NONE KNOWN TO EXIST	

DOLLARS

DOLLARS—EISENHOWER, 1971–1978

In 1971, following the death of President Eisenhower, a dollar piece with his likeness on the obverse, backed by an adaptation of the Apollo 11 insignia, was placed into circulation. Our astronauts had landed on the moon just two years earlier and this was commemorated by the reverse. Frank Gasparro, chief engraver of the Mint, was its designer. Due to the greatly increased price of silver bullion it was not possible to mint this coin as a "silver dollar." Its size was equivalent to that of earlier silver dollars but the composition bore little resemblance to the old standard. Two versions were struck: a collector's edition with an 80% silver content and ordinary circulating coins with an outer layer of three parts copper and one part nickel enclosing an interior of pure copper. The former had a weight of 24.68 grams. Both have a 38.1mm. diameter. In 1976 a special reverse design was applied, featuring a representation of the Liberty Bell superimposed against the moon, in connection with the Bicentennial. The obverse carried a double date, "1776–1976." Some silverclad specimens were struck, their specifications the same as stated above. In the following year the original reverse was reinstated. The final year of production was 1978.

DATE	MINTAGE	MS-60 UNC.	PRF-65 PROOF
☐ 1971 Copper-Nickel Clad	47,799,000	3.50	
☐ 1971D Copper-Nickel Clad	68,587,424	2.50	
☐ 1971S Silver Clad	11,133,764	6.50	8.50
☐ 1972 Copper-Nickel Clad	75,390,000	3.00	

Mint Mark Below
Head on Obverse

Bicentennial
1776–1976 Reverse

DATE	MINTAGE	MS-60 UNC.	PRF-65 PROOF
☐ 1972D Copper-Nickel Clad	92,548,511	3.00	
☐ 1972S Silver Clad	4,004,657	6.00	8.50
☐ 1973 Copper-Nickel Clad	2,000,056	12.00	
☐ 1973D Copper-Nickel Clad	2,000,000	12.00	
☐ 1973S Copper-Nickel Clad	2,760,339		9.00
☐ 1973S Silver Clad	1,883,140	8.00	27.00
☐ 1974 Copper-Nickel Clad	27,366,000	3.00	
☐ 1974D Copper-Nickel Clad	45,520,175	3.00	
☐ 1974S Copper-Nickel Clad	2,617,350		7.00
☐ 1974S Silver Clad	3,216,420	7.00	8.50
☐ 1976 Copper-Nickel Clad Variety I	4,021,250	5.50	
☐ 1976 Copper-Nickel Clad Variety II	113,325,000	2.50	
☐ 1976D Copper-Nickel Clad Variety I	21,048,650	4.50	
☐ 1976D Copper-Nickel Clad Variety II	82,179,355	2.75	
☐ 1976S Copper-Nickel Clad Variety I	2,845,390		9.00
☐ 1976S Copper-Nickel Clad Variety II	4,149,675		7.00
☐ 1976S Silver Clad (40%)	4,239,460	12.00	14.00
☐ 1977 Copper-Nickel Clad	12,598,220	4.50	
☐ 1977D Copper-Nickel Clad	32,985,000	3.00	
☐ 1977S Copper-Nickel Clad	3,250,895		7.50
☐ 1978 Copper-Nickel Clad	25,702,000	2.50	
☐ 1978D Copper-Nickel Clad	33,012,890	2.50	
☐ 1978S Copper-Nickel Clad	3,127,781		8.50

DOLLARS—SUSAN B. ANTHONY, 1979–1981; 1999

In 1979 the Eisenhower dollar was replaced by one picturing Susan B. Anthony, agitator for female suffrage in the earlier part of this century. The new coin, the target of much controversy, had the distinction of a number of "firsts":

• First general issue U.S. coin to picture a female (excluding mythological and symbolic types)
• First nongold dollar coin of small size
• First general issue U.S. coin with noncircular edge

The Anthony dollar measures 26.5mm., or about the size of a quarter. To avoid its confusion with coins of that denomination, the edge was not made circular but squared out into sections. Its composition is: exterior, three parts copper to one part nickel; interior, pure copper. The weight is 8.1 grams. On the reverse appears the Apollo 11 insignia used for the Eisenhower dollar. Public dissatisfaction with the coin has placed its future in doubt. The designer was Frank Gasparro.

DATE	MINTAGE	MS-60 UNC.	PRF-65 PROOF
☐ 1979P Copper-Nickel Clad	360,200,000	1.30	
☐ 1979D Copper-Nickel Clad	287,000,000	1.40	
☐ 1979S Copper-Nickel Clad Variety I	110,000,000	1.50	9.50
☐ 1979S Copper-Nickel Clad Variety II Proof Only	3,677,000		95.00
☐ 1980P	27,600,000	1.50	
☐ 1980D	41,595,000	1.50	
☐ 1980S	20,425,000	1.50	9.00
☐ 1981P	2,995,000	5.00	
☐ 1981D	3,237,631	5.00	
☐ 1981S Variety I	3,500,000	5.00	8.50
☐ 1981S Variety II			165.00
☐ 1999P	29,592,000	2.00	
☐ 1999D	11,766,000	2.00	

DOLLARS—SACAGAWEA, 2000–2001

The golden dollar's front has Sacagawea portrayed in three-quarter profile. On her back, Sacagawea carries Jean Baptiste, her infant son. Six months pregnant when she joined the Lewis and Clark expedition, Sacagawea gave birth to Jean Baptiste early in the journey.

In rendering Sacagawea, Goodacre included the large, dark eyes attributed to her in Shoshone legends. Goodacre also used a present-day Shoshone college student as her model.

DATE	MINTAGE	MS-60 UNC.	PRF-65 PROOF
☐ 2000P	768,120,000	1.50	
☐ 2000D	517,906,000	1.50	
☐ 2000S			9.50
☐ 2001P	61,466,000	2.00	
☐ 2001D	69,920,000	2.00	
☐ 2001S			10.00
☐ 2002P Not Made for General Circulation		2.75	
☐ 2002D Not Made for General Circulation		2.75	
☐ 2002S			9.00

GOLD DOLLARS, 1849–1889

No gold dollars were struck in the Mint's early years. It was felt (logically enough, based upon conditions that existed then) that silver would serve adequately for this denomination and that gold should be restricted to coins of a higher face value. However, a series of events occurred, following the California gold strikes of 1849, which rendered gold dollars a necessity. Chief among them was the growing practice of citizens, especially in the West, to trade with bullion rather than coinage. So in 1849 a gold dollar was introduced.

Designed by James Longacre, the gold dollar carried a Liberty head on the obverse and was backed by a simple reverse featuring a wreath and the numeral 1 in Arabic. A series of stars encircled the obverse portrait. As this coin was, by necessity, of diminutive size, elaborate designing was not possible. The Liberty gold dollar weighed 1.672 grams and was composed of 90% gold and 10% copper. It had a diameter of 13mm. The mint mark appears below the wreath. In 1854 the obverse was given over to an Indian Head and the coin made flatter, its diameter increased to 15mm. The weight was unaltered. There was a further change in 1856 when a new die was cast for the obverse, showing the Indian Head a bit larger. This was the final variety for the gold dollar, whose last year of coining was 1889. The gold content by weight for all three types was .04837 of an ounce.

PLEASE NOTE: THE PRICES THAT ARE LISTED REFLECT A GOLD SPOT PRICE OF $360.00 PER OUNCE.

GOLD DOLLARS—LIBERTY HEAD WITH CORONET, SMALL SIZE, 1849–1854

DATE	MINTAGE	ABP IN F-12	F-12 FINE	EF-40 EX. FINE	MS-60 UNC.
☐ 1849 (4 Varieties)	688,600	85.00	120.00	150.00	375.00
☐ 1849C Closed Wreath	11,634	200.00	280.00	900.00	8000.00
☐ 1849C Open Wreath	4 Known			EXTREMELY RARE	
☐ 1849D	21,588	220.00	260.00	800.00	4200.00
☐ 1849O	215,000	110.00	130.00	210.00	1200.00
☐ 1850	481,953	80.00	130.00	160.00	475.00
☐ 1850C	6,966	250.00	375.00	910.00	9000.00
☐ 1850D	8,382	250.00	360.00	900.00	9000.00
☐ 1850O	14,000	135.00	210.00	350.00	3500.00
☐ 1851	3,317,671	80.00	110.00	150.00	350.00
☐ 1851C	41,267	175.00	250.00	650.00	2100.00
☐ 1851D	9,832	200.00	275.00	760.00	5000.00
☐ 1851O	290,000	100.00	125.00	175.00	600.00
☐ 1852	2,045,351	80.00	90.00	160.00	300.00
☐ 1852C	9,434	185.00	240.00	750.00	4000.00
☐ 1852D	6,360	225.00	310.00	1100.00	8000.00
☐ 1852O	140,000	90.00	125.00	210.00	1100.00
☐ 1853	4,076,051	85.00	120.00	150.00	350.00
☐ 1853C	11,515	175.00	260.00	1100.00	5200.00
☐ 1853D	6,583	250.00	325.00	950.00	9000.00
☐ 1853O	290,000	100.00	110.00	190.00	600.00
☐ 1854	855,502	100.00	110.00	150.00	425.00
☐ 1854D	2,935	400.00	560.00	1800.00	12000.00
☐ 1854S	14,635	185.00	240.00	400.00	2500.00

GOLD DOLLARS—SMALL INDIAN HEAD, FEATHER HEADDRESS, LARGE SIZE, 1854–1856

Mint Mark Below Wreath on Reverse

DATE	MINTAGE	ABP IN F-12	F-12 FINE	EF-40 EX. FINE	MS-60 UNC.	PROOF-65
☐ 1854	783,943	140.00	200.00	400.00	2500.00	176000.00*
☐ 1854C	4				UNKNOWN	
☐ 1855	758,269	225.00	325.00	410.00	2300.00	121000.00*
☐ 1855C	8,903	500.00	650.00	2300.00	20000.00	
☐ 1855D	1,811	1000.00	1400.00	4000.00	30000.00	
☐ 1855O	55,000	275.00	370.00	550.00	5000.00	
☐ 1856S	24,600	300.00	375.00	910.00	6400.00	

*Pittman Sale, Oct. 1997.

GOLD DOLLARS—LARGE LIBERTY HEAD, FEATHER HEADDRESS, LARGE SIZE, 1856–1889

Mint Mark Below Wreath on Reverse

DATE	ABP IN F-12	F-12 FINE	EF-40 EX. FINE	MS-60 UNC.	PRF-65 PROOF
☐ 1856 Upright 5 (1,762,936)					
	100.00	140.00	190.00	600.00	
☐ 1856 Slant 5 (1,762,936)					
	100.00	120.00	175.00	400.00	36000.00
☐ 1856D (1,460)					
	1800.00	2300.00	6000.00	32000.00	
☐ 1857 (774,789)					
	100.00	120.00	140.00	315.00	21500.00
☐ 1857C (13,280)					
	250.00	350.00	1200.00	12000.00	
☐ 1857D (3,533)					
	215.00	310.00	1700.00	12000.00	
☐ 1857S (10,000)					
	200.00	320.00	750.00	6000.00	
☐ 1858 (117,995)					
	85.00	100.00	150.00	300.00	20000.00
☐ 1858D (3,477)					
	310.00	430.00	1300.00	10000.00	
☐ 1858S (10,000)					
	240.00	300.00	500.00	5800.00	

DATE	ABP IN F-12	F-12 FINE	EF-40 EX. FINE	MS-60 UNC.	PRF-65 PROOF
☐ 1859	(168,244)				
	85.00	110.00	200.00	300.00	14000.00
☐ 1859C	(5,235)				
	225.00	300.00	1500.00	17000.00	
☐ 1859D	(4,952)				
	350.00	625.00	1200.00	10000.00	
☐ 1859S	(15,000)				
	150.00	200.00	450.00	6000.00	
☐ 1860	(36,688)				
	90.00	130.00	200.00	400.00	14000.00
☐ 1860D	(1,566)				
	1400.00	1700.00	3700.00	24000.00	
☐ 1860S	(13,000)				
	225.00	275.00	440.00	2000.00	
☐ 1861	(527,499)				
	90.00	100.00	145.00	300.00	15000.00
☐ 1861D	3500.00	4000.00	8000.00	32000.00	
☐ 1862	(1,326,865)				
	85.00	100.00	200.00	300.00	16000.00
☐ 1863	(6,250)				
	250.00	300.00	900.00	3900.00	15500.00
☐ 1864	(5,950)				
	200.00	250.00	350.00	1000.00	22000.00
☐ 1865	(3,725)				
	200.00	300.00	450.00	1500.00	14000.00
☐ 1866	(7,180)				
	200.00	300.00	400.00	810.00	14000.00
☐ 1867	(5,250)				
	225.00	200.00	410.00	1000.00	15000.00
☐ 1868	(10,525)				
	200.00	240.00	320.00	750.00	15500.00
☐ 1869	(5,925)				
	250.00	325.00	500.00	750.00	14000.00
☐ 1870	(6,335)				
	195.00	235.00	350.00	600.00	14000.00
☐ 1870S	(3,000)				
	225.00	280.00	675.00	3000.00	
☐ 1871	(3,930)				
	200.00	230.00	300.00	600.00	16000.00
☐ 1872	(3,530)				
	200.00	230.00	340.00	950.00	16500.00

DATE	ABP IN F-12	F-12 FINE	EF-40 EX. FINE	MS-60 UNC.	PRF-65 PROOF
☐ 1873 Open 3	(125,125) 95.00	120.00	145.00	325.00	
☐ 1873 Closed 3	225.00	290.00	710.00	1700.00	21000.00
☐ 1874	(198,820) 100.00	120.00	150.00	300.00	18000.00
☐ 1875	(420) 1000.00	1600.00	3300.00	5500.00	36000.00
☐ 1876	(3,245) 140.00	190.00	300.00	550.00	16000.00
☐ 1877	(3,920) 110.00	150.00	300.00	750.00	18000.00
☐ 1878	(3,020) 120.00	170.00	300.00	600.00	14000.00
☐ 1879	(3,030) 125.00	150.00	210.00	525.00	11000.00
☐ 1880	(1,636) 110.00	130.00	175.00	400.00	16500.00
☐ 1881	(7,660) 110.00	130.00	180.00	400.00	12500.00
☐ 1882	(5,040) 110.00	140.00	200.00	450.00	9200.00
☐ 1883	(10,840) 110.00	125.00	180.00	380.00	9250.00
☐ 1884	(6,206) 110.00	130.00	180.00	400.00	10500.00
☐ 1885	(12,205) 110.00	130.00	200.00	375.00	9000.00
☐ 1886	(6,016) 110.00	130.00	200.00	380.00	9000.00
☐ 1887	(8,543) 110.00	130.00	200.00	400.00	9500.00
☐ 1888	(16,080) 110.00	130.00	200.00	400.00	9500.00
☐ 1889	(30,729) 110.00	130.00	200.00	350.00	9000.00

Note: Many gold dollars in the 1880s were hoarded and appear in gem, prooflike condition. Beware of these pieces being sold as proofs.

QUARTER EAGLES— $2.50 GOLD PIECES

The $2.50 gold piece, authorized on April 2, 1792, was known as a "Quarter Eagle" (i.e., the quarter part of an Eagle or $10 gold piece). Striking was not begun until 1796. As early production was extremely limited—in no year were as many as 10,000 struck until 1834—these are scarce and valuable coins. Designed by Robert Scot, the original type featured a capped Liberty on the obverse and shield eagle reverse. The portrait is quite different than that used on silver coinage and in general the engraving may be said to be somewhat superior. No wording other than LIBERTY adorns the obverse, with UNITED STATES OF AMERICA on the reverse. The composition was .9167 gold to .0833 copper, or more than nine-tenths gold, with a weight of 4.37 grams and a diameter which varied slightly but normally was about 20mm.

There are two obverse types, one with and one without a circular border of stars. In 1808 the portrait, while retaining the cap, was entirely redesigned. It was shifted around to face left instead of right, the cap was deemphasized, Liberty's features were redrawn in an effort at greater femininity, her hair was made curlier, and the eagle was likewise refurbished. John Reish was the designer. From 1809 to 1820 no quarter eagles were minted. When the series was resumed in 1821 it was with modified obverse and reverse types and the diameter had shrunk to 18.5mm. However, the coin contained fully as much gold as previously and the decreased diameter was compensated for by a slight increase in thickness.

The obverse was changed in 1834 to the so-called Classic Head type, a more stylish rendition of Liberty, designed by the Mint's chief designer, William Kneass (pronounced Niece). The weight was reduced to 4.18 grams and the composition altered to contain less than nine-tenths gold: .8992 to .1008 copper. The diameter was 18.2mm. Christian Gobrecht made

414

some alterations to this design in 1840 but it was not materially changed. However, the gold content was increased to an even .900 and the diameter brought down to 18mm. Total gold content by weight was .12094. This design remained in use for sixty-seven years, surpassed for longevity only by the Lincoln penny (1909–present).

An interesting variation occurred in 1848, the so-called California Quarter Eagle. In that year Colonel Mason, the Military Governor of California, shipped about 230 ounces of gold to Secretary of War Marcy in Washington, D.C. Marcy had the bullion melted down and struck into Quarter Eagles, distinguished by the abbreviation CAL. above the eagle's head on the reverse. This was not an integral part of the design but was stamped separately. As little more than 1,000 specimens were struck, it became a choice collector's item. Purchasers should be on guard against fakes. The Gobrecht Quarter Eagle was discontinued in 1907. Specimens dated after 1900, and some earlier ones, are valued primarily for their bullion content.

PLEASE NOTE: THE PRICES THAT ARE LISTED REFLECT A GOLD SPOT PRICE OF $360.00 PER OUNCE.

QUARTER EAGLES—LIBERTY CAP, 1796–1807

1796
No Stars

1797–1807
With Stars

1796–1807

DATE	MINTAGE	ABP IN F-12	F-12 FINE	EF-40 EX. FINE	MS-60 UNC.
☐ 1796 No Stars	963	6500.00	9000.00	40000.00	140000.00
☐ 1796 With Stars	432	6000.00	8000.00	25000.00	120000.00
☐ 1797	427	5800.00	8000.00	12000.00	120000.00
☐ 1798	1,094	2250.00	3000.00	8000.00	45000.00
☐ 1802 over 1	3,033	2250.00	2700.00	5800.00	20000.00
☐ 1804, 14 Star Reverse	3,327	2100.00	3100.00	6000.00	25000.00
☐ 1804, 13 Star Reverse	140000.00	17000.00	60000.00	250000.00	

DATE	MINTAGE	ABP IN F-12	F-12 FINE	EF-40 EX. FINE	MS-60 UNC.
☐ 1805	1,781	2300.00	3000.00	5000.00	25000.00
☐ 1806 over 4	1,616	2500.00	3300.00	6000.00	22500.00
☐ 1806 over 5		4000.00	6000.00		RARE
☐ 1807	6,812	2250.00	2850.00	4500.00	20000.00

QUARTER EAGLES—BUST TYPE, TURBAN HEAD, 1808–1834

1808
Draped
Bust
Round Cap

1821–1834
Undraped
Liberty
Round Cap

1808–1834
Motto
Over Eagle

DATE	MINTAGE	ABP IN F-12	F-12 FINE	EF-40 EX. FINE	MS-60 UNC.
☐ 1808	2,710	7000.00	10000.00	20000.00	60000.00
REDUCED SIZE (18.5mm. dia.)					
☐ 1821	6,448	2500.00	2900.00	4500.00	20000.00
☐ 1824 over 21	2,600	2800.00	3000.00	4500.00	17000.00
☐ 1825	4,434	2400.00	2600.00	4300.00	14000.00
☐ 1826 over 25	760	3000.00	4000.00	5000.00	38000.00
☐ 1827	2,800	3000.00	4000.00	6000.00	18000.00
☐ 1829	3,403	2800.00	3200.00	3800.00	10000.00
☐ 1830	4,540	2800.00	3200.00	3800.00	11000.00
☐ 1831	4,520	2800.00	3200.00	3800.00	11000.00
☐ 1832	4,400	2800.00	3200.00	3800.00	12000.00
☐ 1833	4,160	2800.00	3200.00	3800.00	12500.00
☐ 1834 Motto	4,000	5000.00	6200.00	14000.00	37500.00

QUARTER EAGLES—LIBERTY HEAD WITH RIBBONS, 1834–1839 NO MOTTO OVER EAGLE

Mint Mark is Above Date on Obverse

DATE	MINTAGE	ABP IN F-12	F-12 FINE	EF-40 EX. FINE	MS-60 UNC.
☐ 1834 No Motto	112,234	200.00	225.00	390.00	1750.00
☐ 1835	131,402	200.00	225.00	390.00	2200.00
☐ 1836	547,986	200.00	225.00	390.00	2000.00
☐ 1837	45,080	200.00	225.00	390.00	3000.00
☐ 1838	47,030	200.00	225.00	390.00	2200.00
☐ 1838C	7,908	500.00	600.00	1900.00	30000.00
☐ 1839	27,021	185.00	200.00	500.00	6000.00
☐ 1839C	18,173	350.00	450.00	1900.00	25000.00
☐ 1839D	13,674	450.00	550.00	2600.00	26500.00
☐ 1839O	17,781	300.00	350.00	900.00	5500.00

QUARTER EAGLES—LIBERTY HEAD WITH CORONET, 1840–1907

Mint Mark is Below Eagle on Reverse

DATE	MINTAGE	ABP IN F-12	F-12 FINE	EF-40 EX. FINE	MS-60 UNC.
☐ 1840	18,859	130.00	150.00	710.00	7000.00
☐ 1840C	12,838	300.00	340.00	1100.00	12500.00
☐ 1840D	3,532	800.00	950.00	9000.00	RARE
☐ 1840O	26,200	150.00	180.00	700.00	12000.00
☐ 1841				PROOF—125000.00	
☐ 1841C	10,297	275.00	350.00	1000.00	20000.00
☐ 1841D	4,164	650.00	810.00	3000.00	26000.00

DATE	MINTAGE	ABP IN F-12	F-12 FINE	EF-40 EX. FINE	MS-60 UNC.
☐ 1842	2,823	350.00	440.00	2500.00	30000.00
☐ 1842C	6,737	600.00	600.00	2500.00	24000.00
☐ 1842D	4,643	750.00	850.00	2700.00	30000.00
☐ 1842O	19,800	210.00	260.00	1150.00	15000.00
☐ 1843	100,546	120.00	140.00	210.00	2000.00
☐ 1843C Small Date	26,096	1000.00	1300.00	6000.00	25000.00
☐ 1843C Large Date	26,096	250.00	360.00	1000.00	9000.00
☐ 1843D	36,209	250.00	400.00	1200.00	10000.00
☐ 1843O Small Date	368,002	130.00	165.00	270.00	2000.00
☐ 1843O Large Date	368,002	175.00	210.00	500.00	9000.00
☐ 1844	6,784	210.00	255.00	760.00	7500.00
☐ 1844C	11,622	350.00	450.00	1500.00	24000.00
☐ 1844D	17,332	350.00	460.00	1100.00	10000.00
☐ 1845	91,051	130.00	185.00	310.00	1500.00
☐ 1845D	19,460	400.00	500.00	1160.00	14000.00
☐ 1845O	4,000	600.00	710.00	1800.00	18000.00
☐ 1846	21,598	150.00	200.00	500.00	6500.00
☐ 1846C	4,808	450.00	600.00	1700.00	20000.00
☐ 1846D	19,303	400.00	500.00	1000.00	10000.00
☐ 1846O	66,000	150.00	185.00	500.00	6000.00
☐ 1847	29,814	120.00	160.00	360.00	4500.00
☐ 1847C	23,226	270.00	320.00	900.00	7000.00
☐ 1847D	15,784	325.00	400.00	1000.00	10000.00
☐ 1847O	124,000	130.00	175.00	400.00	4500.00
☐ 1848	8,886	250.00	290.00	850.00	6500.00
☐ 1848 CAL. above Eagle	1,389	4500.00	6600.00	15000.00	36000.00
☐ 1848C	16,788	350.00	400.00	1200.00	14000.00
☐ 1848D	13,771	320.00	410.00	1000.00	10000.00
☐ 1849	23,294	160.00	210.00	460.00	3000.00
☐ 1849C	10,220	350.00	400.00	1400.00	20000.00
☐ 1849D	10,945	400.00	410.00	1300.00	18000.00
☐ 1850	252,923	85.00	120.00	210.00	1500.00
☐ 1850C	9,148	335.00	400.00	14000.00	20000.00
☐ 1850D	12,148	350.00	410.00	11000.00	15000.00
☐ 1850O	84,000	125.00	100.00	450.00	5000.00
☐ 1851	1,372,748	85.00	120.00	180.00	400.00
☐ 1851C	14,923	350.00	410.00	1150.00	14000.00
☐ 1851D	11,264	375.00	450.00	1200.00	14000.00
☐ 1851O	148,000	100.00	140.00	210.00	5000.00

DATE	MINTAGE	ABP IN F-12	F-12 FINE	EF-40 EX. FINE	MS-60 UNC.
☐ 1852	1,159,681	110.00	140.00	180.00	400.00
☐ 1852C	9,772	250.00	400.00	1300.00	22000.00
☐ 1852D	4,078	450.00	500.00	2600.00	22000.00

DATE	ABP IN F-12	F-12 FINE	EF-40 EX. FINE	MS-60 UNC.	PRF-63 PROOF
☐ 1852O	(140,000)				
	115.00	140.00	295.00	5000.00	
☐ 1853	(1,404,668)				
	100.00	135.00	165.00	350.00	
☐ 1853D	(3,178)				
	600.00	650.00	2600.00	20000.00	
☐ 1854	(596,258)				
	100.00	130.00	185.00	375.00	
☐ 1854C	(7,295)				
	300.00	410.00	1750.00	18000.00	
☐ 1854D	(1,760)				
	1200.00	1850.00	6000.00	36000.00	
☐ 1854O	(153,000)				
	100.00	140.00	260.00	1600.00	
☐ 1854S	(246)	EXTREMELY RARE—EF-40—65000.00			
☐ 1855	(235,480)				
	110.00	140.00	160.00	385.00	
☐ 1855C	(3,677)				
	500.00	675.00	3200.00	35000.00	
☐ 1855D	(1,123)				
	1600.00	2000.00	7000.00	32000.00	
☐ 1856	(384,240)				
	110.00	130.00	180.00	360.00	
☐ 1856C	(7,913)				
	300.00	450.00	2000.00	20000.00	
☐ 1856D	(874)				
	3200.00	4000.00	10000.00	60000.00	
☐ 1856O	(21,100)				
	120.00	160.00	750.00	7600.00	
☐ 1856S	(71,120)				
	100.00	140.00	400.00	6000.00	
☐ 1857	(214,130)				
	100.00	125.00	200.00	360.00	28000.00
☐ 1857D	(2,364)				
	450.00	600.00	1900.00	15000.00	

DATE	ABP IN F-12	F-12 FINE	EF-40 EX. FINE	MS-60 UNC.	PRF-63 PROOF
☐ 1857O	(34,000)				
	100.00	150.00	310.00	5000.00	
☐ 1857S	(68,000)				
	100.00	140.00	350.00	8000.00	
☐ 1858	(47,377)				
	100.00	130.00	215.00	1300.00	21000.00
☐ 1858C	(9,056)				
	275.00	320.00	1200.00	10000.00	
☐ 1859 Reverse of 1858					
	150.00	200.00	410.00	3600.00	
☐ 1859	(39,444)				
	100.00	120.00	275.00	1200.00	16000.00
☐ 1859D	(2,244)				
	400.00	600.00	2300.00	26000.00	
☐ 1859S	(15,200)				
	175.00	210.00	800.00	8850.00	
☐ 1860 Reverse of 1858					
	1400.00	1700.00	2400.00	10000.00	
☐ 1860	(22,675)				
	120.00	175.00	300.00	1100.00	14000.00
☐ 1860C	(7,469)				
	300.00	400.00	1600.00	26000.00	
☐ 1860S	(35,600)				
	130.00	190.00	650.00	4100.00	
☐ 1861 Reverse of 1858					
	300.00	600.00	1200.00	5000.00	
☐ 1861	(1,272,518)				
	110.00	140.00	170.00	340.00	8000.00
☐ 1861S	(24,000)				
	200.00	265.00	900.00	6000.00	
☐ 1862	(112,353)				
	110.00	130.00	275.00	1400.00	10000.00
☐ 1862 2 over 1					
	450.00	600.00	2100.00	12000.00	
☐ 1862S	(8,000)				
	400.00	600.00	2000.00	20000.00	
☐ 1863			30 PROOFS ONLY—PROOF 63—55000.00		
☐ 1863S	(10,800)				
	300.00	425.00	1600.00	20000.00	
☐ 1864	(2,874)				
	3000.00	3000.00	12000.00	RARE	
☐ 1865	(1,545)				
	1800.00	2400.00	8200.00	RARE	

DATE	ABP IN F-12	F-12 FINE	EF-40 EX. FINE	MS-60 UNC.	PRF-63 PROOF
☐ 1865S	(23,376)				
	125.00	175.00	600.00	6000.00	
☐ 1866	(3,110)				
	450.00	600.00	3250.00	17500.00	
☐ 1866S	(38,461)				
	175.00	220.00	900.00	8000.00	
☐ 1867	(3,250)				
	170.00	225.00	575.00	3500.00	9000.00
☐ 1867S	(28,000)				
	150.00	185.00	650.00	5000.00	
☐ 1868	(3,625)				
	130.00	170.00	350.00	3000.00	11000.00
☐ 1868S	(34,000)				
	120.00	200.00	500.00	6000.00	
☐ 1869	(4,343)				
	130.00	170.00	350.00	3500.00	8500.00
☐ 1869S	(29,500)				
	125.00	165.00	450.00	5500.00	
☐ 1870	(4,555)				
	130.00	160.00	380.00	3250.00	12500.00
☐ 1870S	(16,000)				
	125.00	165.00	400.00	5250.00	
☐ 1871	(5,350)				
	135.00	165.00	310.00	2200.00	12000.00
☐ 1871S	(22,000.00)				
	120.00	140.00	340.00	2500.00	
☐ 1872	(3,030)				
	210.00	250.00	675.00	6000.00	11500.00
☐ 1872S	(18,000)				
	120.00	160.00	450.00	5000.00	
☐ 1873 Open 3	(178,025)				
	110.00	140.00	200.00	375.00	
☐ 1873 Closed 3					
	120.00	140.00	200.00	600.00	8000.00
☐ 1873S	(27,000)				
	130.00	175.00	450.00	2400.00	
☐ 1874	(3,940)				
	150.00	180.00	375.00	2500.00	9500.00
☐ 1875	(420)				
	2000.00	2500.00	5000.00	20000.00	35000.00
☐ 1875S	(11,600)				
	100.00	140.00	340.00	4000.00	
☐ 1876	(4,221)				
	150.00	180.00	550.00	3500.00	8250.00

DATE	ABP IN F-12	F-12 FINE	EF-40 EX. FINE	MS-60 UNC.	PRF-63 PROOF
☐ 1876S	(5,000)				
	150.00	185.00	550.00	4000.00	
☐ 1877	(1,652)				
	250.00	300.00	600.00	3500.00	12000.00
☐ 1877S	(35,000)				
	115.00	140.00	180.00	700.00	
☐ 1878	(286,260)				
	90.00	135.00	175.00	300.00	10500.00
☐ 1878S	(55,000)				
	115.00	140.00	175.00	375.00	
☐ 1879	(88,900)				
	110.00	135.00	175.00	340.00	7500.00
☐ 1879S	(43,500)				
	125.00	150.00	230.00	2250.00	
☐ 1880	(2,996)				
	115.00	150.00	325.00	1400.00	7800.00
☐ 1881	(680)				
	600.00	800.00	2500.00	10000.00	
☐ 1882	(4,040)				
	120.00	160.00	260.00	735.00	7000.00
☐ 1883	(1,960)				
	130.00	200.00	400.00	2000.00	6500.00
☐ 1884	(1,993)				
	120.00	185.00	400.00	1600.00	6500.00
☐ 1885	(887)				
	325.00	410.00	1600.00	4500.00	
☐ 1886	(4,088)				
	115.00	150.00	250.00	1200.00	6500.00
☐ 1887	(6,282)				
	115.00	160.00	230.00	1100.00	5500.00
☐ 1888	(16,098)				
	120.00	160.00	225.00	400.00	5250.00
☐ 1889	(17,648)				
	120.00	160.00	225.00	400.00	6500.00
☐ 1890	(8,813)				
	120.00	160.00	225.00	500.00	6000.00
☐ 1891	(11,040)				
	120.00	160.00	185.00	400.00	6000.00
☐ 1892	(2,545)				
	125.00	160.00	250.00	1000.00	5500.00
☐ 1893	(30,106)				
	100.00	140.00	180.00	300.00	5250.00

DATE	ABP IN F-12	F-12 FINE	EF-40 EX. FINE	MS-60 UNC.	PRF-63 PROOF
☐ 1894	(4,122) 100.00	150.00	250.00	600.00	5500.00
☐ 1895	(6,119) 100.00	140.00	200.00	400.00	5500.00
☐ 1896	(19,202) 100.00	125.00	170.00	300.00	5500.00
☐ 1898	(24,165) 100.00	125.00	170.00	300.00	5000.00
☐ 1899	(27,350) 100.00	125.00	160.00	300.00	5000.00
☐ 1900	(67,205) 100.00	150.00	200.00	425.00	5000.00
☐ 1901	(91,323) 100.00	150.00	160.00	310.00	5000.00
☐ 1902	(133,733) 100.00	120.00	160.00	310.00	5000.00
☐ 1903	(201,257) 100.00	125.00	160.00	300.00	5000.00
☐ 1904	(160,960) 100.00	125.00	160.00	300.00	5000.00
☐ 1905	(217,944) 100.00	125.00	160.00	300.00	5000.00
☐ 1906	(179,490) 100.00	125.00	160.00	300.00	5000.00
☐ 1907	(336,448) 100.00	125.00	160.00	300.00	5000.00

Note: Specimens dated 1905S are counterfeits, made either by die striking or applying a false mint mark to a genuine 1905.

QUARTER EAGLES—INDIAN HEAD, 1908–1929

The Quarter Eagle was redesigned in 1908 by Bela Lyon Pratt. Liberty was removed from its obverse and replaced by a portrait of an Indian wearing a war bonnet. A standing eagle adorned the reverse. The coin has no raised edge and the designs plus inscriptions are stamped in incuse, or recessed beneath the surface, rather than being shown in high relief. The composition is .900 gold, .100 copper, with a weight of 4.18 grams. Its diameter is 18mm. with total gold content by weight remaining at .12094 ounce. Quarter Eagles were last struck in 1929, the year of this nation's financial difficulties.

Mint Mark is to Left of Value on Reverse

DATE	ABP IN VF-20	VF-20 V. FINE	EF-40 EX. FINE	MS-60 UNC.	PRF-65 PROOF
☐ 1908	(565,057)				
	115.00	130.00	150.00	250.00	14000.00
☐ 1909	(441,899)				
	115.00	130.00	150.00	300.00	22000.00
☐ 1910	(492,682)				
	115.00	130.00	150.00	250.00	14000.00
☐ 1911	(404,191)				
	115.00	130.00	150.00	250.00	14000.00
☐ 1911D	(55,680)				
	400.00	650.00	900.00	3000.00	
☐ 1912	(616,197)				
	115.00	130.00	160.00	300.00	14500.00
☐ 1913	(722,165)				
	115.00	130.00	160.00	275.00	14000.00
☐ 1914	(240,117)				
	125.00	155.00	200.00	500.00	16000.00
☐ 1914D	(448,000)				
	115.00	130.00	165.00	300.00	
☐ 1915	(606,100)				
	115.00	135.00	160.00	225.00	14000.00
☐ 1925D	(578,000)				
	115.00	135.00	160.00	220.00	
☐ 1926	(446,000)				
	115.00	150.00	175.00	250.00	
☐ 1927	(388,000)				
	115.00	150.00	175.00	250.00	
☐ 1928	(416,000)				
	115.00	150.00	175.00	250.00	
☐ 1929	(532,000)				
	115.00	150.00	175.00	250.00	

$3.00 GOLD PIECES

LIBERTY HEAD WITH FEATHER HEADDRESS, 1854–1889

Introduction and apparent public acceptance of the gold dollar in 1849 led to speculation on the possible usefulness of gold coinage in other denominations. The $3 gold piece, composed of nine-tenths gold with an alloy of one-tenth copper, was introduced in 1854. It carried an Indian head on the obverse and a wreathed reverse. Its diameter was 20.5mm. and the weight 5.015 grams. Though the $3 gold piece continued to be struck until 1889 it had become obvious as early as pre–Civil War years that no great demand or popularity was enjoyed by this coin. The designer was James Longacre. In 1854 the word DOLLARS was set in smaller characters than subsequently. Total gold content by weight was .14512 ounce.

PLEASE NOTE: THE PRICES THAT ARE LISTED REFLECT A GOLD SPOT PRICE OF $360.00 PER OUNCE.

Mint Mark is
Below Wreath
on Reverse

DATE	ABP IN VF-20	VF-20 V. FINE	EF-40 EX. FINE	MS-60 UNC.	PRF-65 PROOF
☐ 1854	(136,618) 350.00	500.00	650.00	1900.00	50000.00
☐ 1854D	(1,120) 5500.00	7000.00	14000.00	75000.00	
☐ 1854O	(24,000) 500.00	900.00	1500.00	25000.00	

425

DATE	ABP IN VF-20	VF-20 V. FINE	EF-40 EX. FINE	MS-60 UNC.	PRF-65 PROOF
☐ 1855	(50,555)				
	400.00	500.00	650.00	2500.00	47500.00
☐ 1855S	(6,000)				
	675.00	1000.00	1750.00	20000.00	
☐ 1856	(26,010)				
	400.00	550.00	625.00	2100.00	42500.00
☐ 1856S*	(34,500)				
	425.00	550.00	1000.00	9500.00	
☐ 1857	(20,891)				
	350.00	500.00	650.00	2600.00	37500.00
☐ 1857S	(14,000)				
	550.00	700.00	1700.00	18000.00	
☐ 1858	(2,133)				
	550.00	650.00	1200.00	7000.00	35000.00
☐ 1859	(15,638)				
	400.00	500.00	625.00	2100.00	35000.00
☐ 1860	(7,155)				
	300.00	450.00	650.00	2250.00	35000.00
☐ 1860S	(7,000)				
	575.00	700.00	1500.00	15000.00	
☐ 1861	(6,072)				
	450.00	525.00	825.00	2600.00	38500.00
☐ 1862	(5,785)				
	450.00	525.00	750.00	2700.00	35000.00
☐ 1863	(5,039)				
	525.00	650.00	775.00	2900.00	34000.00
☐ 1864	(2,680)				
	550.00	700.00	750.00	2700.00	34000.00
☐ 1865	(1,165)				
	700.00	1100.00	2000.00	12000.00	34000.00
☐ 1866	(4,030)				
	525.00	700.00	800.00	2850.00	35000.00
☐ 1867	(2,650)				
	525.00	700.00	825.00	2700.00	33000.00
☐ 1868	(4,875)				
	525.00	750.00	825.00	2700.00	33000.00
☐ 1869	(2,525)				
	550.00	750.00	850.00	4000.00	33000.00
☐ 1870	(3,535)				
	475.00	700.00	800.00	4000.00	32000.00

*Note: Found in Small, Medium, and Large "S" Varieties.

DATE	ABP IN VF-20	VF-20 V. FINE	EF-40 EX. FINE	MS-60 UNC.	PRF-65 PROOF
☐ 1870S			950,000.00		
(2) The other piece is in the cornerstone of the San Francisco Mint.					
☐ 1871 (1,330)	550.00	675.00	900.00	3500.00	33000.00
☐ 1872 (2,030)	500.00	700.00	900.00	3500.00	32000.00
☐ 1873 Open 3 (25)		PROOF ONLY			65000.00
☐ 1873 Closed 3 Restrike				40000.00	
☐ 1874 (41,820)	375.00	500.00	600.00	2000.00	33000.00
☐ 1875 Proofs Only (20)					175000.00
☐ 1876 Proofs Only (45)					60000.00
☐ 1877 (1,488)	800.00	1100.00	2600.00	16000.00	37000.00
☐ 1878 (82,324)	400.00	500.00	625.00	1700.00	42000.00
☐ 1879 (3,030)	450.00	610.00	800.00	2100.00	32000.00
☐ 1880 (1,036)	500.00	700.00	1250.00	2200.00	31000.00
☐ 1881 (550)	800.00	1000.00	1900.00	7000.00	26500.00
☐ 1882 (1,540)	550.00	700.00	1000.00	2250.00	27500.00
☐ 1883 (940)	500.00	650.00	1000.00	3500.00	24000.00
☐ 1884 (1,106)	800.00	950.00	1250.00	3500.00	26000.00
☐ 1885 (910)	800.00	900.00	1200.00	3500.00	27500.00
☐ 1886 (1,142)	700.00	850.00	1150.00	3500.00	21000.00
☐ 1887 (6,160)	450.00	700.00	800.00	2250.00	23500.00
☐ 1888 (5,291)	450.00	600.00	750.00	2000.00	19000.00
☐ 1889 (2,429)	450.00	550.00	700.00	2000.00	22500.00

Note: Beware of deceiving counterfeits with the following dates: 1855, 1857, 1878, 1882, and 1888.

STELLA—$4.00 GOLD PIECES

LIBERTY HEAD WITH FLOWING OR COILED HAIR, 1879–1880

In 1879 and 1880 proofs were struck, in limited quantities, of a $4 gold coin that never reached circulation. It was called Stella and was coined not only in gold but various other metals. The gold specimens are extremely valuable. There are two obverse types, one designed by Barber and the other by Morgan.

PLEASE NOTE: THE PRICES THAT ARE LISTED REFLECT A GOLD SPOT PRICE OF $360.00 PER OUNCE.

Flowing Hair

Coiled Hair

DATE	MINTAGE	ABP IN PRF-65	PRF-65 PROOF
☐ 1879 Flowing Hair Proofs Only	415	80000.00	115000.00
☐ 1879 Coiled Hair Proofs Only	10	250000.00	300000.00
☐ 1880 Flowing Hair Proofs Only	15	100000.00	135000.00
☐ 1880 Coiled Hair Proofs Only	10	285000.00	365000.00

428

HALF EAGLES—$5.00 GOLD PIECES, 1795–1929

The Half Eagle or $5 gold piece was authorized on April 2, 1792, and first struck in 1795. It has the distinction of being the first gold coin struck by the U.S. Mint. Production was limited in the early years. Its designer was Robert Scot. The composition was .9167 gold to .0833 copper alloy, yielding a weight of 8.75 grams and a diameter of (generally) 25mm. A capped portrait of Liberty facing right adorned the obverse, with stars and date appearing below the portrait; on the reverse is a spread-winged eagle holding in its beak a wreath, surrounded by the wording UNITED STATES OF AMERICA. Some alterations in the number of stars and size of figures in the date will be observed. These should be taken into close account, as they can have a considerable bearing on value.

In 1807 John Reich redesigned the Half Eagle. The bust, now "capped and draped," was turned around to face left and the eagle modified. A shortened bust was introduced in 1813. A further modification was made in 1829 but with the same basic design retained. By this time the Half Eagle had become an important circulating as well as banking piece, whose significance was to later increase. The year 1834 brought a revised design known as the Classic Head, the work of William Kneass. The weight of this new coin was 8.36 grams and its composition .8992 gold to .1008 copper, with a diameter of 22.5mm. The slogan IN GOD WE TRUST, previously used on the reverse, was dropped, probably because of a shortage of space. This was followed by Gobrecht's Coronet head in 1839, used until 1908. Its gold content was raised slightly to nine-tenths and the copper reduced to one-tenth. Gold content by weight was .24187 ounce. There are small- and large-date varieties of this coin.

429

In 1866, following the Civil War, IN GOD WE TRUST was added to the rather cramped space between the eagle's head and the legend UNITED STATES OF AMERICA. Composition was as before but the weight was changed to 8.359 grams and the diameter reduced to 21.6mm. One of the longest lived of coin designs, it remained in use a full seventy years, to be replaced by Pratt's Indian Head in 1908.

PLEASE NOTE: THE PRICES THAT ARE LISTED RE-FLECT A GOLD SPOT PRICE OF $360.00 PER OUNCE.

HALF EAGLES—LIBERTY HEAD, 1795–1807 EAGLE ON REVERSE

Head Right
1795–1807

1795–1807
Large Eagle

1795–1798
Small Eagle

DATE	MINTAGE	ABP IN F-12	F-12 FINE	EF-40 EX. FINE	MS-60 UNC.
☐ 1795 Small Eagle	8,707	3200.00	5000.00	11000.00	36000.00
☐ 1795 Large Eagle		6000.00	7600.00	16000.00	74000.00
☐ 1796 over 95 Small Eagle	3,399	4000.00	5800.00	13000.00	55000.00
☐ 1797 over 95 Large Eagle	6,406	5500.00	7000.00	18000.00	115000.00
☐ 1798 Small Eagle	6 Known			EXTREMELY RARE	
☐ 1798 Large Eagle, All Types	24,867	950.00	1500.00	3200.00	13000.00
☐ 1799	7,451	1250.00	1800.00	4000.00	15000.00
☐ 1800	37,620	950.00	1150.00	2300.00	7000.00
☐ 1802 over 1	53,176	950.00	1150.00	2300.00	6600.00
☐ 1803 over 2	33,506	950.00	1150.00	2300.00	6500.00
☐ 1804 Small and Large 8	30,475	950.00	1100.00	2500.00	8500.00
☐ 1805	33,183	950.00	1250.00	2500.00	6600.00
☐ 1806 Round and Pointed Top 6	64,093	950.00	1400.00	3000.00	10000.00
☐ 1807 Head Right	33,496	950.00	1325.00	2600.00	6500.00

HALF EAGLES—DRAPED BUST, 1807–1812, VALUE 5D ON REVERSE

HEAD
LEFT

"Round Cap"

DATE	MINTAGE	ABP IN F-12	F-12 FINE	EF-40 EX. FINE	MS-60 UNC.
☐ 1807	50,597	1000.00	1300.00	2350.00	6000.00
☐ 1808	55,578	1000.00	1500.00	2800.00	5500.00
☐ 1809/8	33,875	1000.00	1300.00	2350.00	5500.00
☐ 1810 (4 varieties)	100,287	1000.00	1300.00	2350.00	6500.00
☐ 1811	99,581	1000.00	1300.00	2350.00	5500.00
☐ 1812	58,087	1000.00	1300.00	2200.00	5500.00

HALF EAGLES—LIBERTY HEAD, ROUND CAP, 1813–1834 MOTTO OVER EAGLE

DATE	MINTAGE	ABP IN F-12	F-12 FINE	EF-40 EX. FINE	MS-60 UNC.
☐ 1813	95,428	1200.00	1600.00	2400.00	6000.00
☐ 1814 over 13	15,454	1400.00	1800.00	2900.00	8500.00
☐ 1815	635			EXTREMELY RARE	
☐ 1818	48,588	1250.00	1680.00	3000.00	8500.00
☐ 1819	51,723			RARE	60000.00
☐ 1820	263,806	1400.00	1680.00	3000.00	10000.00
☐ 1821	34,641	1850.00	2600.00	15000.00	35000.00
☐ 1822			Only 3 Known—EXTREMELY RARE		
☐ 1823	14,485	1350.00	1750.00	3600.00	18000.00

DATE	MINTAGE	ABP IN F-12	F-12 FINE	EF-40 EX. FINE	MS-60 UNC.
☐ 1824	17,340	3000.00	5000.00	13000.00	35000.00
☐ 1825 over 21	29,060	3000.00	5000.00	10000.00	32000.00
☐ 1825 over 24					EXTREMELY RARE
☐ 1826	18,069	2400.00	3200.00	7600.00	30000.00
☐ 1827	24,913	3750.00	4900.00	10000.00	35000.00
☐ 1828	28,029	4000.00	5100.00	16000.00	65000.00
☐ 1828 over 27		2800.00	5000.00	15000.00	120000.00
☐ 1829 Small Date	57,442				RARE
☐ 1829 Large Date					VERY RARE
☐ 1830	126,351	2400.00	3800.00	5500.00	18000.00
☐ 1831	140,594	2400.00	4000.00	8000.00	18000.00
☐ 1832*	157,487	2400.00	3800.00	7200.00	20000.00
☐ 1833	193,630	2250.00	3000.00	5900.00	16000.00
☐ 1834**	50,141	2250.00	3900.00	6800.00	21000.00

*1832 Square Based 2, 13 Stars **1834 Crosslet 4: MS-60 $32000.00

HALF EAGLES—LIBERTY HEAD WITH RIBBON, 1834–1838 NO MOTTO OVER EAGLE

4
Plain 4

4
Crosslet 4

Mint Mark is Above
Date on Obverse

DATE	MINTAGE	ABP IN F-12	F-12 FINE	EF-40 EX. FINE	MS-60 UNC.
☐ 1834 Plain 4*	682,028	165.00	250.00	420.00	3000.00
☐ 1835	371,534	165.00	250.00	430.00	2700.00
☐ 1836	553,147	150.00	200.00	430.00	2400.00
☐ 1837	207,121	165.00	210.00	430.00	3600.00
☐ 1838	286,588	165.00	210.00	430.00	3400.00
☐ 1838C	12,913	700.00	800.00	3400.00	40000.00
☐ 1838D	20,583	600.00	900.00	3400.00	25000.00

*1834 Crosslet 4 worth more: MS-60 Unc. $17500.00

HALF EAGLES—LIBERTY HEAD WITH CORONET, 1839–1908

1839–1908

1839–66
No Motto

1866–1908
With Motto

DATE	ABP IN F-12	F-12 FINE	EF-40 EX. FINE	MS-60 UNC.	PRF-65 PROOF
☐ 1839	(118,143) 200.00	300.00	450.00	3200.00	
☐ 1839C	(23,467) 475.00	600.00	2600.00	22000.00	
☐ 1839D	(18,939) 500.00	600.00	2200.00	20000.00	
☐ 1840	(137,382) 200.00	275.00	450.00	4000.00	
☐ 1840C	(19,028) 375.00	450.00	2500.00	28000.00	
☐ 1840D	(22,896) 350.00	450.00	1500.00	18000.00	
☐ 1840O	(30,400) 250.00	375.00	1200.00	7000.00	
☐ 1841	(15,833) 200.00	275.00	900.00	6000.00	
☐ 1841C	(21,511) 375.00	350.00	1500.00	22000.00	
☐ 1841D	(30,495) 325.00	400.00	1400.00	14000.00	
☐ 1841O	(50)	2 Known—EXTREMELY RARE			
☐ 1842	(27,578) 200.00	380.00	1000.00	15000.00	
☐ 1842C Large Date	(27,480) 325.00	400.00	1700.00	20000.00	
☐ 1842D Small Date	(59,608) 425.00	500.00	2000.00	15000.00	
☐ 1842O	(16,400) 475.00	550.00	3000.00	22500.00	

DATE	ABP IN F-12	F-12 FINE	EF-40 EX. FINE	MS-60 UNC.	PRF-65 PROOF
☐ 1843	(611,205)				
	120.00	150.00	210.00	1500.00	
☐ 1843C	(44,353)				
	350.00	425.00	1300.00	18000.00	
☐ 1843D	(98,452)				
	300.00	380.00	900.00	9500.00	
☐ 1843O	(101,075)				
	150.00	225.00	1200.00	15000.00	
☐ 1844	(340,330)				
	130.00	175.00	250.00	1800.00	
☐ 1844C	(23,631)				
	350.00	600.00	2800.00	20000.00	
☐ 1844D	(88,982)				
	325.00	450.00	1100.00	12000.00	
☐ 1844O	(364,600)				
	150.00	180.00	325.00	5000.00	
☐ 1845	(417,099)				
	120.00	150.00	210.00	1850.00	
☐ 1845D	(90,629)				
	350.00	500.00	1100.00	12000.00	
☐ 1845O	(41,000)				
	200.00	300.00	750.00	15000.00	
☐ 1846	(395,942)				
	120.00	150.00	215.00	2000.00	
☐ 1846C	(12,995)				
	450.00	550.00	2600.00	23000.00	
☐ 1846D	(80,294)				
	325.00	400.00	1050.00	10750.00	
☐ 1846O	(58,000)				
	200.00	300.00	950.00	12000.00	
☐ 1847	(915,981)				
	120.00	175.00	200.00	1500.00	
☐ 1847 Impression of extra 7				VERY RARE	
☐ 1847C	(84,151)				
	325.00	500.00	1200.00	15000.00	
☐ 1847D	(64,405)				
	325.00	500.00	1050.00	7000.00	
☐ 1847O	(12,000)				
	500.00	700.00	6250.00	20000.00	
☐ 1848	(260,775)				
	120.00	150.00	210.00	1500.00	

DATE	ABP IN F-12	F-12 FINE	EF-40 EX. FINE	MS-60 UNC.	PRF-65 PROOF
☐ 1848C	(64,472) 375.00	450.00	1000.00	20000.00	
☐ 1848D	(47,465) 250.00	450.00	1150.00	14000.00	
☐ 1849	(133,070) 115.00	150.00	250.00	3000.00	
☐ 1849C	(64,823) 300.00	400.00	1100.00	10000.00	
☐ 1849D	(39,036) 350.00	450.00	1200.00	16000.00	
☐ 1850	(64,941) 130.00	200.00	600.00	4000.00	
☐ 1850C	(63,591) 300.00	400.00	1000.00	12000.00	
☐ 1850D	(53,950) 350.00	400.00	1300.00	25000.00	
☐ 1851	(377,505) 115.00	140.00	190.00	2000.00	
☐ 1851C	(49,176) 325.00	400.00	1150.00	16000.00	
☐ 1851D	(62,710) 300.00	400.00	2000.00	14000.00	
☐ 1851O	(41,000) 275.00	300.00	1200.00	14000.00	
☐ 1852	(573,901) 115.00	200.00	500.00	1250.00	
☐ 1852C	(72,574) 275.00	375.00	900.00	8000.00	
☐ 1852D	(91,452) 275.00	375.00	1000.00	11000.00	
☐ 1853	(305,770) 130.00	200.00	500.00	1300.00	
☐ 1853C	(65,571) 325.00	400.00	900.00	7000.00	
☐ 1853D	(89,687) 300.00	400.00	900.00	6500.00	
☐ 1854	(160,675) 125.00	150.00	300.00	1600.00	
☐ 1854C	(39,291) 300.00	400.00	1300.00	10500.00	

DATE	ABP IN F-12	F-12 FINE	EF-40 EX. FINE	MS-60 UNC.	PRF-65 PROOF
☐ 1854D	(56,413)				
	300.00	400.00	1050.00	9000.00	
☐ 1854O	(46,000)				
	190.00	220.00	410.00	8000.00	
☐ 1854S	(268) EXTREMELY RARE—200000.00				
☐ 1855	(117,098)				
	130.00	175.00	220.00	1500.00	
☐ 1855C	(39,788)				
	375.00	500.00	1600.00	18000.00	
☐ 1855D	(22,432)				
	375.00	500.00	1150.00	18000.00	
☐ 1855O	(11,100)				
	300.00	350.00	1800.00	22000.00	
☐ 1855S	(61,000)				
	200.00	250.00	1100.00	14000.00	
☐ 1856	(197,990)				
	120.00	150.00	200.00	1500.00	
☐ 1856C	(28,457)				
	350.00	425.00	1300.00	22000.00	
☐ 1856D	(19,786)				
	365.00	400.00	1200.00	12500.00	
☐ 1856O	(10,000)				
	350.00	400.00	1400.00	15000.00	
☐ 1856S	(105,100)				
	200.00	250.00	650.00	5750.00	
☐ 1857	(98,188)				
	125.00	150.00	300.00	1500.00	
☐ 1857C	(31,360)				
	325.00	350.00	1200.00	12000.00	
☐ 1857D	(17,046)				
	325.00	400.00	1100.00	15000.00	
☐ 1857O	(13,000)				
	325.00	375.00	1200.00	15000.00	
☐ 1857S	(87,000)				
	175.00	225.00	600.00	7500.00	
☐ 1858	(15,136)				
	175.00	250.00	500.00	4000.00	80000.00
☐ 1858C	(38,856)				
	325.00	400.00	1100.00	15000.00	
☐ 1858D	(15,362)				
	325.00	450.00	1150.00	12000.00	

DATE	ABP IN F-12	F-12 FINE	EF-40 EX. FINE	MS-60 UNC.	PRF-65 PROOF
☐ 1858S	(18,600)				
	400.00	475.00	2400.00	20000.00	
☐ 1859	(16,814)				
	200.00	240.00	450.00	5000.00	80000.00
☐ 1859C	(31,487)				
	325.00	375.00	1800.00	20000.00	
☐ 1859D	(10,366)				
	425.00	475.00	1300.00	13000.00	
☐ 1859S	(13,220)				
	500.00	650.00	3700.00	26500.00	
☐ 1860	(19,825)				
	175.00	220.00	400.00	4000.00	75000.00
☐ 1860C	(14,813)				
	425.00	450.00	1900.00	15000.00	
☐ 1860D	(14,635)				
	400.00	450.00	1850.00	18000.00	
☐ 1860S	(21,200)				
	500.00	600.00	1750.00	20000.00	
☐ 1861	(639,950)				
	140.00	180.00	240.00	1400.00	55000.00
☐ 1861C	(6,879)				
	850.00	800.00	4000.00	38000.00	
☐ 1861D	(1,597)				
	2250.00	2750.00	6500.00	45000.00	
☐ 1861S	(9,500)				
	500.00	600.00	4100.00	32500.00	
☐ 1862	(4,465)				
	350.00	410.00	1450.00	17000.00	75000.00
☐ 1862S	(9,500)				
	900.00	1200.00	6000.00	50000.00	
☐ 1863	(2,472)				
	350.00	500.00	3350.00	22500.00	50000.00
☐ 1863S	(17,000)				
	500.00	700.00	4500.00	26000.00	
☐ 1864	(4,220)				
	325.00	400.00	1400.00	15000.00	52500.00
☐ 1864S	(3,888)				
	2600.00	4000.00	15000.00	42000.00	
☐ 1865	(1,295)				
	400.00	600.00	3500.00	23500.00	57500.00

DATE	ABP IN F-12	F-12 FINE	EF-40 EX. FINE	MS-60 UNC.	PRF-65 PROOF
☐ 1865S (27,612)					
	450.00	600.00	2000.00	22000.00	
☐ 1866S No Motto (43,020)					
	600.00	800.00	3500.00	26500.00	
☐ 1866S With Motto* (43,020)					
	450.00	550.00	2600.00	19500.00	
☐ 1866 (6,720)					
	310.00	450.00	1400.00	13000.00	45000.00
☐ 1867 (6,920)					
	200.00	300.00	1400.00	7500.00	45000.00
☐ 1867S (29,000)					
	600.00	800.00	2800.00	21500.00	
☐ 1868 (5,725)					
	240.00	300.00	1000.00	12000.00	37000.00
☐ 1868S (52,000)					
	260.00	375.00	1400.00	20000.00	
☐ 1869 (1,785)					
	400.00	525.00	1700.00	19000.00	40000.00
☐ 1869S (31,000)					
	300.00	460.00	1800.00	20000.00	
☐ 1870 (4,035)					
	300.00	400.00	1700.00	16000.00	47500.00
☐ 1870CC (7,675) UNKNOWN IN UNC.—EF-40—14000.00					
☐ 1870S (17,000)					
	400.00	600.00	2400.00	22500.00	
☐ 1871 (3,230)					
	300.00	450.00	1750.00	14000.00	47500.00
☐ 1871CC (20,770)					
	500.00	700.00	3000.00	37000.00	
☐ 1871S (25,000)					
	300.00	410.00	1200.00	18000.00	
☐ 1872 (1,690)					
	400.00	450.00	1700.00	13000.00	45000.00
☐ 1872CC (16,980)					
	450.00	600.00	4500.00	35000.00	
☐ 1872S (36,400)					
	275.00	350.00	800.00	20000.00	
☐ 1873 (112,505)					
	200.00	310.00	450.00	1200.00	47500.00

*Note: From 1866 to 1908 all have motto "In God We Trust" over eagle on reverse.

DATE	ABP IN F-12	F-12 FINE	EF-40 EX. FINE	MS-60 UNC.	PRF-65 PROOF
☐ 1873CC (7,416)	1000.00	1200.00	11000.00	36000.00	
☐ 1873S (31,000)	350.00	400.00	1150.00	22000.00	
☐ 1874 (3,508)	300.00	400.00	1200.00	15000.00	42500.00
☐ 1874CC (21,198)	400.00	525.00	2000.00	35000.00	
☐ 1874S (16,000)	400.00	500.00	1750.00	19000.00	
☐ 1875 (220) VERY RARE—EF-40—50000.00*					
☐ 1875CC (11,828)	700.00	1000.00	3600.00	40000.00	
☐ 1875S (9,000)	500.00	600.00	2300.00	28000.00	
☐ 1876 (1,477)	400.00	500.00	2000.00	14000.00	45000.00
☐ 1876CC (6,887)	525.00	600.00	4800.00	28000.00	
☐ 1876S (4,000)	600.00	900.00	3600.00	22500.00	
☐ 1877 (1,152)	350.00	450.00	1800.00	10500.00	50000.00
☐ 1877CC (8,680)	400.00	500.00	3000.00	23500.00	
☐ 1877S (26,700)	175.00	240.00	600.00	9000.00	
☐ 1878 (131,740)	160.00	180.00	220.00	500.00	43000.00
☐ 1878CC (9,054)	1000.00	1300.00	7000.00	42500.00	
☐ 1878S (144,700)	140.00	185.00	200.00	1000.00	
☐ 1879 (301,950)	140.00	185.00	200.00	425.00	37500.00
☐ 1879CC (17,281)	275.00	350.00	1500.00	15000.00	
☐ 1879S (426,200)	140.00	180.00	240.00	1100.00	

*Note: Only 20 proofs struck in 1875.

DATE	ABP IN F-12	F-12 FINE	EF-40 EX. FINE	MS-60 UNC.	PRF-65 PROOF
☐ 1880 (3,166,436)	100.00	130.00	160.00	250.00	42500.00
☐ 1880CC (51,017)	200.00	250.00	700.00	12000.00	
☐ 1880S (1,348,900)	120.00	150.00	175.00	250.00	
☐ 1881 (5,708,800)	110.00	140.00	175.00	250.00	38500.00
☐ 1881CC (13,886)	300.00	400.00	1400.00	20000.00	
☐ 1881S (969,000)	105.00	140.00	175.00	240.00	
☐ 1882 (21,514,560)	105.00	140.00	175.00	250.00	38500.00
☐ 1882CC (82,817)	200.00	275.00	430.00	7000.00	
☐ 1882S (969,000)	100.00	140.00	175.00	275.00	
☐ 1883 (233,440)	100.00	140.00	175.00	300.00	35000.00
☐ 1883CC (12,958)	200.00	400.00	875.00	19000.00	
☐ 1883S (83,200)	110.00	140.00	220.00	1000.00	
☐ 1884 (191,048)	110.00	140.00	185.00	1000.00	30000.00
☐ 1884CC (16,402)	275.00	375.00	900.00	18000.00	
☐ 1884S (177,000)	110.00	150.00	200.00	350.00	
☐ 1885 (601,506)	110.00	140.00	185.00	250.00	33000.00
☐ 1885S (1,211,500)	110.00	140.00	185.00	250.00	
☐ 1886 (388,432)	110.00	150.00	185.00	300.00	35000.00
☐ 1886S (3,268,000)	110.00	140.00	185.00	250.00	
☐ 1887 (87) Proof Only				VERY RARE	140000.00
☐ 1887S (1,912,000)	110.00	150.00	185.00	250.00	

DATE	ABP IN F-12	F-12 FINE	EF-40 EX. FINE	MS-60 UNC.	PRF-65 PROOF
☐ 1888	(18,296) 125.00	145.00	210.00	550.00	26500.00
☐ 1888S	(293,900) 130.00	150.00	225.00	1125.00	
☐ 1889	(7,565) 135.00	160.00	340.00	1000.00	27500.00
☐ 1890	(4,328) 200.00	220.00	500.00	1700.00	29000.00
☐ 1890CC	(53,800) 140.00	190.00	325.00	1050.00	
☐ 1891	(61,413) 130.00	160.00	195.00	475.00	30000.00
☐ 1891CC	(208,000) 120.00	180.00	300.00	700.00	
☐ 1892	(753,572) 105.00	130.00	150.00	230.00	32000.00
☐ 1892CC	(82,968) 150.00	190.00	320.00	1400.00	
☐ 1892O	(10,000) 325.00	375.00	675.00	2800.00	
☐ 1892S	(298,400) 115.00	140.00	185.00	680.00	
☐ 1893	(1,528,197) 100.00	140.00	185.00	240.00	30000.00
☐ 1893CC	(60,000) 150.00	190.00	310.00	1500.00	
☐ 1893O	(110,000) 125.00	160.00	265.00	1000.00	
☐ 1893S	(224,000) 110.00	140.00	190.00	325.00	
☐ 1894	(957,955) 110.00	135.00	200.00	275.00	32500.00
☐ 1894O	(16,660) 130.00	160.00	260.00	1400.00	
☐ 1894S	(55,900) 130.00	160.00	320.00	2350.00	
☐ 1895	(1,345,936) 110.00	140.00	185.00	230.00	26500.00
☐ 1895S	(112,000) 115.00	140.00	300.00	2900.00	

DATE	ABP IN F-12	F-12 FINE	EF-40 EX. FINE	MS-60 UNC.	PRF-65 PROOF
☐ 1896	(59,063)				
	120.00	140.00	175.00	300.00	28500.00
☐ 1896S	(115,400)				
	140.00	160.00	270.00	1250.00	
☐ 1897	(867,883)				
	115.00	150.00	175.00	230.00	30000.00
☐ 1897S	(345,000)				
	115.00	140.00	215.00	850.00	
☐ 1898	(633,495)				
	115.00	150.00	175.00	240.00	25000.00
☐ 1898S	(1,397,400)				
	115.00	140.00	180.00	250.00	
☐ 1899	(1,710,729)				
	115.00	140.00	180.00	240.00	25000.00
☐ 1899S	(1,545,000)				
	115.00	140.00	180.00	250.00	
☐ 1900	(1,405,730)				
	115.00	140.00	175.00	225.00	25000.00
☐ 1900S	(329,000)				
	115.00	150.00	185.00	375.00	
☐ 1901	(616,040)				
	115.00	150.00	175.00	230.00	25000.00
☐ 1901S	(3,648,000)				
	115.00	150.00	175.00	230.00	
☐ 1901S 1 over 0				325.00	
☐ 1902	(172,562)				
	115.00	140.00	175.00	230.00	26500.00
☐ 1902S	(939,000)				
	115.00	150.00	175.00	240.00	
☐ 1903	(227,024)				
	115.00	150.00	175.00	230.00	25000.00
☐ 1903S	(1,885,000)				
	115.00	150.00	175.00	250.00	
☐ 1904	(392,136)				
	115.00	140.00	175.00	230.00	28000.00
☐ 1904S	(97,000)				
	115.00	150.00	190.00	1200.00	
☐ 1905	(302,308)				
	115.00	140.00	175.00	240.00	28000.00
☐ 1905S	(880,700)				
	115.00	150.00	175.00	575.00	

DATE	ABP IN F-12	F-12 FINE	EF-40 EX. FINE	MS-60 UNC.	PRF-65 PROOF
☐ 1906	(348,820) 115.00	150.00	175.00	230.00	23500.00
☐ 1906D	(320,000) 115.00	150.00	175.00	240.00	
☐ 1906S	(598,000) 115.00	150.00	190.00	325.00	
☐ 1907	(626,192) 115.00	140.00	180.00	225.00	25000.00
☐ 1907D	(888,000) 115.00	150.00	180.00	235.00	
☐ 1908	(421,874) 115.00	140.00	180.00	240.00	

HALF EAGLES—INDIAN HEAD, 1908–1929

Bela Lyon Pratt's Indian Head design replaced the Liberty Head Half Eagle in 1908. Like the Quarter Eagle these coins are uniquely without raised edges and have designs stamped in incuse or recess rather than raised from the surface. A standing eagle adorns the reverse, with mint mark beneath the wording E PLURIBUS UNUM. These Half Eagles contained 90% gold and 10% copper with a weight of 8.359 grams. The diameter is 21.6mm. and the gold content by weight is .24167 ounce each. Striking of Half Eagles was suspended during World War I and not resumed until 1929, their final year of production.

Mint Mark is to Left of Value on Reverse

DATE	ABP IN VF-20	VF-20 V. FINE	EF-40 EX. FINE	MS-60 UNC.	PRF-65 PROOF
☐ 1908	(578,012)				
	150.00	180.00	230.00	350.00	24000.00
☐ 1908D	(148,000)				
	150.00	180.00	230.00	350.00	
☐ 1908S	(82,000)				
	275.00	325.00	390.00	1150.00	
☐ 1909	(627,138)				
	175.00	200.00	240.00	340.00	28500.00
☐ 1909D	(3,423,560)				
	175.00	200.00	240.00	350.00	
☐ 1909O*	(34,200)				
	550.00	650.00	1050.00	7000.00	
☐ 1909S	(297,200)				
	175.00	180.00	230.00	1200.00	
☐ 1910	(604,250)				
	160.00	175.00	200.00	340.00	27500.00
☐ 1910D	(193,600)				
	160.00	175.00	200.00	450.00	
☐ 1910S	(770,200)				
	180.00	200.00	230.00	1200.00	
☐ 1911	(915,139)				
	160.00	175.00	200.00	330.00	25000.00
☐ 1911D	(72,500)				
	275.00	325.00	430.00	3250.00	
☐ 1911S	(1,416,000)				
	170.00	200.00	220.00	490.00	
☐ 1912	(790,144)				
	160.00	175.00	200.00	350.00	25000.00
☐ 1912S	(392,000)				
	160.00	190.00	220.00	1400.00	
☐ 1913	(916,099)				
	160.00	175.00	200.00	330.00	26500.00
☐ 1913S	(408,000)				
	185.00	215.00	250.00	1500.00	
☐ 1914	(247,125)				
	160.00	175.00	195.00	350.00	27500.00
☐ 1914D	(247,000)				
	175.00	200.00	240.00	350.00	
☐ 1914S	(263,000)				
	175.00	185.00	200.00	1500.00	

*Some "O" mint marks are false.

HALF EAGLES—$5.00 GOLD PIECES, 1795–1929 / 445

DATE	ABP IN VF-20	VF-20 V. FINE	EF-40 EX. FINE	MS-60 UNC.	PRF-65 PROOF
☐ 1915*	(588,075) 175.00	200.00	250.00	375.00	35000.00
☐ 1915S	(164,000) 200.00	245.00	350.00	1900.00	
☐ 1916S	(240,000) 175.00	200.00	265.00	600.00	
☐ 1929	(662,000) 2250.00	2650.00	4000.00	6000.00	

*Coins marked 1915D are not authentic.

EAGLES—$10.00 GOLD PIECES, 1795–1907

Gold pieces valued at $10 were released for general circulation in 1795. Despite the large face value and the super-large buying power ($10 in the 1790s was equivalent to about $200 in present-day money), this coin was struck in substantial numbers, chiefly as a banking piece. Though bullion shortages, speculation, and world economic conditions made the Eagle's career far from sedate, it retained great influence throughout most of its history. The first design, conceived by Robert Scot, comprised a capped bust of Liberty facing right with the so-called Small Eagle reverse, depicting an eagle holding a wreath in its beak. The Shield or Heraldic Eagle replaced this type in 1797 and production was stepped up, output reaching more than 37,000 in 1799. The content was .9167 gold to .0833 copper, with a weight of 17.5 grams and diameter generally of 33mm. From 1805 to 1837 no Eagles were struck.

When production resumed in 1838 the portrait of Liberty had undergone a thorough alteration at the hands of Christian Gobrecht. This was the Coronet type, with modified shielded eagle on the reverse. It weighed 16.718 grams with a 9-to-1 gold content (alloyed with copper) and diameter of 27mm. The gold content by weight was .48375 ounces. The slogan E PLURIBUS UNUM, previously used on the reverse, was dropped. For many years no motto appeared on the reverse until the installation, in 1866, of IN GOD WE TRUST. The composition and other specifications remained unaltered. No change was made until 1907 when the Indian Head obverse, designed by Augustus Saint-Gaudens, was introduced.

PLEASE NOTE: THE PRICES THAT ARE LISTED REFLECT A GOLD SPOT PRICE OF $360.00 PER OUNCE.

EAGLES—LIBERTY HEAD, SMALL EAGLE, 1795–1797

DATE	MINTAGE	ABP IN F-12	F-12 FINE	EF-40 EX. FINE	MS-60 UNC.
☐ 1795* 9 Leaves	5,583	15000.00	18000.00	45000.00	165000.00
☐ 1796	4,146	5000.00	7000.00	18000.00	60000.00
☐ 1797 Part of Liberty Head, Small Eagle					
	3,615	6250.00	8000.00	26000.00	125000.00

EAGLES—LIBERTY HEAD, LARGE EAGLE, 1797–1804

4 Stars Right   6 Stars Right   Large Eagle

DATE	MINTAGE	ABP IN F-12	F-12 FINE	EF-40 EX. FINE	MS-60 UNC.
☐ 1797 Large Eagle	10,940	1950.00	2200.00	4600.00	18000.00
☐ 1798 over 97, 9 Stars Left, 4 Right					
	900	4250.00	56000.00	18500.00	75000.00
☐ 1798 over 97, 7 Stars Left, 6 Right					
	842		VERY RARE MS-60—$225,000.00		
☐ 1799	37,449	2000.00	2500.00	5000.00	11000.00
☐ 1800	5,999	2000.00	2500.00	5000.00	18000.00
☐ 1801	44,344	2000.00	2500.00	4100.00	12000.00
☐ 1803	15,017	2000.00	2500.00	4100.00	12000.00
☐ 1804	3,757	2500.00	3400.00	6500.00	30000.00

*Note: 1795 13 Leaves EF-40 $12,000.

EAGLES—LIBERTY HEAD WITH CORONET, 1838–1907

1862

1838–1866
No Motto

Mint Mark is Below Eagle on Reverse

1866–1907
With Motto

DATE	ABP IN F-12	F-12 FINE	EF-40 EX. FINE	MS-60 UNC.	PRF-65 PROOF
☐ 1838 Large Letters	(7,200)				
	500.00	610.00	2800.00	2600.00	
☐ 1839 Large Letters	(25,800)				
	450.00	550.00	1700.00	28000.00	
☐ 1839 Small Letters	(12,447)				
	700.00	850.00	3250.00	23500.00	
☐ 1840	(47,338)				
	240.00	300.00	600.00	11000.00	
☐ 1841	(63,131)				
	225.00	300.00	500.00	8500.00	
☐ 18410	(2,500)				
	900.00	1200.00	4500.00	27500.00	
☐ 1842	(81,507)				
	240.00	300.00	450.00	10000.00	
☐ 18420	(27,400)				
	240.00	300.00	500.00	25000.00	
☐ 1843	(75,462)				
	235.00	325.00	500.00	16000.00	
☐ 18430	(175,162)				
	225.00	300.00	500.00	14000.00	
☐ 1844	(6,361)				
	550.00	650.00	2600.00	20000.00	
☐ 18440	(118,700)				
	225.00	300.00	450.00	18000.00	
☐ 1845	(26,153)				
	350.00		750.00	12500.00	
☐ 18450	(47,500)				
	265.00	350.00	650.00	20000.00	

DATE	ABP IN F-12	F-12 FINE	EF-40 EX. FINE	MS-60 UNC.	PRF-65 PROOF
☐ 1846	(20,095) 385.00	450.00	1000.00	18500.00	
☐ 1846O	(81,780) 250.00	300.00	750.00	12500.00	
☐ 1847	(862,258) 225.00	260.00	300.00	3500.00	
☐ 1847O	(417,099) 225.00	275.00	350.00	4600.00	
☐ 1848	(145,484) 225.00	275.00	450.00	5500.00	
☐ 1848O	(35,850) 325.00	340.00	1000.00	15000.00	
☐ 1849	(653,618) 220.00	260.00	340.00	3500.00	
☐ 1849O	(23,900) 300.00	400.00	1700.00	20000.00	
☐ 1850*	(291,451) 220.00	275.00	400.00	3800.00	
☐ 1850O	(57,500) 235.00	300.00	1000.00	11000.00	
☐ 1851	(176,328) 220.00	300.00	410.00	5000.00	
☐ 1851O	(263,000) 220.00	300.00	410.00	6500.00	
☐ 1852	(263,106) 220.00	300.00	335.00	4000.00	
☐ 1852O	(18,000) 350.00	390.00	950.00	18000.00	
☐ 1853	(201,253) 225.00	275.00	370.00	3800.00	
☐ 1853O	(51,000) 225.00	295.00	410.00	9500.00	
☐ 1854	(54,250) 225.00	295.00	410.00	5600.00	
☐ 1854O	(52,500) 225.00	300.00	675.00	8750.00	
☐ 1854S	(123,826) 225.00	295.00	400.00	12000.00	
☐ 1855	(121,701) 225.00	270.00	350.00	5000.00	60000.00

*Note: Small Date more—MS-60 $10,000.

DATE	ABP IN F-12	F-12 FINE	EF-40 EX. FINE	MS-60 UNC.	PRF-65 PROOF
☐ 1855O	(18,000)				
	250.00	325.00	1400.00	18000.00	
☐ 1855S	(9,000)				
	600.00	700.00	2300.00	25000.00	
☐ 1856	(60,490)				
	220.00	265.00	375.00	5000.00	65000.00
☐ 1856O	(14,500)				
	400.00	450.00	1000.00	10000.00	
☐ 1856S	(26,000)				
	220.00	260.00	500.00	9000.00	
☐ 1857	(16,606)				
	240.00	300.00	1000.00	10750.00	
☐ 1857O	(5,500)				
	475.00	600.00	1750.00	20000.00	
☐ 1857S	(26,000)				
	350.00	350.00	1200.00	10500.00	
☐ 1858*	(2,521)				
	2500.00	3000.00	7500.00		90000.00
☐ 1858O	(20,000)				
	220.00	300.00	650.00	10000.00	
☐ 1858S	(11,800)				
	750.00	850.00	3200.00	29000.00	
☐ 1859	(16,093)				
	220.00	285.00	725.00	10000.00	70000.00
☐ 1859O	(2,300)				
	1600.00	2000.00	7500.00	45000.00	
☐ 1859S	(7,007)				
	900.00	1150.00	4200.00	37000.00	
☐ 1860	(11,783)				
	250.00	300.00	650.00	8000.00	62500.00
☐ 1860O	(11,100)				
	210.00	300.00	750.00	9000.00	
☐ 1860S	(5,500)				
	1500.00	1800.00	5500.00	38000.00	
☐ 1861	(113,233)				
	225.00	260.00	350.00	4000.00	60000.00
☐ 1861S	(15,500)				
	700.00	750.00	2550.00	29500.00	
☐ 1862	(10,995)				
	275.00	270.00	950.00	15000.00	60000.00

*Check for removed mint mark.

DATE	ABP IN F-12	F-12 FINE	EF-40 EX. FINE	MS-60 UNC.	PRF-65 PROOF
☐ 1862S (12,500)	475.00	625.00	2700.00	30000.00	
☐ 1863 (1,248)	2100.00	3100.00	7600.00	42000.00	72000.00
☐ 1863S (10,000)	600.00	750.00	3200.00	30000.00	
☐ 1864 (3,580)	750.00	825.00	2600.00	20000.00	70000.00
☐ 1864S (2,500)	2300.00	2750.00	12000.00	42500.00	
☐ 1865 (4,005)	600.00	775.00	3400.00	29500.00	65000.00
☐ 1865S (16,700)	1700.00	2300.00	11000.00	42000.00	
☐ 1866 With Motto (3,780)	450.00	600.00	1750.00	15000.00	55000.00
☐ 1866S No Motto (8,500)	1200.00	1400.00	2900.00	37000.00	
☐ 1866S With Motto (11,500)	600.00	825.00	3200.00	21500.00	
☐ 1867 (3,140)	600.00	825.00	2400.00	23000.00	55000.00
☐ 1867S (9,000)	900.00	1200.00	5000.00	30000.00	
☐ 1868 (10,655)	275.00	450.00	700.00	18000.00	45000.00
☐ 1868S (13,500)	600.00	700.00	2500.00	21000.00	
☐ 1869 (1,855)	700.00	800.00	2500.00	25000.00	45000.00
☐ 1869S (6,430)	650.00	850.00	2550.00	28000.00	
☐ 1870 (2,535)	400.00	500.00	1200.00	15000.00	50000.00
☐ 1870CC (5,908)	3700.00	4500.00	25000.00	75000.00	
☐ 1870S (8,000)	675.00	800.00	2600.00	24000.00	
☐ 1871 (1,780)	750.00	900.00	2000.00	17500.00	50000.00

DATE		ABP IN F-12	F-12 FINE	EF-40 EX. FINE	MS-60 UNC.	PRF-65 PROOF
☐ 1871CC	(7,185)					
		1100.00	1300.00	4500.00	50000.00	
☐ 1871S	(16,500)					
		600.00	725.00	1850.00	25000.00	
☐ 1872	(1,650)					
		1300.00	1200.00	3250.00	28000.00	60000.00
☐ 1872CC	(5,500)					
		1250.00	1500.00	9000.00	56000.00	
☐ 1872S	(17,300)					
		325.00	445.00	875.00	22000.00	
☐ 1873	(825)					
		2500.00	4000.00	8500.00	45000.00	65000.00
☐ 1873CC	(4,543)					
		1500.00	1900.00	12000.00	44500.00	
☐ 1873S	(12,000)					
		500.00	600.00	2200.00	26000.00	
☐ 1874	(53,160)					
		200.00	240.00	300.00	1900.00	55000.00
☐ 1874CC	(16,767)					
		500.00	600.00	2350.00	28000.00	
☐ 1874S	(10,000)					
		600.00	750.00	3400.00	36000.00	
☐ 1875	(120)				PROOF-65—350000.00	
☐ 1875CC	(7,715)					
		1700.00	2000.00	9000.00	50000.00	
☐ 1876	(732)					
		2000.00	2800.00	6250.00	50000.00	57500.00
☐ 1876CC	(4,696)					
		1500.00	1700.00	6000.00	5000.00	
☐ 1876S	(5,000)					
		600.00	750.00	1800.00	33500.00	
☐ 1877	(817)					
		1350.00	1700.00	3500.00	34000.00	47500.00
☐ 1877CC	(3,332)					
		1350.00	1600.00	4600.00	42500.00	
☐ 1877S	(17,000)					
		325.00	375.00	700.00	22500.00	
☐ 1878	(73,800)					
		200.00	250.00	350.00	1250.00	35000.00
☐ 1878CC	(3,244)					
		1800.00	2400.00	8500.00	3750.00	

DATE	ABP IN F-12	F-12 FINE	EF-40 EX. FINE	MS-60 UNC.	PRF-65 PROOF
☐ 1878S	(26,100) 210.00	325.00	620.00	17000.00	
☐ 1879	(384,770) 200.00	250.00	300.00	800.00	38000.00
☐ 1879CC	(1,762) 2500.00	3000.00	13500.00	42000.00	
☐ 1879O	(1,500) 1350.00	2000.00	3750.00	23500.00	
☐ 1879S	(224,000) 200.00	235.00	290.00	1200.00	
☐ 1880	(1,644,876) 185.00	200.00	270.00	300.00	38000.00
☐ 1880CC	(11,192) 300.00	350.00	750.00	13000.00	
☐ 1880O	(9,500) 200.00	250.00	700.00	10000.00	
☐ 1880S	(506,205) 190.00	230.00	300.00	500.00	
☐ 1881	(3,877,260) 190.00	230.00	300.00	300.00	40000.00
☐ 1881CC	(24,015) 250.00	300.00	500.00	6800.00	
☐ 1881O	(8,350) 200.00	260.00	700.00	8000.00	
☐ 1881S	(970,000) 185.00	220.00	275.00	400.00	
☐ 1882	(2,324,480) 185.00	220.00	275.00	300.00	40000.00
☐ 1882CC	(6,764) 375.00	450.00	1100.00	8500.00	
☐ 1882O	(10,280) 225.00	300.00	550.00	8500.00	
☐ 1882S	(132,000) 200.00	230.00	300.00	450.00	
☐ 1883	(208,740) 200.00	240.00	275.00	300.00	40000.00
☐ 1883CC	(12,000) 285.00	335.00	650.00	12000.00	
☐ 1883O	(800) 1000.00	1300.00	7000.00	25000.00	

DATE	ABP IN F-12	F-12 FINE	EF-40 EX. FINE	MS-60 UNC.	PRF-65 PROOF
☐ 1883S	(38,000)				
	190.00	230.00	300.00	1400.00	
☐ 1884	(76,017)				
	190.00	225.00	280.00	810.00	38000.00
☐ 1884CC	(9,925)				
	300.00	400.00	850.00	10000.00	
☐ 1884S	(124,250)				
	190.00	225.00	300.00	700.00	
☐ 1885	(124,527)				
	180.00	200.00	300.00	425.00	40000.00
☐ 1885S	(228,000)				
	210.00	240.00	300.00	400.00	
☐ 1886	(236,160)				
	180.00	225.00	275.00	400.00	38000.00
☐ 1886S	(826,000)				
	190.00	220.00	275.00	375.00	
☐ 1887	(53,680)				
	200.00	225.00	300.00	825.00	35000.00
☐ 1887S	(817,000)				
	190.00	220.00	285.00	300.00	
☐ 1888	(132,996)				
	200.00	250.00	300.00	800.00	40000.00
☐ 1888O	(21,335)				
	175.00	210.00	300.00	575.00	
☐ 1888S	(648,700)				
	180.00	220.00	285.00	300.00	
☐ 1889	(4,485)				
	230.00	290.00	450.00	3250.00	38000.00
☐ 1889S	(425,400)				
	185.00	215.00	300.00	300.00	
☐ 1890	(58,043)				
	200.00	235.00	300.00	900.00	45000.00
☐ 1890CC	(17,500)				
	250.00	300.00	450.00	2500.00	
☐ 1891	(91,868)				
	190.00	235.00	300.00	335.00	35000.00
☐ 1891CC	(103,732)				
	250.00	285.00	400.00	750.00	
☐ 1892	(797,552)				
	200.00	225.00	290.00	350.00	38000.00

EAGLES—$10.00 GOLD PIECES, 1795–1907 / 455

DATE	ABP IN F-12	F-12 FINE	EF-40 EX. FINE	MS-60 UNC.	PRF-65 PROOF
☐ 1892CC (40,000)	250.00	300.00	400.00	3500.00	
☐ 1892O (28,688)	200.00	225.00	290.00	410.00	
☐ 1892S (115,500)	200.00	235.00	300.00	425.00	
☐ 1893 (1,840,895)	180.00	220.00	270.00	300.00	45000.00
☐ 1893CC (14,000)	250.00	300.00	610.00	4000.00	
☐ 1893O (17,000)	200.00	230.00	310.00	600.00	
☐ 1893S (141,350)	195.00	240.00	275.00	500.00	
☐ 1894 (2,470,782)	195.00	225.00	300.00	375.00	45000.00
☐ 1894O (197,500)	195.00	220.00	300.00	950.00	
☐ 1894S (25,000)	210.00	265.00	410.00	3000.00	
☐ 1895 (567,826)	190.00	225.00	275.00	320.00	35000.00
☐ 1895O (98,000)	200.00	260.00	380.00	500.00	
☐ 1895S (49,000)	215.00	250.00	370.00	2650.00	
☐ 1896 (76,348)	215.00	230.00	325.00	350.00	35000.00
☐ 1896S (123,750)	200.00	240.00	325.00	3000.00	
☐ 1897 (1,000,159)	200.00	220.00	270.00	300.00	45000.00
☐ 1897O (42,500)	200.00	225.00	300.00	800.00	
☐ 1897S (234,750)	200.00	240.00	310.00	875.00	
☐ 1898 (812,197)	180.00	200.00	270.00	300.00	35000.00
☐ 1898S (473,600)	190.00	220.00	275.00	400.00	

DATE	ABP IN F-12	F-12 FINE	EF-40 EX. FINE	MS-60 UNC.	PRF-65 PROOF
☐ 1899	(1,262,305)				
	200.00	225.00	270.00	300.00	35000.00
☐ 1899O	(37,047)				
	210.00	250.00	325.00	500.00	
☐ 1899S	(841,000)				
	200.00	230.00	290.00	300.00	35000.00
☐ 1900	(293,960)				
	200.00	225.00	270.00	325.00	35000.00
☐ 1900S	(81,000)				
	210.00	240.00	300.00	1000.00	
☐ 1901	(1,718,825)				
	190.00	220.00	275.00	340.00	38000.00
☐ 1901O	(72,041)				
	190.00	230.00	275.00	400.00	
☐ 1901S	(2,812,750)				
	185.00	210.00	275.00	325.00	
☐ 1902	(82,513)				
	200.00	230.00	270.00	325.00	35000.00
☐ 1902S	(469,500)				
	190.00	220.00	275.00	300.00	
☐ 1903	(125,926)				
	180.00	225.00	270.00	340.00	35000.00
☐ 1903O	(112,771)				
	220.00	220.00	300.00	375.00	
☐ 1903S	(518,620)				
	190.00	225.00	270.00	350.00	
☐ 1904	(162,038)				
	200.00	225.00	300.00	340.00	38000.00
☐ 1904O	(108,950)				
	210.00	240.00	270.00	390.00	
☐ 1905	(201,078)				
	200.00	220.00	275.00	325.00	40000.00
☐ 1905S	(369,250)				
	200.00	225.00	280.00	1275.00	
☐ 1906	(165,496)				
	200.00	230.00	270.00	315.00	40000.00
☐ 1906D	(981,000)				
	200.00	230.00	270.00	315.00	
☐ 1906O	(86,895)				
	210.00	240.00	300.00	625.00	

DATE	ABP IN F-12	F-12 FINE	EF-40 EX. FINE	MS-60 UNC.	PRF-65 PROOF
☐ 1906S	(457,000) 200.00	260.00	300.00	550.00	
☐ 1907	(1,203,973) 200.00	225.00	265.00	315.00	35000.00
☐ 1907D	(1,020,000) 200.00	225.00	265.00	350.00	
☐ 1907S	(210,000) 200.00	225.00	275.00	700.00	

EAGLES—INDIAN HEAD, 1907–1933

Augustus Saint-Gaudens, a noted sculptor and really the first artist of international repute to design an American coin, strove to inject a touch of creative feeling in coin design. True to the artistic spirit of the times he sacrificed such supposedly old-fashioned qualities as balance to achieve imagination of line and composition. His eagle, on the reverse, is totally stylized, its strength and symmetry purposely overemphasized. At first the motto IN GOD WE TRUST was omitted, owing to President Theodore Roosevelt's opinion that the name of God was not suitable for use on coinage in any context. He was overruled by Congress in 1908 and the motto appeared shortly thereafter. Striking of Eagles, which had reached as high as nearly $4\frac{1}{2}$ million pieces in a single year ($45,000,000 face value), was discontinued in 1933. The Saint-Gaudens Eagle contained 90% gold and 10% copper, with a diameter of 27mm. and a weight of 16.718 grams. The bullion weight is .48375 of an ounce.

1907–1908 Without Motto

1907–1933

1908–1933 With Motto

Mint Mark is Left of Value on Reverse

DATE	ABP IN VERY FINE	VERY FINE	EF-40 EX. FINE	MS-60 UNC.	PRF-65 PROOF
☐ 1907 Without Periods (239,406)					
	300.00	350.00	425.00	600.00	
☐ 1907 Wire Rim With Periods Before and After U.S.A.					(500)
				9000.00	
☐ 1907 Rolled Rim, Periods (42)				34000.00	
☐ 1908 No Motto (33,500)					
	300.00	350.00	425.00	750.00	
☐ 1908 With Motto (341,486)					
	300.00	360.00	420.00	600.00	35000.00
☐ 1908D No Motto (210,000)					
	300.00	350.00	400.00	850.00	
☐ 1908D (386,500)					
	275.00	325.00	410.00	875.00	
☐ 1908S (59,850)					
	325.00	390.00	425.00	2000.00	
☐ 1909 (184,863)					
	295.00	335.00	385.00	500.00	40000.00
☐ 1909D (121,540)					
	295.00	335.00	385.00	800.00	
☐ 1909S (292,350)					
	295.00	335.00	385.00	700.00	
☐ 1910 (318,704)					
	295.00	325.00	385.00	490.00	40000.00
☐ 1910D (2,356,640)					
	285.00	325.00	400.00	500.00	
☐ 1910S (811,000)					
	285.00	300.00	400.00	800.00	
☐ 1911 (505,595)					
	285.00	300.00	375.00	500.00	38500.00
☐ 1911D (30,100)					
	400.00	510.00	700.00	4250.00	
☐ 1911S (51,000)					
	350.00	400.00	475.00	1000.00	
☐ 1912 (405,083)					
	280.00	340.00	395.00	500.00	42000.00
☐ 1912S (300,000)					
	285.00	340.00	400.00	1000.00	
☐ 1913 (442,071)					
	285.00	340.00	375.00	550.00	40000.00

DATE	ABP IN VERY FINE	VERY FINE	EF-40 EX. FINE	MS-60 UNC.	PRF-65 PROOF
☐ 1913S	(66,000) 400.00	475.00	650.00	4250.00	
☐ 1914	(151,050) 285.00	335.00	400.00	500.00	42000.00
☐ 1914D	(343,500) 285.00	315.00	375.00	510.00	
☐ 1914S	(208,000) 285.00	335.00	400.00	700.00	
☐ 1915	(351,075) 285.00	325.00	380.00	510.00	42000.00
☐ 1915S	(59,000) 375.00	475.00	575.00	3000.00	
☐ 1916S	(138,500) 285.00	350.00	425.00	750.00	
☐ 1920S	(126,500) 4500.00	5500.00	7200.00	15250.00	
☐ 1926	(1,014,000) 285.00	325.00	375.00	525.00	
☐ 1930S	(96,000) 3500.00	3650.00	5000.00	7800.00	
☐ 1932	(1,463,000) 285.00	325.00	350.00	500.00	
☐ 1933	(312,500)		30000.00	67500.00	

Note: The rare dates of this series are heavily counterfeited. Be sure that you buy from a reputable dealer.

DOUBLE EAGLES— $20.00 GOLD PIECES

The Double Eagle or $20 gold piece was the largest denomination coin issued for regular use by the U.S. Mint. It was introduced in 1849, as a direct result of the California gold strikes. Discovery of gold at Sutter's Mill had not only made vast new supplies available to the government, but focused increased attention on gold as a medium of exchange. Necessity for a $20 face value coin was further prompted by the fact that the Treasury Department was not yet issuing paper currency.

These coins are known as Double Eagles, as a result of being twice the size of Eagles or $10 gold pieces. Their composition was exactly the same as the lower denomination gold coins, .900 fine, or nine parts of 24K gold alloyed with one part copper. The Double Eagle contained .96750 of an ounce of pure gold, or just a slight fraction under one full ounce. With the copper content added, the coin's weight was more than an ounce, making it not only our highest denomination coin but the heaviest physically. However, it was smaller in diameter than the silver $1, at 34mm.

The first Double Eagles carried a portrait of Liberty facing left, by James B. Longacre, with a heraldic eagle on the reverse. Two significant changes were made during the use of this design, which was removed in 1907. In 1866 the motto IN GOD WE TRUST was added above the eagle, and in 1877 the statement of value (on the reverse) was changed from TWENTY D. to TWENTY DOLLARS.

PLEASE NOTE: THE PRICES THAT ARE LISTED REFLECT A GOLD SPOT PRICE OF $360.00 PER OUNCE.

DOUBLE EAGLES—LIBERTY HEAD, 1849–1866

Mint Mark is Below Eagle on Reverse

DATE	ABP IN VF-20	VF-20 V. FINE	EF-40 EX. FINE	MS-60 UNC.	PRF-65 PROOF
☐ 1849		UNIQUE—Only 1 Known in U.S. Mint Collection			
☐ 1850	(1,170,261) 450.00	625.00	900.00	6250.00	
☐ 1850O	(141,000) 550.00	750.000	1750.00	32500.00	
☐ 1851	(2,087,155) 450.00	650.00	775.00	4000.00	
☐ 1851O	(315,000) 500.00	650.00	800.00	16500.00	
☐ 1852	(2,053,026) 450.00	600.00	725.00	3000.00	
☐ 1852O	(190,000) 500.00	625.00	725.00	14500.00	
☐ 1853	(1,261,326) 450.00	600.00	610.00	5000.00	
☐ 1853O	(71,000) 540.00	650.00	1000.00	36500.00	
☐ 1854	(757,899) 450.00	610.00	650.00	5000.00	
☐ 1854O	(3,250)	20000.00	40000.00		
☐ 1854S	(141,469) 500.00	675.00	1000.00	6250.00	
☐ 1855	(364,666) 500.00	625.00	700.00	7100.00	
☐ 1855O	(8,000) 1650.00	2400.00	4800.00	62500.00	
☐ 1855S	(879,675) 500.00	725.00	1000.00	7000.00	
☐ 1856	(329,878) 450.00	600.00	700.00	8250.00	

DATE	ABP IN VF-20	VF-20 V. FINE	EF-40 EX. FINE	MS-60 UNC.	PRF-65 PROOF
☐ 1856O	(2,250) EXTREMELY RARE—EF-40—45000.00				
☐ 1856S	(1,189,750)				
	450.00	600.00	1000.00	6000.00	
☐ 1857	(439,375)				
	450.00	550.00	650.00	4000.00	
☐ 1857O	(30,000)				
	700.00	875.00	1500.00	16000.00	
☐ 1857S	(970,500)				
	450.00	675.00	1000.00	3000.00	
☐ 1858	(211,714)				
	500.00	700.00	775.00	5000.00	
☐ 1858O	(35,250)				
	900.00	1200.00	1700.00	15000.00	
☐ 1858S	(846,710)				
	450.00	700.00	1000.00	10500.00	
☐ 1859	(43,597)				
	700.00	1000.00	2100.00	30000.00	125000.00
☐ 1859S	(636,445)				
	450.00	725.00	950.00	6000.00	
☐ 1859O	(9,100)				
	2500.00	3200.00	6100.00	62500.00	
☐ 1860	(577,670)				
	450.00	625.00	650.00	3600.00	115000.00
☐ 1860O	(6,600)				
	2000.00	3200.00	7000.00	42000.00	
☐ 1860S	(544,950)				
	450.00	1150.00	1500.00	7250.00	
☐ 1861	(2,976,453)				
	450.00	550.00	600.00	2500.00	115000.00
☐ 1861O	(5,000)				
	1000.00	1400.00	3200.00	38500.00	
☐ 1861S	(768,000)				
	450.00	1000.00	1400.00	10500.00	
☐ 1862	(92,133)				
	550.00	800.00	1400.00	10500.00	115000.00
☐ 1862S	(854,173)				
	450.00	800.00	1300.00	13000.00	
☐ 1863	(142,790)				
	450.00	700.00	1100.00	12000.00	115000.00
☐ 1863S	(966,570)				
	450.00	710.00	1000.00	8000.00	

DATE	ABP IN VF-20	VF-20 V. FINE	EF-40 EX. FINE	MS-60 UNC.	PRF-65 PROOF
☐ 1864	(204,285) 500.00	600.00	725.00	8750.00	110000.00
☐ 1864S	(793,660) 600.00	800.00	1300.00	9500.00	
☐ 1865	(351,200) 500.00	600.00	750.00	6000.00	110000.00
☐ 1865S	(1,042,500) 500.00	575.00	750.00	4000.00	
☐ 1866S	(842,250) 1000.00	1500.00	3000.00	22500.00	

DOUBLE EAGLES—LIBERTY HEAD, 1866–1876, WITH MOTTO AND "TWENTY D" ON REVERSE

Mint Mark is Below Eagle on Reverse

DATE	ABP IN VF-20	VF-20 V. FINE	EF-40 EX. FINE	MS-60 UNC.	PRF-65 PROOF
☐ 1866	(698,775) 500.00	565.00	650.00	6000.00	100000.00
☐ 1866S	(842,250) 450.00	525.00	650.00	17000.00	
☐ 1867	(238,760) 450.00	535.00	650.00	1850.00	
☐ 1867S	(920,250) 450.00	510.00	650.00	16000.00	
☐ 1868	(98,600) 625.00	750.00	900.00	8000.00	100000.00
☐ 1868S	(837,500) 450.00	525.00	675.00	10000.00	
☐ 1869	(175,155) 450.00	600.00	710.00	5000.00	100000.00

DATE	ABP IN VF-20	VF-20 V. FINE	EF-40 EX. FINE	MS-60 UNC.	PRF-65 PROOF
☐ 1869S	(686,750)				
	450.00	525.00	570.00	4750.00	
☐ 1870	(155,185)				
	500.00	600.00	750.00	7500.00	12000.00
☐ 1870CC	(3,789)		100000.00		
☐ 1870S	(982,000)				
	425.00	550.00	600.00	5000.00	
☐ 1871	(80,150)				
	500.00	600.00	750.00	3750.00	100000.00
☐ 1871CC	(14,687)				
	1700.00	2200.00	4400.00	38000.00	
☐ 1871S	(928,000)				
	450.00	525.00	600.00	3500.00	
☐ 1872	(251,880)				
	450.00	525.00	600.00	2400.00	100000.00
☐ 1872CC	(29,650)				
	800.00	1000.00	1300.00	25000.00	
☐ 1872S	(780,000)				
	400.00	500.00	600.00	2400.00	
☐ 1873	(1,709,825)				
	450.00	525.00	600.00	1000.00	100000.00
☐ 1873CC	(22,410)				
	600.00	800.00	1750.00	25000.00	
☐ 1873S	(1,040,600)				
	450.00	500.00	650.00	1550.00	
☐ 1874	(366,800)				
	465.00	525.00	600.00	1600.00	100000.00
☐ 1874CC	(115,085)				
	525.00	575.00	700.00	8000.00	
☐ 1874S	(1,241,000)				
	450.00	525.00	600.00	1400.00	
☐ 1875	(295,740)				
	450.00	510.00	600.00	1000.00	125000.00
☐ 1875CC	(111,151)				
	550.00	600.00	710.00	2500.00	
☐ 1875S	(1,230,000)				
	450.00	525.00	600.00	1000.00	
☐ 1876	(583,905)				
	450.00	525.00	600.00	875.00	100000.00
☐ 1876CC	(138,441)				
	600.00	650.00	800.00	4500.00	

DATE	ABP IN VF-20	VF-20 V. FINE	EF-40 EX. FINE	MS-60 UNC.	PRF-65 PROOF
☐ 1876S	(1,597,000)				
	450.00	535.00	625.00	850.00	

Note: 1861 and 1861S both with A. C. Paquet Reverse; 61-5 Rare; 61 Ex. Rare

DOUBLE EAGLES—LIBERTY, 1877–1907, WITH MOTTO AND "TWENTY DOLLARS" ON REVERSE

Mint Mark is Below Eagle on Reverse

DATE	ABP IN VF-20	VF-20 V. FINE	EF-40 EX. FINE	MS-60 UNC.	PRF-65 PROOF
☐ 1877	(397,670)				
	450.00	500.00	520.00	750.00	75000.00
☐ 1877CC	(42,565)				
	550.00	720.00	850.00	15000.00	
☐ 1877S	(1,735,000)				
	450.00	500.00	650.00	775.00	
☐ 1878	(534,645)				
	450.00	500.00	600.00	700.00	75000.00
☐ 1878CC	(13,180)				
	700.00	850.00	1200.00	19500.00	
☐ 1878S	(1,739,000)				
	450.00	485.00	550.00	1000.00	
☐ 1879	(2,075,630)				
	450.00	500.00	550.00	900.00	75000.00
☐ 1879CC	(10,708)				
	800.00	1000.00	1450.00	23000.00	
☐ 1879O	(2,325)				
	2000.00	3200.00	4500.00	35000.00	
☐ 1879S	(1,223,800)				
	450.00	500.00	550.00	1150.00	

DATE	ABP IN VF-20	VF-20 V. FINE	EF-40 EX. FINE	MS-60 UNC.	PRF-65 PROOF
☐ 1880	(51,456)				
	450.00	525.00	550.00	3000.00	75000.00
☐ 1880S	(836,000)				
	425.00	500.00	550.00	1000.00	
☐ 1881	(2,260)				
	2500.00	3400.00	7000.00	40000.00	80000.00
☐ 1881S	(727,000)				
	425.00	500.00	600.00	1000.00	
☐ 1882	(630)				
	4500.00	8000.00	15000.00	52000.00	90000.00
☐ 1882CC	(39,140)				
	500.00	650.00	800.00	6000.00	
☐ 1882S	(1,125,000)				
	425.00	500.00	550.00	800.00	
☐ 1883 Proofs Only (40)				PRF-65	200000.00
☐ 1883CC	(59,962)				
	550.00	650.00	700.00	3800.00	
☐ 1883S	(1,189,000)				
	425.00	500.00	550.00	725.00	
☐ 1884 Proofs Only (71)				PRF-65	85000.00
☐ 1884CC	(81,139)				
	525.00	625.00	710.00	2400.00	
☐ 1884S	(916,000)				
	450.00	500.00	550.00	700.00	
☐ 1885	(828)				
	4000.00	5100.00	6500.00	35000.00	
☐ 1885CC	(9,450)				
	750.00	1000.00	1500.00	12000.00	
☐ 1885S	(683,500)				
	425.00	500.00	550.00	710.00	
☐ 1886	(1,106)				
	5000.00	6000.00	11000.00	42500.00	75000.00
☐ 1887 Proofs Only (121)				PRF-65	65000.00
☐ 1887S	(283,000)				
	435.00	500.00	600.00	700.00	
☐ 1888	(226,266)				
	435.00	500.00	550.00	710.00	65000.00
☐ 1888S	(859,600)				
	435.00	500.00	550.00	675.00	
☐ 1889	(44,111)				
	425.00	475.00	550.00	750.00	60000.00

DATE	ABP IN VF-20	VF-20 V. FINE	EF-40 EX. FINE	MS-60 UNC.	PRF-65 PROOF
☐ 1889CC	(30,945)				
	575.00	650.00	810.00	3500.00	
☐ 1889S	(774,700)				
	435.00	475.00	550.00	650.00	
☐ 1890	(75,995)				
	435.00	475.00	575.00	650.00	55000.00
☐ 1890CC	(91,209)				
	500.00	650.00	710.00	2600.00	
☐ 1890S	(802,750)				
	435.00	475.00	575.00	650.00	
☐ 1891	(1,442)				
	2200.00	2800.00	4100.00	22000.00	50000.00
☐ 1891CC	(5,000)				
	1000.00	1500.00	2550.00	13000.00	
☐ 1891S	(1,288,125)				
	435.00	475.00	500.00	650.00	
☐ 1892	(4,523)				
	650.00	800.00	1300.00	5000.00	50000.00
☐ 1892CC	(27,265)				
	500.00	600.00	800.00	3000.00	
☐ 1892S	(930,150)				
	435.00	475.00	500.00	600.00	
☐ 1893	(344,399)				
	450.00	475.00	500.00	600.00	50000.00
☐ 1893CC	(18,402)				
	600.00	675.00	800.00	2250.00	
☐ 1893S	(996,175)				
	435.00	475.00	510.00	600.00	
☐ 1894	(1,368,990)				
	450.00	450.00	500.00	600.00	50000.00
☐ 1894S	(1,048,550)				
	435.00	450.00	550.00	650.00	
☐ 1895	(1,114,656)				
	450.00	450.00	500.00	600.00	50000.00
☐ 1895S	(1,143,500)				
	435.00	450.00	500.00	625.00	
☐ 1896	(792,663)				
	435.00	450.00	500.00	600.00	50000.00
☐ 1896S	(1,403,925)				
	435.00	450.00	475.00	650.00	

DATE	ABP IN VF-20	VF-20 V. FINE	EF-40 EX. FINE	MS-60 UNC.	PRF-65 PROOF
☐ 1897	(1,383,261)				
	415.00	450.00	510.00	600.00	50000.00
☐ 1897S	(1,470,250)				
	415.00	425.00	525.00	600.00	
☐ 1898	(170,470)				
	415.00	450.00	525.00	750.00	50000.00
☐ 1898S	(2,575,175)				
	415.00	450.00	510.00	600.00	
☐ 1899	(1,669,384)				
	415.00	450.00	475.00	600.00	50000.00
☐ 1899S	(2,010,300)				
	415.00	450.00	500.00	650.00	
☐ 1900	(1,874,584)				
	415.00	425.00	500.00	600.00	50000.00
☐ 1900S	(2,459,500)				
	415.00	450.00	500.00	600.00	
☐ 1901	(111,526)				
	415.00	435.00	475.00	610.00	50000.00
☐ 1901S	(1,596,000)				
	415.00	450.00	500.00	600.00	
☐ 1902	(31,254)				
	415.00	475.00	550.00	950.00	50000.00
☐ 1902S	(1,753,625)				
	415.00	425.00	475.00	600.00	50000.00
☐ 1903	(287,428)				
	415.00	475.00	550.00	600.00	50000.00
☐ 1903S	(954,000)				
	415.00	465.00	500.00	625.00	
☐ 1904	(6,256,797)				
	400.00	450.00	500.00	600.00	50000.00
☐ 1904S	(5,134,175)				
	400.00	450.00	500.00	600.00	
☐ 1905	(59,011)				
	415.00	450.00	550.00	1200.00	50000.00
☐ 1905S	(1,813,000)				
	415.00	450.00	550.00	600.00	
☐ 1906	(69,690)				
	415.00	450.00	550.00	800.00	50000.00
☐ 1906D	(620,250)				
	400.00	450.00	475.00	600.00	

DATE	ABP IN VF-20	VF-20 V. FINE	EF-40 EX. FINE	MS-60 UNC.	PRF-65 PROOF
☐ 1906S	(2,065,750)				
	450.00	500.00	575.00	650.00	
☐ 1907	(1,451,864)				
	450.00	500.00	575.00	650.00	50000.00
☐ 1907D	(842,250)				
	450.00	485.00	525.00	600.00	
☐ 1907S	(2,165,800)				
	450.00	500.00	550.00	600.00	

DOUBLE EAGLES—$20.00 GOLD PIECES, 1907–1933

The Longacre Liberty design was replaced by the Saint-Gaudens in 1907, featuring a striding figure of Liberty holding a torch on the obverse and an eagle in flight on the reverse. A fact seldom mentioned is that this, of all representations of Liberty on our coins, was the only full-face likeness, the others being profiles or semiprofiles. Composition and weight remained as previously. The motto IN GOD WE TRUST, at first omitted on request of Theodore Roosevelt, was added by an Act of Congress in 1908. Striking of Double Eagles ceased in 1933. This final version of the mighty coin had a 90% gold/10% copper composition, with a weight of 33.436 grams (of which .96750 of an ounce was pure gold—almost a full ounce). Its diameter was 34mm.

As a speculative item for gold investors, the Double Eagle has enjoyed greater popularity and media publicity in recent months than ever in its history. This should not be surprising, as it contains very nearly an exact ounce of gold and its worth as bullion can be figured easily based upon daily gold quotations.

DOUBLE EAGLE LIBERTY STANDING
"ST. GAUDENS" ROMAN NUMERALS MCMVII

Roman Numeral High Relief, Wire Rim,
Plain Edge, 14 Rays over Capitol.
Three Folds on Liberty's skirt

DATE	ABP IN VF-20	VF-20 V. FINE	EF-40 EX. FINE	MS-60 UNC.	PRF-65 CH. PROOF
☐ 1907-MCMVII Ex. High Relief—Lettered Edge					
			SOTHEBY'S SALE 1996—825000.00		
☐ 1907-MCMVII Ex. High Relief—Plain Edge				VERY RARE:	
			NORWEB Proof 67 sold for $1.21 million		
☐ 1907 Flat Rim*					
	2500.00	3000.00	4000.00	8000.00	
☐ 1907 Wire Rim* (11,250)					
	2500.00	3000.00	4000.00	8000.00	

*Note: Separate mintage figures were not kept on the 1907 flat rim and wire rim varieties.

DOUBLE EAGLES—LIBERTY STANDING
"ST. GAUDENS," 1907–1908
DATE IN ARABIC NUMERALS,
NO MOTTO ON REVERSE

Mint Mark is Out on Obverse

DATE	MINTAGE	ABP IN VF-20	VF-20 V. FINE	EF-40 EX. FINE	MS-60 UNC.
☐ 1907*	361,667	415.00	430.00	475.00	600.00
☐ 1908	4,271,551	415.00	430.00	475.00	600.00

*Note: Small Letters on Edge, Large Letter on Edge—Unique.

DOUBLE EAGLES—LIBERTY STANDING "ST. GAUDENS," 1908–1933 WITH MOTTO ON REVERSE

Motto
IN GOD
WE TRUST

Mint Mark is Out on Obverse

DATE	ABP IN VF-20	VF-20 V. FINE	EF-40 EX. FINE	MS-60 UNC.	PRF-65 PROOF
☐ 1908D	(663,750)				
	400.00	450.00	475.00	600.00	
☐ 1908	(156,359)				
	400.00	425.00	475.00	575.00	37500.00
☐ 1908D	(349,500)				
	375.00	410.00	475.00	550.00	
☐ 1908S	(22,000)				
	600.00	725.00	950.00	3850.00	
☐ 1909	(161,282)				
	400.00	450.00	575.00	700.00	47500.00
☐ 1909 over 8					
	475.00	550.00	585.00	1400.00	
☐ 1909D	(52,500)				
	400.00	450.00	600.00	1400.00	
☐ 1909S	(2,774,925)				
	385.00	425.00	450.00	525.00	
☐ 1910	(482,167)				
	385.00	425.00	450.00	525.00	45000.00
☐ 1910D	(429,000)				
	385.00	425.00	450.00	525.00	
☐ 1910S	(2,128,250)				
	385.00	425.00	465.00	550.00	
☐ 1911	(197,350)				
	400.00	450.00	550.00	600.00	38500.00
☐ 1911D	(846,500)				
	385.00	425.00	500.00	575.00	
☐ 1911S	(775,750)				
	385.00	425.00	450.00	525.00	

DATE	ABP IN VF-20	VF-20 V. FINE	EF-40 EX. FINE	MS-60 UNC.	PRF-65 PROOF
☐ 1912	(149,824)				
	400.00	450.00	475.00	575.00	41500.00
☐ 1913	(168,838)				
	400.00	425.00	475.00	575.00	42000.00
☐ 1913D	(393,500)				
	385.00	425.00	450.00	510.00	
☐ 1913S	(34,000)				
	375.00	460.00	500.00	1250.00	
☐ 1914	(95,320)				
	350.00	425.00	450.00	800.00	45000.00
☐ 1914D	(453,000)				
	350.00	425.00	450.00	600.00	
☐ 1914S	(1,498,000)				
	375.00	425.00	450.00	550.00	
☐ 1915	(152,050)				
	375.00	425.00	450.00	550.00	50000.00
☐ 1915S	(567,500)				
	375.00	425.00	450.00	525.00	
☐ 1916S	(796,000)				
	375.00	425.00	450.00	525.00	
☐ 1920	(228,250)				
	375.00	425.00	450.00	550.00	
☐ 1920S	(558,000)				
	4500.00	6000.00	8000.00	27500.00	
☐ 1921	(528,500)				
	5500.00	7000.00	11000.00	40000.00	
☐ 1922	(1,375,500)				
	365.00	425.00	500.00	575.00	
☐ 1922S	(2,658,000)				
	350.00	400.00	500.00	875.00	
☐ 1923	(566,000)				
	365.00	425.00	500.00	575.00	
☐ 1923D	(1,702,000)				
	365.00	425.00	500.00	550.00	
☐ 1924	(4,323,500)				
	365.00	425.00	500.00	575.00	
☐ 1924D	(3,049,500)				
	700.00	800.00	900.00	2500.00	
☐ 1924S	(2,927,500)				
	600.00	750.00	1000.00	2250.00	

DATE	ABP IN VERY FINE	VERY FINE	EF-40 EX. FINE	MS-60 UNC.	PRF-65 PROOF
☐ 1925	(2,831,750) 365.00	400.00	475.00	550.00	
☐ 1925D	(2,938,500) 850.00	1000.00	1400.00	2750.00	
☐ 1925S	(2,776,500) 700.00	800.00	1000.00	6000.00	
☐ 1926	(816,750) 400.00	475.00	550.00	625.00	
☐ 1926D	(481,000) 1500.00	1850.00	2700.00	7150.00	
☐ 1926S	(2,041,500) 650.00	700.00	900.00	2000.00	
☐ 1927	(2,946,750) 400.00	475.00	550.00	625.00	
☐ 1927D	(180,000)		MS-65—725,000.00		
☐ 1927S	(3,107,000) 2400.00	3700.00	3700.00	12500.00	
☐ 1928	(8,816,000) 365.00	450.00	525.00	575.00	
☐ 1929	(1,779,750) 3000.00	4250.00	6500.00	9000.00	
☐ 1930S	(74,000.00) 4000.00	7000.00	9000.00	20000.00	
☐ 1931	(2,938,250) 4000.00	8000.00	10000.00	16500.00	
☐ 1931D	(106,500) 4500.00	5000.00	7250.00	12500.00	
☐ 1932	(1,101,750) 6250.00	7000.00	10000.00	12000.00	
☐ 1933*	(445,525)				

*Note: Never placed in circulation because of gold recall legislation.

COMMEMORATIVE COINAGE

Commemorative coinage—that is, coins whose designs present a departure from the normal types for their denomination—was first struck in the ancient world. Roman emperors delighted in issuing coins portraying members of the family or topical events; they served an important propaganda purpose. Commemorative coins must be distinguished from medals, as the former have a stated face value and can be spent as money while the latter serve a decorative function only. During the Mint's first century it coined no commemoratives whatever. Its first was the Columbian half dollar of 1892, issued in connection with the Columbia Exposition. To date the total has reached 158 pieces, of which one is a silver dollar; one a silver quarter; 143 are half dollars (comprising 48 major types); two are $2.50 gold pieces; two are $50 gold pieces; and nine are $1 gold pieces. There is some objection to including the $50 Quintuple Eagles as commemorative *coins*, as regular coins of this denomination were never issued. They do, however, bear a statement of face value and are spendable.

Commemorative coins are issued by a special Act of Congress and overseen by a committee established for the purpose. Sale of commemoratives is made to the public (and coin dealers) at an advance in price over the face value, this advance being excused on grounds that specimens supplied as choice and uncirculated have, presumably, sufficient collector appeal to be worth more than their stated denomination. While commemoratives have certainly not all advanced in price at a comparable pace, all have shown very healthy increases and proved excellent investments for their original or early purchasers.

A pair of medals is traditionally collected in conjunction with commemorative silver coins and careful note should be taken of them: the Octagonal North American Centennial, 1828–1925, designed by Opus Fraser, struck on thick and thin planchets in a total issue of 40,000 (the latter are scarcer); and the Wilson dollar, designed by George T. Morgan of Morgan dollar fame in connection with the opening of the Philippine Mint. The 2 Kroner commemoratives of 1936 issued by Sweden are also frequently collected with our commemoratives, though small in size and quite plentiful, as they relate to the Delaware Tercentenary, or 300th anniversary.

The extent to which commemorative coins have been used as money is not precisely determined but is thought to be very limited. As the original owners paid a premium for these coins it is not likely that many—except in time of dire need—would have cared to exchange them merely at face value. It should not automatically be presumed that specimens in less than Uncirculated condition were indeed used as money and passed through many hands. Their substandard preservation could well be the result of injury, ill-advised cleaning or mounting procedures, or wear received from handling in traveling from collection to collection. Nevertheless, discriminating buyers expect commemoratives to be in Uncirculated state and anything inferior is worth much less (the discount being sharper than for a circulating coin).

The existence of proofs among the commemorative series has aroused much debate. Commemoratives are occasionally seen as proofs, notably the Columbian and Isabella quarters, but this is no evidence that all or even a majority of commemoratives were available in proof state. It is easy to be confused on this point, as well-struck Uncirculated specimens frequently have a prooflike appearance.

The gold commemorative series began not long after the silver, in 1903. Far fewer gold commemoratives were issued, as the large physical size necessary for impressive designing resulted in a coin of very high face value. Experiments were made with $1 gold commemoratives, which some critics called puny, and goliaths of $50 denomination, which were indeed eye-catching but well beyond the budget of most citizens in those days. The value of these pieces in Extremely Fine condition is about one-third the price for Uncirculated—ample proof that most buying activity originates with numismatists rather than bullion speculators.

EARLY COMMEMORATIVE COINS, 1892–1954
COLUMBIAN EXPOSITION (Silver $.25)

Comparatively little notice was at first taken of this handsome commemorative, because the Columbian Exposition (at which it was issued) had already produced a commemorative and a larger one, in fifty-cent denomination. The Isabella quarter dollar, originally sold at the exposition for $1, soon became a popular favorite of collectors. Agitation for it was made by the fair's Board of Lady Managers, which may explain why it portrays a female on the obverse—Isabella of Spain, who helped finance Columbus' voyage round the world—and a symbol of "female industry" on its reverse. The coin was designed by C. E. Barber and struck in 1893.

DATE	MINTAGE	ABP IN MS-60	MS-60 UNC.	MS-65 UNC.
☐ 1893	24,214	300.00	600.00	3000.00

COLUMBIAN EXPOSITION (Silver $.50)

DATE	MINTAGE	ABP IN MS-60	MS-60 UNC.	MS-65 UNC.
☐ 1892	950,000	28.00	35.00	1000.00
☐ 1893	1,550,405	28.00	35.00	1200.00

LAFAYETTE MONUMENT (Silver $1.00)

The celebrated Lafayette dollar holds a special rank among commemoratives, being the first $1 denomination coin of its sort and the first to portray an American president. On its obverse is a profile bust of General Lafayette (the French officer so instrumental to our efforts in ending colonial domination) over which a profile of Washington is superimposed. The reverse carries a fine equestrian likeness of Lafayette, adapted from a statue put up in Paris as a gift from the American people. This coin was designed by C. E. Barber and struck in 1900. It was sold originally at twice the face value, with proceeds going to the Lafayette Memorial Commission.

DATE	MINTAGE	ABP IN MS-60	MS-60 UNC.	MS-65 UNC.
☐ 1900	36,026	400.00	600.00	9000.00

LOUISIANA PURCHASE EXPOSITION (Gold $1.00)

1903–Jefferson

1903–McKinley

DATE	MINTAGE	ABP IN MS-60	MS-60 UNC.	MS-65 UNC.
☐ 1903 Jefferson	17,500	270.00	450.00	2400.00
☐ 1903 McKinley	17,500	260.00	425.00	2600.00

LEWIS AND CLARK EXPOSITION (Gold $1.00)

DATE	MINTAGE	ABP IN MS-60	MS-60 UNC.	MS-65 UNC.
☐ 1904	10,025	480.00	800.00	6500.00
☐ 1905	10,041	600.00	1000.00	14000.00

PANAMA-PACIFIC EXPOSITION (Silver $.50)

DATE	MINTAGE	ABP IN MS-60	MS-60 UNC.	MS-65 UNC.
☐ 1915S	27,134	220.00	400.00	2200.00

PANAMA-PACIFIC EXPOSITION (Gold $2.50)

DATE	MINTAGE	ABP IN MS-60	MS-60 UNC.	MS-65 UNC.
☐ 1915S	6,766	950.00	1800.00	5500.00

PANAMA-PACIFIC EXPOSITION (Gold $1.00)

Panama-Pacific

DATE	MINTAGE	ABP IN MS-60	MS-60 UNC.	MS-65 UNC.
☐ 1915S	15,000	275.00	400.00	2000.00

PANAMA-PACIFIC EXPOSITION (Gold $50.00)

This huge coin, containing nearly $2\frac{1}{2}$ ounces of gold, was not the world's largest gold piece but by far the most substantial coin of that metal struck by the U.S. government. (To give some indication of changes in the market from 1915, the date of issue, until today, $50 worth of gold today is about one-sixth of an ounce.) It was issued for the Panama-Pacific Exposition and was struck in two varieties, one with round and one with octagonal edge, the former being somewhat scarcer and more valuable. Minerva is pictured on the obverse and the Athenian state symbol, the owl, representative of wisdom, on the reverse. The place of issue was San Francisco and the designer Robert Aitken. This is definitely not a piece for bullion speculators as its value is many times that of the gold content and under no circumstances would a $50 Panama-Pacific—or any U.S. gold commemorative—be melted down.

ROUND

DATE	MINTAGE	ABP IN MS-60	MS-60 UNC.	MS-65 UNC.
☐ 1915S	483	18000.00	30000.00	125000.00

OCTAGONAL

DATE	MINTAGE	ABP IN MS-60	MS-60 UNC.	MS-65 UNC.
☐ 1915S	645	16000.00	25000.00	115000.00
☐ COMPLETE SET, 50.00 Gold Round and Octagonal, 2.50 and 1.00 Gold and Half Dollar Silver		50000.00	90000.00	19000.00
☐ DOUBLE SET IN ORIGINAL FRAME—Superior Sale, January 1985—				160,000.00

Note: The double sets were authorized Mint issues. They consisted of two specimens of each coin, mounted so that both sides could be seen. The original price in 1915 was $400.

McKINLEY MEMORIAL (Gold $1.00)

DATE	MINTAGE	ABP IN MS-60	MS-60 UNC.	MS-65 UNC.
☐ 1916	10,003	300.00	400.00	1800.00
☐ 1917	8,004	400.00	625.00	3000.00

ILLINOIS CENTENNIAL (Silver $.50)

DATE	MINTAGE	ABP IN MS-60	MS-60 UNC.	MS-65 UNC.
☐ 1918	100,058	75.00	110.00	550.00

MAINE CENTENNIAL (Silver $.50)

DATE	MINTAGE	ABP IN MS-60	MS-60 UNC.	MS-65 UNC.
☐ 1920	50,028	75.00	100.00	625.00

PILGRIM TERCENTENARY (Silver $.50)

DATE	MINTAGE	ABP IN MS-60	MS-60 UNC.	MS-65 UNC.
☐ 1920	152,112	50.00	80.00	475.00
☐ 1921	20,053	85.00	140.00	725.00

MISSOURI CENTENNIAL (Silver $.50)

DATE	MINTAGE	ABP IN MS-60	MS-60 UNC.	MS-65 UNC.
☐ 1921	15,428	300.00	500.00	6500.00
☐ 1921 Same with 2 × 4 (Above 1821)				
	5,000	325.00	500.00	6250.00

ALABAMA CENTENNIAL (Silver $.50)

DATE	MINTAGE	ABP IN MS-60	MS-60 UNC.	MS-65 UNC.
☐ 1921	59,038	160.00	350.00	2250.00
☐ 1921 Same with 2 × 2 on Obverse				
	6,006	200.00	350.00	2600.00

GRANT MEMORIAL (Silver $.50)

DATE	MINTAGE	ABP IN MS-60	MS-60 UNC.	MS-65 UNC.
☐ 1922	67,405	75.00	120.00	825.00
☐ 1922 Same with Star on Obverse				
	4,256	650.00	1000.00	7500.00

GRANT MEMORIAL (Gold $1.00)

1922–Grant

DATE	MINTAGE	ABP IN MS-60	MS-60 UNC.	MS-65 UNC.
☐ 1922	5,016	850.00	1400.00	2850.00
☐ 1922 Same with Star	5,000	900.00	1400.00	2800.00

MONROE DOCTRINE CENTENNIAL (Silver $.50)

DATE	MINTAGE	ABP IN MS-60	MS-60 UNC.	MS-65 UNC.
☐ 1923S	274,077	28.00	50.00	2650.00

HUGUENOT-WALLOON TERCENTENARY (Silver $.50)

DATE	MINTAGE	ABP IN MS-60	MS-60 UNC.	MS-65 UNC.
☐ 1924	142,080	40.00	120.00	575.00

LEXINGTON-CONCORD SESQUICENTENNIAL (Silver $.50)

DATE	MINTAGE	ABP IN MS-60	MS-60 UNC.	MS-65 UNC.
☐ 1925	162,013	40.00	100.00	700.00

STONE MOUNTAIN MEMORIAL (Silver $.50)

DATE	MINTAGE	ABP IN MS-60	MS-60 UNC.	MS-65 UNC.
☐ 1925	1,314,709	20.00	50.00	225.00

CALIFORNIA DIAMOND JUBILEE (Silver $.50)

DATE	MINTAGE	ABP IN MS-60	MS-60 UNC.	MS-65 UNC.
☐ 1925S	86,594	70.00	140.00	880.00

FORT VANCOUVER CENTENNIAL (Silver $.50)

DATE	MINTAGE	ABP IN MS-60	MS-60 UNC.	MS-65 UNC.
☐ 1925	14,944	150.00	340.00	1275.00

AMERICAN INDEPENDENCE
SESQUICENTENNIAL (Silver $.50)

DATE	MINTAGE	ABP IN MS-60	MS-60 UNC.	MS-65 UNC.
☐ 1926	141,120	60.00	100.00	5250.00

AMERICAN INDEPENDENCE
SESQUICENTENNIAL (Gold $2.50)

Philadelphia

DATE	MINTAGE	ABP IN MS-60	MS-60 UNC.	MS-65 UNC.
☐ 1926	46,019	200.00	375.00	3850.00

OREGON TRAIL MEMORIAL (Silver $.50)

DATE	MINTAGE	ABP IN MS-60	MS-60 UNC.	MS-65 UNC.
☐ 1926	47,955	70.00	110.00	210.00
☐ 1926S	83,055	70.00	110.00	210.00
☐ 1928	6,028	110.00	185.00	325.00
☐ 1933D	5,008	160.00	250.00	435.00

DATE	MINTAGE	ABP IN MS-60	MS-60 UNC.	MS-65 UNC.
☐ 1934D	7,006	100.00	165.00	290.00
☐ 1936	10,006	75.00	130.00	225.00
☐ 1936S	5,006	100.00	145.00	275.00
☐ 1937D	12,008	100.00	150.00	200.00
☐ 1938 Set PDS	6,005	400.00	600.00	825.00
☐ 1939 Set PDS	3,004	850.00	1200.00	2200.00

VERMONT-BENNINGTON SESQUICENTENNIAL
(Silver $.50)

DATE	MINTAGE	ABP IN MS-60	MS-60 UNC.	MS-65 UNC.
☐ 1927	28,162	125.00	180.00	875.00

HAWAII DISCOVERY SESQUICENTENNIAL
(Silver $.50)

DATE	MINTAGE	ABP IN MS-60	MS-60 UNC.	MS-65 UNC.
☐ 1928	9,958	1000.00	1400.00	5000.00

MARYLAND TERCENTENARY (Silver $.50)

DATE	MINTAGE	ABP IN MS-60	MS-60 UNC.	MS-65 UNC.
☐ 1934	25,015	95.00	125.00	400.00

TEXAS INDEPENDENCE CENTENNIAL (Silver $.50)

DATE	MINTAGE	ABP IN MS-60	MS-60 UNC.	MS-65 UNC.
☐ 1934	61,413	60.00	120.00	195.00
☐ 1935 Set PDS	10,007	200.00	325.00	500.00
☐ 1936 Set PDS	9,039	200.00	325.00	500.00
☐ 1937 Set PDS	6,605	215.00	325.00	500.00
☐ 1938 Set PDS	3,775	400.00	650.00	1000.00

DANIEL BOONE BICENTENNIAL (Silver $.50)

DATE	MINTAGE	ABP IN MS-60	MS-60 UNC.	MS-65 UNC.
☐ 1934	10,007	65.00	100.00	200.00
☐ 1935 Set PDS	5,005	150.00	300.00	475.00

DATE	MINTAGE	ABP IN MS-60	MS-60 UNC.	MS-65 UNC.
☐ 1935 Set (1934 Reverse)				
	2,003	400.00	700.00	2000.00
☐ 1936 Set PDS	5,006	175.00	300.00	525.00
☐ 1937 Set PDS	2,506	185.00	700.00	1200.00
☐ 1938 Set PDS	2,100	375.00	900.00	1600.00

CONNECTICUT TERCENTENNARY (Silver $.50)

DATE	MINTAGE	ABP IN MS-60	MS-60 UNC.	MS-65 UNC.
☐ 1935	25,018	110.00	200.00	600.00

ARKANSAS CENTENNIAL (Silver $.50)

DATE	MINTAGE	ABP IN MS-60	MS-60 UNC.	MS-65 UNC.
☐ 1936 Single Coin		60.00	85.00	300.00
☐ 1935 Set PDS	5,505	180.00	250.00	750.00
☐ 1936 Set PDS	9,660	150.00	250.00	1200.00
☐ 1937 Set PDS	5,505	160.00	250.00	1200.00
☐ 1938 Set PDS	3,155	250.00	400.00	2200.00
☐ 1939 Set PDS	2,104	400.00	700.00	3000.00

ARKANSAS-ROBINSON (Silver $.50)

DATE	MINTAGE	ABP IN MS-60	MS-60 UNC.	MS-65 UNC.
☐ 1936	25,265	50.00	85.00	300.00

HUDSON, NEW YORK, SESQUICENTENNIAL (Silver $.50)

DATE	MINTAGE	ABP IN MS-60	MS-60 UNC.	MS-65 UNC.
☐ 1935	10,008	275.00	550.00	1400.00

CALIFORNIA-PACIFIC EXPOSITION, SAN DIEGO (Silver $.50)

DATE	MINTAGE	ABP IN MS-60	MS-60 UNC.	MS-65 UNC.
☐ 1935S	70,132	40.00	80.00	125.00
☐ 1936D	30,082	45.00	80.00	125.00

OLD SPANISH TRAIL (Silver $.50)

DATE	MINTAGE	ABP IN MS-60	MS-60 UNC.	MS-65 UNC.
☐ 1935	10,008	500.00	825.00	1100.00

PROVIDENCE, RHODE ISLAND, TERCENTENNARY (Silver $.50)

DATE	MINTAGE	ABP IN MS-60	MS-60 UNC.	MS-65 UNC.
☐ 1936		50.00	95.00	230.00
☐ 1936 Set	15,010	150.00	250.00	725.00

CLEVELAND CENTENNIAL AND GREAT LAKES EXPOSITION (Silver $.50)

DATE	MINTAGE	ABP IN MS-60	MS-60 UNC.	MS-65 UNC.
☐ 1936	50,030	50.00	75.00	250.00

WISCONSIN TERRITORIAL CENTENNIAL
(Silver $.50)

DATE	MINTAGE	ABP IN MS-60	MS-60 UNC.	MS-65 UNC.
☐ 1936	25,015	120.00	175.00	240.00

CINCINNATI MUSIC CENTER (Silver $.50)

DATE	MINTAGE	ABP IN MS-60	MS-60 UNC.	MS-65 UNC.
☐ 1936		150.00	250.00	575.00
☐ 1936 Set PDS	5,005	550.00	750.00	1800.00

LONG ISLAND TERCENTENARY (Silver $.50)

DATE	MINTAGE	ABP IN MS-60	MS-60 UNC.	MS-65 UNC.
☐ 1936	81,826	60.00	85.00	450.00

YORK COUNTY, MAINE, TERCENTENARY
(Silver $.50)

DATE	MINTAGE	ABP IN MS-60	MS-60 UNC.	MS-65 UNC.
☐ 1936	25,015	100.00	150.00	225.00

BRIDGEPORT, CONNECTICUT, CENTENNIAL
(Silver $.50)

DATE	MINTAGE	ABP IN MS-60	MS-60 UNC.	MS-65 UNC.
☐ 1936	25,015	70.00	115.00	285.00

LYNCHBURG, VIRGINIA, SESQUICENTENNIAL
(Silver $.50)

DATE	MINTAGE	ABP IN MS-60	MS-60 UNC.	MS-65 UNC.
☐ 1936	20,013	80.00	155.00	320.00

ALBANY, NEW YORK, CHARTER 250TH ANNIVERSARY (Silver $.50)

DATE	MINTAGE	ABP IN MS-60	MS-60 UNC.	MS-65 UNC.
☐ 1936	17,671	150.00	210.00	375.00

ELGIN, ILLINOIS, PIONEER MEMORIAL (Silver $.50)

DATE	MINTAGE	ABP IN MS-60	MS-60 UNC.	MS-65 UNC.
☐ 1936	20,015	140.00	200.00	240.00

SAN FRANCISCO–OAKLAND BAY BRIDGE (Silver $.50)

DATE	MINTAGE	ABP IN MS-60	MS-60 UNC.	MS-65 UNC.
☐ 1936	71,424	85.00	150.00	325.00

COLUMBIA, SOUTH CAROLINA, SESQUICENTENNIAL (Silver $.50)

DATE	MINTAGE	ABP IN MS-60	MS-60 UNC.	MS-65 UNC.
☐ 1936		120.00	160.00	220.00
☐ 1936 Set PDS	8,009	310.00	525.00	675.00

DELAWARE TERCENTENARY (Silver $.50)

DATE	MINTAGE	ABP IN MS-60	MS-60 UNC.	MS-65 UNC.
☐ 1936	20,993	150.00	220.00	345.00

BATTLE OF GETTYSBURG 75TH ANNIVERSARY (Silver $.50)

DATE	MINTAGE	ABP IN MS-60	MS-60 UNC.	MS-65 UNC.
☐ 1936	26,030	175.00	300.00	560.00

NORFOLK, VIRGINIA, BICENTENNIAL AND TERCENTENARY (Silver $.50)

DATE	MINTAGE	ABP IN MS-60	MS-60 UNC.	MS-65 UNC.
☐ 1936	16,936	250.00	360.00	450.00

ROANOKE COLONIZATION 350TH ANNIVERSARY (Silver $.50)

DATE	MINTAGE	ABP IN MS-60	MS-60 UNC.	MS-65 UNC.
☐ 1937	29,030	140.00	180.00	250.00

BATTLE OF ANTIETAM 75TH ANNIVERSARY (Silver $.50)

DATE	MINTAGE	ABP IN MS-60	MS-60 UNC.	MS-65 UNC.
☐ 1937	18,028	270.00	435.00	600.00

NEW ROCHELLE, NEW YORK, 250TH ANNIVERSARY (Silver $.50)

DATE	MINTAGE	ABP IN MS-60	MS-60 UNC.	MS-65 UNC.
☐ 1938	15,226	200.00	300.00	375.00

IOWA STATEHOOD CENTENNIAL (Silver $.50)

DATE	MINTAGE	ABP IN MS-60	MS-60 UNC.	MS-65 UNC.
☐ 1946	100,057	50.00	90.00	130.00

BOOKER T. WASHINGTON MEMORIAL ($.50)

DATE	MINTAGE	ABP IN MS-60	MS-60 UNC.	MS-65 UNC.
☐ 1946		16.00	20.00	40.00
☐ 1946 Set PDS	200,113	20.00	40.00	140.00
☐ 1947 Set PDS	100,017	30.00	70.00	270.00
☐ 1948 Set PDS	8,005	60.00	120.00	190.00
☐ 1949 Set PDS	6,004	120.00	210.00	300.00
☐ 1950 Set PDS	6,004	75.00	100.00	170.00
☐ 1951 Set PDS	7,004	65.00	115.00	180.00

BOOKER T. WASHINGTON–
GEORGE WASHINGTON CARVER (Silver $.50)

DATE	MINTAGE	ABP IN MS-60	MS-60 UNC.	MS-65 UNC.
☐ 1951		15.00	20.00	60.00
☐ 1951 Set PDS	10,004	45.00	80.00	500.00
☐ 1952 Set PDS	8,006	45.00	75.00	410.00
☐ 1953 Set PDS	8,003	55.00	80.00	550.00
☐ 1954 Set PDS	12,006	55.00	80.00	485.00

MODERN COMMEMORATIVE COINS, 1982 TO DATE

Note: Regarding ABP prices, dealers will usually discount for coins that are not in the original packaging.

GEORGE WASHINGTON'S BIRTHDAY 250TH ANNIVERSARY (Silver $.50)

The U.S. resumed its commemorative coin program with this silver half dollar in 1982, after a lapse of twenty-eight years. The reason for its long suspension was that the value of silver far exceeded the traditional face values of commemorative coins. However, since commemoratives are issued for collectors and not for circulation, it was finally decided that the public would not object to low face values. The year 1982 marked the 250th anniversary of George Washington's birth. This was considered an appropriate occasion for resumption of the commemorative series. This coin is .900 silver and has the same specifications as earlier silver commemorative half dollars, and likewise the same as circulating half dollars up to 1964. The obverse carries an equestrian portrait of Washington looking left, with a view of Mount Vernon on the reverse. The artistic style was designed to conform, at least generally, to that of the majority of earlier commemorative halves.

DATE	MINTAGE	ABP	MS-65 UNC.	PRF-65 PROOF
☐ 1982S Proofs Only	4,894,044	3.50		6.00
☐ 1982D	2,210,458	3.50	5.75	

OLYMPIAD GAMES XXIII, LOS ANGELES (Silver $1.00)

The set of two commemorative silver dollars issued in 1983 and 1984 for the Los Angeles Olympic Games marked the first $1 silver commemoratives in more than eighty years. Enormous publicity and controversy surrounded these coins, concerning their designs, face values, and the method of distributing them to the public. The first coin, dated 1983, pictures a discus thrower on the obverse with a profile bust of an eagle on the reverse. The second, dated 1984, shows the entrance to the Los Angeles Coliseum (site of the 1984 games) on the obverse, and a full-length eagle on the reverse. These coins have the same specifications as the standard U.S. silver dollar, last struck in 1935, and contain approximately three-fourths of an ounce of .999+ silver. Debate arose over whether or not they should show a face value and, if so, the amount. It was decided that they should have a $1 face value, in spite of the fact that they contain several times that value in silver. This virtually insured that they—unlike some commemoratives of the past—will never end up in circulation. Yet they are legal tender, and could be passed at $1 if an owner desired.

DATE	MINTAGE	ABP	MS-65 UNC.	PRF-65 PROOF
☐ 1983P	294,543	6.00	12.00	
☐ 1983S	1,751,039	5.00	12.00	16.00
☐ 1983D	174,014	7.50	12.00	
☐ 1984P	217,954	10.00	14.00	
☐ 1984S	1,917,885	15.00	24.00	16.00
☐ 1984D	116,675	15.00	25.00	

OLYMPIAD GAMES XXIII, LOS ANGELES
(Gold $10.00)

This $10 gold commemorative, carrying the date 1984, marked U.S. re-entry into commemorative gold—which many forecasters claimed would never occur. Issuance of a gold commemorative under modern circumstances called for a drastic change in approach. Traditionally (prior to the Gold Recall Act of 1933), our gold commemoratives contained slightly less than their face value in gold, just as did our gold circulating coins. With today's much higher gold prices, the Los Angeles XXIII Olympiad $10 gold commemorative contains about twenty times its face value in gold. They were distributed to the public at prices which took this factor into account, as well as including a handling fee (which many persons in the numismatic community charged to be exorbitant). A pair of torch bearers is shown on the obverse, symbolizing the ceremony of "lighting the Olympic flame" to open the games. The American eagle symbol with stars, arrows, and branches is pictured on the reverse. This coin has the same specifications used in striking circulating $10 gold pieces, prior to their discontinuance.

DATE	MINTAGE	ABP	MS-65 UNC.	PRF-65 PROOF
☐ 1984P	33,309	200.00		275.00
☐ 1984D	34,533	200.00		250.00
☐ 1984S	48,551	185.00		235.00
☐ 1984W*	456,971	200.00	220.00	235.00

*Note: "W" mint mark indicates West Point, New York.

STATUE OF LIBERTY–ELLIS ISLAND CENTENNIAL (Clad $.50)

The U.S. Statue of Liberty Coin Program honored the centennial of the Statue of Liberty and Ellis Island. It was the most successful commemorative coin program in the history of the Mint. More than 15 million gold, silver, and clad Liberty coins were sold, raising more than $83 million in surcharges used to renovate the Statue of Liberty and Ellis Island.

DATE	MINTAGE	ABP	MS-65 UNC.	PRF-65 PROOF
☐ 1986D	928,008	3.50	5.75	
☐ 1986S	6,925,627	4.00		6.00

STATUE OF LIBERTY–ELLIS ISLAND CENTENNIAL (Silver $1.00)

The Statue of Liberty commemorative silver dollar, .900 Fine: This beautiful coin commemorates and celebrates the Statue of Liberty. The obverse portrays a classic likeness of our Lady of Liberty standing on Ellis Island. The reverse shows the Torch of Liberty with the famous inscription inviting all of those who love and look for freedom.

DATE	MINTAGE	ABP	MS-65 UNC.	PRF-65 PROOF
☐ 1986P	723,635	9.00	12.00	
☐ 1986S	6,414,638	9.00		12.00

STATUE OF LIBERTY–ELLIS ISLAND CENTENNIAL (Gold Half Eagle)

The Statue of Liberty $5 gold commemorative: The obverse depicts the head of the Statue of Liberty and the date. The reverse is a version of a flying eagle.

DATE	MINTAGE	ABP	MS-65 UNC.	PRF-65 PROOF
☐ 1986W	499,261	60.00	85.00	120.00

CONSTITUTION BICENTENNIAL (Silver $1.00)

The U.S. Constitution Coin Program commemorated the bicentennial of the Constitution. More than $52.6 million in surcharges was raised from the sale of more than 4 million gold and silver coins. All surcharges went to reduce the national debt.

The Constitution silver dollar commemorative, .900 Fine: The obverse shows a quill pen and the words WE THE PEOPLE superimposed over the Constitution document. The reverse depicts a group of "We the People."

DATE	MINTAGE	ABP	MS-65 UNC.	PRF-65 PROOF
☐ 1987P	451,629	6.00	11.00	
☐ 1987S	2,747,116	6.00		12.00

CONSTITUTION BICENTENNIAL (Gold Half Eagle)

The Constitution $5 gold commemorative: The obverse depicts a flying eagle with a superimposed quill pen. The reverse again shows the quill pen over which is superimposed WE THE PEOPLE.

DATE	MINTAGE	ABP	MS-65 UNC.	PRF-65 PROOF
☐ 1987W	865,884	90.00	110.00	130.00

OLYMPIAD GAMES XXIV, CALGARY, SEOUL (Silver $1.00)

The 1988 U.S. Olympic Coin Program was created to raise money for the U.S. Olympic Committee to fund Olympic and amateur training programs. More than $22.9 million, generated by the sale of the 1.9 million Olympic gold and silver coins, was contributed to the U.S. Olympic Committee.

DATE	MINTAGE	ABP	MS-65 UNC.	PRF-65 PROOF
☐ 1988D	191,368	7.00	12.00	
☐ 1988S	1,359,366	6.00		10.00

OLYMPIAD GAMES XXIV, CALGARY, SEOUL
(Gold Half Eagle)

DATE	MINTAGE	ABP	MS-65 UNC.	PRF-65 PROOF
☐ 1988W	344,378	95.00	115.00	165.00

BICENTENNIAL OF CONGRESS (Clad Half Dollar)

This coin program commemorated the bicentennial of the U.S. Congress. More than $14.6 million in surcharges was raised from the sale of more than 2 million gold, silver, and clad Congressional coins to restore and preserve public areas of the U.S. Capitol.

DATE	MINTAGE	ABP	MS-65 UNC.	PRF-65 PROOF
☐ 1989D	163,753	7.00	10.00	
☐ 1989S	767,897	3.00		6.00

BICENTENNIAL OF CONGRESS (Silver $1.00)

DATE	MINTAGE	ABP	MS-65 UNC.	PRF-65 PROOF
☐ 1989D	135,203	10.00	15.00	
☐ 1989S	762,198	9.00		12.00

BICENTENNIAL OF CONGRESS
(Gold Half Eagle)

DATE	MINTAGE	ABP	MS-65 UNC.	PRF-65 PROOF
☐ 1989W	211,589	80.00	115.00	115.00

EISENHOWER BIRTHDAY CENTENNIAL
(Silver $1.00)

The 1990 Dwight David Eisenhower commemorative coin celebrated the 100th anniversary of the birth of the 34th president of the United States, and honored his military career and peacetime leadership. More than 1.3 million Eisenhower centennial silver dollar coins were sold, generating more than $9.7 million in surcharges to reduce the national debt.

DATE	ABP	MS-65 UNC.	PRF-65 PROOF
☐ 1990P	10.00		15.00
☐ 1990W	8.00	14.00	

MOUNT RUSHMORE 50TH ANNIVERSARY
(Clad Half Dollar)

The Mount Rushmore anniversary coins commemorated the 50th anniversary of the completion of the historic Mount Rushmore National Monument. Approximately $12 million in surcharges raised from the sale of these coins has been paid to the Mount Rushmore National Memorial Society to assist in efforts to improve, enlarge, and renovate the Memorial.

DATE	ABP	MS-65 UNC.	PRF-65 PROOF
☐ 1991D	10.00	14.00	
☐ 1991S	9.00		13.00

MOUNT RUSHMORE 50TH ANNIVERSARY
(Silver $1.00)

DATE	ABP	MS-65 UNC.	PRF-65 PROOF
☐ 1991P	20.00	25.00	
☐ 1991S	20.00		25.00

MOUNT RUSHMORE 50TH ANNIVERSARY
(Gold Half Eagle)

DATE	ABP	MS-65 UNC.	PRF-65 PROOF
☐ 1991W	100.00	135.00	160.00

KOREAN WAR 38TH ANNIVERSARY
(Silver $1.00)

The Korean War Memorial coin commemorated the 38th anniversary of the end of the Korean War. A surcharge of $7 per coin sold was designated to assist in the construction of the Korean War Veterans Memorial to be built in Washington, D.C. More than $5.8 million was raised from the sale of more than 830,000 coins. President Bush participated in the ground-breaking ceremony for the Memorial on June 14, 1992 (Flag Day).

DATE	ABP	MS-65 UNC.	PRF-65 PROOF
☐ 1991D	11.00	16.00	
☐ 1991S	12.00		18.00

UNITED SERVICE ORGANIZATION'S 50TH ANNIVERSARY (Silver $1.00)

The United Services Organization coin commemorated the 50th anniversary of the USO and honored its continuing commitment to serve the needs of America's Armed Forces at home and abroad. Sales of the silver dollar resulted in more than $3.1 million in surcharges divided equally between the USO (to fund the organization's many programs worldwide for the members of the United States military and their families) and the Treasury Department (to reduce the national debt).

DATE	ABP	MS-65 UNC.	PRF-65 PROOF
☐ 1991D	12.00	16.00	
☐ 1991S	9.00		16.00

OLYMPIAD GAMES XXV, ALBERTVILLE, BARCELONA (Clad $.50)

Designs for the 1992 U.S. Olympic gold $5, silver $1, and clad $.50 coins were selected after an open coin design competition held by the U.S. Mint. Surcharges included in the price of each coin were paid to the United States Olympic Committee to train and finance U.S. Olympic athletes. More than 1.4 million coins were sold, resulting in more than $9 million in contributions to the U.S. Olympic Committee.

DATE	ABP	MS-65 UNC.	PRF-65 PROOF
☐ 1992P	4.00	6.00	
☐ 1992S	6.00		9.00

OLYMPIAD GAMES XXV, ALBERTVILLE, BARCELONA (Silver $1.00)

DATE	ABP	MS-65 UNC.	PRF-65 PROOF
☐ 1992D	17.00	25.00	
☐ 1992S	18.00		28.00

OLYMPIAD GAMES XXV, ALBERTVILLE, BARCELONA (Gold Half Eagle)

DATE	ABP	MS-65 UNC.	PRF-65 PROOF
☐ 1992W	90.00	130.00	135.00

WHITE HOUSE BICENTENNIAL (Silver $1.00)

The Silver Dollar Coin Program commemorated the 200th anniversary of the laying of the White House cornerstone. The authorized mintage of 500,000 coins, with a surcharge of $10 per coin, sold out within the pre-issue period. Surcharges of $5 million went to the White House Endowment Fund to maintain the historic public rooms of the White House and to support the White House collection of fine art and historic furnishings.

OBVERSE   REVERSE

DATE	ABP	MS-65 UNC.	PRF-65 PROOF
☐ 1992D	22.00	24.00	
☐ 1992W	20.00		25.00

COLUMBUS DISCOVERY QUINCENTENNIAL
(Clad $.50)

The Columbus Quincentenary Coin Program celebrated the 500th anniversary of the discovery of America by Christopher Columbus. Sales of the coins raised more than $7.6 million in surcharges to endow the Christopher Columbus Fellowship Foundation. The Foundation will award fellowships to promote "new discoveries in all fields of endeavor for the benefit of mankind."

OBVERSE   REVERSE

DATE	ABP	MS-65 UNC.	PRF-65 PROOF
☐ 1992D	10.00	13.00	
☐ 1992S	10.00		13.00

COLUMBUS DISCOVERY QUINCENTENNIAL
(Silver $1.00)

OBVERSE   REVERSE

DATE	ABP	MS-65 UNC.	PRF-65 PROOF
☐ 1992P	9.00		26.00
☐ 1992D	9.00	22.00	

COLUMBUS DISCOVERY QUINCENTENNIAL
(Gold Half Eagle)

OBVERSE   REVERSE

DATE	ABP	MS-65 UNC.	PRF-65 PROOF
☐ 1992W	110.00	135.00	150.00

BILL OF RIGHTS—JAMES MADISON (Clad $.50)

The gold $5, silver $1, and silver $.50 coins commemorate the first ten amendments to the Constitution of the United States, known as the Bill of Rights, and the role that James Madison, the fourth president of the United States, played in supporting their adoption. Sales of the coins raised more than $9 million in surcharges for the James Madison Memorial Fellowship Trust Fund to encourage teaching and graduate study of the Constitution of the United States.

OBVERSE   REVERSE

DATE	ABP	MS-65 UNC.	PRF-65 PROOF
☐ 1993S	8.00		13.00
☐ 1993W	9.50	14.00	

BILL OF RIGHTS—JAMES MADISON
(Silver $1.00)

OBVERSE   REVERSE

DATE	ABP	MS-65 UNC.	PRF-65 PROOF
☐ 1993D	11.00	16.00	
☐ 1993S	11.00		16.00

BILL OF RIGHTS—JAMES MADISON
(Gold Half Eagle)

OBVERSE   REVERSE

DATE	ABP	MS-65 UNC.	PRF-65 PROOF
☐ 1993W	100.00	160.00	140.00

WW II 50TH ANNIVERSARY
(Clad $.50)

The gold $5, silver $1, and clad $.50 coins commemorate the involvement of the United States in World War II. Sales of the coins raised more than $7 million in surcharges to help fund the construction of a memorial in Washington, D.C. to honor members of the Armed Forces of the United States who served in World War II, and to create a United States D-Day and Battle of Normandy Memorial in Normandy, France.

OBVERSE

REVERSE

DATE	ABP	MS-65 UNC.	PRF-65 PROOF
☐ 1993P	7.00	10.00	14.00

WW II 50TH ANNIVERSARY
(Silver $1.00)

OBVERSE

REVERSE

DATE	ABP	MS-65 UNC.	PRF-65 PROOF
☐ 1993D	18.00	23.00	
☐ 1993W	19.00		26.00

WW II 50TH ANNIVERSARY
(Gold Half Eagle)

OBVERSE   REVERSE

DATE	ABP	MS-65 UNC.	PRF-65 PROOF
☐ 1993W	130.00	175.00	140.00

WORLD CUP SOCCER (Clad $.50)

Obverse (L) and Reverse (R) of 1994 World Cup Cupro-Nickel Half Dollar

The World Cup commemorative coins, established by Public Law 102-281, authorized the Mint to produce gold $5, silver $1, and clad $.50 coins to celebrate the World Cup, which was staged for the first time ever in the United States. Surcharges included in the price of each coin were paid to World Cup USA 1994, Inc. for organizing and staging the 1994 World Cup, and to fund scholarships through the United States Soccer Federation Foundation. The World Cup coins were available individually, in sets, and in special Host City venue editions featuring the nine sites where the World Cup games were played.

DATE	ABP	MS-65 UNC.	PRF-65 PROOF
☐ 1994D	6.00	8.00	
☐ 1994P	8.00		12.00

WORLD CUP SOCCER
(Silver $1.00)

Obverse (L) and Reverse (R) of 1994 World Cup Silver Dollar Coin

DATE	ABP	MS-65 UNC.	PRF-65 PROOF
☐ 1994D	15.00	24.00	
☐ 1994S	20.00		28.00

WORLD CUP SOCCER
(Gold Half Eagle)

Obverse (L) and Reverse (R) of 1994 World Cup Gold Five Dollar Coin

DATE	ABP	MS-65 UNC.	PRF-65 PROOF
☐ 1994W	125.00	150.00	140.00

THOMAS JEFFERSON BIRTHDAY 250TH ANNIVERSARY (Silver $1.00)

OBVERSE   REVERSE

Public Law 103-186 signed by President Clinton on December 14, 1993, authorized the Mint to produce silver dollars to commemorate the 250th anniversary of the birth of Thomas Jefferson on April 13, 1743. The Thomas Jefferson Coin and Currency Set provided a brief history of Jefferson's role in establishing America's decimal coinage system, from his earliest thoughts on the subject to Congressional approval of Jefferson's plan, and his role in establishing the first U.S. Mint. Surcharges included in the price of each coin were paid to the Thomas Jefferson Memorial Foundation to help fund educational programs and restoration of Monticello, Jefferson's primary residence, and to the Corporation for Jefferson's Poplar Forest to help fund restoration of Jefferson's retreat home. This program sold out during the pre-issue period with surcharges paid as follows: The Thomas Jefferson Memorial Foundation had received $5 million and Jefferson's Poplar Forest had received $714,630 as of June 27, 1994.

DATE	ABP	MS-65 CH. UNC.	PRF-65 CH. PROOF
☐ 1994P	25.00	30.00	
☐ 1994S	18.00		20.00

WOMEN IN MILITARY SERVICE FOR AMERICA MEMORIAL (Silver $1.00)

Authorized by Congress in 1986, The Women in Military Service For America Memorial will document the history of American servicewomen. The memorial will provide an unprecedented tribute to military women, at the same time encouraging Americans of all ages to learn about the women who have defended America throughout history.

The Women in Military Service For America Memorial Foundation (WIMSA) has taken on the task of raising the funds required to build the memorial, which according to legislation must be built without federal funds. To date, WIMSA has nearly $11 million available for the memorial, but an additional $5 million is needed before construction can begin. The memorial is to be built at the gateway to Arlington National Cemetery.

- **The exterior** will incorporate the existing 1930s neoclassical hemicycle, which serves as the ornamental gateway to Arlington National Cemetery. Restoration and adaptation will allow for a memorial structure above ground and an educational center below.
- **The terrace** will feature an arc of glass "pages" inscribed with quotations about or from servicewomen. Acting as skylights, the glass panels will dramatically reflect the quotations on the walls of the gallery below.
- **The Court of Honor** will center around a waterfall and reflecting pool. A continuous stream of water will gather to form a waterfall, and from there flow into a narrow channel leading to a circular reflecting pool. The flow of water will symbolize the "singular voices" of American servicewomen coming together as a "chorus of voices."
- Visitors will be able to access a **computer register** that will feature the name and picture of each registered servicewoman with service details and their most memorable experience. To date 100,000 women have registered and WIMSA expects to register an additional 400,000 by the time the memorial is dedicated.

Surcharges from the 500,000 Women in Military Service For America Memorial commemorative silver dollars will